Women, Enterprise, Craft

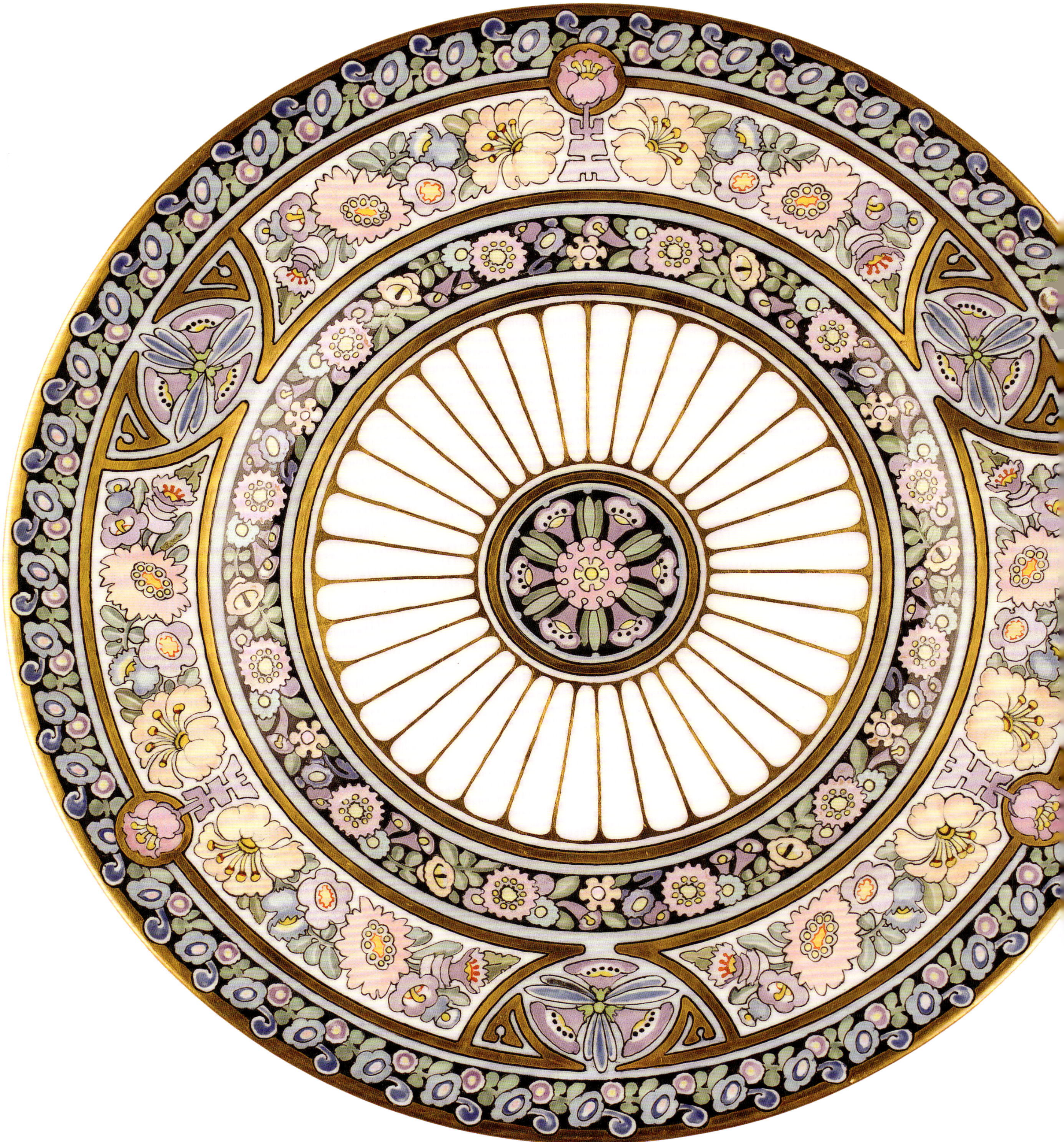

Women, Enterprise, *Craft*

Chicago's Atlan Ceramic Art Club, 1893–1923

Sharon S. Darling

RIT Press • Rochester, New York

Women, Enterprise, Craft:
Chicago's Atlan Ceramic Art Club, 1893–1923

Published and distributed by:

RIT Press
90 Lomb Memorial Drive
Rochester, New York 14623
https://press.rit.edu

Printed in the United States of America

Cover: Cup and saucer with Chinese-inspired floral bands, Lillie E. Cole, 1905. Although Cole's final exhibition with the Atlan Club was in 1904, she continued painting in the Atlan style. Signed: LECole cipher/1905. Blank: Limoges/W. G. & Co./France. (saucer, d: 4⅝"; cup, h: 2¼") *Photo*: Private collection.

Designed by Steve Boerner

ISBN 978-1-956313-07-9 (print)
ISBN 978-1-956313-11-6 (electronic)

Library of Congress Cataloging-in-Publication Data
Names: Darling, Sharon S., author.
Title: Women, enterprise, craft : Chicago's Atlan Ceramic Art Club, 1893–1923 / Sharon S. Darling.
Description: Rochester, New York : RIT Press, [2024] | Series: Arts and crafts movement series | Includes bibliographical references and index.
Identifiers: LCCN 2023056465 | ISBN 9781956313079 (hardcover) | ISBN 9781956313116 (pdf)
Subjects: LCSH: Atlan Ceramic Art Club (Chicago, Ill.) | China painting—Illinois—Chicago—19th century. | China painting—Illinois—Chicago—20th century.
Classification: LCC NK4605.5.U63 A853 2024 | DDC 738.09773/11—dc23/eng/20240130
LC record available at https://lccn.loc.gov/202305646

Frontispiece: Plate, Helen Frazee, ca. 1900. Signed: Frazee. (d: 10¼") Photo courtesy of Chicago History Museum, i174280_pm.

We gather on the traditional territory of the Onöndowa'ga:' or "the people of the Great Hill." In English, they are known as Seneca people, "the keeper of the western door." They are one of the six nations that make up the sovereign Haudenosaunee Confederacy.

We honor the land on which RIT was built and recognize the unique relationship that the Indigenous stewards have with this land. That relationship is the core of their traditions, cultures, and histories. We recognize the history of genocide, colonization, and assimilation of Indigenous people that took place on this land. Mindful of these histories, we work towards understanding, acknowledging, and ultimately reconciliation.

For Mikell

Arts and Crafts Movement Series
Bruce A. Austin, *Series Editor*

The Arts and Crafts Movement series is a forum for significant, accessible original scholarship focusing on multidimensional elements of the decorative arts movement popular from 1875 to 1920. Authors employ diverse methods to prepare compelling narratives exploring and contextualizing enduring Arts and Crafts subjects. The series enhances and expands understanding of the Movement, including historical, social, economic, political, biographical, and aesthetic analyses.

Additional titles in the Arts and Crafts Movement Series:

The Splendid Disarray of Beauty: The Boys, the Tiles, the Joy of Cathedral Oaks—A Study in Arts and Crafts Community by Richard D. Mohr

A Symbiotic Partnership: Marrying Commerce to Education at Gustav Stickleys 1903 Arts and Crafts Exhibitions by Bruce A. Austin

Contents

Introduction

In 1902, the members of the Atlan Ceramic Art Club were invited to show their overglaze decorated porcelain in the Art Institute of Chicago's first annual Arts and Crafts exhibition. With 751 exhibitors from around the United States, the exhibition included metalwork, jewelry, and household furnishings, along with ceramics by such renowned craftworkers as Susan S. Frackelton, George E. Ohr, Hugh C. Robertson, and Artus Van Briggle, and vitrines of Teco, Grueby, Newcomb, and Rookwood pottery. The Atlan Club, with fifty examples by its seventeen female members, was the major exhibitor of overglaze decorated ceramics.

The first exhibition of the Chicago Arts and Crafts Society, at the Art Institute of Chicago in 1898, also included work by the Atlan Club. It was the first public showing of the women's work after, as a club, they adopted a new and advanced style of china painting featuring stylized ornamentation that would set them apart from traditional china painters. Nor was it their first time exhibiting at a major American art museum: the Atlan Club's annual exhibitions had been held at the Art Institute of Chicago since 1894 and would continue through 1922. Despite the club's lengthy history, few collectors and curators have heard of the Atlan Ceramic Art Club or acknowledge porcelain decorated overglaze in the abstract "conventional" style, as a significant part of the Arts and Crafts movement. The present work shares the story of how the Atlan Club's all-female membership elevated Chicago as a center of china painting during the Arts and Crafts movement by examining its history—its founding, evolution, and demise—and its influence on decorative ceramics in the United States during the first quarter of the twentieth century.

The Atlan Ceramic Art Club was an elite association organized by fifteen of Chicago's most talented female china painters who were eager to exhibit their work at the 1893 Chicago World's Fair. Under

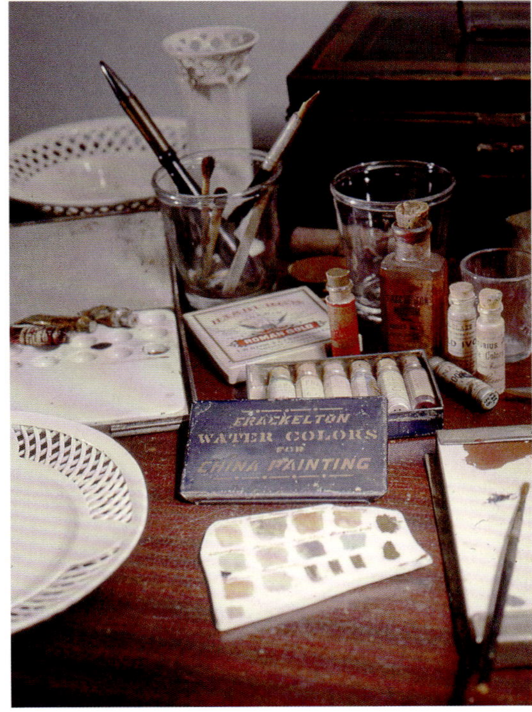

0.0 The tools of the china painter. Mineral colors came in vials of powder that required mixing with oil. Special brushes, with fine tips made from sable or squirrel hair, were used to apply the paint to porcelain blanks. Like many china painters with a national reputation, Susan S. Frackelton, founder of the National League of Mineral Painters, offered her own line of mineral colors. Her Artist's Box is in the collection of the Milwaukee County Historical Society. Hasburg's Roman Gold paint was manufactured in Chicago. *Photo*: Author's collection.

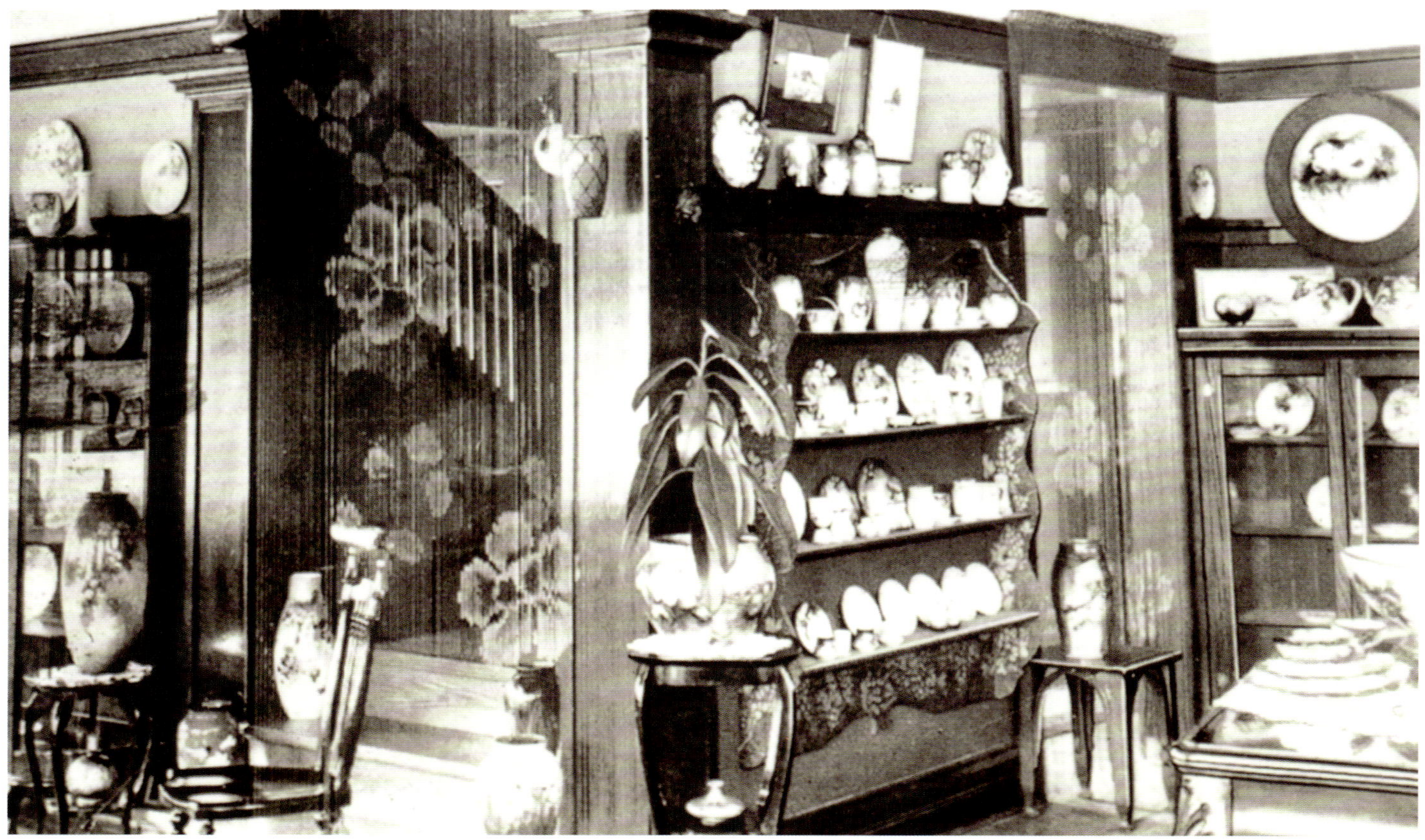

0.1 The home studio of Chicago china decorator Emily Hoggins Chase (1868–1957). An Art Institute of Chicago graduate, Chase offered lessons and hand-painted ceramics from 1891 through 1919, when she and her husband returned to their native England. *Photo*: Chicago History Museum.

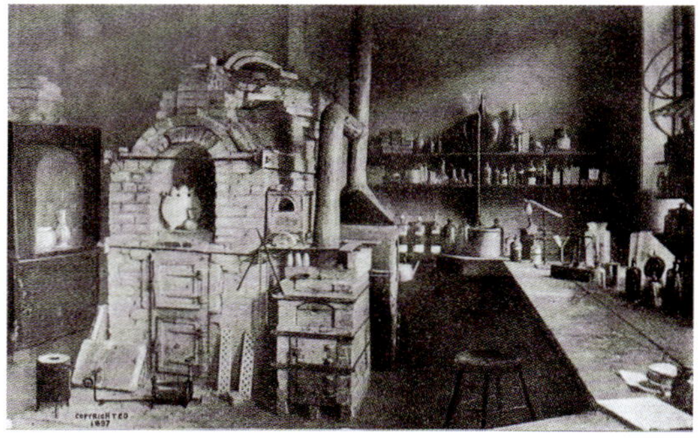

0.2 The ceramic color laboratory of Chicago chemist John W. Hasburg in 1897. His company manufactured a wide variety of mineral paints, including the popular Roman Gold. *Source*: John W. Hasburg, "A Glimpse into The Manufacture of Ceramic Colors," *Arts for America*, November 15, 1898.

the untiring leadership of its founder, Florence Steward, the club remained active for thirty years. The abstract style of overglaze decoration developed by Atlan Club members and applied with superb technical skill brought regional, national, and even international recognition as they pioneered the study of appropriate designs for china and sought to develop an original "American style" of ceramic decoration. Abandoning in 1898 the so-called naturalistic approach—plump roses, cherubs, lots of gold—that typified their work, going forward, club members painted exclusively in the stylized "conventional" style that would be adopted by progressive ceramic decorators during the Arts and Crafts movement.

When the club was launched in 1893, Chicago was the midwestern center of the "china craze" that developed in the United States after the 1876 Philadelphia Centennial, where impressive ceramics displays from France, Great Britain, and the Far East inspired American men and women to try their hand at decorating porcelain ("china painting") or making pottery as a pastime, livelihood, or art form. China painting became so popular that one writer speculated, "In almost every family in our larger cities one member at least has taken up pottery or porcelain painting."[1]

Boston, Chicago, Cincinnati, Indianapolis, Kansas City, New York, and Philadelphia were china painting centers, although enthusiasts were active across the country. Chicago, as the country's transportation hub and its second-largest city, claimed a strong industrial complex as well as a network of national retailers, wholesalers, and mail-order firms. It was also home to a fast-growing, substantial middle class eager to furnish its houses and apartments with artistically decorated porcelain that was unique yet affordable. Although men as well as women worked as china painters, females predominated, with various levels of involvement ranging from hobbyists to self-supporting professionals.

Reenforcing the growing popularity of hand-painted wares was the spreading influence of the Arts and Crafts movement, which encouraged people to make art a part of their daily lives and to surround themselves with household objects that combined beauty with utility. Hand-decorated ceramics not only beautified domestic interiors but provided their creators a satisfying outlet for creative expression. In the 1890s, inspired by the British movement, Arts and Crafts principles found a sympathetic audience among Chicago art workers, educators, and others involved in progressive cultural and social reforms. Ideas of craftwork and simplicity, appreciation of the inherent beauty of the material, looking to nature for inspiration—core characteristics of the Arts and Crafts movement—paralleled the emergence of the feminist movement that encouraged women to develop their individual talents and become self-reliant. In many ways, china painting was a link between the earlier Aesthetic movement, which recognized beauty in household art, and the Arts and Crafts movement, which encouraged participation in the production of art. In their design work, the women would abandon the romantic, often Japanese-inspired motifs found in the era of the "artful home" for a modern design attitude that advocated abstracted motifs and simple, uncluttered settings.

Although the basic techniques of china painting (also known as mineral painting) were those involved in watercolor and oil painting, it also included complex technical aspects of kiln loading and firing at correct temperatures. Dry powdered mineral paints, which were simply colored glass ground to a very fine powder, were mixed with a medium, usually oil based; they were applied by brush to a previously fired glazed surface, usually porcelain but sometimes pottery, of a shape called a "blank." The porcelain or pottery was then refired to a temperature that caused the paint to melt and combine chemically with the glaze of the ware, making the decoration permanent and indelible. The paints were colored by adding the oxide of a metal, such as oxide of cobalt for blues, oxide of tin for white, and so on.[2]

Because the process of firing materially altered the colors and

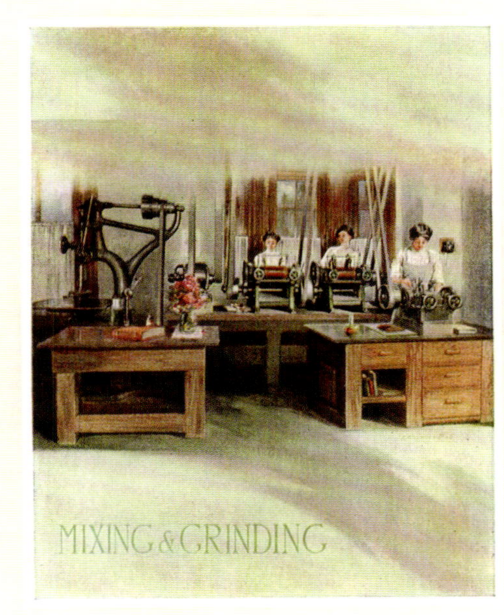

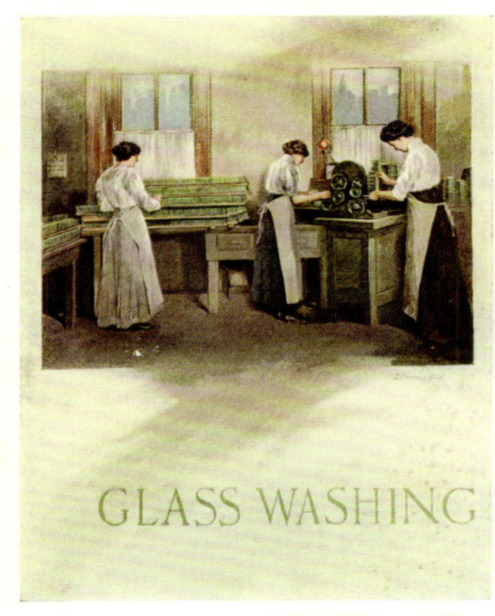

0.3A AND B Producing the gold used in china painting at the John W. Hasburg Company in Chicago. Women employees were featured in the photos illustrating *Hasburg's Golds: A Glittering Trail* in 1913. *Photo*: Tim Ingram.

shades of mineral paint, it required some knowledge of technique. Too much medium or indiscriminate mixing of colors was often followed by disaster when fired in the kiln, where regulation of temperature was also required. A competent professional china painter would possess skill in drawing, painting, design, and color theory; an understanding of chemistry; and the technical competence needed to load, fire, and troubleshoot an often-temperamental ceramic kiln. Although they drew on the standard techniques of the fine arts, china painters "developed a wholly separate category of creative expression that involved knowledge of design history, the natural world, psychology, and geometry," concluded Ellen Paul Denker, one of the first ceramics historians to note the significance of china painting in the origins of the Arts and Crafts and feminist movements.[3]

China painting, which had many more practitioners than art pottery, was widely presented as an art form in museum exhibitions and was the subject of specialty publications, along with newspaper and magazine articles, in the decades between 1880 and 1920. In exhibitions, jurors used the same criteria to vet overglaze decorated porcelain or pottery as that used in selecting art pottery, handwrought metalwork, and similar artistic productions. Hand-painted china as a research subject, however, has been largely ignored by ceramics scholars and Arts and Crafts collectors, who have focused on art pottery produced during this period. As Cynthia A. Brandimarte pointed out in her informative essay on the American china painter and her work, the topic of china painting is often considered "an inconsequential 'artistic' field, important solely for its eventual harvest of art potters," with few pieces considered museum worthy.[4]

Apart from Wendy Kaplan's "The Art That Is Life" exhibition (1987), hand-painted porcelain and its practitioners, although celebrated in their day, are typically excluded from major American Arts and Crafts exhibitions and publications.[5] To date, the Chicago History Museum is the only American museum with a significant collection of work by members of the Atlan Ceramic Art Club. The Art Institute of Chicago, which hosted the club's annual exhibitions for twenty-nine years, holds two porcelain vases decorated overglaze by members of the club.[6] Atlan Club members exhibited an average of two hundred pieces at each of their exhibitions over thirty years, but work signed by Atlan members is now rare; pieces identified with the Atlan logo and year, as required for exhibition, are even rarer. Unlike art pottery, whose sturdy bodies often took the form of vases and sculptural artwork, porcelain decorated during the era was predominantly tableware—plates, bowls, pitchers, tea sets—subject to breakage during daily use. As one arrogant Chicago art critic predicted in 1895, "Of course the china painting craze, among young women, results in much bad work, but the material used is fortunately fragile, so there is little danger of homes becoming overcrowded with it, or of its going down to posterity."[7]

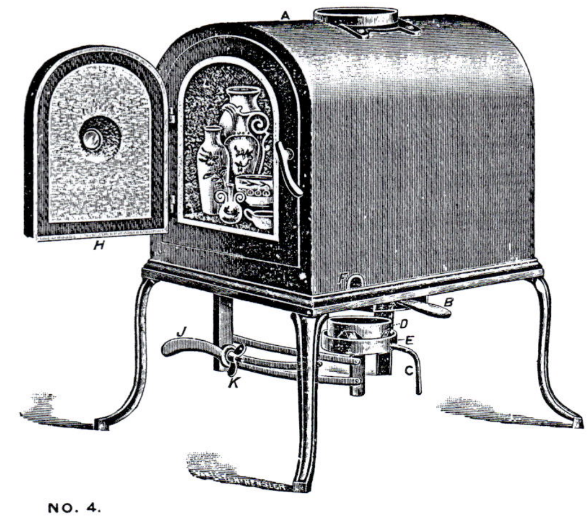

0.4 Revelation china kiln of the type used by decorators for firing hand-painted porcelain in their studios around 1901. *Photo:* Tim Ingram.

Chapter One

A Few of the "Better Artists"

We have quite a number of earnest workers; now let us gather them together for concerted effort toward educational progress. This can be accomplished by seeking cooperation of the better artists.
—Mrs. Florence Steward, "1893–1902 The History of the Atlan Ceramic Art Club of Chicago, Ill.," 1902

It is late January, less than four months until the World's Columbian Exposition opens in Chicago in May 1893. Florence Pratt, an avid china decorator, has invited some of Chicago's best-known female painters to dinner at her home to share an idea: why not form a club—a small club of the city's "better artists"—with the goal of encouraging a higher standard of ceramic decoration? By limiting membership to a select group known for originality and excellent craftsmanship, they could improve their own skills and, optimistically, raise the status of china painting as an art.

It did not take much persuasion. In February, fifteen women met in the studio that Louise Anderson shared with her sister Emma Anderson Kittredge in the Tower of the Auditorium Building to organize the Atlan Art Club.[1] As their first order of business, they agreed to exhibit their wares as a club at the upcoming World's Fair. The members also proposed Florence Pratt as president, but she declined; she needed to be free to do the work required to secure space and coordinate their exhibition at the World's Fair, opening in only sixty days, but agreed to serve as secretary-treasurer. Veteran painter Cornelia Mann agreed to serve as president; she had been appointed curator of ceramics by the Illinois Woman's Exposition Board, the official group selecting work by Illinois women, and could smooth the way for the club's exhibition.

Emma Anderson Kittredge was elected vice president; Cornelia Linsted and Roxana Preuszner were appointed "councilors," or coaches, to provide critical feedback to members on their work. At Mann's suggestion, Susan S. Frackelton, president of the National League of Mineral Painters, through whose offices the neophyte club could obtain desirable space in the Woman's Building, was elected honorary president for the ensuing year.[2]

Club members chose the name Atlan through a suggestion contained in a translation of an ancient Egyptian text written on clay, read

Atlan Founders

Eva Eliza Adams
Louise Compton Anderson
Lucy "Lillie" Elizabeth Cole
Mabel Caroline Dibble
Belle Foster
Nellie L. DeGolyer Greenleaf (Mrs. Walter)
Mary Helen Stevens Humphrey (Mrs. Edward L.)
Emma Anderson Kittredge
Cornelia Burns Linsted (Mrs. D. B.)
Cornelia Hooker Mann (Mrs. Washington L.)
Letitia McIntyre
Grace Harriet Peck
Roxana Beecher Preuszner (Mrs. Carl)
Florence Pratt Steward (Mrs. Le Roy T.)
Julia C. Richardson Wells (Mrs. Melancthon W.)

to the group by Florence Pratt. In its closest interpretation, Atlan was the name of a unique center of learning where rare arts were taught to a select few; its school was surrounded by a labyrinth of beautiful walks through which one had to pass to access this knowledge. Although Steward did not reveal the source of her document, it appears that the Atlan Art Club's name was inspired by theories regarding the lost continent of Atlantis that proliferated after the 1882 publication of Ignatius L. Donnelly's pseudo-archaeological bestseller, *Atlantis: The Antediluvian World*. Donnelly, who considered Plato's account of Atlantis to be largely factual, suggested that it had been the site of a people possessing superior culture and technology from which all the world's ancient civilizations descended before that island disappeared into the sea. The Atlan club's link to Atlantis was confirmed in 1895. In the *Ceramic Monthly*, an unidentified club member lyrically attributed "the fabled Atlantis, famous in song and story," as the source of the forms and methods of ancient Egyptian art that inspired them to emulate "those qualities which enabled the Egyptian tribes to crystalize their crude dreams of the beautiful into historical values for the student of the present."[3]

Equating this tale with the challenges they navigated to become skilled artists, the women unanimously adopted the name. It also inspired the selection of a club motto: "Patience, Persistence, Progress," a constant reminder that all three elements were necessary for success in the trying art of mineral painting, where surprises and disappointments in chemical combinations during firing were frequent occurrences. Symbolically, they would place a distinctive red stamp—the oblique crossing of the three P initials of the motto, with the word Atlan underneath—on the bottom of all pieces exhibited by club members.

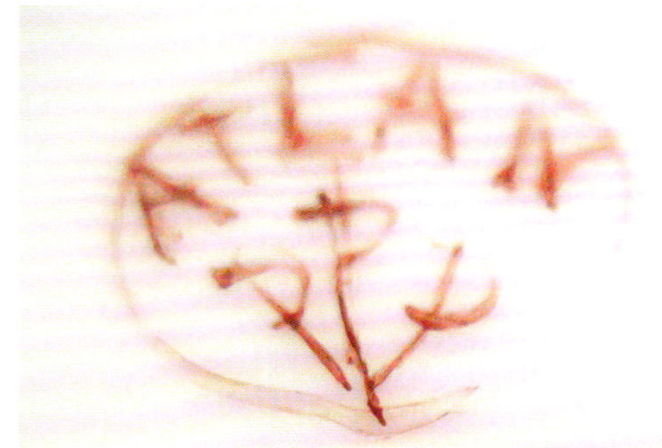

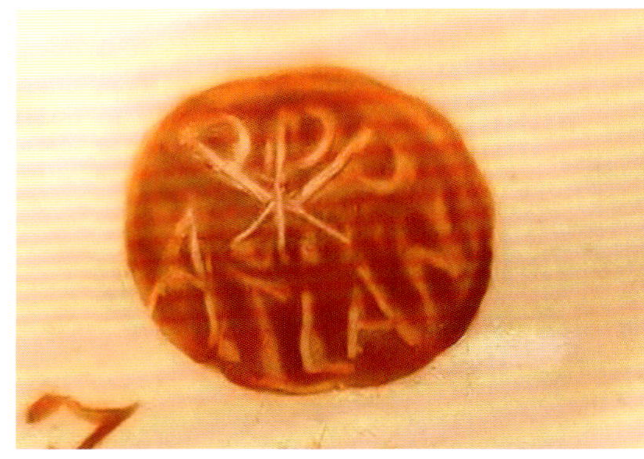

1.1.A AND B Two variations of the original Atlan logo, which featured three crossed *P*s and "Atlan" enclosed in a red circle.

Cornelia Hooker Mann, 1893–1894

Cornelia Hooker Mann (1849–1895), a talented china painter and teacher, was a founding member and the first president of the Atlan Ceramic Club in 1893, serving a two-year term. At the time, she was considered one of the finest artists in the city, excelling in etched effects in color over gold and bronze;[1] unable to find bronze in the United States, she experimented for years until she learned how to make her own bronzes and colored golds and invented several new shades.[2] She excelled in painting delicate seaweeds and birds with downy plumage, as well as portrait work; her rose jars were "dreams of beauty," and she painted forget-me-nots "as poets idealize them."[3]

Cornelia was among the organizers of the Chicago Ceramic Association in 1892. During the 1893 Chicago World's Fair, she was appointed Curator of Ceramics by the Illinois Woman's Board, who later presented her with a gold badge as a testimonial of her efficient services. She received two awards, one for the "Marcia Louise Vase" and another for her "Beautifully Painted Collection."[4]

Born in Cape Vincent, New York, Cornelia Hooker grew up in Milwaukee, Wisconsin, where her father was a prominent grain dealer. She attended Milwaukee Female College, a progressive school that followed Catherine Beecher's curriculum for educating women for teaching and similar professions. By 1870, Cornelia was operating her own school, most likely teaching china painting.[5] After marrying bookkeeper Washington Lafayette Mann in 1871, she moved with her husband to Chicago, where

For harmony, they chose "Egyptian red" and blue as their official club colors and a deep red carnation as its official flower, and they adopted an insignia pin in the form of an Egyptian lamp, whose flame symbolized the light of knowledge and the heat connected with mineral painting. A badge of red and blue ribbons printed with the club's name and motto printed in Egyptian letters would be worn at all Atlan Club functions.[4]

A constitution and by-laws were adopted. The constitution provided for a broad interpretation of decoration and materials, including metal and glass as well as porcelain and pottery, along with the optimistic goal of founding an American School of Art. Membership would be limited to twenty-five. The requirement for full membership, besides knowledge of mineral painting, was the favorable approval of two pieces of work executed without the aid of an instructor. Applicants had to undergo two ballots; one black ball would drop them from consideration.

An advisory committee, composed of prominent Chicago society and clubwomen active in the arts, was organized to support and promote the club. Among them were the wives of Judge Henry M. Shepard; financier Ferdinand W. Peck; industrialists Nathaniel H. Blatchford, Erskine M. Phelps, and Milton H. Wilson; newspaper publishers Herman H. Kohlsaat and William Penn Nixon; Henry O. Shepard, founder of the trade magazine, *Inland Printer* and proponent of industrial arts; and Dr. Frank W. Gunsaulus, noted pastor and president of the Armour Institute of Technology. Besides being potential customers, advisory members would assist in fundraising by hosting social events, lending prestige by their presence at sales and exhibitions, and encouraging patronage by affluent Chicagoans.

---

he was credit manager for a large clothier until launching his own clothing manufacturing company. In 1890, the couple built a stylish house, designed by prominent architects Flanders & Zimmerman, on Vincennes Avenue. She began accepting local china painting students in 1891.[6]

In November 1894, the Chicago Ceramic Association announced that Cornelia, who had "recently suffered pecuniary losses" and was seriously ill, was compelled to sell the "Marcia Louise Vase," for which "chances" were being taken by a local jeweler.[7] She died, age forty-five, in April 1895. "Enthusiastic, talented, untrammeled by family cares, ill health, or want of means; encouraged by a companion who fully appreciated his wife's ability, it is no wonder that by years of conscientious study, Mrs. Mann became a leader in Ceramic art," recalled the editor of *Ceramic Monthly*, noting that "the loss of wealth and the beautiful home she had designed, would have crushed a woman less talented."[8]

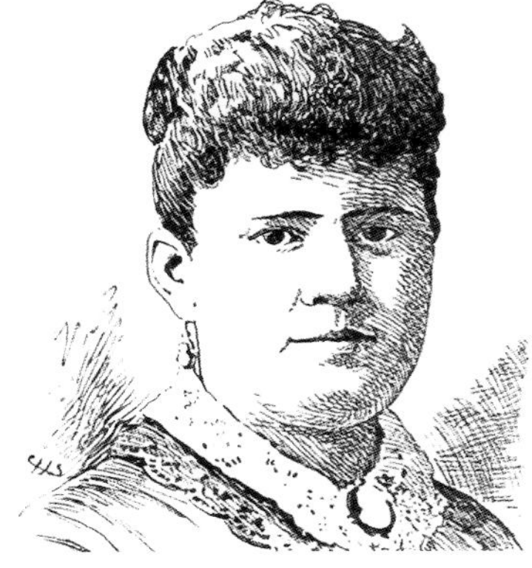

Cornelia Hooker Mann, first president of the Atlan Ceramic Art Club, 1893. *Source*: *Ceramic Monthly* 1, no. 4 (May 1895).

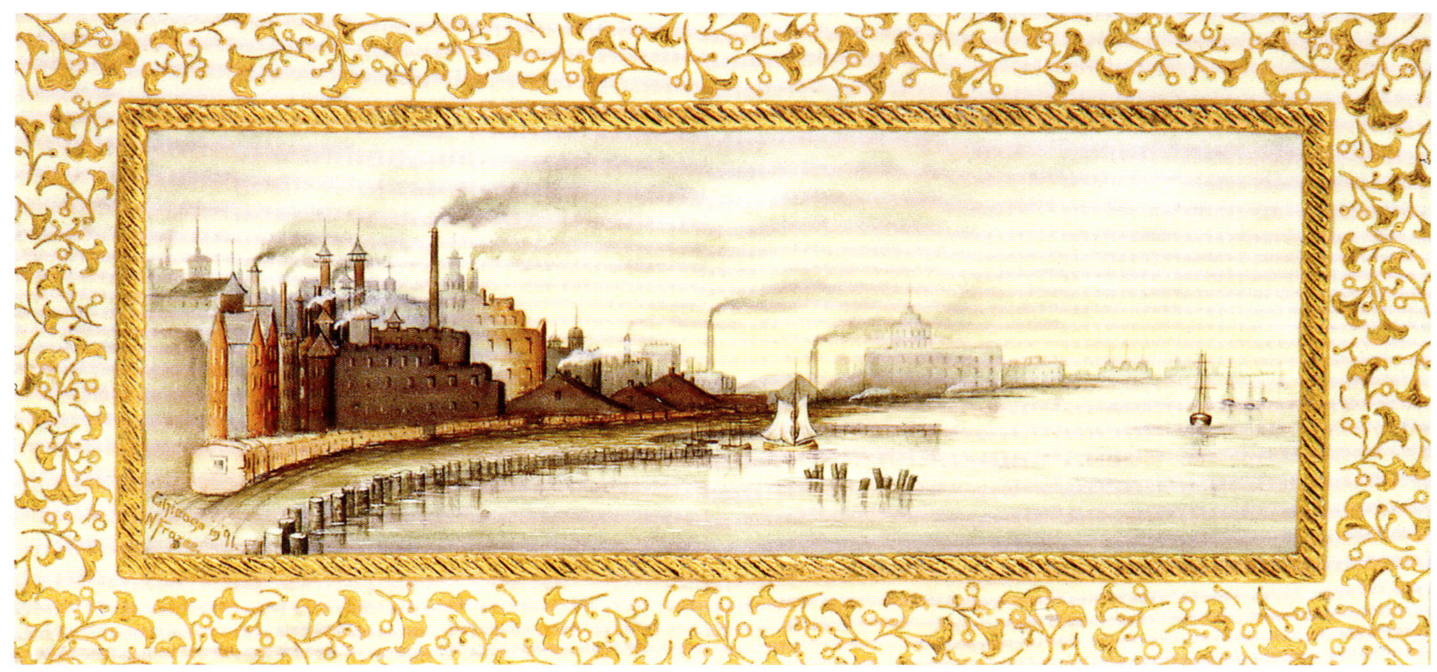

1.2 "Chicago in '91," Helen Frazee, 1891. This porcelain plaque, with a view of the city's smoky lakefront skyline, was one of the items Frazee exhibited at the 1893 World's Columbian Exposition in Chicago. She joined the Atlan Club in August 1893. Signed lower left: Chicago in '91/H. Frazee. (6″ × 12″) *Photo*: Chicago History Museum.

As a small club, Atlan would not compete with the Chicago Ceramic Association formed the previous year by several hundred artists and amateurs. It could, however, ally itself with the recently organized National League of Mineral Painters, that had already appointed Florence Pratt as its treasurer and director in charge of coordinating the World's Fair exhibits coming from the various regional ceramic clubs represented in the league.[5]

The following six weeks before the opening of the World's Columbian Exposition were busy ones as the women prepared for the club's first exhibition. Members selected the best examples of their work, which were then consolidated in Mabel C. Dibble's china painting studio. Eva E. Adams later recalled how "with untiring energy and wonderful patience," Dibble "packed, listed and cared for each exhibitor's piece."[6]

When the fair opened, the Atlan Club's work could be seen in three large cases of the National League of Mineral Painters in the Woman's Building.[7] Nearby were pieces decorated by ceramist Susan S. Frackelton of Wisconsin, the Columbian Ceramic Society of Chicago, and the Chicago Exchange for Woman's Work, a philanthropic society that began promoting china painting in the early 1880s.

Several Atlan members had such well-established reputations that examples of their work were chosen to beautify special rooms at the fair. Cornelia Mann's pitcher-shaped vase, described as "the first piece of Royal Worcester decorated in Illinois," graced the Reception Room in the Illinois Building; her large "Marcia Louise Vase," considered one of the handsomest ceramic pieces at the exposition, was featured in the Library of the Woman's Building. The large vase, painted in honor of Mrs. Marcia Louise Gould, president of the Illinois Woman's Exposition Board, had been made of pearly, translucent Belleek porcelain perfected by the Ceramic Art Company (Willets Manufacturing Co., later Lenox) of Trenton, New Jersey, making it "purely American," in contrast to the imported porcelain forms typically decorated by china painters (see fig. 1.3).[8] Also in the same room were items decorated by Atlan members Louise Anderson, Nellie Greenleaf, Emma Anderson Kittredge, and Grace H. Peck.[9] In the Chicago Room in the Woman's Building could be seen "exquisite china" painted by Mabel C. Dibble, Grace H. Peck, and Louise Anderson, who also exhibited an oak table ornamented with pyrographic work.[10]

Through Cornelia Mann's connections, the Atlan Art Club gained the privilege of hosting a reception in the Woman's Building, under the auspices of the Board of Lady Managers, in honor of the officers of the National League of Mineral Painters.[11] More than two thousand invitations were issued to national and state representatives of mineral painting clubs and hosts of Chicago friends. Mrs. Henry M. Shepard, chair of the club's advisory board, gave a brilliant address of welcome at the event, which was heralded with congratulatory letters and telegrams.[12] Susan S. Frackelton, the league's president, urged the necessity of developing a national style in china painting.[13]

Despite the hurried circumstances, the collective and individual work of Atlan Club members earned more awards than any other club at the fair. Thirty-one medals were given to the clubs forming the National League of Mineral Painters; out of this number, eighteen went to Atlan members, eight to Honorary President Susan S. Frackelton. "Eight of its members had cabinets of individual work there," recalled Mabel C. Dibble, "seven of them won medals and diplomas, as indeed did nearly every member who exhibited with the club proper."[14]

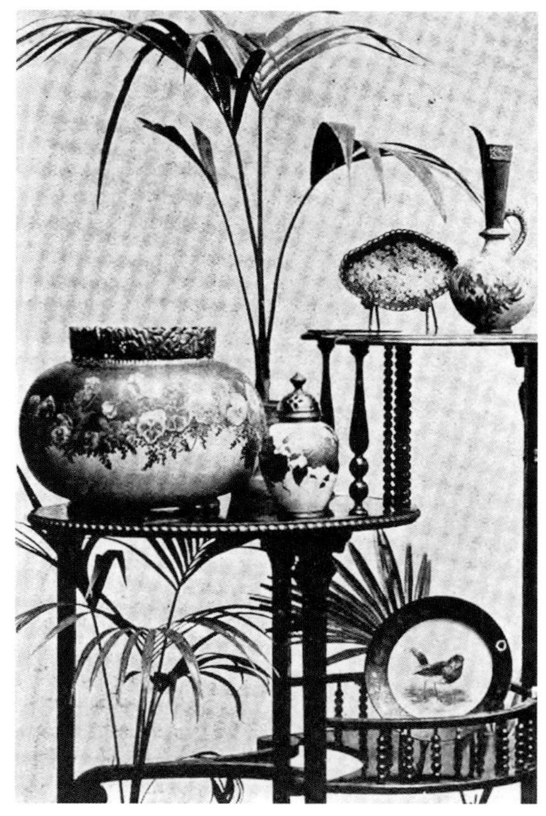

1.3 (top) Cornelia Mann's hand-painted china shown in the Woman's Building at the 1893 Chicago World's Fair. The large Belleek porcelain "Marcia Louise Vase," decorated with pansies, is center left. Mann received two awards, one for this vase and another for her "Beautifully Painted Collection." *Source*: "In Memoriam," *Ceramic Monthly* 1, no. 4 (May 1895): 9.

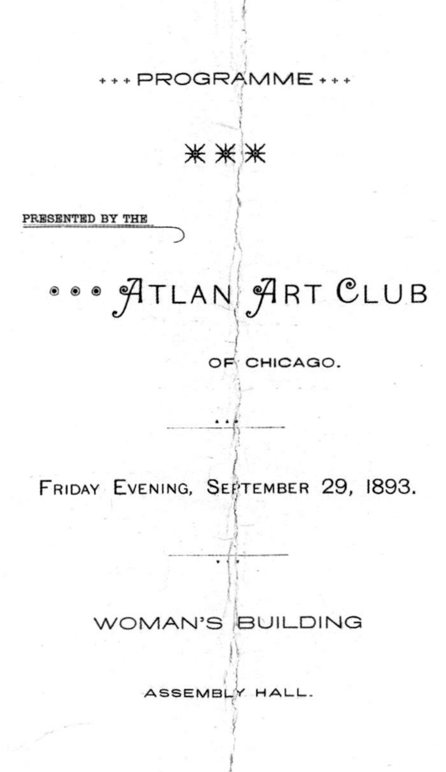

PROGRAMME

PRESENTED BY THE

ATLAN ART CLUB

OF CHICAGO.

FRIDAY EVENING, SEPTEMBER 29, 1893.

WOMAN'S BUILDING

ASSEMBLY HALL.

1.4 (bottom) Mrs. Henry M. Shepard, chairman of the Atlan Art Club's Advisory Board, welcomed guests to their reception in the Woman's Building at the 1893 Chicago World's Fair. Susan S. Frackelton, president of the National League of Mineral Painters, was the featured speaker. *Source*: Programme Presented by the Atlan Art Club of Chicago, September 29, 1893, Woman's Building, in Frazee Family Papers (manuscript) 1858–1922, folder 2, Chicago History Museum.

Chapter Two

"Ceramics Their Fad"

In the Chicago ceramic studios there are artists who devote their entire time to filling orders for private families. Many society ladies who have studied art abroad prefer to have their china decorated at home. The growing interest in china painting manifested by society people is a most gratifying evidence of appreciation of the artistic and beautiful.
—"Ceramics Their Fad," *Clay Record* 1, no. 3 (August 12, 1892): 84

In August 1892, the *Clay Record*, the Chicago-based journal chronicling the clay industry, claimed one thousand china painters among those who considered "Ceramics Their Fad" in and about the city of Chicago. Among them were seventy teachers and several studios where orders were filled for customers, many from outside cities and towns.[1] The article made clear that interest in ceramics was not a new phenomenon, but a thriving business that evolved over two decades.

Chicago women offered lessons in porcelain decoration "for daily profit and pleasure" in home studios as early as 1874,[2] while the Ladies' Art Association, under the auspices of the Chicago Society of Decorative Art, sponsored classes and a salesroom for "ladies dependent upon their own exertions" by 1881.[3] China painting was also a staple course in Chicago's fledging art academies, including the Academy of Design (reborn as the Art Institute of Chicago in 1878), the Chicago Athenaeum, and the South Side School of Art. Economic

2.1 Bill head for Western China Decorating Works, operated by Frederick L. Grunewald and George R. Busher in 1896. Founded by Grunewald in 1877, the firm sold china painting supplies, fired porcelain and pottery for amateurs, and sponsored annual exhibitions through the 1890s. *Photo*: Tim Ingram.

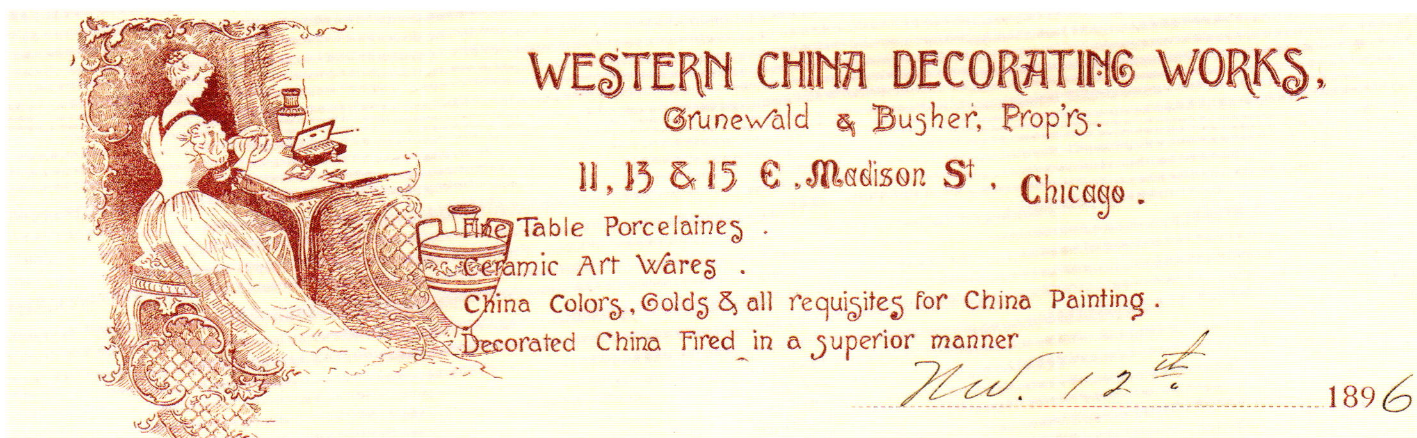

need and the lack of social services beyond one's family were strong incentives for many women to turn their skill in china decoration into a respectable source of employment. China decoration was perceived as a genteel profession—and, realistically, one of the few occupations available to women.[4]

By 1877, local interest in Chicago was sufficient for German émigré Frederick L. Grunewald, "the high priest of the ceramic cult," to open the Western China Decorating Works, where he installed the first kiln for firing china in "the West" and carried a complete line of mineral paints and supplies along with undecorated white porcelain tableware, tiles, and plaques.[5] Because American porcelain factories were still in their infancy, most of the blanks used by decorators were imported from France or Germany, where they were turned out in huge quantities by factories in Limoges or Berlin. In 1882, the firm began sponsoring annual exhibitions, open to amateurs and professionals alike, that drew hundreds of entries from men and women throughout the Midwest. Its weeklong exhibitions were thronged with visitors, primarily women, eager to see and compare the work submitted by professional European-trained decorators, local teachers and their pupils, and hobbyists. Local art critics and national periodicals, including the *China Decorator* (1888–1895), based in New York, and the *Ceramic Monthly* (1895–1899), launched in Chicago, reviewed its exhibitions, singling out painters whose work demonstrated originality or exceptional skill. After 1898, Burley & Tyrrell (renamed Burley & Co. in 1907), the city's largest importer of ceramics, sponsored annual exhibitions while offering the largest variety of white china for decorating.[6]

Self-instruction was available in the form of manuals such as *China Painting: A Practical Manual for the Use of Amateurs in the Decoration of Hard Porcelain*, published by M. Louise McLaughlin of Cincinnati in 1877, followed in 1886 by *Tried by Fire: A Work on China-Painting*, by Susan S. Frackelton, a Milwaukee china painter and teacher.[7] That same year, Frackelton patented one of the first portable gas kilns for china decorators, making it safer for artists to fire their work in their studios or at home—an invention that allowed many women to make china painting a career instead of a pastime.[8] Some women who would become celebrated china decorators and teachers—for example, Adelaide A. Robineau, editor of *Keramic Studio*—were entirely self-taught. By the opening of the 1893 World's Fair, some 25,000 American women were engaged in china painting, with Chicago, New York, and Cincinnati being the largest centers, although participants were active throughout the country.[9]

While most Chicago china painters worked in home studios, many of the city's professional ceramic teachers rented studios in its "china painting district," which encompassed the Atheneum, Auditorium, Marshall Field, and Venetian Buildings, all close to the Art Institute

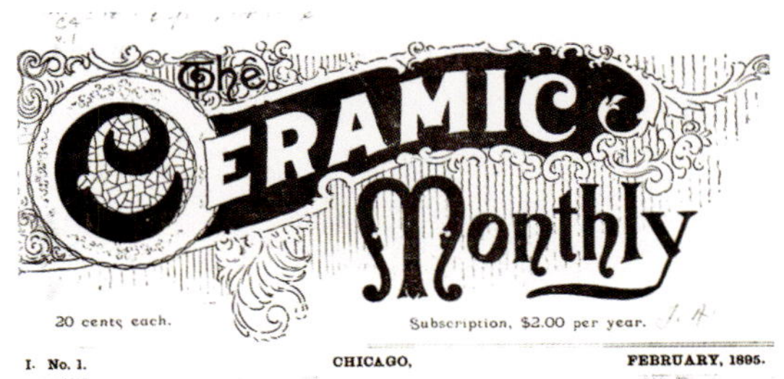

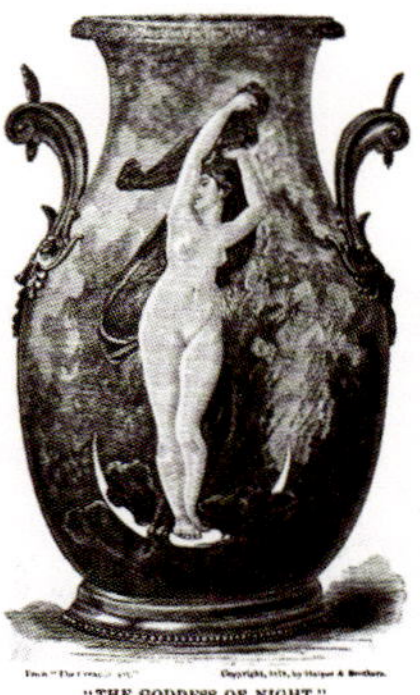

2.2 Published in Chicago, the *Ceramic Monthly* offered instructional articles on china painting, activities of ceramic clubs, decorative designs, and advertisements for supplies and local teachers, 1895–1899.

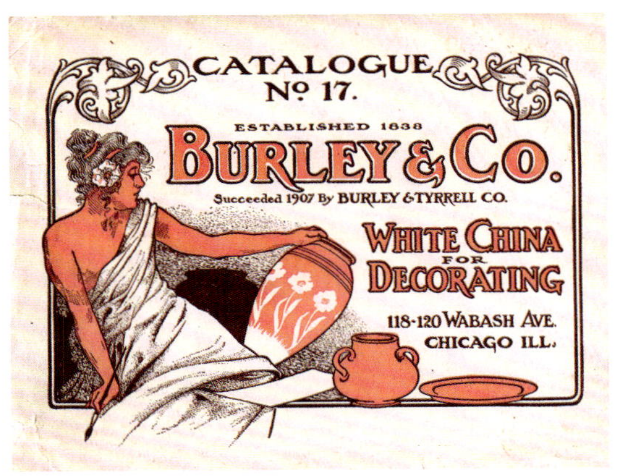

2.3 Burley & Co., formerly Burley & Tyrrell, was Chicago's largest importer of ceramics and glassware. It sold huge quantities of blank china and offered custom china decorating for private households, hotels, and railroads. Between 1898 and 1916, Burley sponsored exhibitions of hand-painted china that drew entries from throughout the United States. *Photo*: Tim Ingram.

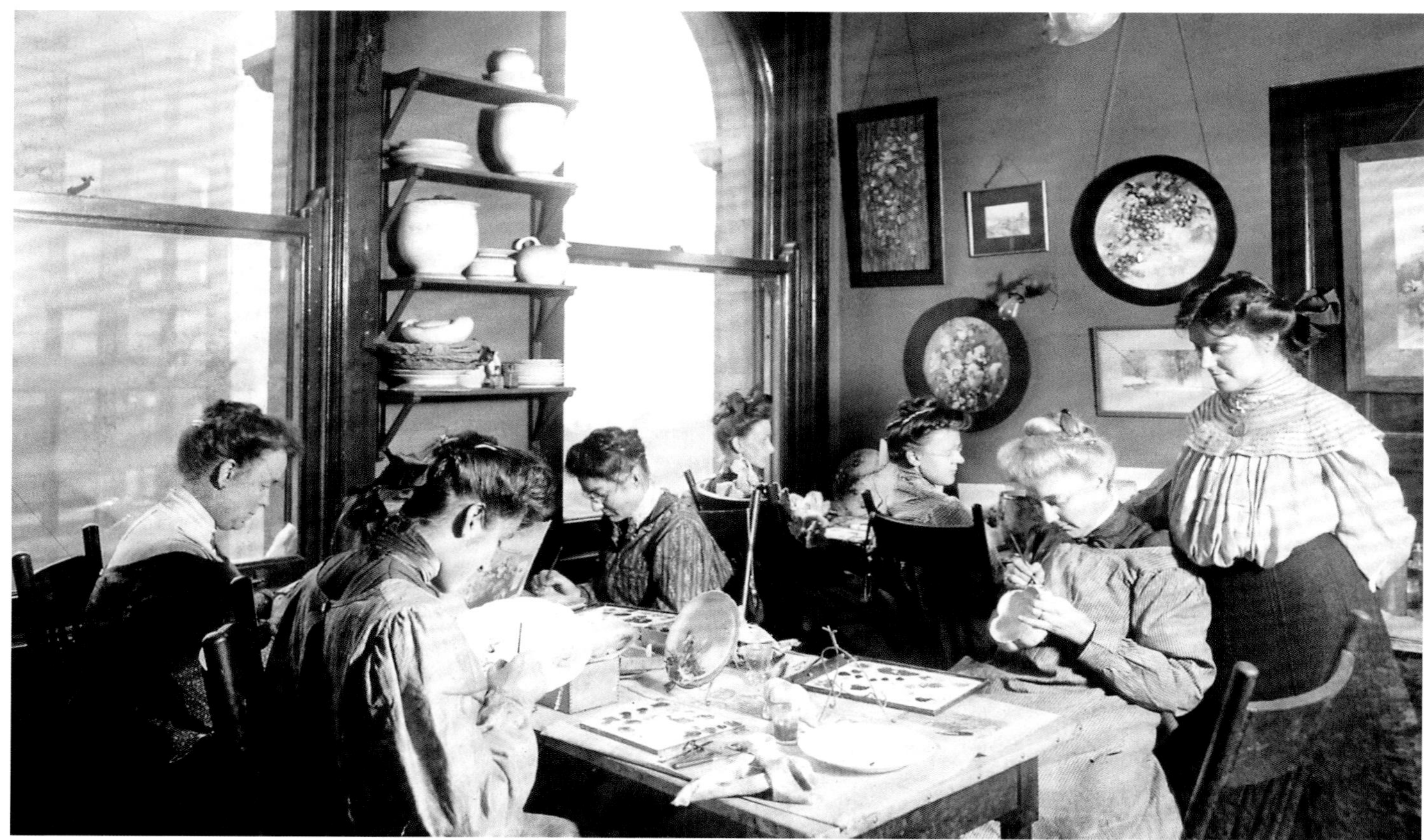

2.4 A china decorating class in the studio of Jeanne M. Stewart (1868–1960) in the Marshall Field Building, Chicago. A popular teacher, Stewart was known for her naturalistic fruits and flowers. *Photo*: Author's collection.

of Chicago, in the downtown business and cultural area defined as "the Loop" by the elevated train that encircled it. The seven-story Athenaeum Building (1886–1929), on E. Van Buren Street, between Washington Street and Wabash Avenue, functioned as a cultural center dedicated to education, art, and allied industries; its facilities included a gymnasium, auditorium, library, reading rooms, classrooms, and an upper story fitted with studios for artists.[10] The Marshall Field Building (D. H. Burnham, 1895–1930), on the northwest corner of Washington and Wabash, housed china painting studios amid offices occupied by physicians, dentists, druggists, architects, and the John Crerar Library, a free public library dedicated to the sciences. Similarly, between Washington and State Streets, the elegant thirteen-story Venetian Building (Holabird & Roche, 1892–1959) also contained a mix of artists' studios and medical offices.

Still standing at the corner of Michigan Avenue and Congress Parkway, the Auditorium Building (Adler & Sullivan, 1889) was built as a combination theater, hotel, and office building. In 1893, the tenth, eleventh, and twelfth floors of its nineteen-story tower were almost exclusively occupied by china painting teachers.[11] On the tenth floor, a group of artists known as the "tenth-floor colony" occupied studios with interconnecting doors, which they opened to create a long corridor ideal for hosting china painting exhibitions and receptions.[12] Both the Athenaeum and Auditorium Buildings had been built by private corporations financed by Ferdinand W. Peck (1848–1924), a wealthy Chicago businessman, philanthropist, and tireless promoter of the arts and their role in public education.

Chicago's china painting community was well established by January 1892, when a group of ambitious artists organized the Chicago Ceramic Association with the aim of securing a creditable exhibition at the upcoming World's Columbian Exposition. Within four months, the association, whose membership included men as well as women, counted 250 enthusiastic members.[13] Among them were all fifteen future Atlan Art Club members, including Roxana Beecher Preuszner, the association's vice president, and Mabel C. Dibble, its corresponding secretary.

Roxana Preuszner, eldest of the Atlan Club's founders at age 53, was a pioneer in the city's ceramics community. The widow of a Civil War veteran, she attended the Academy of Design before being appointed the school's first teacher of china painting in 1878.[14] By 1881, she was teaching classes in painting and pottery in her own studio. In addition to teaching "overglaze" decoration used in china painting, Preuszner, at her own expense, paid for the first kiln in the city for firing pottery with "underglaze" decoration of the type being made by M. Louise McLaughlin and the Rookwood Pottery in Cincinnati. The kiln allowed Chicago women to take their productions downtown for firing, relieving them of the necessity of shipping their work to Cincinnati.[15] Like many of the city's professional china painters, Preuszner held studio receptions showcasing the oil and watercolor pictures, pastel portraits, pottery, and china painted by herself and her pupils.[16]

Mabel C. Dibble, one of the younger Atlan members at 35, was already a well-known teacher by 1890, when she and her pupils exhibited work at the Western Decorating Works. Raised by a widowed mother who encouraged her evident artistic talent, Dibble was, by all accounts, an independent and confident businesswoman. In addition to operating a successful china painting studio, she managed the Chicago office of the *Ceramic Monthly* china painting journal after it moved to New York City, and, after 1899, served as the Chicago Ceramic Association's correspondent for the magazine's successor, *Keramic Studio*, the official publication of the National League of Mineral Painters.

Dibble, like most of the women in the Atlan Club, came of age after the Civil War in a country experiencing rapid industrialization, waves of economic recession, and, more specifically, the emergence of the feminist movement. The term "New Woman," first used in 1894, came to stand for the progress middle- to upper-class women were making toward self-sufficiency and the shift in the focus of their energies from home to workplace. Debates, both pro and con, raged in print and pulpit regarding the proper role of women; but at the same

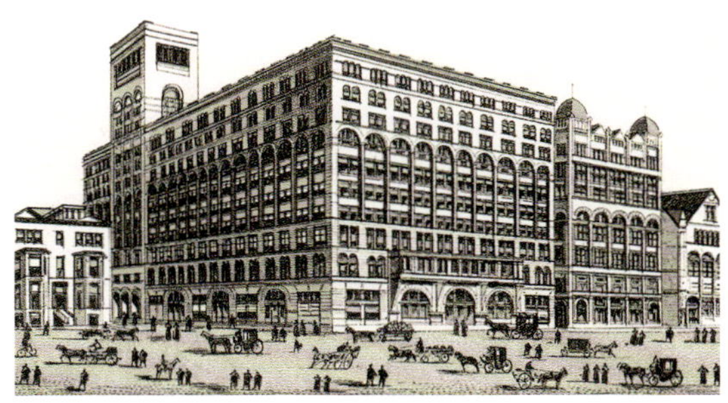

2.5 Many of Chicago's best-known professional china painters had studios in the Tower of the Auditorium Building, located in the heart of Chicago's china painting district. Public transportation was available in the form of streetcars, horse-drawn carriages, and later electrified train—Chicago's famous "L." *Photo*: Author's collection.

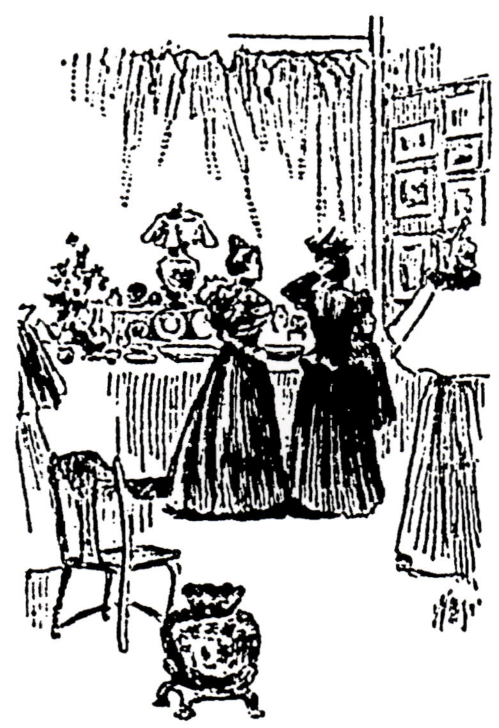

2.6 Visitors viewing ceramics during an open house and sale hosted by the "colony" of china painters with studios in the Auditorium Tower, 1895. *Source*: "Tenth-Floor Colony Exhibit," *Chicago Record*, November 8, 1895, 3.

time, there was widespread agreement that women should be trained to be self-supporting. While many single young women identified paid work as a major vehicle of woman's emancipation, others, including Dibble, had no choice: it was their sole means of survival. But they also selflessly took on leadership roles in women's clubs and civic organizations that sought to improve social conditions, secure political equality, or enhance the quality of life, as in her case, through art.

The Atlan Club's fifteen founding members, who ranged in age from twenty to fifty-three years, comprised an elite microcosm of the many middle- and upper-middle-class women who decorated china in Chicago. Most of the women were single, divorced, or widowed, and china decorating was their primary source of income; several were supporting elderly parents or dependent siblings; most were childless, but some had grown children. For some, china painting provided personal "pin money" or discretionary household income that contributed to a more comfortable life. Just three women were married; of these, one was living in reduced circumstances after her husband's business failed; the other two had husbands whose jobs required extensive time away from home or travel, allowing the women time to develop their hobby or business.

Of the founding members whose family histories are known, only three were born in Illinois and, of these, just one in Chicago; five were born in New York State; three came from families that migrated from New York to Wisconsin. Nearly all had landed in Chicago in the 1860s and 1870s, accompanying parents or husbands attracted by economic prospects inherent in a rapidly growing city. By 1870, Chicago was the nation's second-largest city; by 1890, it was a major industrial metropolis with a population of more than one million. As the "crossroads of America," it offered a heady mix of commerce, industry, art, culture, and opportunity for ambitious women.[17]

Most of the Atlan women were popular teachers of china painting; several painted portraits and landscapes as well as porcelain; some excelled in a variety of crafts, including pyrography, pottery, and embroidery. Most studied painting and design at one of Chicago's fledgling art academies; others developed their talent through private lessons or instruction manuals; several had studied art in Europe. A few were talented "amateurs," in the phrasing of the day, who enjoyed painting for personal pleasure and to beautify the interiors of their homes. All demonstrated artistic ability far beyond the dabbling in drawing and painting popularly associated with female education. Although many of its members developed strong friendships, the Atlan Ceramic Art Club was not a social club but a professional association of women, reminiscent of a medieval guild, in which members were dedicated to a specific craft, with standards defined for work and performance and acceptance based upon artistic talent, rather than social status.

Chapter Three

The Second Exhibition

A high standard of excellence was observed throughout the collection, which embraced a number of pieces that had been exhibited at The Fair, and of which some took medals. The collection showed what rare work could be produced in Chicago.
—"An Artistic Affair," *Inter Ocean* (Chicago), December 15, 1893, 4

On December 12, 1893, following the closing of the World's Fair, the Atlan Art Club held an informal reception at the residence of Eva E. Adams. The event combined a social function with an exhibition and sale of the members' art china. The club's display of china—all appropriate as gifts for the holiday season—filled three large rooms. The local *Inter Ocean* newspaper, which appealed to an upscale readership, described the collection as large, varied, artistic, and tasteful, with "much originality apparent in many of the ornamental articles, most of which were useful as well," and indicative of "what rare work could be produced in Chicago."[1] Several pieces had been exhibited at the Columbian Exposition, including some that took medals.

In the receiving line were the club's officers: President Cornelia Mann, Vice President Emma Anderson Kittredge, Secretary-Treasurer Florence Pratt, and councilors Eva E. Adams and Henrietta Zeublin, a new member. Adams, the hostess, was one of several Atlan members who worked discreetly as "private professionals," in that they did not rely upon teaching or selling their work for their primary financial support. A minister's daughter orphaned at a young age, she had the good fortune to be adopted by her affluent stepmother who sent her to the prestigious Dearborn Female Seminary, where she excelled in art and music. Adams maintained a private studio in the family's large residence on Chicago's nearby South Side.

The club's president, the well-connected Cornelia Mann, was the daughter of a prominent Milwaukee grain dealer. She was a close friend and perhaps a former teacher or pupil of ceramist Susan S. Frackelton, since, as Mrs. Washington L. Mann, she was one of the two women to whom Frackelton dedicated her classic instruction manual, *Tried by Fire: A Work on China- Painting*, in 1886. After their marriage in 1871, Cornelia and her husband moved to Chicago, where, despite years of conscientious study, she did not become a professional instructor until "adversity entered her life" through the loss of wealth and her beautiful home due to her husband's financial reverses.[2] By the time she became an Atlan member in 1893, she had "long been known in the West as a serious artistic worker of extraordinary skill."[3]

Florence Jane Donovan Wilcox Pratt, the club's energetic organizer, was a graduate of the Academy of Design, where she took classes in drawing, painting, design, and china painting before perfecting her skills and offering lessons. Born in New York, Florence had been brought as a child to Wisconsin, where her mother supported the family by operating a millinery shop in Waukesha. After marrying in 1871, Florence moved to Chicago; later, as a divorcee, she married real estate developer Ezra Huntington Pratt in 1891. During their brief marriage, Florence became increasingly self-sufficient as she offered lessons and developed a national reputation as an excellent china decorator. In 1894, she was treasurer of the National Leage of Mineral Painters, while Cornelia Mann was an honorary vice president.

The club's social connections and sales success contributed to its

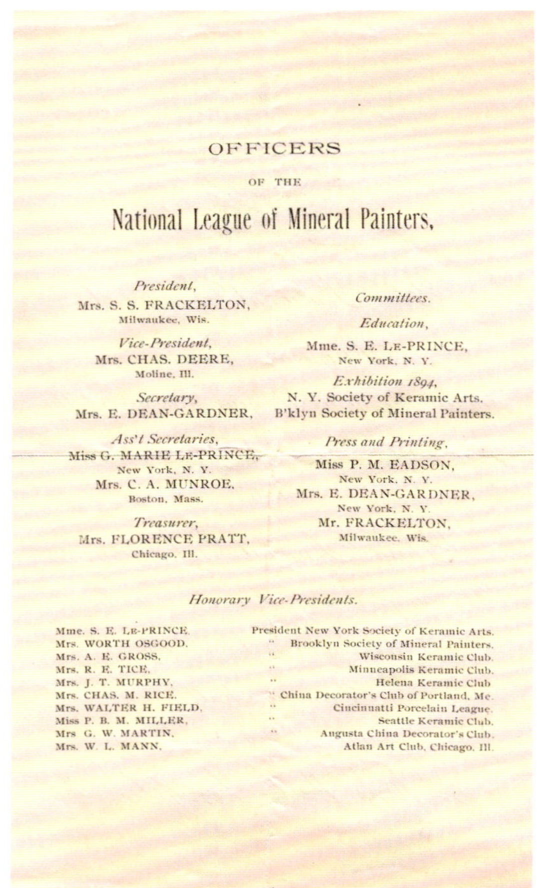

OFFICERS

OF THE

National League of Mineral Painters,

President,
Mrs. S. S. FRACKELTON,
Milwaukee, Wis.

Vice-President,
Mrs. CHAS. DEERE,
Moline, Ill.

Secretary,
Mrs. E. DEAN-GARDNER,

Ass't Secretaries,
Miss G. MARIE LE-PRINCE,
New York, N. Y.
Mrs. C. A. MUNROE,
Boston, Mass.

Treasurer,
Mrs. FLORENCE PRATT,
Chicago, Ill.

Committees.

Education,
Mme. S. E. LE-PRINCE,
New York, N. Y.

Exhibition 1894,
N. Y. Society of Keramic Arts.
B'klyn Society of Mineral Painters.

Press and Printing,
Miss P. M. EADSON,
New York, N. Y.
Mrs. E. DEAN-GARDNER,
New York, N. Y.
Mr. FRACKELTON,
Milwaukee, Wis.

Honorary Vice-Presidents.

Mme. S. E. LE-PRINCE.	President New York Society of Keramic Arts.
Mrs. WORTH OSGOOD.	" Brooklyn Society of Mineral Painters.
Mrs. A. E. GROSS,	" Wisconsin Keramic Club.
Mrs. R. E. TICE,	" Minneapolis Keramic Club.
Mrs. J. T. MURPHY,	" Helena Keramic Club
Mrs. CHAS. M. RICE.	" China Decorator's Club of Portland, Me.
Mrs. WALTER H. FIELD,	" Cincinnatti Porcelain League.
Miss P. B. M. MILLER,	" Seattle Keramic Club.
Mrs G. W. MARTIN,	" Augusta China Decorator's Club.
Mrs. W. L. MANN,	Atlan Art Club, Chicago, Ill.

3.1 Florence Pratt [Steward] was treasurer and Cornelia Mann was honorary vice president of the National League of Mineral Painters in 1894, when the Atlan Art Club withdrew from membership in the federation of ceramics clubs. Many Atlan members continued to exhibit with the Chicago Ceramic Association, whose members retained a leadership role in in the League. Invitation to the Third Annual Exhibition of the National League of Mineral Painters, Carnegie Hall, New York, December 13, 1894. *Photo*: Wisconsin Historical Society, Susan Goodrich Frackelton Papers, 1848–1932.

Eva Eliza Adams, 1893–1904

Eva Eliza Adams (1853–1943) was a founding member of the Atlan Ceramic Art Club. In December 1893, following the closing of the World's Columbian Exposition, she hosted the Atlan Club's second exhibition, a reception and sale, at her family's spacious home on Wabash Avenue. Eva was the club's president in 1894, when the club installed its first exhibition at the Art Institute of Chicago, and again in 1900–1901, when the club sent its exhibitions to Paris and the Buffalo Pan-American Exposition. She last exhibited with the club in 1904.

Eva was born in 1853 in Dubuque, Iowa; her mother died not long after her birth. She spent her earliest years with the family of an uncle and her maternal grandmother while her father completed his divinity degree. Rev. William A. Adams took young Eva with him to Chicago, where he married Sarah Cherrie in July 1862; their happiness was short-lived, as Rev. Adams died just two years later.

In Chicago, Eva lived with her stepmother and the affluent Cherrie family for six decades. They shared a house with the family of Mary J. Cherrie Dolph, Sarah's widowed sister, in a fashionable Chicago neighborhood near Chicago's main business district. Eva graduated from Dearborn Female Seminary, a private school for girls, in 1873. Blessed with a lovely soprano voice, she studied at the Chicago Conservatory of Music and participated in musicales for many years.[1]

In 1881, Sarah's brother, Robert M. Cherrie, an iron and coal merchant who owned Pine Lake Iron Company, built a blast furnace at Ironton in Charlevoix County, Michigan. At the same time, with several investors, he formed a stock company to purchase a large track of land on Pine Lake (renamed Lake Charlevoix, 1926) that they developed into the Chicago Summer Resort Company for their families and friends. Eva and

growing reputation. Between March 1893 and May 1894, more than a dozen women joined the club, including teachers Helen Frazee and Nellie A. Cross, both of whom had exhibited work in the Woman's Building at the Fair. Although adept at painting china, Nellie A. Cross made a specialty of decorating glass tableware; she installed a kiln made especially for firing glass in the studio she shared with Atlan members Louise Anderson and Emma Anderson Kittredge in the Auditorium Building Tower.[4] In 1894, when the Anderson sisters moved to the artist colony housed in the Tree Studio Building (Parfitt Brothers, 1894) on Ohio Street, Cross shared the Auditorium studio with Helen Frazee. "Mrs. Cross has a large class in glass painting," reported local fine arts journal, *Arts for America*, "while Mrs. Frazee's work is of such variety that it covers nearly the whole range of ceramic decoration. They both make a specialty of order work."[5]

In September 1894, the Atlan Club withdrew from membership in the National League of Mineral Painters so that they could apply to join the Art Institute of Chicago as an affiliated club with exhibition privileges, and, coincidently, a large local audience. A committee of three—Eva E. Adams, Henrietta Zeublin, and Lillie E. Cole—successfully negotiated with institute officials, who granted the Atlan Art Club an annual club membership, with members placed on the invitation list by the payment of two dollars each. The date of December 18th was agreed upon for the opening reception of a one-week exhibition of club members' work. Around this time, the word "Ceramic" was added to the club's name to differentiate it from other art clubs in the city.[6]

Sarah spent their summers at the Cherrie family compound named Sweet Briar Farm.[2]

In the 1890s, Eva moved with family members into a substantial new residence on Kenmore Avenue on Chicago's north side, where all were listed in the *Chicago Blue Book*, a select listing of genteel Chicago society. In 1906, Eva toured Europe for several months, returning via New York in late April 1906.[3]

Eva must have maintained a home studio, as she was not listed as an artist in Chicago city directories until 1910, when she joined Mabel C. Dibble, a former Atlan member, in her studio in the Marshall Field Building. Following Dibble's death in November 1917, Eva wrote a tribute to her memory that was published in *Keramic Studio*.[4]

By 1920 Eva was spending much of the year at Sweet Briar Farm in Charlevoix. There, on October 18, 1928, Eva, at the age of 75, married widower Frederick William Sass. A retired Congregational minister, Rev. Sass was a graduate of Chicago's Moody Bible Institute who had held pastorates in various Michigan cities from 1913 until his retirement in 1920.[5]

In Michigan, Eva pursued her interests in art and music. In 1941, she contributed a watercolor picture and "an interesting exhibit" of her china painting to the first exhibition of the Petoskey Artists Association organized by members of the local artist's colony.[6] Eva, age eighty-nine, passed away in her Charlevoix home on January 8, 1943.[7]

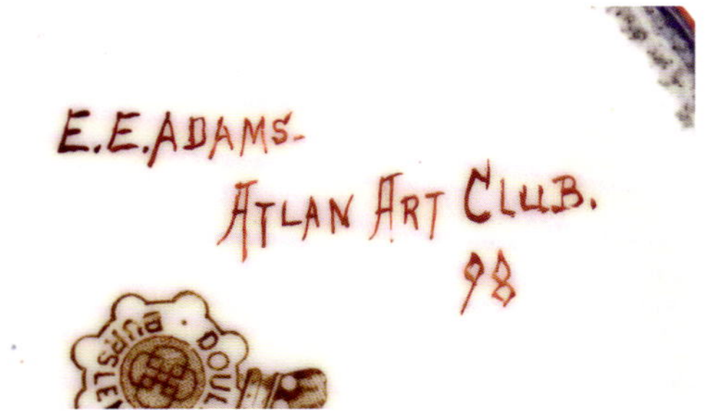

Maker's mark: Eva Eliza Adams. *Source*: Author's collection.

Chapter Four

The Art Institute of Chicago

Now the Atlan Club steps forward and are given one of the galleries in the Art Institute for their exhibition and it was my good fortune to hear one of the prominent officers of the Institute remark that "It was an exceptionally fine exhibition and the Institute was proud of it.

—"The Atlan Club Exhibition," *Arts for America* 3, no. 7 (January 1895): 201

Some 1,500 invitations were issued for the opening reception of the Atlan Club's third exhibition, its first at the Art Institute of Chicago, scheduled for Tuesday, December 18, through Friday, December 21, 1894.

In preparation, the best work of members was collected, including pieces that had been displayed in previous exhibitions. As it was the Art Institute's first exhibition of locally decorated porcelains, the museum's management team—Director William M. R. French, Vice President James H. Dole, and Secretary Newton H. Carpenter—took a great personal interest in its installation, finding much to admire and commend, while, as Atlan members were quite aware, silently regarding it as an experiment that might prove very temporary.[1]

At the opening reception, attended by "a great many society ladies and a goodly number of people interested in art," Eva E. Adams, the club's president, received guests, while club members explained the especially attractive features of the exhibition, which included ceramics and complementary embroideries.[2] Following the protocol of the day, married or widowed members were identified using their husband's names—for example, Florence Steward as Mrs. Le Roy T. Steward or Helen Frazee as Mrs. A. A. Frazee; the names of unmarried women were usually preceded by "Miss."

The *Inter Ocean* commented on the work of each of the fifteen exhibitors, providing insight into the wide variety of decorative items exhibited by Atlan Club members. Most of the exhibition ceramics were decorated with naturalistic flowers—roses, lilacs, lilies, pansies—various fruits, quite a few cupids, and lots of gold. Mabel C. Dibble's tête-à-tête set in pale green with a band of white clover in gold with delicate traceries was singled out as "particularly excellent" in design, painting, and coloring. Henrietta Zeublin and Nellie Greenleaf demonstrated their mastery of portraiture on porcelain, while

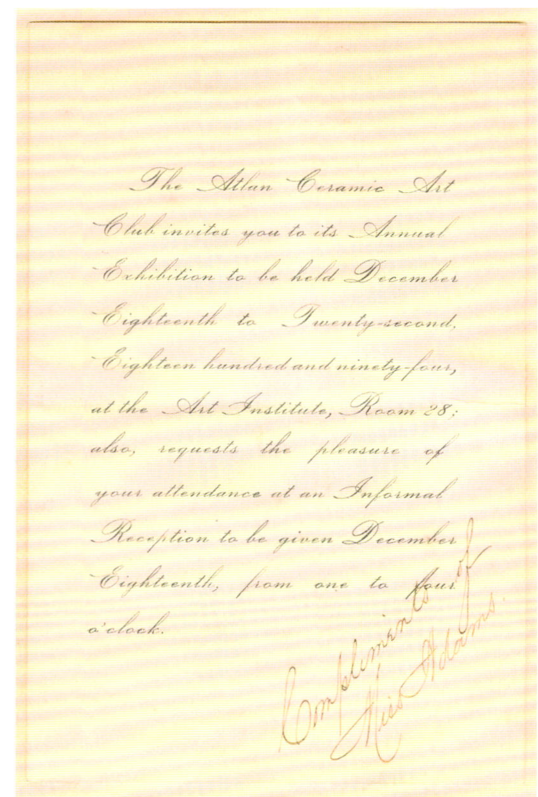

The Atlan Ceramic Art Club invites you to its Annual Exhibition to be held December Eighteenth to Twenty-second, Eighteen hundred and ninety-four, at the Art Institute, Room 28: also, requests the pleasure of your attendance at an Informal Reception to be given December Eighteenth, from one to four o'clock.

Compliments of Miss Adams.

4.1 Eva E. Adams was the club's president when the Atlan Ceramic Art Club issued 1,500 invitations to its first exhibition at the Art Institute of Chicago in December 1894. *Photo*: Author's collection.

Louise Anderson displayed an exquisite "Marie Antoinette style" plate. Nellie A. Cross exhibited a large collection of decorated glass.[3]

A reviewer for *Arts for America* proclaimed, "Ceramics have indeed taken rapid strides in Chicago," and noted the technical achievements of some of its members: Louise Anderson manufactured her own gold and enamels and did her own firing; Mabel C. Dibble had discovered the secret of making a dark rich green enamel, which a large manufacturer was putting on the market labeled with her name (Dibble Green).[4] Made from powdered glass, vitreous enamel (also called porcelain enamel) was applied by brush to the glaze-fired porcelain surface; when fired, it melted, flowed, and then hardened to a smooth, durable coating with a slightly raised effect, as well as richness of color and gloss.

Pleased by the public's response, the Art Institute board extended an invitation to again exhibit at the museum, this time extending free membership tickets to Atlan Ceramic Art Club members.[5] When the club's next exhibition opened in 1895, the liberal *Chicago Chronicle* cheekily heralded the Atlan Club's triumphal entry into the city's lakefront museum, observing that the "high and mighty men" running the Art Institute had rather frowned upon the china painters and "dinner set decorators" until the Atlan exhibition proved so creditable and attracted so much attention.[6] Few could have predicted that the Atlan Club's exhibits would continue annually for twenty-seven years.

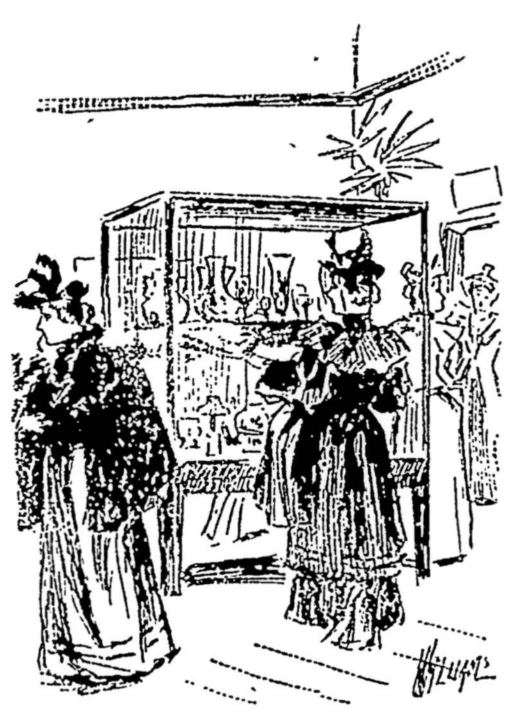

4.2 Fashionable women admiring the hand-painted china displayed in the Atlan Club's first exhibition at the Art Institute of Chicago in 1894. *Source*: "The Atlan Ceramic Exhibition," *Chicago Record*, December 19, 1894, 7.

It is important to remember that pieces contributed by Atlan Club members to exhibitions at the Art Institute, Chicago Ceramic Association, and various studio receptions were for sale, and that proceeds from such sales were important sources of livelihood for the women. For steady income, most relied on filling custom orders, teaching classes, and giving private lessons, often supplemented by selling porcelain blanks, painting supplies, and watercolor designs suitable for copying. In 1896, the price per lesson varied from $1 to $2.50 (about $35–$89 today),[7] with some of the "better artists" able to earn as much as $2,000 ($71,230) a year, a respectable middle-class income.[8] But they had to be skilled artists as well as savvy small business operators. As the editors of *Keramic Studio* routinely pointed out, independent decorators had to do work that set them apart from standardized factory work and commercial studios, both in quality of design and in execution. Commercial china decorating operations, such as Pickard China Studio of Chicago or Ceramic Art Company of Trenton, New Jersey, had marketing and sales organizations and wholesaled their work to department stores, retail china shops, and jewelers across the country. Employing dozens of talented artists, such firms could guarantee retailers a steady stream of moderately priced decorated ware in a variety of popular styles and patterns.

The output of professional china painters, like those in the Atlan Club, was much smaller, being limited to original patterns, which

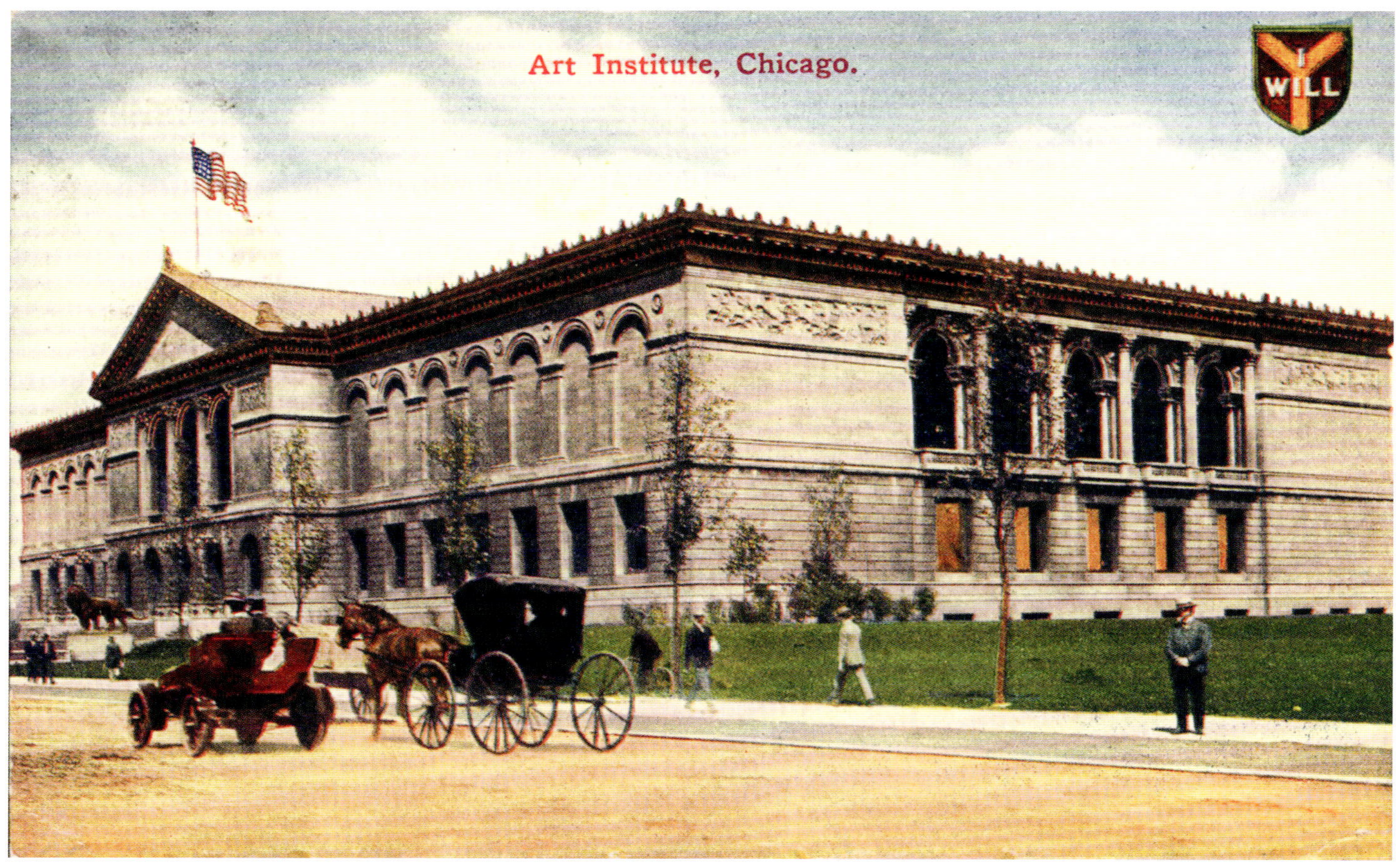

4.3 The Art Institute of Chicago, founded as both a museum and school for the fine arts, found its permanent home in 1893, when it moved into a building built jointly with the city of Chicago for the World's Columbian Exposition at the intersection of Michigan Avenue and Adams Street. *Photo*: Author's collection.

made it time-consuming and therefore more expensive. Work was largely "on order" from customers or produced for exhibition. To sell their work, china painters relied upon word-of-mouth recommendations from satisfied customers, the positive publicity gained from exhibition reviews, and mentions in newspapers and periodicals to build their reputations, call attention to their work, draw customers to their studios, and secure students for their classes. Teaching and selling designs provided a reliable income; however, exhibitions offered sales, invaluable publicity, and credibility, allowing potential customers and students to view and compare their work. Gaining admittance to a highly respected cultural institution like the Art Institute of Chicago was a major incentive for membership and, thus, the future survival of the Atlan Ceramic Art Club.

Chapter Five

Only the Current Year

The exhibition of hand-painted china by members of the Atlan Club, now in progress at the Art Institute, is one of the most important events in its class in the history of the city.
—"Ceramics," *Inter Ocean* (Chicago), November 22, 1896, 35

In May 1896, the Atlan Ceramic Art Club radically revised its exhibition guidelines. In addition to demanding original, independent work, members unanimously agreed that, beginning that year, only work produced during the current calendar year could be offered for exhibition. The result would be a smaller annual display, given that additional time would be required to produce the elaborate work intended solely for the annual exhibition. Because most members were teachers, whose income derived from time spent with pupils or upon order work, it also meant a financial sacrifice.

As previously agreed, each member would exhibit at least three, or, if small, six, pieces each year, with all work approved by a special committee. As an incentive to begin painting early, those failing to complete at least two pieces before the club's spring meeting would be fined 50 cents (about $18) for each missing piece. The members also agreed to use the proceeds of their study fund to hire instructors to help them improve the quality and originality of their work.[1] Money in the fund had been raised through a well-attended musicale held the previous year at the imposing mansion of Mrs. Ferdinand W. Peck, a member of their advisory committee.[2]

The club's fourth annual exhibition that November was smaller, displayed in just six large cases. With nearly one thousand people at the three hour opening reception, it proved difficult for guests to examine the works in detail, owing to the throngs in front of the displays.[3] Regardless, the reviewer from *Inter Ocean* effused, "The exhibition of hand-painted china by members of the Atlan Club, now in progress at the Art Institute, is one of the most important events in its class in the history of the city.[4] In contrast, the art critic from the conservative *Chicago Daily Tribune* found "nothing strikingly original." He did agree, however, that "everything exhibited showed a technical excellence superior to that generally displayed in work of this sort."[5]

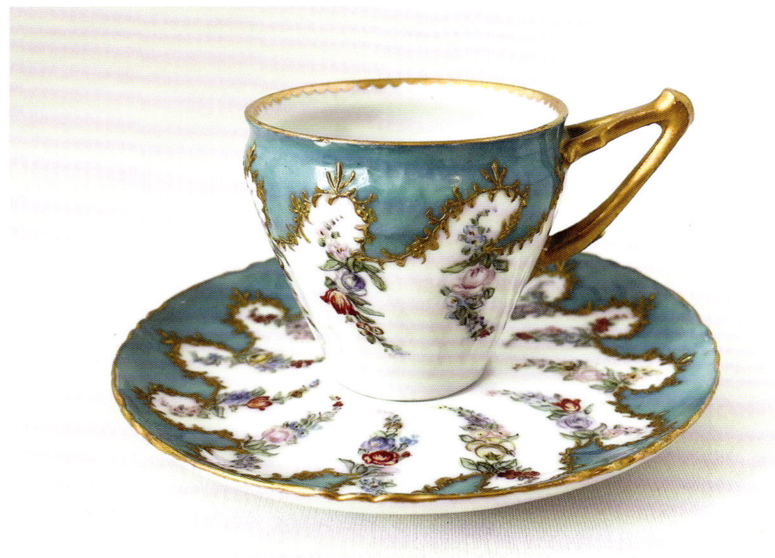

5.1 After-dinner coffee cup and saucer with floral swags and ribbons of gold, Lillie E. Cole, 1896. Cole excelled at small "Dresden flowers" inspired by rococo revival–style porcelain imported from Dresden, Germany. Signed: Atlan/PPP in circle/Ceramic/LC [Lille Cole]/1896. (cup, h: 2"; saucer, d: 5½") *Photo*: Private collection.

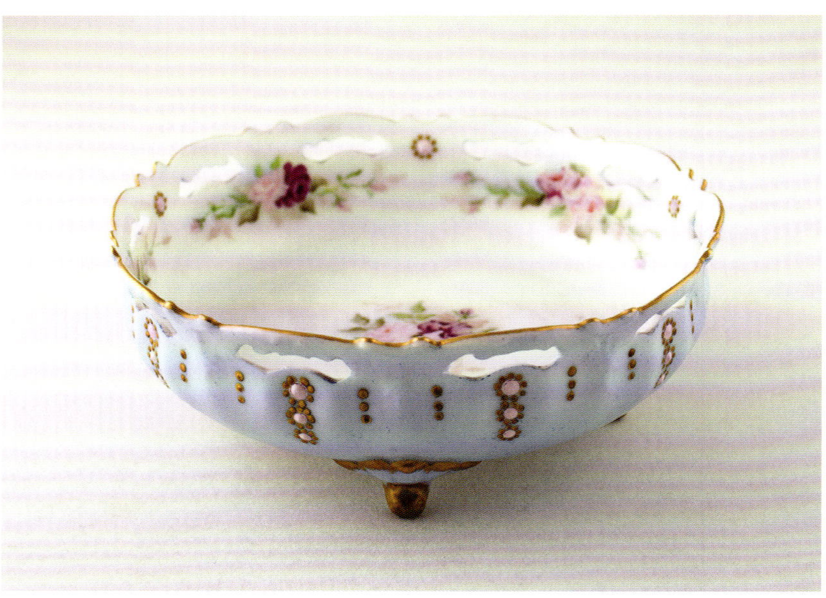

5.2 Footed bowl, Mabel C. Dibble, 1896. Painted two years before Atlan Club members adopted the conventional style, the interior features clusters of naturalistic roses, while the exterior has rows of raised enamel dots over pale blue luster glaze. Signed: MD [Mabel Dibble]/'96/P.P.P./Atlan, in red. Blank: Leonard/Vienna/Austria. (2¼" × 5½") *Photo*: Robert W. Switzer.

Arts for America complimented the members' noticeable striving for a better understanding of form to achieve a high standard overall but observed that some pieces with almost perfect drawing and coloring were so badly applied that they suggested pictures rather than decorations.[6] Probably typical of pieces shown in 1896 is a raised bowl exhibited by Mabel C. Dibble that features a cluster of naturalistic roses at its center and rose sprigs alternating with raised enamel dots on its interior.

In November 1897, the club's fifth annual exhibition also drew an opening crowd of more than one thousand people. Attracting the most attention was the collection of unique plates being sold for $3 each ($108) during the afternoon, with proceeds benefiting the club's study fund. Henrietta Zeublin, club president, had donated the plates for members to paint and offered a $10 (about $360) prize for the best original border pattern. Helen Frazee's plate took top honors, with those of Mabel C. Dibble and Mary A. Phillips receiving honorable mention.[7] Sales amounted to about $300 (about $10,813), not including orders taken for custom work.[8] The *Inter Ocean*, noting that all the work exhibited had been produced within the past year, commented that it was the first ceramic club to insist upon this requirement, with their example having recently been followed by the New York Society of Keramic Art.[9]

At the end of 1897, the Atlan Ceramic Art Club comprised eighteen women, eight of whom were new members. By its fifth year, it was evident that club membership would be transient, with women resigning due to changes in personal or family circumstances, ill health, death, or lack of commitment to the club's high standards and rigorous rules. Among founding members, Cornelia Mann died in 1895; Emma Anderson Kittredge remarried and gave up painting; Roxana Preuszner abandoned china painting for a new career as a lecturer and superintendent of Kansas's elementary Sunday schools. Early on, officers became aware of the importance of maintaining a lucrative

---

Lucy "Lillie" Elizabeth Cole, 1893–1904

A founding member, Lucy "Lillie" Elizabeth Cole (1852–1915) was born in Lake County, Illinois, shortly after her parents migrated from Chenango County, New York. In Chicago by 1863, her father sold real estate; her mother, an active worker at the Sanitary Fair during the Civil War, served on the boards of various charitable organizations.

Working in a home studio on Ellis Avenue, Lillie, "excelling in Dresden flowers," exhibited her work at annual Western Decorating Works exhibitions from 1889 onward. Her work was displayed with the Atlan Club in the Woman's Building in 1893, and she was one of three Atlan members negotiating exhibition space at the Chicago Art Institute in 1894. By 1897, she was listed as an "artist" in the Chicago City Directory and federal census records.

Lillie served as Atlan Club treasurer, 1896–1897; secretary, 1900–1901; and a councilor, 1898, 1902–1903. She exhibited with the Atlan Club at the National Arts Club in New York, 1899; Paris Exposition, 1900; Pan-American Exposition, 1901; and St. Louis Exposition, 1904. Lillie's "Plate, Chinese," which won second prize in *Keramic Studio*'s competition in designs from historic ornament, was published as the magazine's color supplement in December 1902. Her "Practical Hints on China Painting" was published in *House Beautiful* in June 1904. She was still listed as "artist" in the 1910 federal census.

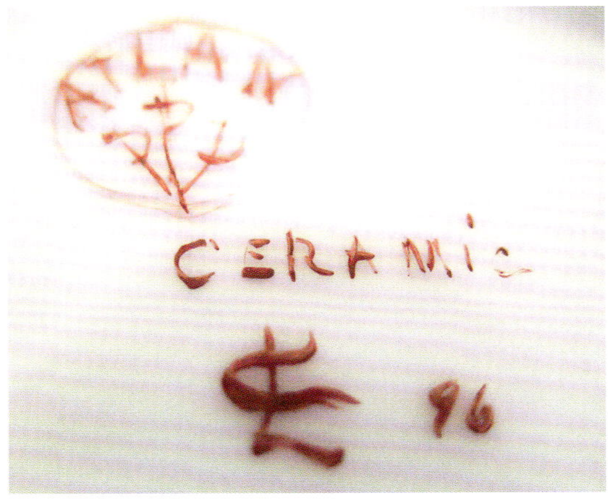

Maker's mark: Lucy "Lillie" Elizabeth Cole. *Photo*: Private collection.

Lillie was also active in the Chicago Ceramic Art Association, the Central Art Association, and the Chicago chapter of the Daughters of the American Revolution. She died following a thyroidectomy at age sixty-three.

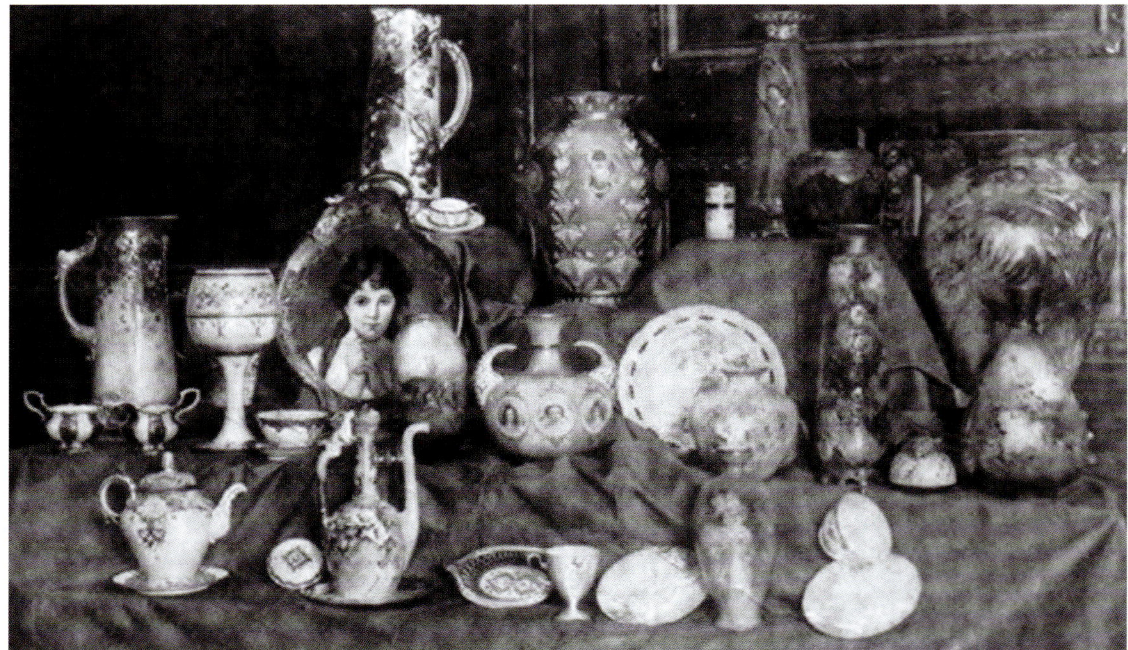

5.3 A case featuring one example of each member's work in the Atlan Club exhibition in 1897, the second year when only pieces completed within the current year could be shown. Mabel C. Dibble's Toasting Goblet (fig. 5.4) is shown in the middle row, second from left. *Source*: "Notes for China Painters," *Art Interchange*, 40, no. 1 (January 1898): 23.

exhibition schedule and promoting a desirable social profile to recruit new members.

Among the new members were five prominent teachers, including Annie S. Marsh, one of the organizers of the Chicago Ceramic Association in 1892 and its first president; two founding Atlans, Grace H. Peck and Lillie E. Cole, had been among her pupils. Helen M. Topping taught painting and drawing in her hometown of Alton, Illinois, before sharing a studio with fellow member Mabel C. Dibble in the Marshall Field Building. Anna Barnes Crane and Marguerite Mills Yeoman maintained studios in the Auditorium Tower, while Adele Lawson gave lessons in her home studio.

In April 1897, the club's founder, Florence Pratt, divorced from E. H. Pratt, married for a third time. Her new husband, Col. LeRoy T. Steward, was one of Chicago's leading citizens. A Civil War veteran active in civic affairs, Steward had served as chairman of the committee on public information during the 1893 World's Fair and played a leading role in the development of the city's lakefront park.[10] At the time of their marriage, he was superintendent in charge of the Chicago Post Office.[11]

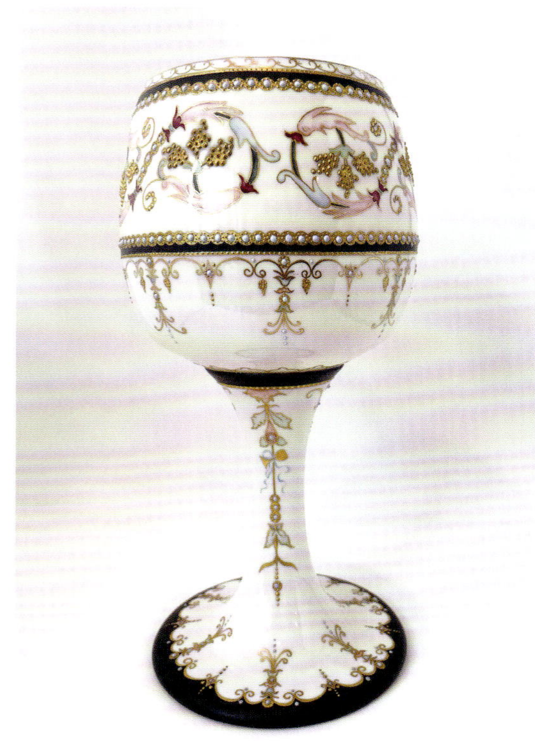

5.4 Toasting Goblet with raised enamel decoration, Mable C. Dibble, 1897. Signed: P.P.P./Atlan in red circle/MCD monogram/1897. Blank: Belleek/Willets. (11″ × 4″) *Photo*: Private collection.

Chapter Six

Adopting a New Style

Not the least interesting china exhibit is made by some amateur china painters. . . . These plates and jugs are really decorative and truly artistic, and Mrs. Koehler and her pupils are equally to be congratulated.

—"Art Life in Chicago," *Inter Ocean* (Chicago), March 27, 1898, 26

In 1898, Atlan Ceramic Art Club members made another radical decision: they abandoned painting china in the "naturalistic" style. As Florence Steward explained, "During this year the members of the club came to a mutual understanding that only porcelains decorated with conventional designs would be offered at an exhibition where we exhibited as a club."[1]

The decision to change their decorative style evolved from a suggestion from William M. R. French (1879–1914), director of the Art Institute. In the words of Florence Steward, "At an exhibition of ceramics held at the Art Institute of Chicago in 1897, in which the club exhibited, the importance of abandoning the naturalistic fashion for a more constructive method, in harmony with the general and broad principles of art, was made clear to the club by the director of the Institute, Mr. French. The club henceforth gave up the naturalistic spray and attacked the problem of training themselves thoroughly in the principles of ornament."[2]

Among decorators of ceramics, the argument between "naturalistic" versus "conventional" styles constituted a debate between classical and modern styles. In this context, "conventional" had a meaning quite different from its daily usage. A conventional approach was essentially an exercise in abstraction, reducing nature to its most elemental forms to be summarized, flattened, and repeated as ornament. It relied upon the artist's training in design and color to guide her in using these basic, usually geometrical, forms to create an appropriate and beautiful design. By contrast, a naturalistic treatment relied on the artist's skill as a copyist to realistically reproduce the beauties of nature and create an illusion of reality. These two distinct approaches to ceramic decoration—conventional and naturalistic—would coexist uneasily for decades.

Since its second year, the club had made efforts to do "something practical" during the winter months. In 1894, to increase their understanding of the scientific basic of mineral painting, members were assigned color tests, which were fired and analyzed; then the women tested, described, and evaluated a series of enamels in varying proportions and mixtures. Some also took a correspondence course of lessons in design from the School of Industrial Art and Technical Design for Women operated by Mrs. Florence E. Cory of New York City.[3]

During the winter of 1895, the club had studied design under Art Institute instructor Grace Long Updyke (1871–1961), who suggested that the women bar "figure work," or representations of people or objects, as being too elaborate for ceramic tableware and adhere to conventional designs as much as possible. In 1897, Director William M. R. French, who considered conventional design the most appropriate form of decoration for china, reinforced this suggestion. The conventional approach to decorative design was already being practiced by students who studied under Louis J. Millet (1856–1923), a celebrated architectural designer associated with the Art Institute of Chicago for more than thirty-two years.[4] After studying architecture and decoration in Paris, he operated Healy & Millet, one of Chicago's most distinguished decorating firms, particularly known for innovative art glass, in partnership with George L. Healy from 1881 through 1899, before continuing the business on his own. His practical experience as a businessman, combined with his artistic accomplishments, made him well qualified to teach a new evening course in applied art, or "decorative designing," at the Art Institute, "for the sake of the improvement of our various manufactures," first offered in January 1886."[5]

Millet, like many Chicago architects and artists of his generation, advocated and applied the British concepts of design popularized by theorists Owen Jones, Christopher Dresser, and Louis F. Day. In his decorative design classes, Millet stressed, in addition to freehand drawing and watercolor skills, the derivation of designs from nature and historical ornament, along with the abstraction of plant forms resulting in a conventionalization of nature that was characterized by a flattening and simplification of natural forms. Millet's course formed the nucleus of the Art Institute's Department of Decorative Design formally established in 1891, and by the mid-1890s, some of his students were applying his "modern" principles of design to ceramic decoration. The romanticism and rich eclecticism associated with the Aesthetic movement's "artful home" were being usurped by a modern design attitude that advocated abstract motifs and simple, uncluttered settings.

"The winter of '98 was truly the beginning of our most serious study," Florence Steward recalled. For instruction, the Atlan Club hired Florence Koehler (1861–1944) to teach them the principles of good design and conventionalization with a view to learning which

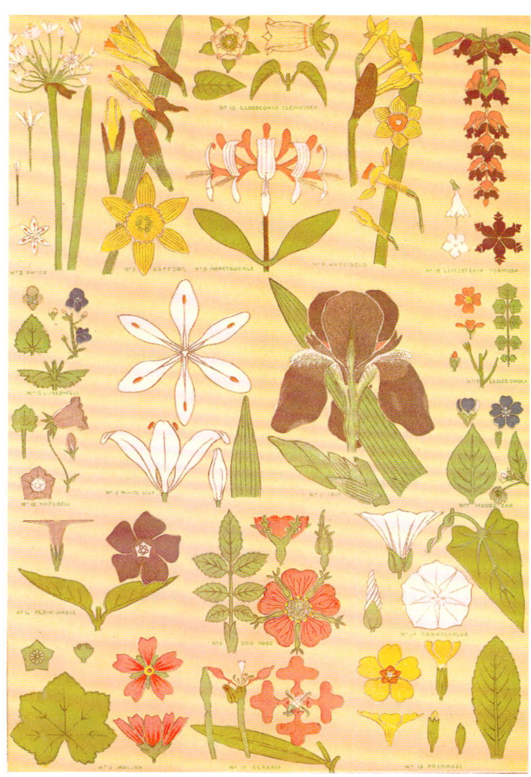

6.1 Christopher Dresser's plate XCVIII, Leaves and Flowers from Nature, in Owen Jones's *The Grammar of Ornament*, illustrated several varieties of flowers to reveal "the inherent structure of design of flora, from the bud to full flower. If nature is one source of conventionalization, geometry is the other. Nature and geometry together generate the ideal motif." *Source*: Owen Jones, *The Grammar of Ornament: Illustrated by Examples from Various Styles of Ornament* (London: B. Quaritch, 1910).

forms would be most suitable for application on porcelain surfaces. Koehler, partner in a successful Chicago interior design business with former colleague Edith Whiteside Sheridan, had taught china painting at the Kansas City Art Association and School of Design before moving to Chicago in 1893.[6] Although a newcomer to Chicago, her work was familiar to several Atlan members who had exhibited their decorated porcelain alongside hers in the Chicago Ceramic Art Association's entry in the Chicago Architectural Club's 1895 exhibition.[7]

Like many art instructors, Koehler advocated the serious study of antique ceramics, which included designing and working in each epoch of "historic ornament" as demonstrated in the artwork of ancient, preindustrial cultures, as the first step in developing appropriate designs. In progressive art schools at the time, the study of historic ornament was considered essential to understanding the principles of good design and developing a style of one's own. Mastery of the historic epochs was a first step in abstracting the art principles illustrated in the ancient masterworks and then applying them as motifs to create an original work of art. The stylized symmetry of the Japanese approach to design—so fashionable at the time in art, fashion, and home furnishings—was another powerful influence.[8]

Often consulted for guidance were publications such as Owen Jones's *The Grammar of Ornament*, a hefty volume with richly colored plates of every period in art from the earliest known to its original publication date in 1856. This seminal design sourcebook by Jones (1809–1874), a British architect, presented his theories on flat patterning, geometry, and abstraction of ornament. As his *Grammar* illustrated, abstract traditions in ornament tended toward geometry, with almost half of the plates showing pure geometrical motifs in either simple or complex forms with a minimum of modeling or shading. In the book's last chapter, titled "Leaves and Flowers from Nature," a colored plate by fellow design theorist Christopher Dresser (1834–1904) illustrated the structure of design of flora, from the bud to full flower, with its inherent geometry, with "true art consisting in idealizing, and not copying, the forms of nature."[9]

Two decades later, British designer and educator Lewis F. Day (1845–1910) published another influential series on ornamental design, including *The Anatomy of Pattern* and *The Planning of Ornament*, both 1887, in which he analyzed the geometry and repetition of patterns inherent in various historic textiles, architecture, and tiles.[10] Like Jones, Dresser, and Day, many instructors in the new field of "decorative design" were convinced that the foundations of good, modern design were to be found in studying the lessons of history and non-Western cultures.. This notion was widely promoted in Chicago, with lectures on ancient pottery and their inherent national characteristics popular topics at the Chicago Ceramic Association, the Chicago Art Institute, and art and women's clubs.

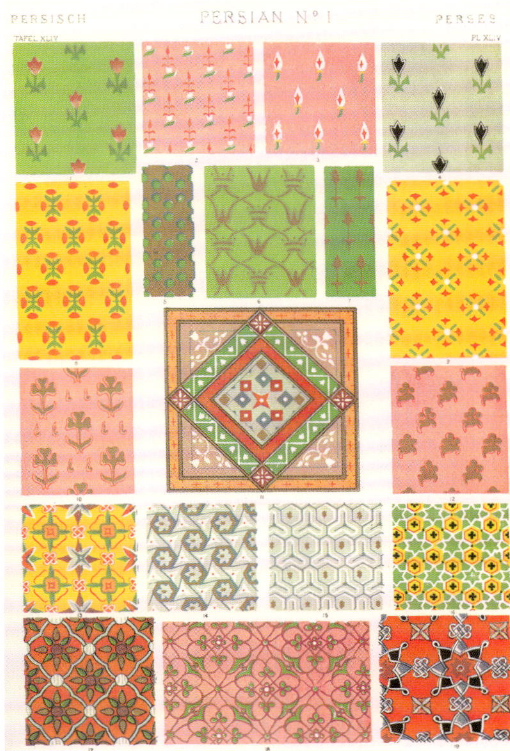

6.2 A typical illustration, this one showing Persian geometric motifs, from Owen Jones, *The Grammar of Ornament*, first published in 1856. *Source*: Owen Jones, *The Grammar of Ornament: Illustrated by Examples from Various Styles of Ornament* (London: B. Quaritch, 1910).

In January 1898, eighteen members of the Atlan Club began their systematic study of historic ornament as applied to china painting under the inspiring leadership of Florence Koehler. Extending into March, the class met weekly for eight class lessons, divided into small groups for technical lessons, and consulted a reading list of books made available at the public library.[11] Club members showed exceptional diligence in faithfully tracing, reading, and submitting designs as they conscientiously studied the different epochs, beginning with Egyptian, followed by Persian, Arabic, Moorish, East Indian, Indo-Persian, Japanese, and Chinese, as illustrated in Jones's *The Grammar of Ornament*. So keen were they to match the enthusiasm and encouragement shown by Koehler, that members sacrificed almost all other work to accomplish as much as possible given the limited time. It quickly proved its worth.

In the spring of 1898, the Chicago Arts and Crafts Society invited the club to exhibit a case of their china in their first exhibition to be held jointly with the Chicago Architectural Club at the Art Institute. A new organization founded in 1897 at Hull House, the settlement house for immigrants founded by Jane Addams and Ellen Gates Starr, the Arts and Crafts Society advocated the integration of art, education, and labor to make them more expressive of the nation's democratic and industrial life. Inspired by a similar reform movement in England, it promoted the revival of handicraft and created a renewed

Florence Cary Koehler
Honorary Member, 1898

Florence Cary Koehler (1861–1944) was a multitalented artist and jeweler who excelled at painting on porcelain, interior design, and metalworking. She was the instructor who, in study courses conducted 1898–1900, introduced Atlan Club members to the study of historic ornament and taught them how to create and apply conventionalized designs on porcelain. She was made an honorary Atlan member in December 1898.[1]

Born in Jackson, Michigan, Florence grew up in Missouri, where she married Frederick Harrison Koehler in Kansas City in February 1884. Announcing their marriage, the local newspaper noted, "Miss Cary came from Brookfield some four years and was at once admitted into the best society—a position she has meritoriously maintained. She is a bright, vivacious, talented young lady, who is sure to attract friends wherever she appears."[2] Her new husband was chief clerk at the Lindell Hotel; later, he worked as a railway ticket broker.[3]

Florence's painting skills were apparently self-taught; however, her work was of "such merit and beauty" that she was hired to teach china painting at the Kansas City Art Association and School of Design in 1892.[4] When fire destroyed the school in January 1893, she and her husband moved to Chicago, where Florence's work was displayed at the World's Fair. When former Kansas City resident Edith Whiteside Sheridan followed a year later, they opened a studio offering china painting and interior design.[5] In December 1895, Florence was invited to spent five months at the Rookwood Pottery in Cincinnati, where she was "singularly successful in the difficult process of painting underglaze."[6] In 1897, Florence was one of the founding members of the Chicago Arts and Crafts Society; the following year, work by her Atlan Club pupils was shown in the society's first exhibition.[7]

By 1897, Helen had tried her hand at making jewelry, which would become her primary passion. That year she spent several months traveling in Europe with a Kansas City protégée,

appreciation of handmade objects as superior to mass-produced goods. By bringing craftworkers, amateurs, and enthusiasts together for lectures, exhibitions, and sales of crafts, the society was influential in improving taste and encouraging artistic production. Unlike its British predecessor, whose products targeted the elite, the Chicago movement aimed to serve the city's rapidly expanding middle class.

The founders of the Chicago Arts and Crafts Society included prominent architects, artists, writers, craftworkers, and social reformers. Among them were Atlan Club members Louise Anderson and her sister Emma Anderson Kittredge, Lillie E. Cole, and Ella Pratt Steele; their instructor, Florence Koehler; and University of Chicago sociologist Charles Zueblin (Charles spelled his surname "Zueblin" rather than "Zeublin") and his journalist wife Rho, son and daughter-in-law of Henrietta Zeublin, the club's current president. Although founding members of the Atlan Club, Anderson and Kittredge soon transferred their allegiance to the Arts and Crafts Society, shifting from decorating china to producing furniture, metalwork, and various handicrafts.

The Chicago Arts and Crafts Society's exhibition would be the Atlan Club's first public display of their porcelain with conventional designs. Described in the catalog as the "Work of the Ceramic Art Club during a short preparatory course of study of the best styles of decorated pottery and porcelain, under Mrs. Koehler," the twenty-one entries included pieces decorated by fifteen members. The pieces

---

Bertha Lynde Holden, studying with prominent Arts and Crafts jewelers, including Alexander Fisher in London.[8] Returning to Chicago in 1898, she shared a studio with craftworker Ella Raymond Waite in the Woman's Temple, where she taught china painting and made jewelry. In addition to instructing the Atlan Club, Florence gave china painting lessons in the New York studio of *Keramic Studio* editor Anna Leonard in 1900 and to the Kansas City Pottery and Porcelain Club in 1902.[9]

Around 1902, and perhaps before, Florence began traveling as a companion to wealthy Chicago socialite and divorcée Emily Crane Chadbourne. Settling in London, Florence worked as a jeweler from 1904 until 1914, when, on her own, she moved to Paris, France.[10] While in Paris, and later in Rome, Italy, Florence's experience and talent in interior design provided a steady income, as wealthy acquaintances relied upon her to fit out their villas and mansions.[11] One of her most devoted art patrons was Mary Elizabeth Sharpe, an American businesswoman, whom she named executor of her will. In 1947, three years after Florence's death in Rome, with the cooperation of the Museum of the Rhode Island School of Design, Sharpe organized a memorial traveling exhibition of her work.[12] Collections of her jewelry, paintings, and decorative arts were donated to the Rhode Island School of Design and Everson Museum of Art; her papers and correspondence are held by the Arthur and Elizabeth Schlesinger Library on the History of Women in America at Harvard.

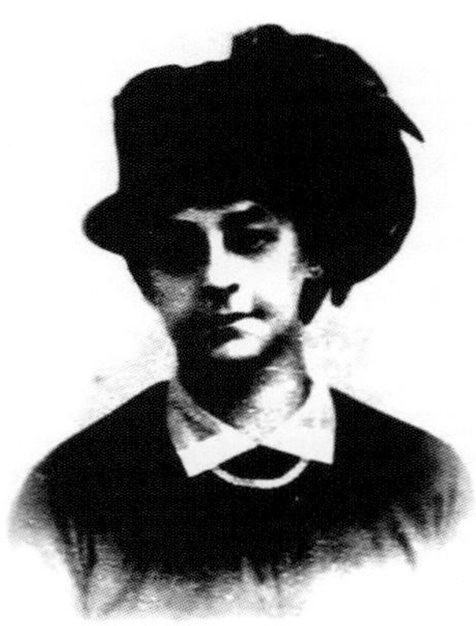

Florence Koehler's passport photo for her 1915 application. *Source*: Ancestry.com.

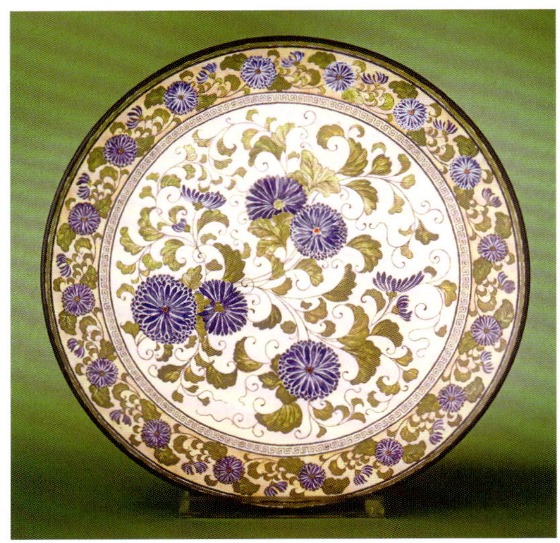

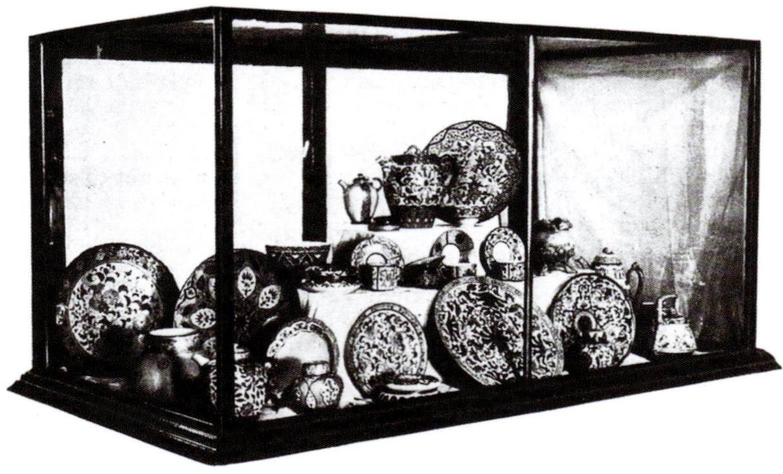

6.3 "Old Japanese" plaque, blue chrysanthemums, Helen Frazee, 1898. Decorated during the study course with Florence Koehler, the plaque was displayed in the Chicago Arts and Crafts Society's first exhibition in March 1898; the Atlan Club's annual exhibition in November 1898; and the 1899 Greater America Exposition in Omaha, Nebraska. It was also illustrated in Mabel C. Dibble's 1899 articles in *Brush and Pencil* (April) and *Keramic Studio* (August). Signed: Frazee/98," and partial label from Greater America Exposition. (d: 12") *Photo*: Chicago History Museum.

6.4 Helen Frazee's "Old Japanese" plaque is visible in the far-left corner in the Atlan Club's case at the Chicago Arts and Crafts Society's first exhibition in March 1898. *Source*: "Exhibit of the Atlan Ceramic Club," *House Beautiful* 4, no. 5 (October 1898): 189.

offered for sale were quite expensive, ranging in price from $7 (about $252) for Lillie E. Cole's "low dish, old China" to $15 ($540) for Helen M. Topping's "bowl, Indian."[12] "The Atlan Club had every reason to congratulate its members on the few choice pieces which so proudly held their own besides their more pretentious neighbors," wrote editor T. Vernette Morse in *Arts for America*.[13] Reviewing the Chicago Arts and Crafts exhibition, *House Beautiful*, a Chicago-based magazine targeting homemakers, praised the exhibit of china decorated in conventional lines by the Atlan Club, "composed of women who rebelled against this naturalistic school," concluding "the entire effect is so infinitely better and stronger that it is worth any amount of trouble to achieve."[14] The *Inter Ocean* critic noted the sharp contrast and artistic superiority of conventional patterns shown in the work of "some amateur china painters" studying under Florence Koehler over the "shocking weakness" of naturalistic designs.[15]

Hull House resident George Twose, president of the Arts and Crafts Society, viewed the exhibition from a higher, ethical perspective. He, like many social reformers, regarded handcraftsmanship as a regenerative force that could bring joy to the worker, reunite art with life, and, in so doing, elevate the public's taste. An everyday object not only revealed the spirit of its maker but influenced the morality of its users. As he explained in his review, "Cups and saucers, pots and pans, tables and chairs, though insignificant in their humble ministering, are important articles when considered in the light of the sensitiveness of man's character and the persistency of their effect."[16] To many practitioners, the movement was primarily one of ideas, not objects; however, few disagreed with British reformer William Morris's dictate: "Have nothing in your houses that you do not know to be useful, or believe to be beautiful."

Following the Atlan Club's successful debut in the Chicago Arts

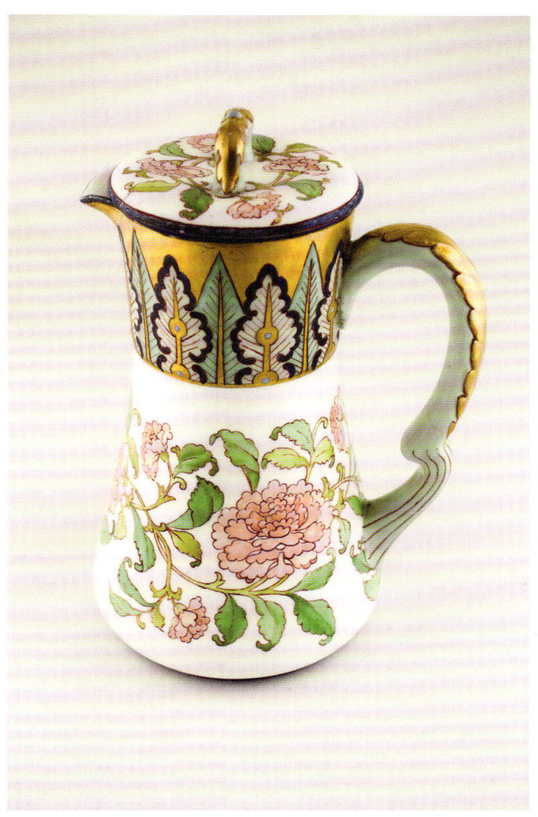

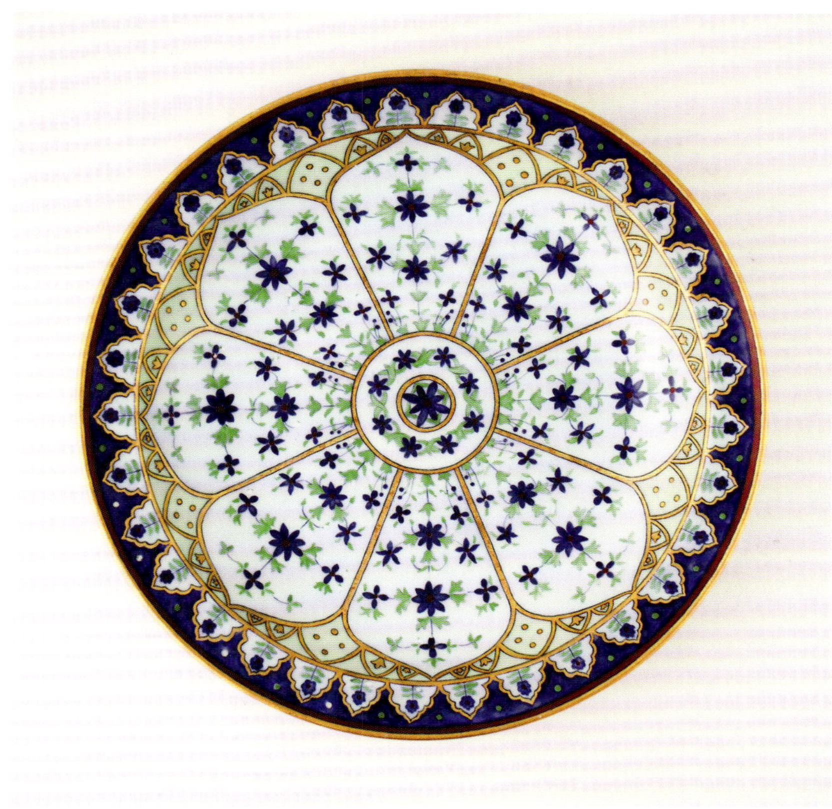

6.5 "Chocolate pot, Chinese," Eva E. Adams, 1898. The pot, with decoration inspired by historic ornament, was listed as "Sold" for $25 ($919) in the Atlan Club's 1898 exhibition catalog. Signed: E. E. Adams/ Atlan Art Club/98. Blank: Doulton/Burslem. (h: 9") *Photo*: Robert W. Switzer.

6.6 "Indo-Persian" low dish, Mabel C. Dibble, 1898. This dish with symmetrical geometric ornamentation was priced at $10 ($368) in the sixth annual Atlan exhibition in 1898. The design and treatment were published in the September 1899 *Keramic Studio* (see fig. 7.4) Signed: Mabel C. Dibble/1898/ Atlan/Indu[sic]-Persian. Blank: Limoges. (d: 8") *Photo*: Robert W. Switzer.

and Crafts exhibition, *Brush and Pencil*, a local magazine promoting the fine and applied arts, requested an article describing the club's work. Mabel C. Dibble, a competent writer, provided a short account of the club's history and aims. She also described their method of study under Koehler, accompanied by photographs of some of the china exhibited at the Art Institute the previous year.[17] Countering criticism that the small club was elite, she acknowledged that its rules were more severe and stricter than those of similar art clubs; its sole purpose was study and progress, compelling each member to show improvement each year. While most teachers, ignorant of advances in design, still pursued naturalistic floral work, Dibble was pleased to report, "In Chicago it is not so, and the club members who are teachers, are gratified by an increased interest among their pupils in the beautiful conventional work so dear to these teachers' hearts."[18]

Atlan members, like many Chicago china painters, abandoned their hot studios during the summer months, but maintained busy exhibition schedules in the spring and fall. In April 1898, they shipped a "small but choice" exhibit of their work to the Trans-Mississippi and International Exposition, the world's fair opening in June in Omaha, Nebraska.[19] In September, they placed a selection of their work in the exhibition sponsored by Thayer & Chandler, successors to the Western Decorating Works. According to Florence Steward, the Atlan exhibit tested the comparative merits of conventional versus naturalistic applications to glazed surfaces. To her dismay, "We were sometimes very disappointed to find that some of the best designs, color schemes and almost perfect technique was given but a glance and turned away from in silence, to rave over a festoon of forget-me-nots, or a cupid balancing on the nose of a teapot, by visitors at this exhibition." Some measure of balm was offered when the editor of the Chicago-based homemaker magazine *House Beautiful* asked for a picture of this exhibit, remarking, "It was the only china exposition that he had cared to look at."[20]

In November, the pieces in the club's sixth annual exhibition were nearly all inspired by their winter study course. For example, Eva E. Adams displayed pieces with Chinese, Japanese, Indian and Moorish designs, including a chocolate pot with a Chinese motif that sold for $25 (about $901). Mabel C. Dibble expanded the range with items based on Indo-Persian, Arabian, and Egyptian motifs. Helen Frazee added a plate in Old Japanese, along with plaques, cups and saucers, and bon bons, all in conventional designs. Mary Humphrey, the club's president, showed fifteen pieces, many with Chinese motifs. A surprising number had already been sold when the exhibition opened.[21]

Opening attendance was in the high hundreds. The radical new style did not go unnoticed. As the *Chicago Daily Tribune*'s art critic reported, "The Atlan Club's study of historic ornament has enabled the members intelligently to adapt and compose conventional decoration of a pure style. Such work is a vast improvement on the usual exhibits of china painting where the decoration consists chiefly of flowers and fruit applied haphazard."[22] Sales amounted to about $300 (about $10,813), not including orders taken.[23]

Florence Steward recorded the public's reaction as noncommittal, considering their departure from naturalistic decoration as experimental; however, their "ART friends," whose opinions counted, were generous with praise and encouragement. In her words, "This chance to test the interest of the public in our departure from floral decoration was indeed valuable, because it brought to us many adverse criticisms that had been in the spirit of kindness, withheld, but now in view of our apparent abandonment of those lines, were freely expressed as a preface to their congratulations that the Atlan Club had entered upon the only style of work that would endure or make for us any lasting name."[24] Abandonment of the naturalistic style, so firmly established among their china painting peers, was a bold move that allowed their work to be perceived as unique and progressive, two traits that appealed to the affluent customers who acquired hand-painted porcelain as household art.

At their December meeting, Atlan members made Florence Koehler an honorary member of the club and adopted a resolution thanking the woman "whose advice and instruction had been the impulse to begin and the sole aid to the furtherance of their studies."[25]

Chapter Seven

Preparing for Paris

If this group of workers goes on in this good way there will be collected in the country many articles known as "Atlan Ware," long after the turns in this globe shall have rolled the living members under. This is no pretty fancy, either, but the logical outcome of the movement.

—James William Pattison, "Ceramics for Paris," *Inter Ocean* (Chicago), November 26, 1899, 19

In January 1899, Atlan Club members began a second winter study with Florence Koehler, this time learning to abstract the essential elements of flowers into design modules to create original designs, while keeping strictly to conventional decoration. Once again, in addition to group instruction, members received a technical lesson, with the club divided into small classes of four or five, with each bringing a piece of china whose design and color would be criticized.[1]

As they pursued their study and research, they had to lay aside their old ideas of decoration; however, as work progressed, they became more and more confident they were learning the true principles of decorative art upon which each could build a unique personal style and, as a group, set a new standard for porcelain painting. Conventionalized decoration, as presented by Owen Jones and the British proponents of "modern design" and interpreted through Florence Koehler involved more than geometry or the stylization of nature; it connoted the creation of an ornament appropriate for the shape of the object being decorated; it implied the eventual creation of a new style of ornament appropriate for its age.

Despite their commitment to conventionalization, a February vote to change the constitution to exclude all work from exhibition not decorated in the conventional style was taken and lost.[2] It seems likely that several members who were known for fine figural subjects and portraits on porcelain were not willing to have their work rejected. Others, dependent on income from their work, may have been reluctant to formally commit to adopting a new design approach that might alienate loyal customers.

Koehler advised the group to work toward developing "an American style of ornament," an idea, noted Florence Steward, that, five years earlier, the Atlan Club had embodied in the preamble of its constitution, as a goal of founding an American School of Art. Even

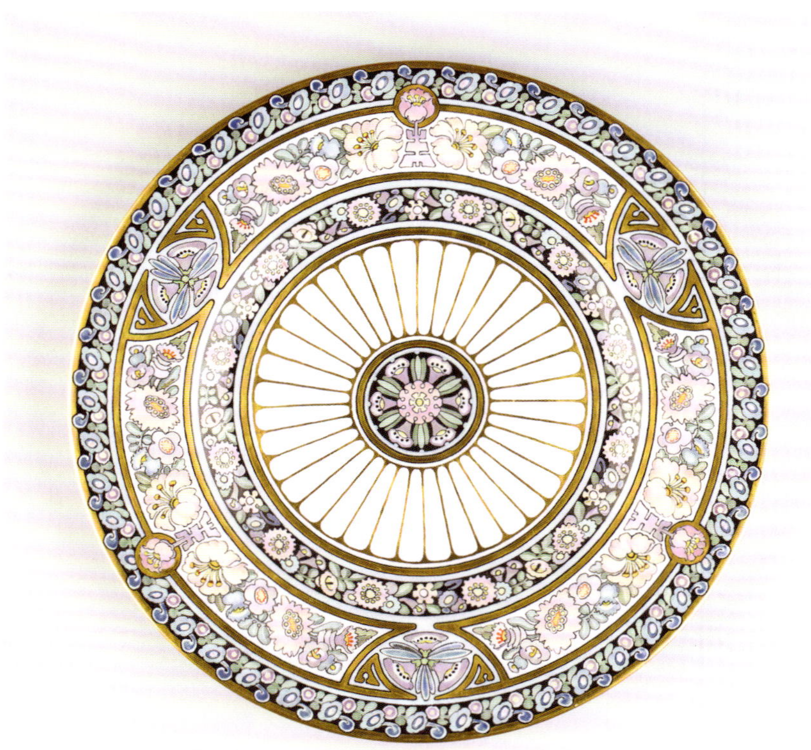

7.1 Plate, Helen Frazee, ca. 1900. A precise geometric control grid was critical in developing the plate's complex conventional layout. This undated plate was kept in Frazee's studio as an example of her work. Signed: Frazee. (d: 10¼") *Photo*: Chicago History Museum, i174280_pm.

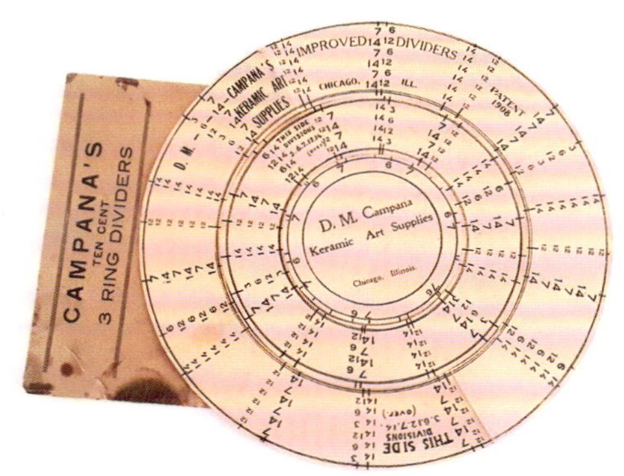

7.2 Paper protractors or dividers were used to accurately divide and mark off the equal number of divisions required for the symmetrical placement of a conventional design on a ceramic surface. Chicago china painter D. M. Campana's art supply company offered various devices to improve precision and expedite preparation. *Photo*: Tim Ingram.

then, the idea had been percolating among progressive ceramic artists for several years; Atlan mentor Susan S. Frackelton had called attention to the need for a national school of ceramic art in *Tried by Fire* as early as 1886.

Steward noted that New York decorative designer Candace Wheeler, while director of women's applied arts at the 1893 World's Fair, in private conversation, had also urged Steward to make every possible effort to induce the Atlan Club to study and originate something that might be called distinctly American in style, saying, "You have a larger number of good workers than in any other Club so there is no reason why you should not take the lead; the work of our New York societies is in no sense as good as yours."[3]

Atlan Club members, along with those of the Chicago Ceramic Association and the National League of Mineral Painters, understood that the creation of a ceramic art that was original and distinctly American depended upon improving the skill of individual china painters to ultimately raise the standard of ceramic art in general. To further this end, it was important for the groups to offer their members instruction in the basics of design, drawing, and color. As a result, all three organizations offered study courses, with members expected to develop and submit designs appropriate for use on ceramics to a committee that would provide feedback in the form of design critiques.

At the time, the Atlans' search for a national style of ceramic decoration coincided with the movement to make Chicago a major center of American art. This was the goal of the Central Art Association, organized in 1894 by many of the city's leading artists and educators to "promote art education among the people" and thereby raise the level of public taste. Under the leadership of novelist Hamlin Garland and sculptor Lorado Taft, the Central Art Association functioned as a Chautauqua-type educational assembly, uniting artists, students, educators, and art lovers in one central organization to encourage native talent and the development of homegrown art. Departments, or "leagues," devoted to various branches of art provided lectures, publications, and traveling exhibitions, while *Arts for America*, the association's national organ, reported its progress. Its ceramic department was staffed by members of the Chicago Ceramic Association, headquartered within the Central Art Association in the Fine Arts Building (S. S. Beman, 1898) on Michigan Avenue across from the Art Institute.

For several years, *Arts for America* awarded gold medals through the Central Art Association's ceramic department in its quest to raise the standard of American art. During the 1896–1897 season, it awarded medals for "the best collection of china showing the greatest variety of styles" at exhibitions sponsored by the Western Decorating Works, National League of Mineral Painters, Chicago Ceramic Association, Atlan Club, and Tennessee Centennial.[4] The Atlan Club's gold medal recipient was Helen Frazee, whose work was "looked upon by everyone as excelling in decorative quality," with a report in *Arts for America* noting, "The range of Mrs. Frazee's subjects is wide, her drawing is excellent and she has the ability to decorate a form instead of painting it."[5]

In May 1899, the National League of Mineral Painters, hosted by the Chicago Ceramic Association, sponsored a three-day Keramic Congress, wherein noted ceramic artists presented papers in conjunction with an exhibition of members' work at the Art Institute of Chicago. By gathering the best work from around the country, league officers hoped to have a large collection from which to select the best pieces for its group display at the Exposition Universelle of 1900 to be held in Paris, France.[6] When the league's Art Institute exhibition closed, most of the pieces, along with a special exhibition put together by the Atlan Club, were sent to the Greater America Exposition in Omaha, where they were displayed in the Department of Fine Arts.[7]

While in Chicago, league members were guests of the Atlan Club at a reception held in the spacious studio Florence Koehler shared with craftworker Ella Raymond Waite in the Woman's Temple (Burnham & Root, 1892–1926), a thirteen-story "skyscraper" housing art studios and offices along with the headquarters of the Woman's Christian Temperance Union. In Koehler's workroom, visitors viewed the sketchbooks of Atlan members and the decorations in different stages of completion, the various color schemes, and the adaptation of the designs to the ceramic shapes. Like most professional china decorators, the women first worked out their designs on paper, then transferred them to the objects using tracing paper or pouncing (pricking holes with a fine needle around the outline of the sketch or pattern, then dusting with powder).

Keramic Studio editors, who were among the visitors, were so impressed they published an illustrated profile of the club in their August 1899 edition. They praised the wonderful handling of colorful enamels by club members, "so like the old Chinese," and the intricate, but charming, drawings of designs adapted from ancient cultures. Singling out the designs of Grace H. Peck, Lillie E. Cole, Helen M. Topping, and Mabel C. Dibble for their "delightful individuality," the editors wrote, "It is the work that will last for ages without wearying one."[8] They told readers to pay close attention to forthcoming illustrations, because designs by Atlan members would complement *Keramic Studio*'s series on historic ornament and its application to modern ceramic shapes. As promised, Helen Frazee's design and treatment for a plate appeared in August, followed in September by Mabel C. Dibble's

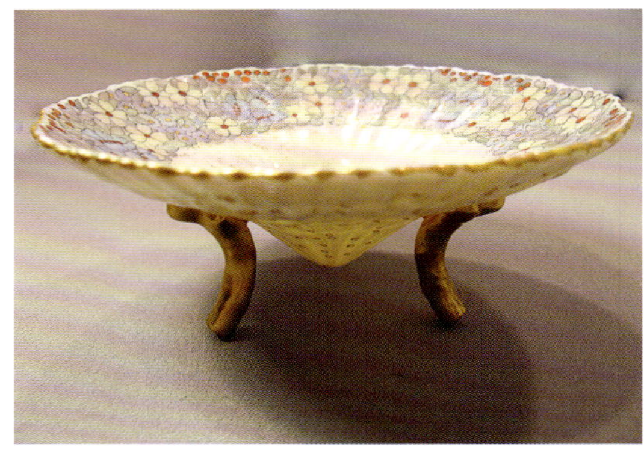

7.3. Footed dish with a floral band, Florence Steward, ca. 1898. Marked Atlan but undated, the Belleek porcelain blank was illustrated in Willets Manufacturing Company's 1898 catalog. Signed: F. Steward/Atlan. (2″ × 4¾″) *Photo*: Private collection.

Helen Maria Topping, 1895–1907

After joining the Atlan Club in 1895, Helen Maria Topping (1863–1907) was a councilor, 1897–1900, and its secretary, 1902–1903. She served as treasurer of the Chicago Ceramic Art Association in 1897 and was a member of the Central Art Association.

Helen was born in Alton, Illinois, where her father was a hardware merchant. After studying at the Monticello Seminary in Godfrey, Illinois, and graduating from Alton High School in 1880, she gave lessons in music, painting, and drawing in her family's home. She was an enthusiastic member of the Alton Opera Company and a successful musician.

After spending the winter of 1886 with an aunt in Chicago, she remained in the city. She was one of the organizers of the Chicago Ceramic Art Association in 1892 and occasionally delivered lectures on china painting techniques to members. She had a china painting studio in Steinway Hall by September 1896, when the *Ceramic Monthly* published a profile of Topping, who, "as a teacher and exhibitor," was "well known to the Chicago art public." After 1897, Topping shared a studio in the Marshall Field Building with Atlan member Mabel C. Dibble.

In 1898, her "bowl, Indian" and Satsuma water pot were among items displayed by Atlan Club members in the first Chicago Arts and Crafts Society exhibition. Her work was also shown in the 1900 Paris Exposition; the 1901 Pan-American Exposition in Buffalo, New York; and the 1904 St. Louis World's Fair.

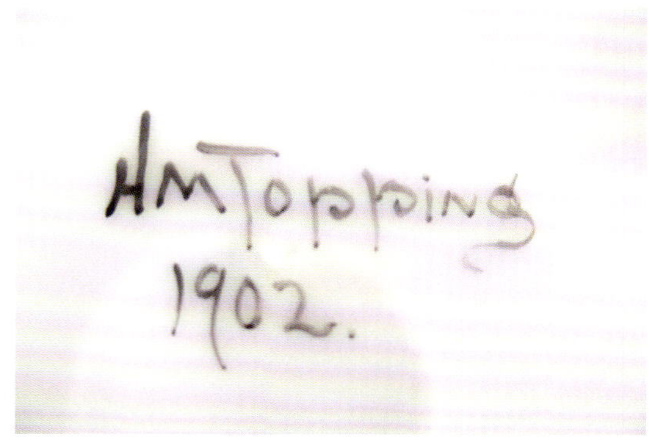

Maker's mark: Helen Maria Topping. *Photo*: Private collection.

Topping died in Chicago from pneumonia at age forty-three in 1907. When she was buried with a Christian Science service, the *Alton Evening Telegraph* described her as "enthusiastic and animated, and interested in every good cause," and noted, "She was possessed of rare talent, and the many art treasures of her own design and creation will be silent reminders of the beautiful spirit which pervaded her art, which she so deeply loved and cherished."[1]

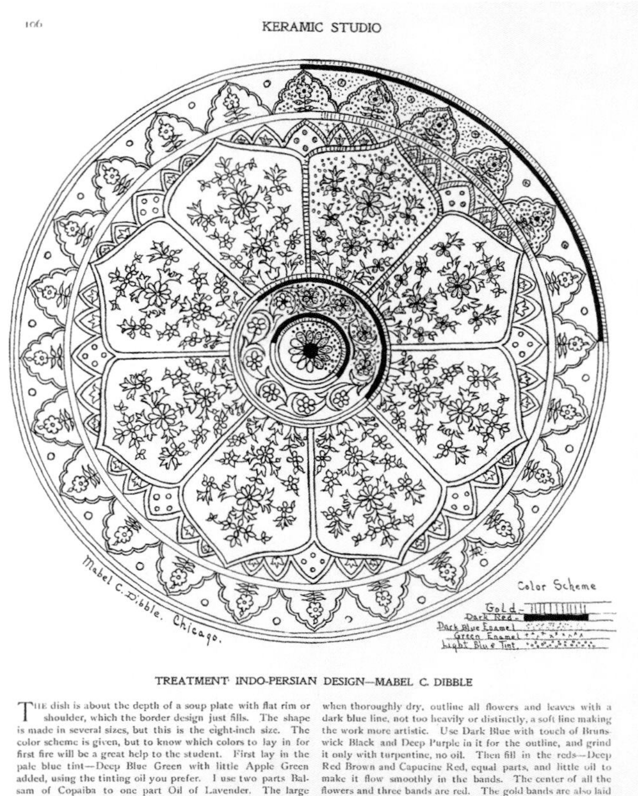

106 KERAMIC STUDIO

TREATMENT INDO-PERSIAN DESIGN—MABEL C. DIBBLE

The dish is about the depth of a soup plate with flat rim or shoulder, which the border design just fills. The shape is made in several sizes, but this is the eight-inch size. The color scheme is given, but to know which colors to lay in for first fire will be a great help to the student. First lay in the pale blue tint—Deep Blue Green with little Apple Green added, using the tinting oil you prefer. I use two parts Balsam of Copaiba to one part Oil of Lavender. The large panels, two center bands, and small panels in border all have background of the pale blue. Wipe the design out carefully, when thoroughly dry, outline all flowers and leaves with a dark blue line, not too heavily or distinctly, a soft line making the work more artistic. Use Dark Blue with touch of Brunswick Black and Deep Purple in it for the outline, and grind it only with turpentine, no oil. Then fill in the reds—Deep Red Brown and Capucine Red, equal parts, and little oil to make it flow smoothly in the bands. The center of all the flowers and three bands are red. The gold bands are also laid in for the first fire, and a line of gold around each little green circle in the border. The dish is now ready for first fire, and

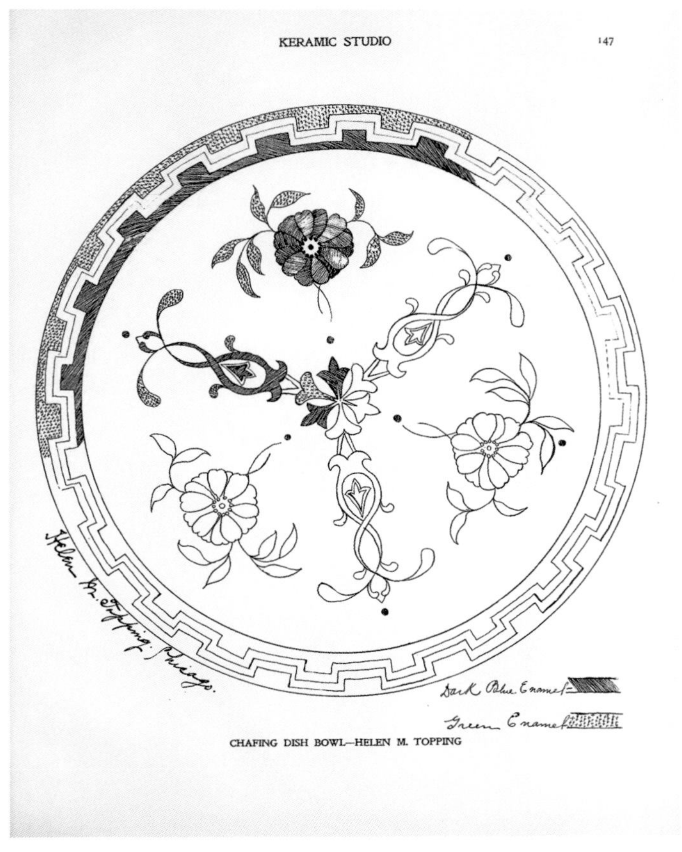

KERAMIC STUDIO 147

CHAFING DISH BOWL—HELEN M. TOPPING

7.4. (left) Mabel C. Dibble's design and treatment for her low dish with "Indo-Persian Design," incorporating conventionalized flowers with geometric symmetry, was published in *Keramic Studio* in September 1899. The actual plate is shown as fig. 6.6. *Source*: *Keramic Studio* 1, no. 5 (September 1899): 106.

7.5 (right) Helen M. Topping's design, "suggested by the Chinese," for a shallow chafing-dish bowl was published in the November 1899 issue of *Keramic Studio*. Her treatment featured dark blue enamel flowers with pale yellow centers and apple-green leaves and a central trefoil design on a center tinted all over with a soft gray tone. Source: *Keramic Studio* 1, no. 7 (November 1899): 146–147.

design for an Indo-Persian dish, first shown at the Chicago Arts and Crafts exhibition. Frazee's bonbon dish, plate, and cup came out in October 1899; Helen M. Topping's design for a chafing-dish bowl appeared in November.[9]

Since the first of the year, Atlan Club members had been preparing and executing work for the club's entry in the upcoming world's fair, the Exposition Universelle of 1900, the first major European exhibition of American hand-painted porcelain and glazed pottery. The club, which had been granted space in the Palace of Industries, was the only American ceramic club granted accommodations for an individual exhibit. To help defray the large expense of exhibiting the club's work in Paris, Ella Pratt Steele, who joined in 1896, hosted a successful "Palmistry reception" at her stylish residence on Ellis Avenue in early November. Two of Steele's friends gave palm readings, Eva E. Adams sang, and a Miss Richards gave several recitations, while various Atlan members presided over the tea table.[10]

When the Chicago Ceramic Association opened its seventh annual exhibition, its first at the Art Institute, on November 10, 1899, and not, as usual, at the Auditorium Building in December, its timing perturbed Atlan members.[11] "Many are confusing the Atlan Ceramic Art club's exhibition, at which the work that will go to the Paris exposition will be shown, with the ceramics exhibit now on view at the Art Institute," reported *Inter Ocean*, "The Atlan club wishes to announce that its display will not be placed on exhibition until Nov. 21."[12]

A special feature of the Atlan Club's seventh exhibition was the "Paris case," a custom-built showcase holding the ceramics selected by Florence D. Koehler that would be sent to the 1900 exposition.[13] Local art critic James William Pattison was impressed by the "architectural" treatment of the pieces, with designs respecting the severely simple porcelain shapes. Noting that the designs were of two sorts, original and adapted, he singled out Helen Frazee's large, full-bodied "Peacock Vase" (Persian) as one of the most important articles in the room, "because of its individuality as well as for the ingenuity displayed in conventionalization of peacock forms."[14] The *New York Times*, identifying the Atlan exhibit as "one of the rarest and by no means the least costly of the exhibits that Chicago will send to the Paris Exposition," described the collection to be "superb in coloring and workmanship . . . Every piece is declared by connoisseurs to be of the highest class of ceramic work."[15]

The *Chicago Times-Herald* considered the Atlan showing "the best exhibit of local ceramic work yet made," finding it refreshingly "free from examples of porcelain embellished with irrelevant nosegays, fish, fowl, and, save the mark, human faces and figures."[16] The reporter for the *Art Interchange*, a national magazine for amateur artists, appeared more impressed by the women's amity than by their "mixed styles in conventional treatment," commenting, "Those who do not appreciate the aims of this zealous band of workers realize that they reflect credit on Chicago. Devotion to an ideal that carries fifteen to twenty people through seven year's work without friction or disagreement, merits success and is worthy of emulating."[17]

Mabel C. Dibble, Chicago correspondent for *Keramic Studio* happily reported, "The club members surely should feel satisfied that their progress the past year has not only been noted but appreciated, for never has the Atlan exhibit awakened so much interest, especially among artists and critics. The attendance during the two weeks has been good, the sales very satisfactory and particularly have the comments and praise of the strangers within our gates warmed our hearts, their first surprise over the total absence of all floral decoration—so closely connected with china painting in all minds—having passed away."[18]

When the annual exhibit closed, Mary Humphrey, the club president, had the dubious honor of spending several weeks on packing and logistics before the work was shipped to Paris.

Chapter Eight

International Recognition

It is evident that within the last ten years, America has done much toward the furtherance of its ceramic art. At least one-fourth of the section of varied industries is devoted to ceramics. The Atlan Ceramic Art Club occupies a prominent place.

—"Ceramic Art at the Exposition," *Brooklyn Daily Eagle* (Brooklyn, NY), July 8, 1900, 24

The Exposition Universelle, better known as the 1900 Paris Exposition, was held from April 14 through November 12, 1900. After being buoyed by positive feedback at home, American china decorators found disappointment in Paris—indeed, received a "black eye," according to *Keramic Studio*—when exposition judges excluded from gold medal competition most of the American overglaze ceramic work. While the decoration was American workmanship, it was on wares of foreign manufacture. While giving American pottery makers a much-needed stimulus, the practice disqualified many talented artists.[1] Despite such limitations, Dedham Pottery, Susan S. Frackelton, the National League of Mineral Painters, Newcomb Pottery, and the Atlan Club were awarded bronze metals.[2]

"The shapes sent over from Europe for our 'amateurs' to use are mostly abominable," declared James William Pattison, reviewing the ceramics shown at the Paris exposition for Chicago's *Inter Ocean*. "Pray, make your own pots and vases, ladies and gentlemen, and then we can judge of your talent. However, as we must content ourselves today with the decoration of this mongrel pottery, it must be stated that the results are in some cases excellent, because talent will tell even against odds."[3]

More specifically, Milton B. Marks, in the *Art Interchange*, claimed the Atlan Club's work demonstrated "the highest degree of artistic and decorative skill" and exemplified the progress being made in ceramic art in America. He was suitably impressed by the "decidedly progressive movement" demonstrated by the fact that all the pieces had been done within the last year.[4]

In January 1900, club members began another "winter campaign" with Florence Koehler, this time focusing on color, while holding them strictly to original designs. This was viewed "with mingled feelings of the tremendousness of the task," recalled Florence Steward, "yet intense curiosity as to how we should manage it, but with-all,

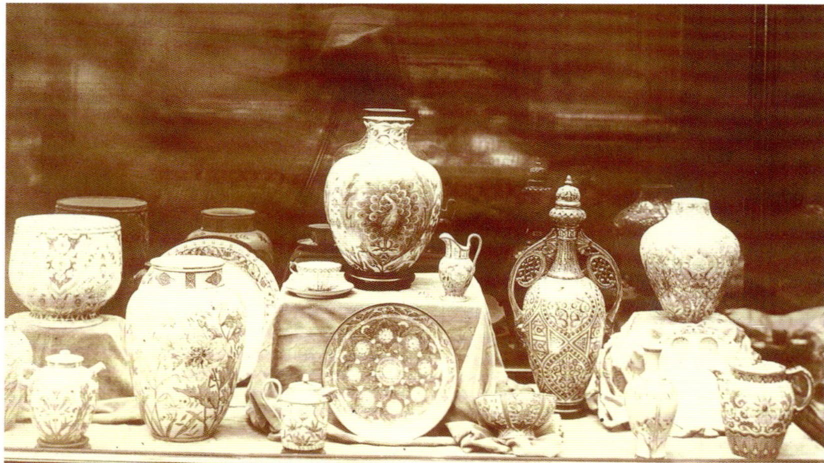

8.1 One of the two "Paris cases," arranged to show at least one piece by each Atlan member, in the 1899 exhibition at the Chicago Art Institute. James William Pattison, art critic for *Inter Ocean*, considered Helen Frazee's "Peacock Vase (Persian)," elevated at center, one of the most important articles in the exhibition, "because of its individuality as well as for the ingenuity displayed in conventionalization of peacock forms." *Photo*: Chicago History Museum, i073071_pm.

never doubting that we would ultimately succeed."[5] By then, Atlan members had adopted Koehler's method of applying enamels "flat" to the porcelain surface, treating it more as a medium to paint with, rather than using it sparingly for highlights or ornamental relief, as had been the custom among china painters.

That same winter, inspired by the Atlan Club's success, the Chicago Ceramic Association hired Art Institute design instructor Louis J. Millet to teach a Saturday morning study course on "organic ornament," envisioning decoration appropriate for the ceramic form, with local ceramic expert John W. Hasburg teaching the practical application of conventional designs, tools, and materials in the afternoon.[6]

In the spring, Atlan member Grace H. Peck spent time in New York City sketching porcelains displayed at the Metropolitan Museum of Art and studying art publications available at the city's libraries. Noting her visit, *Keramic Studio* reported, "she is a disciple of Mrs. Koehler, and her interesting work on exhibition at Mrs. Leonard's studio has been much admired."[7] At the time, Florence Koehler was giving lessons in the studio of *Keramic Studio* coeditor Anna B. Leonard, who hosted a private showing of Koehler's work, along with that of several Atlan pupils, for the New York Society of Keramic Art.[8] Peck and Eva E. Adams also had pieces in the National Arts Club exhibition, where, "of the decorated porcelain, the best was that exhibited by Miss Grace Peck, of the Atlan Club, Chicago, and by Miss Eva E. Adams, of the same city," according to the *Artist*, a monthly arts and crafts magazine.[9]

While the Atlan Club was acquiring national and international reputations, its members were not necessarily heroines at home. In a letter to the editor of the *Art Interchange*, one reader complained about the un-American character of the china with its foreign designs sent to Paris, and "the misdirected efforts shown in the work of Mrs. Florence Koehler." A Chicago china painter wrote, "The most mischievous results are being seen here in the exploitation of the work of the Atlan

KERAMIC STUDIO

JARDINIERE Mrs. S. E. Zeublin — CHOP PLATTER Eva E. Adams — VASE Mrs. A. A. Frazee — VASE Mrs. E. C. Humphrey — VASE AND PLATE Lillie E. Cole

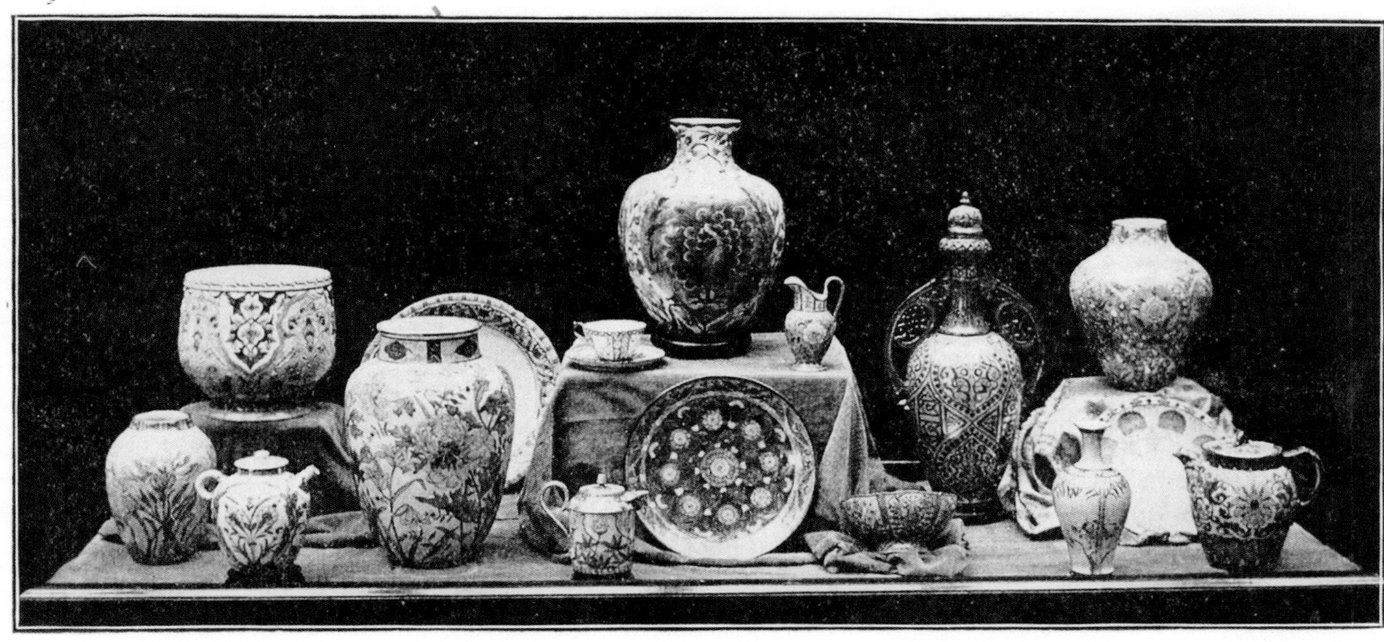

VASE Mrs. R. M. McCreery — VASE Mabel C. Dibble — CUP AND SAUCER Mrs. Adele Lawson — PITCHER Mrs. F. M. Sessions — SMALL VASE Mrs. F. M. Steele

TEA POT Helen M. Topping — HOT WATER PITCHER Grace H. Peck — PLACQUE AND BOWL Mrs. L. T. Stewart — CHOCOLATE POT Mary A. Phillips

8.2 The Paris case, with ceramics identified by their decorators, featured in *Keramic Studio* in February 1900. *Source*: *Keramic Studio* 1, no. 10 (February 1900): 204. *Photo*: Tim Ingram.

Club, of this city, as original work. Workers who formerly did good work are wholly at sea and discouraged over such laudation."[10]

In truth, originating, preparing, and repeating units of precisely placed conventional motifs, particularly on a three-dimensional object, did require more time and skill to create than naturalistic designs, which could be placed at random on porcelain surfaces. Time was money; many decorators feared they would not be able to compete in the marketplace if conventional decoration became the buyer's preference; but not to worry, much to the dismay of *Keramic Studio*, most customers, particularly those in small towns, still preferred the familiar fruits and flowers over the modern abstract designs.

When Atlan members showed pieces in the Chicago Arts and Crafts Society's third exhibit, held in the Woman's Temple in 1900, *House Beautiful* reviewer Mary Adams wrote that several areas of work showed decided advances, including that of the china of the Atlan Ceramic Art Club. Noting the beauty and originality of Atlan pieces and that members had studied "oriental potteries" under the guidance of Florence Koehler, Adams declared, "This has revolutionized china-decorating, so far as the Atlan band is concerned, and the result is a happy one."[11]

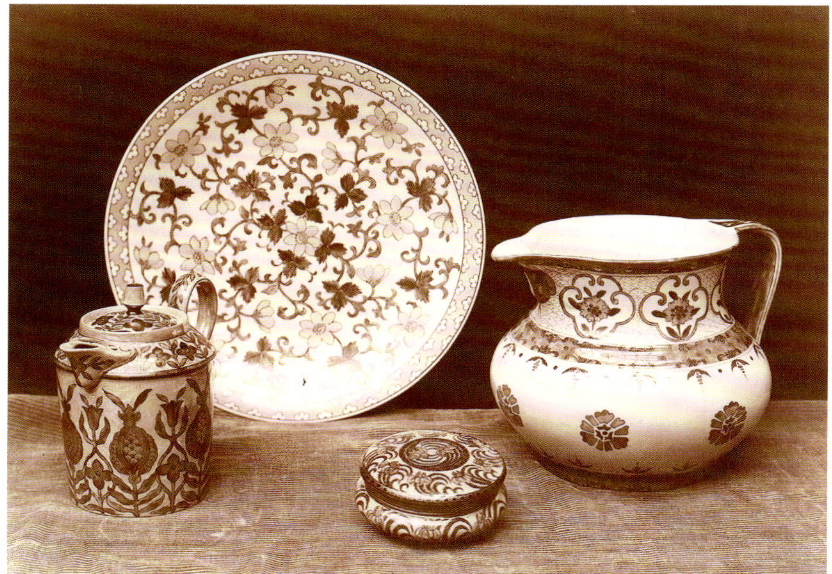

8.3 The Atlan Club's exhibition in October 1900 included, left to right: a hot water pot decorated by Lillie E. Cole; a plate by Beulah L. Frazer; a bonbon box by Helen Frazee; and a pitcher in blue and green enamels by Mabel C. Dibble. This photo was one of the illustrations in Mabel Dibble's review published in the January 1901 issue of *Keramic Studio*. The design and treatment for Frazer's plate, mistakenly attributed to Helen Frazee, was published in the April 1901 issue of *Keramic Studio*. *Photo*: Chicago History Museum, ICHI-073071_pm.

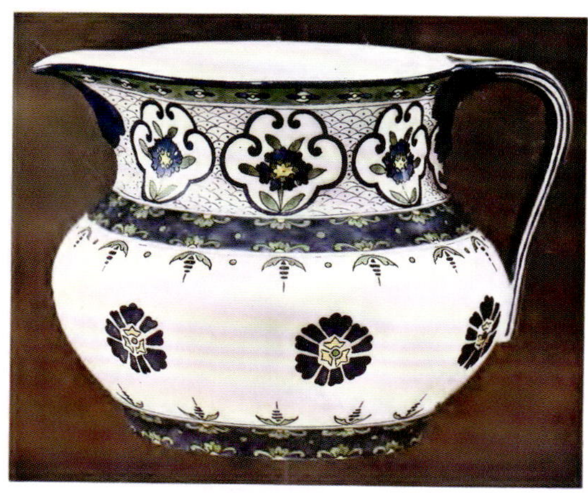

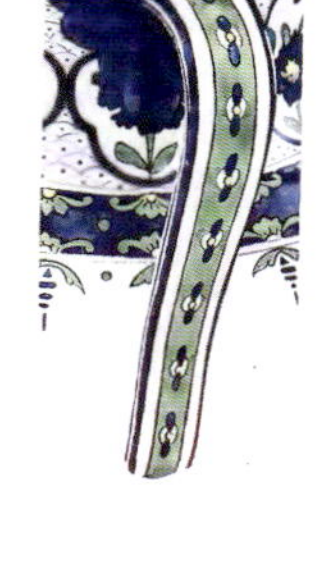

8.4 Mabel C. Dibble's porcelain pitcher, decorated with blue and green enamels in 1900, was a color supplement in the April 1901 issue of *Keramic Studio*. *Source*: *Keramic Studio* 2, no. 12 (April 1901): 254, and supplement.

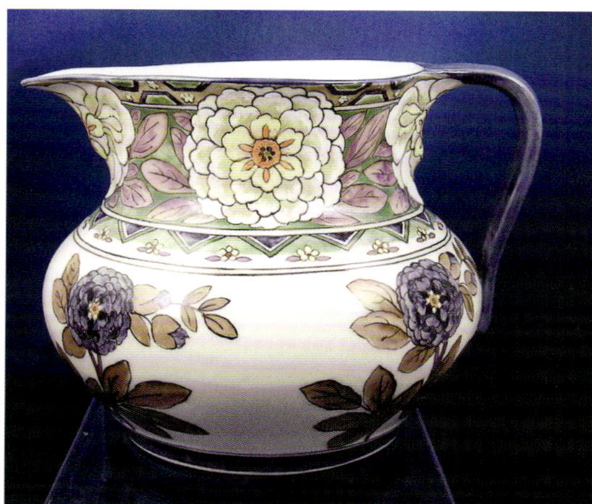

8.5 Pitcher with conventional floral decoration, Helen M. Topping, ca. 1900. It may have been one of the two pitchers "loaned by Miss Waite" shown in the Atlan Club's 1900 exhibition. Bookbinder Ella R. Waite shared her studio in the Woman's Temple with Atlan Club instructor Florence Koehler. Topping also exhibited with the Chicago Ceramic Association and the Chicago Arts and Crafts Society. Signed: H. M. Topping. Blank: JP/L/France. *Photo*: Dark Flowers Antiques.

At the opening of the Atlan Club's eighth annual exhibit, on October 30, 1900, women representing the exclusive Fortnightly women's club and the Art Institute's influential Antiquarian Society assisted in receiving the hundreds of guests. "Women admirers of ceramics have shown an unusual interest in the exhibition of the Atlan Club, considered the best that has been made by the club since its organization eight years ago," the *Chicago Daily Tribune* reported.[12]

Keramic Studio, in a review written by Mabel C. Dibble, mentioned the originality shown in decoration resulting from Koehler's study course developing designs based on flowers and also noted the success of experiments on Chinese celadon ware using enamel paints in

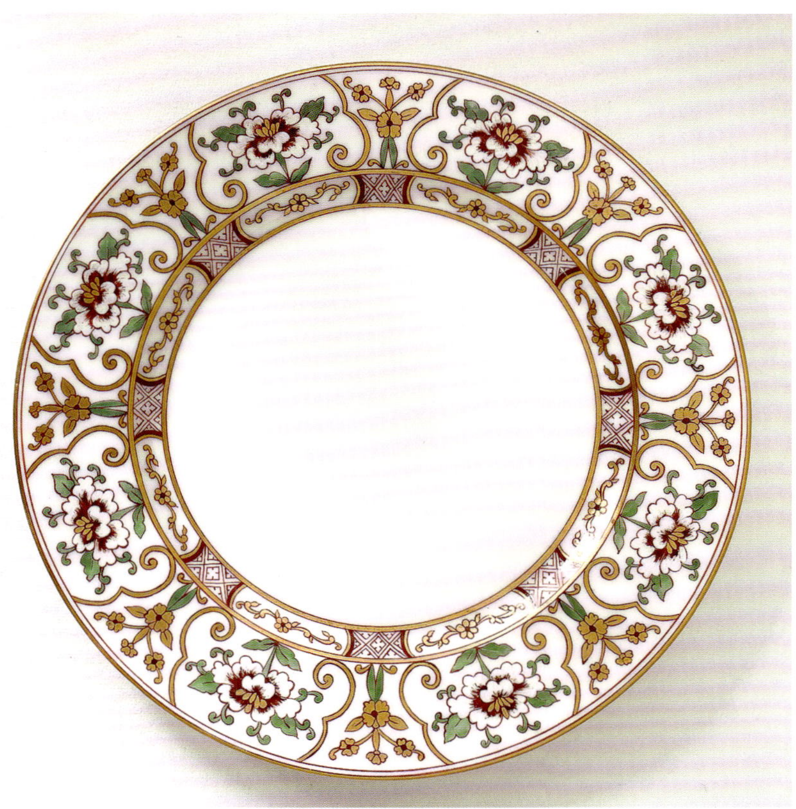

8.6 "Chinese" dinner plate, Mabel C. Dibble, 1900. This French porcelain plate was priced at $5, or $60 ($2,180) per dozen, in the eighth Atlan Club exhibition in 1900. The design, published as a "Chinese Design for Plate," was the April 1904 *Keramic Studio* Color Supplement. It was also illustrated as a design for enamel work in Clarabel Childs Filkins, *The China Painters ABC: A Primer for Beginners*, 1915. Signed: Mabel C. Dibble/Atlan Club/Art Institute/1900. Blank: T & V/France. (d: 9⅝") *Photo*: Private collection.

low relief.[13] The *Art Interchange* was more critical, "Throughout the display was seen the careful workmanship and patient application which has brought the club to its present high position among the china painters' organizations of America. There is, still, however, too close a following of Oriental and remote styles of decoration to entitle the workers to be called original, but hope is found in the breaking away from these styles which some of the members show in their exhibits." Also mentioned was Florence Hart Miner's attractive exhibit that replaced ceramics with a beaten silver bowl, beaten copper frame, and Egyptian-inspired necklace.[14]

The work of Gertrude "May" McCrystle, exhibiting for the first time, received special mention from the *Art Interchange* reviewer, who wrote, "The exhibit of Mrs. McCrystle was individual, artistic, lacking the sameness that seemed to be the drawback of this style of work."[15] Already known to members, McCrystle was elected to a two-year term as vice president shortly after joining the club.

Another new member, Matilda Middleton, working in a home studio, advertised "order work a specialty" in the Atlan catalog in 1900; a few months later, she opened a studio in the Woman's Temple.[16] Middleton had supported herself as a professional artist since 1898, when she returned to Chicago from a year in Paris, where she became known for her exquisite miniatures.[17]

Chapter Nine

A Busy Exhibition Schedule

From year to year its quality has improved in beauty of design and perfection of workmanship, and since the success of its exhibition in Paris last year the club has an international reputation.
—Harriet Monroe, Clipping in Art Institute Scrapbook, October 31, 1901

In January 1901, the Atlan Club members began a final study course to develop their skills in design and color with Florence Koehler, with bimonthly lessons continuing through the year, until she left in April to tour Japan.[1] It appears that, for the first time, the club's study course included associate members, a pool of women from whom candidates for active membership could be chosen.[2]

When the Paris exhibition was returned to Chicago, it was sent to New York City, where it was displayed in the art rooms of prominent jeweler Tiffany & Co. The club's work remained on display until April, when pieces were needed for the Atlan Club's exhibition in Buffalo, New York, where the Pan-American Exposition was opening on May 1, 1901.

The arrangement with Tiffany's had been facilitated by Susan Gale Cooke (1846–1932), former secretary of the Board of Lady Managers at the 1893 Chicago World's Fair, who also played an influential role in coordinating women's exhibits at the Paris exposition. When the widowed Cooke married William H. Parlin in New York in June 1901, the Atlan Club presented her with a set of plates, with each member decorating one, and made her an honorary member in recognition of her unflagging interest and efforts on behalf of the club in Chicago and in France.[3]

At the Pan-American Exposition, the Atlan Club exhibition, despite its obscure placement, carried off more honors than any other club's exhibition of ceramics, receiving Honorable Mention—the highest honor awarded to china painters—and a Diploma for the club.[4] Eva E. Adams, Mabel C. Dibble, and Matilda Middleton also received individual awards. Other ceramic decorators recognized for Honorable Mention were Cora M. Day of Indianapolis; Susan S. Frackelton of Milwaukee; and Marshall Fry of New York.[5]

In May 1901, the club sent a loan exhibition to Indiana for display

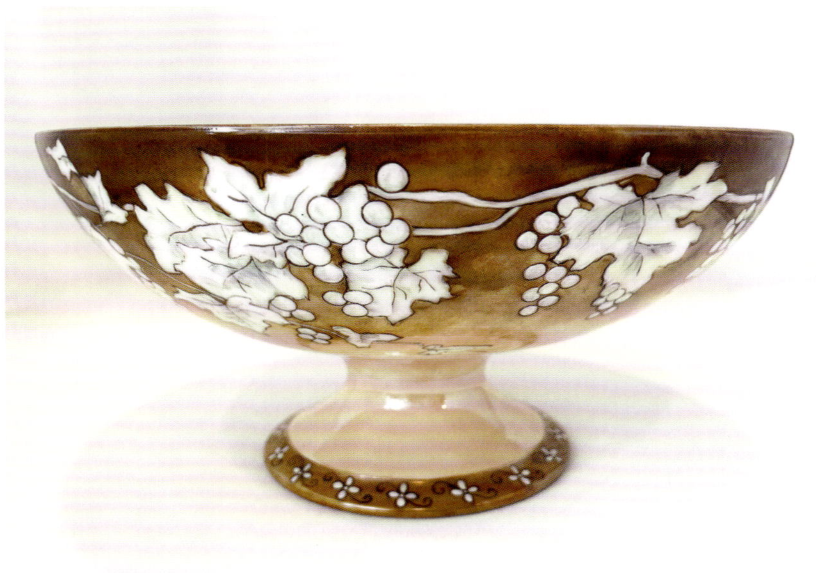

9.1 Footed fruit bowl with luster glaze, Mabel C. Dibble, 1901. Offered for $15 ($539) in the 1901 Atlan Club exhibition, the fruit dish features a flat-white leaf motif reminiscent of those illustrated in the section on Nature in Owen Jones's *Grammar of Ornament*. Luster glazes were made from the same minerals as overglaze colors but mixed with balsam of sulfur and thinned oil of turpentine, applied thinly with a brush. When fired, the result was a lustrous and iridescent effect. Signed: Mabel C. Dibble/1901/Atlan Club. Blank: Haviland/ France. (5″ × 10″) *Photo*: Mikell C. Darling.

in the Richmond Art Association's annual art exhibition, which had expanded to include decorated china, pottery, and student work from local art and manual training departments. Atlan members would continue to exhibit their work in the small city of Richmond, where a thriving art movement was supported by a strong industrial economy, for several years. In addition to advertising the club, this and similar regional exhibitions promoted sales and drew attention to Atlan members who were teachers, drawing students to their classes in Chicago.

The Atlan Club's ninth exhibition, in October 1901, was under the direction of Eva E. Adams, who was again president, replacing Henrietta Zeublin, who resigned following the sudden death of her husband. "Women in light dresses hurried from one part of the exhibition to another, explaining the work on the jardinière and the tobacco jar, and telling why the ink well with its blue rosebuds was worth so much more than the fish set," observed the reviewer from the local *Inter Ocean*.[6] Florence Steward, who consistently provided an attention-getting entry, displayed a series of twelve small plaques decorated with conventionalized flowers, along with a plaque and two vases painted "on biscuit" (unglazed white porcelain). The catalog's expanded teachers' directory included advertisements for classes in conventional decoration taught by nine Atlan members, including Helen Frazee, Mary Humphrey, Mary A. Phillips, and Helen M. Topping, who offered additional specialties like figural painting or miniatures on ivory.[7]

Local newspaper coverage reinforced the club's enviable reputation. The *Chicago Chronicle* described the club as "an organization purely Chicago and yet one which wields influences throughout America."[8] William Vernon, in the *Chicago American*, declared each piece "a work of art."[9] Chicago journalist Harriet Monroe agreed, "From year to year its quality has improved in beauty of design and perfection of workmanship, and since the success of its exhibition in Paris last year the club has an international reputation."[10] On a national level, *Keramic Studio* declared the exhibition to be the best the club had yet made, with "each year showing more originality and exquisite coloring, the workmanship on many pieces beyond criticism."[11]

After the Atlan exhibition closed, members Lillie E. Cole, Helen M. Topping, Grace H. Peck, and Matilda Middleton entered a selection of their pieces in the Chicago Arts and Crafts Society's annual exhibition in the Woman's Temple.[12] "The china shows some fine pieces in conventional all-over patterns in peculiarly soft colors," reported the *Minneapolis Journal*.[13] Among the metalwork exhibitors was their instructor, Florence Koehler, who had begun crafting exotic jewelry.

The club also accepted an invitation from Oscar Lovell Triggs, a strong proponent of local Arts and Crafts activity, to install a permanent exhibition of its decorated china in the new salesrooms of the Industrial Art League, with the league retaining twenty percent of the sales price of each piece sold.[14] A new organization whose goal was "the democratization of art," the league worked to train industrial designers by sponsoring manual training classes and model workshops. Triggs, a professor at the University of Chicago and a league founder, was a key thinker in the city's efforts to integrate art, education, and labor.[15] "The Atlan Ceramic Club has a very attractive permanent exhibit," he wrote in 1902, describing the league's rooms in his influential *Chapters in the History of the Arts and Crafts Movement*.[16]

Even as the Atlan Club was attaining Arts and Crafts glory at the Art Institute and Industrial Art League, its members were neglecting artistic trends prominent in Chicago at the time—trends that might have given them lasting recognition as key Arts and Crafts contributors. Of particular importance was the growing influence of Arthur Wesley Dow (1857–1922), who made significant artistic and intellectual contributions to the Arts and Crafts movement through his teaching and publications based on Japanese principles of art. His highly influential *Composition: A Series of Exercises in Art Structure for the Use of Students and Teachers* (Boston: J. M. Bowles, 1899) was used in art classes for decades.

In Dow's system, the designer started with a sparse, asymmetrical grid of vertical and horizontal lines, then developed a pattern or mosaic of "design units" of varying tones that were manipulated to form a final highly generic design of perspective-less flatness.[17] The finished product was highly abstract—flat, decorative, and modern; his approach was universal, in that it could be applied to any medium.[18] This "additive" approach was adopted by many of the potters and art potteries associated with the American Arts and Crafts movement. In contrast, Atlan Club members practiced the then-popular "subtractive" form of conventionalization that began with a recognizable

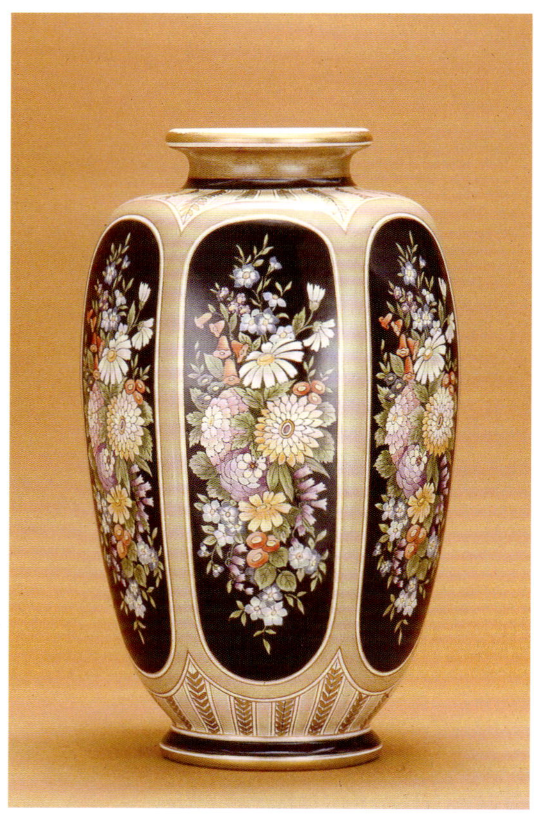

9.2 Satsuma vase with oblong black cartouches filled with multicolored flowers, Matilda Middleton, undated. If this was the vase Middleton exhibited in 1901, it was priced at $20 ($698). A copy of this vase, attributed to Mary Helen Hatch, assistant professor of drawing and painting, was illustrated in the 1918 *Drake University Record* 15, no. 3, 74. Her colleague, china painting instructor Loula Electra Hart, studied with Middleton, Helen Frazee, Mabel C. Dibble, and Helga M. Peterson in Chicago. Signed: Middleton. (h: 14½") *Photo*: Author's collection.

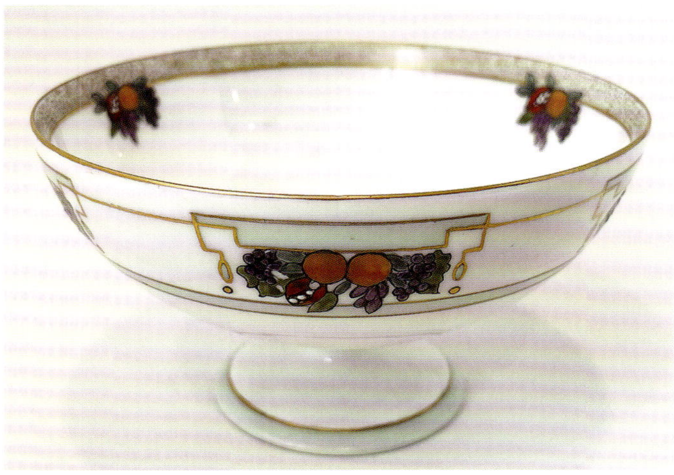

9.3 Footed dish with fruit motif, Mabel C. Dibble, 1913. Signed: Mabel C. Dibble/1913/Chicago. Blank: France. (2¾″× 4¾″) *Photo*: Private collection.

Mabel Caroline Dibble, 1893–1909

A founding member of the Atlan Club, Mabel Caroline Dibble (1858–1917) was one of the best-known and most highly respected instructors of china painting in her day. She served as secretary of the club, 1896–1899, and as a councilor in 1895, 1900, and 1901. In 1899, she wrote "The Atlan Ceramic Club of Chicago" overview for *Brush and Pencil*.[1]

Mabel was born in Milwaukee, Wisconsin, in 1858. Her father, a dry goods merchant, died when she was four years old. Her widowed mother moved the family to Dubuque, Iowa; after Mabel graduated from high school, they moved to Chicago around 1875. Mabel did not formally study art until she was an adult, when she took drawing and charcoal lessons with W. K. Bigelow in Chicago. Her first formal instruction was studying design with Art Institute instructor Louis J. Millet, chief critic for study classes conducted by the Chicago Ceramic Art Association after 1892.[2] One of the founders of the association, she served as its first corresponding secretary.

Mabel began teaching china painting in the 1880s and, along with her students, displayed work in annual Western China Decorating Works exhibitions.[3] Her work was well known by 1892, when *Clay Record* commented "Miss Dibble's work is marked by an originality that is charming."[4] In 1893, she exhibited with the Atlan Club at the Chicago World's Fair, where her fruit set won a medal.[5] In 1895, she developed a rich dark-green enamel marketed as "Dibble Green."[6]

In 1896, Mabel opened a studio in the Marshall Field Building, sharing it with fellow Atlan members Grace Peck, Helen M. Topping, and Eva E. Adams. In addition to teaching classes in china painting and watercolors, with "conventional work a specialty," she offered custom work, original designs for sale or rent, and instructions by mail.[7] She occasionally taught classes for ceramics clubs beyond Chicago.

Mabel exhibited with the Atlan Club and won awards at the 1900 Paris Exposition, 1901 Pan-American Exposition, and 1904 St. Louis World's Fair, in addition to participating in the club's regional exhibitions. Her last exhibition as a club member was in 1909.

In 1909, Mable was invited to become a member of the Royal Society of Arts in London. The following year, she became a member of the Boston Arts and Crafts Society; she was the first woman in "the West" to be named a Master Craftsman.[8] She exhibited her work in Arts and Crafts exhibitions in Chicago, Boston, New York, Detroit, and Minneapolis, as well as in the galleries of the Chicago Artists' Guild, which she joined in 1915.[9]

Keramic Studio published at least fifteen of Mabel's designs, 1899–1918. It devoted its October 1906 issue almost exclusively to her work, calling her "one of the leading disciples of the Conventional school."[10] In 1911 she published *How to Use Enamels on China*, paying special attention to decoration of Satsuma ware,[11] which she sold, along with her own line of colored enamels, through her studio. That same year, some of her designs were featured in the album for enamel workers published by the Anglo-French Art Co.[12]

Around 1915, Mabel began spending the summer months with Eva E. Adams at Sweet Briar Farm in Charlevoix, Michigan. She was fifty-nine when she died in Chicago on November 7, 1917. "A Tribute to Mabel C. Dibble," written by Adams, appeared in *Keramic Studio* in March 1918. "Students from distant parts of the country have come to her for advice and instruction. The testimonials which have come to me during the past few weeks fill volumes, all emphasizing the value of such a friendship."[13]

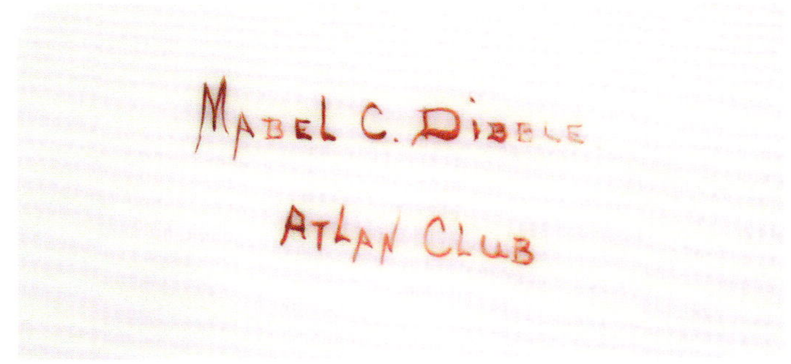

Maker's mark: Mabel Caroline Dibble. *Photo*: Private collection.

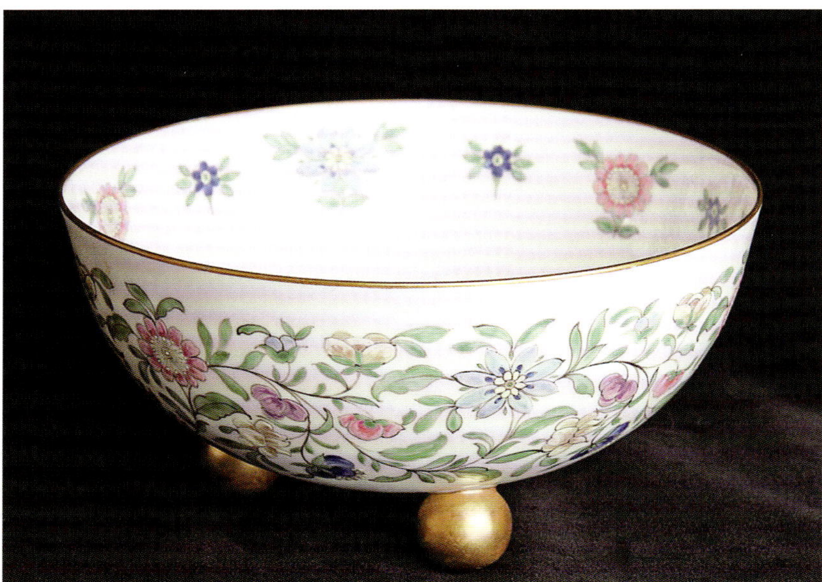

9.4 Footed bowl with conventionalized flowers, Grace H. Peck, 1898–1900. Signed: G. H. Peck. Blank: H & Co. (3⅛" × 6") *Photo*: Private collection.

object, usually a fruit or flower, that they reduced to its basic components, then flattened, removing anything not necessary to identify the species (say, the leaves of a flower). These they arranged, and often repeated symmetrically, to create an original design whose origin remained identifiable.

By 1900, Dow's work and publications were known in Chicago. As early as August 1899, Chicago artist Mabel Key presented Dow's method in an article entitled "A New System of Art Education: Arranged and Directed by Arthur W. Dow" published in *Brush and Pencil*. The previous month, according to Key, one of Dow's instructors had successfully demonstrated his method during a teacher training course sponsored by the Prang Educational Company.[19] Dow himself lectured at Hull House in March 1900; shortly thereafter, Mary Camp Scovel, one of his students, began teaching his system in the teacher training department at the Chicago Art Institute.[20]

While it seems likely that Florence Steward and members of the Atlan Club would have been aware of Dow, his design philosophies and methods were largely ignored. Steward, in her study courses, continued to teach and perpetuate the distinctive Atlan "style" that had brought fame to the club. Although their designs became more colorful, bolder, and more "modern" over the years, Atlan Club members continued to utilize the abstractly unified, yet ornamentally complex designs based on theories rooted in the work of British design theorists of the previous century. The crisp, controlled, conventional and semi-conventional decoration on Atlan ceramics differed considerably from the subtle, highly abstracted Dow-inspired motifs increasingly applied on art pottery by their contemporaries and now considered the norm for Arts and Crafts ceramics.

Grace Harriet Peck, 1893–1901

A founding member of the Atlan Art Club, Grace Harriet Peck (1865–1931) was a councilor in 1897–1899 and showed her work with the club in the 1900 Paris exposition and 1901 Pan-American Exposition. Active in the Chicago Ceramic Art Association, she served as its treasurer, 1895–1896. Although she ceased exhibiting with the Atlan Club after 1901, she occasionally exhibited in Chicago Arts and Crafts exhibitions.

Born in Buffalo, New York, Grace was brought to Bloomington, Illinois, as a young child in the 1860s; the family moved to Chicago in the 1870s. She was skilled in china painting by 1888, when she assisted at a reception in the studio of her teacher, Mrs. John W. Marsh; by 1890, her work in Western China Decorating Works exhibitions often drew media attention. "Miss Grace Peck of Chicago is an earnest and clever woman who has made unto herself a name by her Doulton and old ivory tints. These Mr. Gruenwald [*sic*] of Chicago has called Pecksonian," a critic wrote in 1892. "For two years Miss Peck has been all the rage in Chicago, and her "inimitable Doulton" and "delectable flowers" have brought her more orders than she could fill."[1]

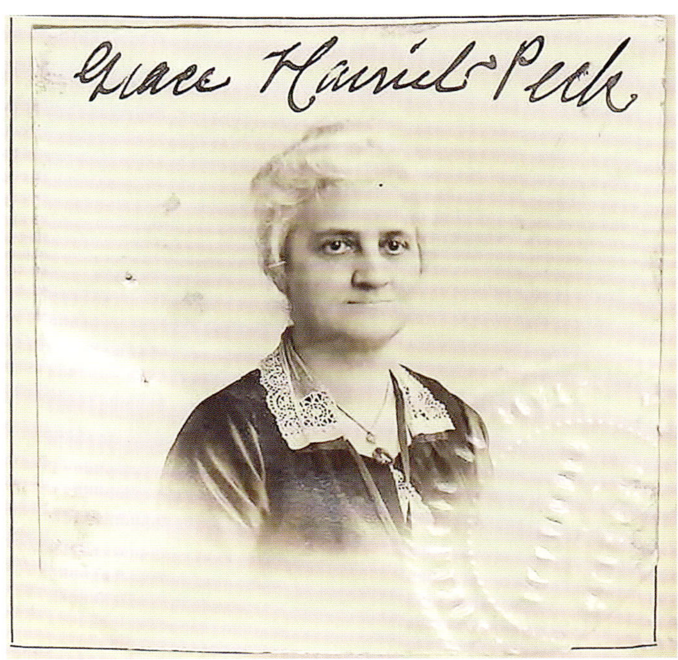

Grace Harriet Peck's passport photo, 1922. *Source*: Ancestry.com.

Grace's work was exhibited in the Woman's Building at the 1893 Chicago World's Fair. At the time, the *China Decorator* called her "a well-known teacher of china painting," who reported the meetings of the Chicago Ceramic Club.[2] Her exhibition "was greatly admired by everybody. Her forte lies in decoration, and her paste work is scarcely equaled by the best decorators."[3] She shared a studio in the Marshall Field Building with fellow Atlan member Mabel C. Dibble, 1896–1898; after that, she worked in a home studio. Grace and her sister Theodora, a schoolteacher, lived with her widowed father, then with a widowed aunt.

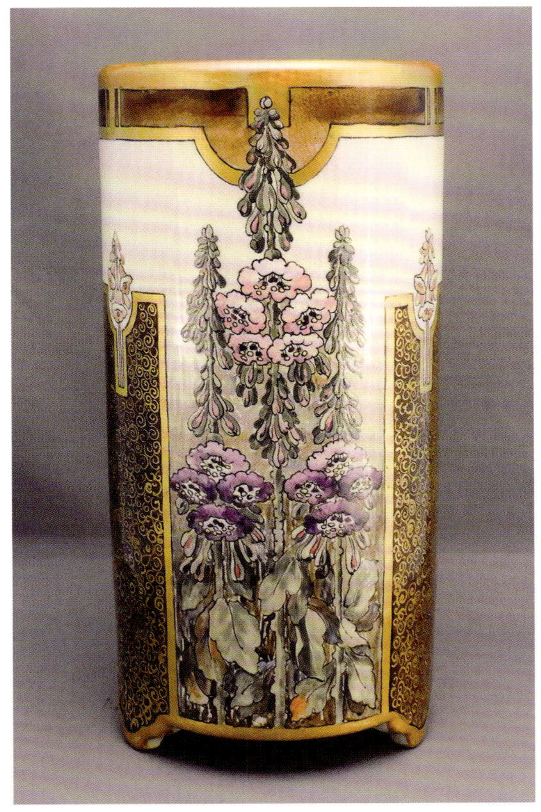

9.5 Satsuma vase, Grace H. Peck, ca. 1910–1917. Signed: G. H. Peck. (8½" × 4") *Photo*: Dark Flowers Antiques.

Grace spent three months in England in 1898; she returned to study art, 1910–1912. She toured England, Europe, and Holland in 1922.[4] During her travels, she became interested in antique textiles and began embroidering unique table linens to complement hand-painted porcelain, which she had stopped painting during World War I. In October 1923, Grace told a *Christian Science Monitor* journalist, "For my china I studied what Egyptians, Chinese, Persians and Indians have done, and in embroideries, what the English have done, and in textiles, the French and Italians. I take note of their disposition of form and conventionalization and adapt these things to my sense of the needs of tableware or embroidery."[5] In 1924, she returned to England to study at the Royal School of Art Needlework. Grace died, age sixty-six, in Chicago on September 28, 1931.

Chapter Ten

The First Decade

We shall watch the annual growth as we continue to press forward, aiming to win a first place, as a Club among associated Artists, and deserving to be named as pioneers who blazed the path and pointed the way for recognition, and as American Ceramic Painters, to attain the coveted place where artists who use mineral color and enamel shall be given an important place in American history of ornament.

—Mrs. Florence Steward, "1893–1902 The History of the Atlan Ceramic Art Club of Chicago, Ill.," 1902

In 1902, Florence Steward celebrated the Atlan Ceramic Art Club's first decade by writing a detailed 130 page history upon invitation from the Chicago Historical Society (now the Chicago History Museum), the city's oldest cultural organization. At the time, the society was primarily a library and research institution housed in an imposing granite-clad fireproof building on North Dearborn Street.

The club had nineteen members. Of these, five—Eva E. Adams, Lillie E. Cole, Mabel C. Dibble, Mary Humphrey, and Florence Steward—were founding members. Since 1893, twenty members had resigned and four had been dropped for nonpayment of dues. There were two associate members and one life member, with Florence Steward elected to that role in 1901. Five honorary members included Susan S. Frackelton; Florence Koehler; Susan Gale Cooke and Mary Lockwood, influential lady managers at the 1893 fair; and Bessie B. Bennett, decorative design instructor at the Art Institute of Chicago.[1] The club still retained an advisory board composed of some of Chicago's most prominent ladies, although they were not listed by name. Going forward, the club would accept nonresident members if their conventional work was up to the standards required for membership. In this new category were Florence Hart Miner, who was living in Wisconsin, and four women who were among founders of the Kansas City Keramic Club, whose members had also studied under Florence Koehler the previous winter. Modeled after the Atlan Club when organized in 1899, the Kansas City club counted among its members women who had studied china painting with Franz B. Aulich in Chicago, Marshall Fry in New York City, and local expert Dorothea Warren (later O'Hara) before she moved to New York.[2]

10.1 Variations of the Atlan logo appeared before 1902. The circle was eliminated, the crossed *P*s were linked with the word "Atlan," and it was usually drawn in black rather than red.

In 1902, rather than hold its own exhibition, the Atlan Club accepted an invitation to join with the Alumni Association of Decorative Designers of the Art Institute of Chicago, which was sponsoring a large and important exhibition of artistic handicrafts opening on December 16. Officially titled the First Exhibition of Original Designs for Decorations and Examples of Art Crafts Having Distinct Artistic Merit (but commonly referred to as Arts and Crafts exhibitions), the show, with 751 entries, was a microcosm of the finest output of the Arts and Crafts movement at its peak in the United States. One could view (and often buy) art glass, basketry, books, furniture, graphics, leatherwork, metalwork, textiles, designs for interiors, and decorative accessories crafted in Chicago and far beyond. Local artisans Bessie B. Bennett, Robert R. Jarvie, Jessie M. Preston, and Christia M. Reade exhibited metalwork and jewelry; the Kalo Shop and the Wilro Shop showed leatherwork; Blue Sky Press displayed its books; and Ellen Gates Starr and Peter Verburg showed volumes bound at Hull House. The extensive display of art pottery included Teco pottery lamp bases made by Gates Potteries and "Blue and Grey" pottery by Susan S. Frackelton, both of Chicago. Substantial commercial operations—Grueby Faience Company, Boston; Newcomb College, New Orleans; Rookwood Pottery Co., Cincinnati—sent outstanding examples, as did individual potters, including Theophilus Brouwer of New York; George E. Ohr, Mississippi; Hugh C. Robertson, Massachusetts; and Artus Van Briggle, Colorado. It proved so successful that it became an annual affair. At the time, however, the exhibition received sparse newspaper coverage. The *Chicago Tribune*'s art critic was impressed by its positive effect on museum attendance, with nearly nine thousand visitors in mid-December, when attendance typically dropped dramatically; perhaps the public had gone there "in search of Christmas presents," given that 125 pieces were sold. "Those who have taste and ambition of that sort should be stimulated by the assurance of a market for their wares; and that means improvement and extension of artistic handiwork," he concluded.[3] The *Inter Ocean*'s brief overview gave the Atlan Club a bold subhead, followed by a sentence mentioning its "large and interesting exhibition."[4]

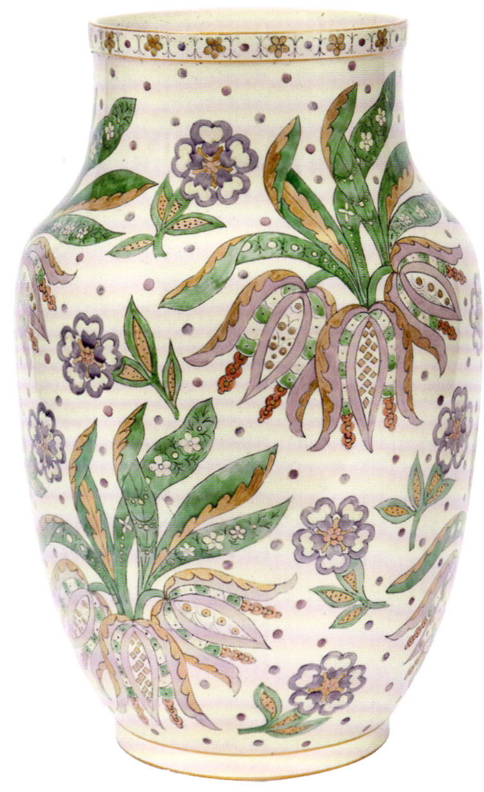

10.2 "Tulip Vase," Eva E. Adams, 1902. This sizable vase was included in the Atlan Club's entry in the first annual Arts and Crafts exhibition at the Art Institute of Chicago in 1902. Signed: Eva E. Adams/Atlan Art Club/Chicago/1902. (h: 14¼"). *Photo*: Treadway Toomey Auctions.

The Atlan Club, with fifty examples by seventeen members, was the only large exhibitor of overglaze decorated porcelain. Descriptions, though sparse, indicate the vases, plaques, bowls, plates, and other serving pieces were decorated in conventionalized patterns incorporating Chinese, Japanese, Moorish, or fruit motifs.[5] The smaller number of pieces per person may have resulted from entries being vetted by the Jury of Selection, composed of Art Institute alumni. The Atlan entry included pieces by four members of the Kansas City Keramic Club, which reciprocated by including Atlan members from Chicago in its second annual exhibition.[6]

On a national level, the Atlan Club's contribution to the handicraft revival was recognized by the *Chautauquan*, a magazine of the adult education institution, in its nine-article series on the Arts and Crafts movement. In 1903, discussing the "Education of Producer and

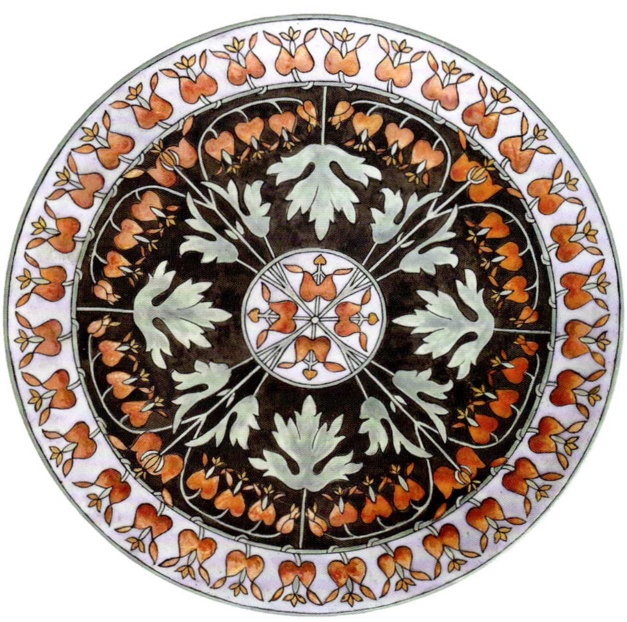

10.3 "Plaque, bleeding heart," Florence Steward, 1902. The plaque was one of two items Steward showed with the Atlan Club in the Art Institute's first annual Arts and Crafts exhibition in December 1902. The reverse is signed: "Mrs. Helen D. Irons With Christmas Greetings 1902/Florence Steward." Helen Irons is presumed to be a relative of Atlan Club member Katherine R. Irons. (d: 10") *Photo*: Private collection.

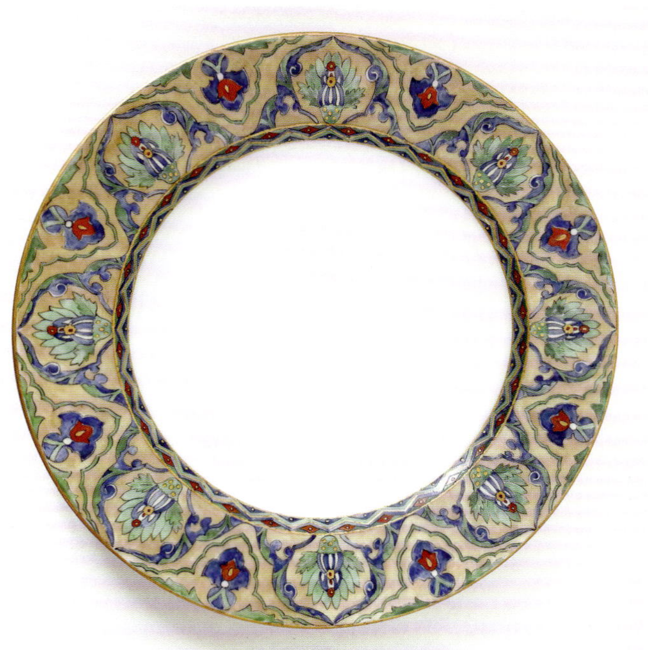

10.4 Plate, Helen M. Topping, 1902. The colorful border was influenced by her study of historic ornament. Topping's advertisements in *House Beautiful* promised "conventional designs for tableware given special attention." Signed: H M Topping/1902. Blank: France. (d: 8⅗") *Photo*: Private collection.

Consumer," Rho Fisk Zueblin called attention to the club's artistic proficiency, noting, "The Atlan Ceramic Art Club, of Chicago, amateur china decorators, in the past six years, owing to systematic study of design under Mrs. Florence Koehler, has turned its technical gifts from quite commonplace and mistaken china painting to a rare standard of beauty, excellence, and originality."[7] The author spoke from firsthand knowledge: she was the daughter-in-law of Harriett Zeublin, the club's former president. By this time, Atlan members were in high demand as teachers or lecturers. Mabel C. Dibble and Helen Frazee were particularly popular, their reputations enhanced by their conventional designs appearing frequently in *Keramic Studio*. Students and teachers of china painting in small towns often traveled to Chicago to study conventional design with an Atlan member; some stayed several days to take in the full range of available instruction, studying conventional decoration with an Atlan member; the naturalistic style with Franz B. Aulich, famous for roses, or Jeanne Stewart, known for fruits; and figure painting with Dominic M. Campana.

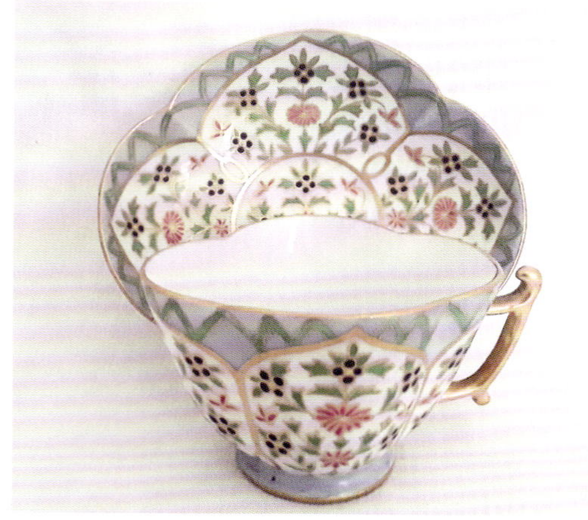

10.5 Cup and saucer, Mary A. Phillips, 1902. Phillips showed this set, along with two vases, with the Atlan Club in the first annual Arts and Crafts exhibition at the Art Institute of Chicago in 1902. Signed: M. A. Phillips/1902/Atlan. Mark: T & V. (cup: 3" × ¾"; saucer: 1" × 4⅝"). *Photo*: Private collection.

Chapter Eleven

Pottery and Art Crafts

It is proposed to have courses in pottery connected with china-painting societies. This is as it should be, for china painters then will no longer be dependent upon "shop" designs in pottery, but each artist can design her own piece and thus give individuality to her work.

—"Another Occupation for Women," *Inter Ocean* (Chicago). March 6, 1903, 7

"The Atlans are anxious to undertake the manufacture of their own shapes, and have already commenced to experiment in this direction. But thus far the work consists in the decoration of such porcelain and fine pottery as the market supplies—French, English, and American ware," wrote journalist James William Pattison in 1899 in the *Art Amateur*, a magazine devoted to household art.[1] While some of the club's winter study classes included sessions involving clay modeling, emphasis had been on understanding the clay process and evolution of forms in order to design appropriate decoration for three-dimensional shapes.

This changed in 1903 when club members tried their hand at pottery making in the plant of Swedish architect Swen Linderoth, proprietor of the Alhambra Ceramic Works. A successful producer of porcelain filter tubes (used in water purification), Linderoth also made blank vases and plaques for china decorators and taught art students to make pottery and underglaze decorated ware.[2] "A very important addition has been made to the activities of this plant recently," *Brick* magazine reported in July 1903, "It is now the seat of ceramic endeavor of the celebrated Atlan Ceramic Art Club."[3] Club members were spending Thursday afternoons making their own pottery on the potter's wheel, conducting all the operations from start to finish themselves, with work intended for a special display at the upcoming St. Louis World's Fair.

Although Atlan Club catalogs occasionally listed pieces as "pottery," they did not indicate who made the shapes. At the time, many china decorators were experimenting with pottery. Some planned to expand the range of courses they could offer their students; others wanted simpler and more attractive shapes than those available from commercial vendors; a few even aspired to master the entire process of ceramic production. It appears that the group experiment at the Alhambra Ceramic Works lasted only one season; however, at least one Atlan member found it inspirational. Matilda Middleton began teaching pottery classes on Monday and Wednesday evenings in the workshops at Hull House, where she later became a resident.[4]

In December 1903, Atlan Club's eleventh annual exhibition was held in conjunction with the second annual Arts and Crafts exhibition held at the Art Institute. The Atlan Club's entry included porcelain decorated by thirteen women, including five from Kansas City.[5] The exhibition also included pottery and porcelain decorated by members of the Chicago Ceramic Association, the Chicago Arts and Crafts Society, and students at the Art Institute of Chicago. Earlier in the year, the institute had installed a kiln and began offering classes on Saturday mornings. On exhibition were pieces modeled, glazed, decorated, and fired by young women attending classes at the school.

The early part of 1904 was devoted to preparations for the Atlan Club's exhibition at the St. Louis World's Fair, officially the Louisiana Purchase Exposition, opening on April 30. According to Mabel C. Dibble, the club was honored with an invitation to exhibit in the Fine Arts Building at the exposition, "without expense to them of any kind for case, space, and placing, and they had a very fine and well placed exhibit there."[6]

Although we do not know whether any of the ceramic bodies in the club's exhibition were made by members, contemporary printed sources provide some indication of what was exhibited. *Keramic Studio* noted that sales at the exposition included a mayonnaise bowl by Eva E. Adams, a saki pot by Mabel C. Dibble, and a milk pitcher by Beulah Frazer, all with overglaze decoration.[7] Later, describing ceramics shown at the fair, *Keramic Studio* complimented the members, "whose careful execution and good taste in an oriental style of decoration are so well known."[8]

Although an Atlan exhibition was on the Art Institute's calendar for November 1904, it did not take place; however, a group of members did exhibit their work under the club's name in the third annual Arts and Crafts exhibition at the Art Institute in December. A very large show, its 655 entries represented craftworkers around the country. Gustav Stickley (1858–1942) was a major exhibitor, showing furniture, metalwork, and textiles made in his workshops in Syracuse, New York. The Deerfield Society of Arts and Crafts, Whittier Home Association of Arts and Crafts, and Women's Art Association of Canada sent handwoven textiles and baskets. Well-known Chicago craftworkers included Bessie B. Bennett, Robert R. Jarvie, Leonide C. Lavaron, Jessie M. Preston, and James Winn displaying handwrought metalwork and jewelry; the Kalo Shop, Swastica Shop, and Wilro Shop showing leatherwork; and the Hull House Shops exhibiting metalwork and pottery.[9]

The club's entry consisted of twenty-four items by ten exhibitors. "The Atlan China [*sic*] Club exhibit is disappointingly small," commented Elizabeth Emery in *House Beautiful*.[10] Exhibiting under their

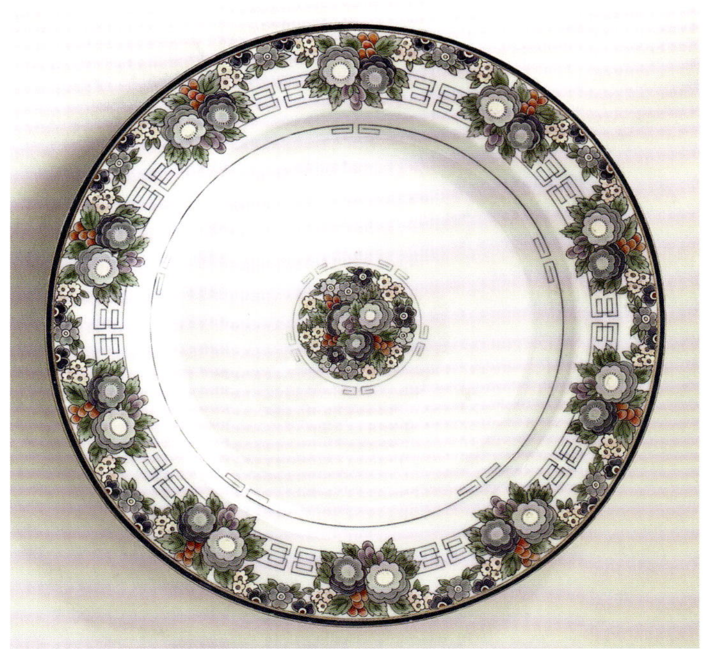

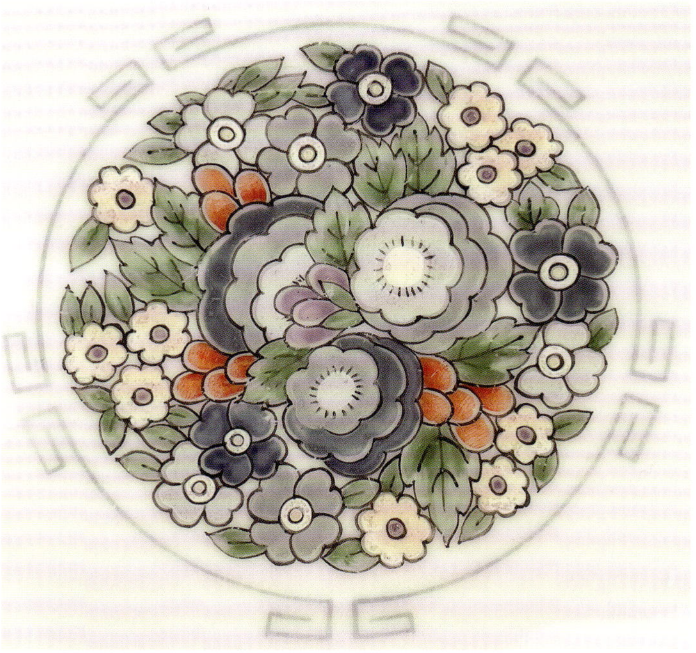

11.1A AND B Charger with Chinese-inspired clusters of flowers, Matilda Middleton, ca. 1908. Exhibited in the 1908 Kansas City exhibition, the charger was illustrated in the February 1908 *Keramic Studio* article on "The Ceramic Crafts at the National Society of Craftsmen Exhibition" in New York. It was also the *Keramic Studio* Color Supplement for August 1909. Later, it was illustrated as a design for enamel work in Clarabel Childs Filkins, *The China Painters A B C* (Buffalo: Courier Company, 1915). Signed: -Middleton.-. (d: 12") *Photo*: Private collection.

Matilda Middleton, 1900–1903

A highly skilled porcelain artist, Matilda Middleton (1863–1923) was an Atlan Club exhibitor from 1900 through 1903, serving as a councilor, 1901–1902. She was no longer a member in 1908, when she received the Atlan Ceramic Art Club Prize for the best original plate design in conventional overglaze ornament in that year's Arts and Crafts exhibition at the Art Institute of Chicago. She entered her work in Chicago Arts and Crafts exhibitions through 1915.

Matilda was born in Chicago in 1863, the same year her parents migrated from Ireland. In Chicago, Thomas worked as an upholsterer until his wife launched a successful lace curtain laundry, which he expanded to include carpets. In 1898 he was appointed a deputy U.S. marshal, a post he held until 1919. Matilda was the second of seven children.

Matilda's early education and art training is unknown; however, her talent was evident by December 1895, when the Streator, Illinois, *Times* observed that Miss Middleton, "the artist," had returned to Chicago after visiting a married sister. Matilda sailed for France in August 1897; when she returned home in July 1898 via Yonkers, New York, the *Statesman* noted, "Miss Matilda Middleton, well known in Paris through her exquisite miniatures, has returned to her home in Chicago and has opened a studio there."[1]

Her first studio was in the Middleton family home in suburban Woodland Park, an address she used when advertising "order work a specialty" in the

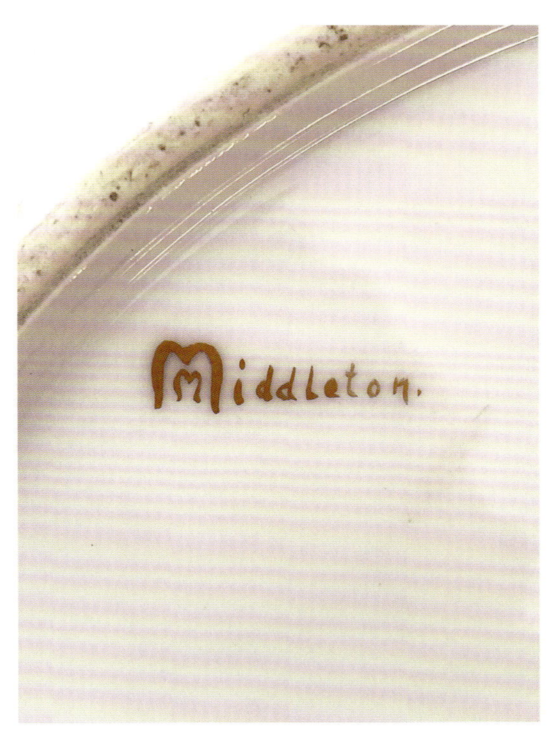

Maker's mark: Matilda Middleton. *Photo*: Private collection.

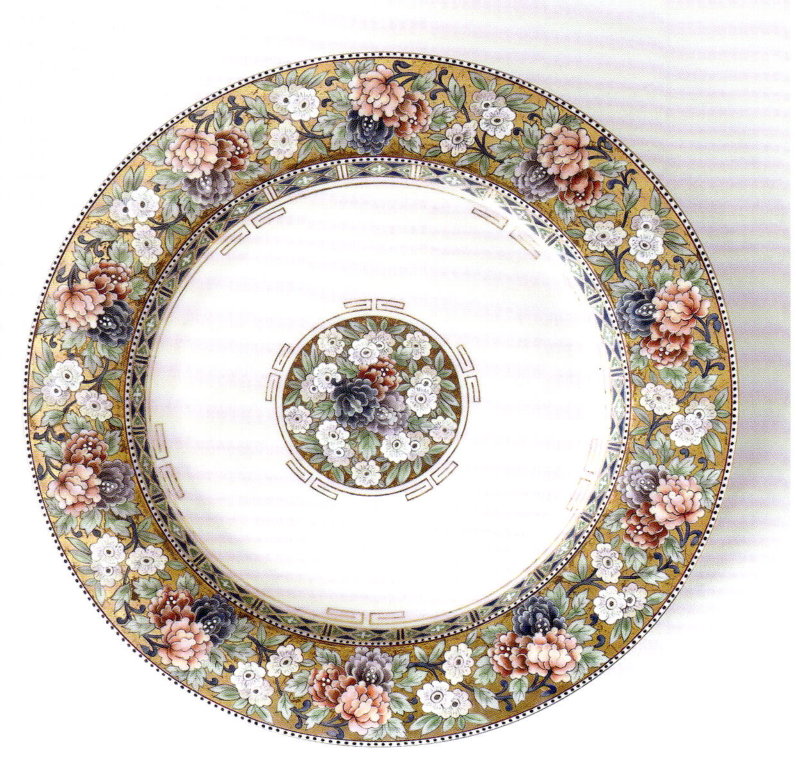

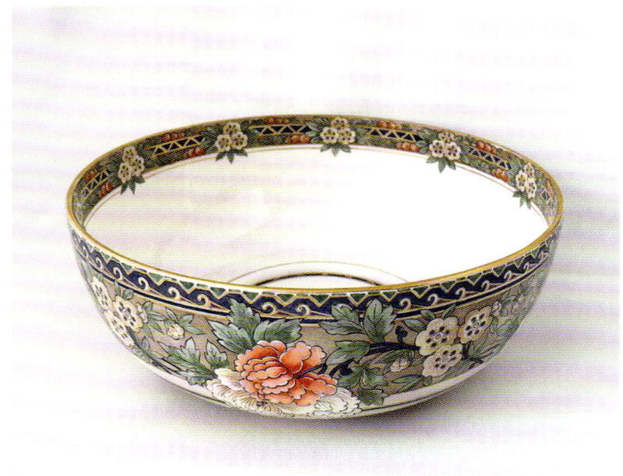

11.2 Bowl with "Chinese feeling" flowers, Matilda Middleton, 1908–1918. Signed: Middleton. Blank: Willets Belleek. (4" × 9¾") *Photo*: Private collection.

11.3 Charger with Chinese-inspired motif, Matilda Middleton, ca. 1911. Although she occasionally used Satsuma, Middleton preferred plain white china. "Nothing looks so well on the white tablecloth as white china," she told the writer of an article featuring her work in the June 1911 *Arts and Decoration*. Signed: Middleton. (d: 12") *Photo*: Private collection.

Atlan Club's exhibition catalog in 1900. Matilda soon opened a studio in the Woman's Temple, where she exhibited her work in the 1900 exhibition held by the Chicago Arts and Crafts Society, of which she was a member. During the winter of 1903–1904, and perhaps others, she taught evening classes in pottery at Hull House, the social settlement cofounded by Jane Addams, where the Arts and Crafts Society had been founded in 1897.[2]

By 1906, Matilda shared a studio in the Athenaeum Building with Atlan Club colleague May McCrystle; in 1910, she was sharing the studio with another member, Caroline Blodgett. In addition to exhibiting in regional Arts and Crafts exhibitions and state fairs, where she usually won top honors, Matilda participated in national art-craft exhibitions, including those sponsored by the Boston Arts and Crafts Society and the National Society of Craftsmen, New York. After November 1908, when her work won first prize in a *Keramic Studio* competition, her conventionalized designs appeared regularly in the magazine, including a full-color supplement in February 1909.

By then, Matilda was so widely known as a teacher and designer that aspiring china painters and teachers studied and emulated her work. In 1909, in Springfield, Illinois, members of the Amateur Art Study Club discussed and reviewed illustrations of her work in flat enamels and admired "exquisite pieces" of her work proudly displayed by a member.[3]

In June 1911, *Arts and Decoration* published "The Ceramic Work of Matilda Middleton: Chinese Motifs and Methods Characteristic."[4] Describing her work as "distinctly individual and of the first rank," author Dorothy Biddle commented that Middleton's interest in and use of Chinese motifs and methods was evident in almost all her decoration. Although she occasionally used Satsuma ware, she preferred plain white porcelain, which she rarely or never hid with any tint save in the decorative design.

After 1911, as a member of the Artists' Guild of Chicago, Matilda's work was featured in its galleries and salesroom in the Fine Arts Building. She won the guild's top prize for decorated china in 1917 and for lamps in 1919. In 1921, a special exhibition featured her work on luster china and glass.

After their mother's death in 1911, Matilda and her sister Amy moved into an apartment in Hull House, where Matilda may have continued to teach ceramics. She died there, age fifty-nine, on June 4, 1923.

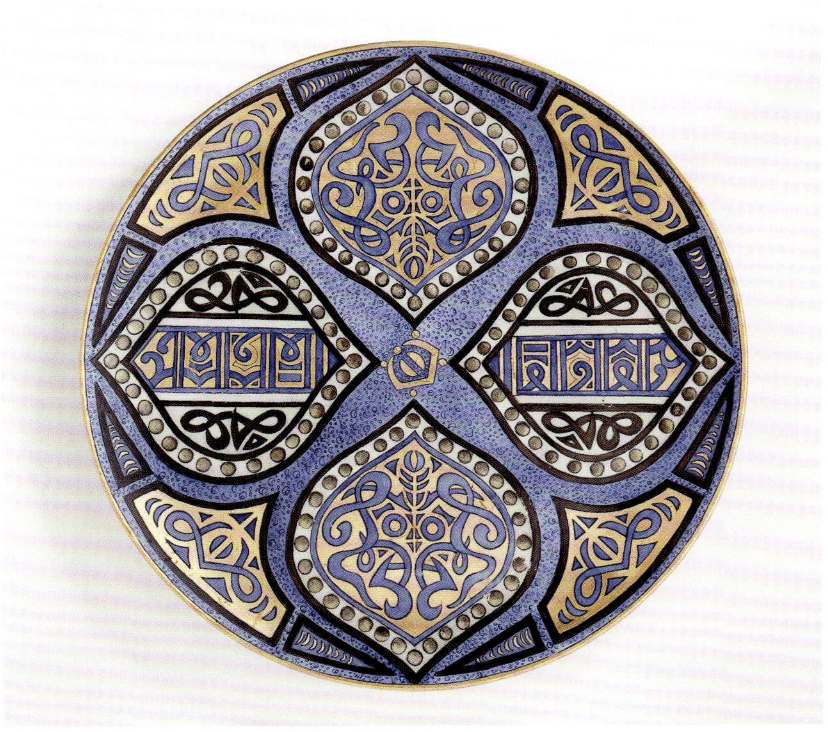

11.4 Plate with Arabesque motif, Katharine R. Irons, 1904. Likely decorated for the 1904 Atlan Club exhibition that did not take place; however, the plate was not included in the Atlan entry in that year's Arts and Crafts exhibition at the Chicago Art Institute. Signed: Katharine R. Irons/Chicago/11-1904/PPP/Atlan. (d: 12") *Photo*: Private collection.

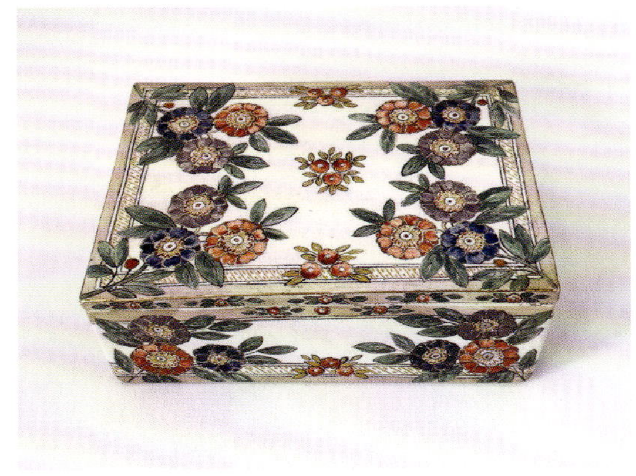

11.5 Satsuma box with conventionalized zinnias, Helen M. Topping, 1904. This may have been the box Topping exhibited under her own name in the 1904 Arts and Crafts exhibition at the Chicago Art Institute. Satsuma ware tended to show crazing as it aged. Signed: H. M. Topping/1904. (1⅗"× 4¾") *Photo*: Private collection.

own names were Helen Frazee, who showed a teapot and plate; Grace H. Peck, who presented several examples of decorated Japanese Satsuma ware; Helen M. Topping, who exhibited a box and a bowl; and Matilda Middleton, who showed a china bowl, a dish, and two books.[11]

The Atlan display was indeed underwhelming compared with the French Government's selection of 108 ceramics from its display at the St. Louis World's Fair and the 24 pieces of underglaze decorated porcelain made from American clays by Adelaide A. Robineau, the celebrated New York china painter, potter, and editor of *Keramic Studio*.

Three years of small, lackluster annual exhibits—with the average number of Atlan exhibition pieces declining from 133 to 30—under the leadership of a mysterious "Mrs. McIntyre," who was president during 1903 and 1904 (despite never having exhibited her work), took its toll. The club lost several of its most loyal and talented members, including founding members Eva E. Adams, Lillie E. Cole, and Grace H. Peck; Matilda Middleton and Helen M. Topping also dropped out. Most, however, continued to exhibit in Arts and Crafts exhibitions and with the Chicago Ceramic Art Association, whose shows opened simultaneously at the Art Institute.

Professional members relied upon the sales, publicity, and name recognition generated by the club's exhibitions to enhance their reputations and attract students; Atlan exhibiting as a subset of another organization generated neither. Why abide by all those club rules and work so hard when the payback was not worth it?

Chapter Twelve

Renaissance

In conventionalization you have changed nature for a special purpose—to fit a given space, or into some specific scheme of color. It is not nature now, it is ornament.

—Florence Steward, *Flat Enamel Decoration on China*, 1907, 31

In 1905, the Atlan Club quickly revived under the experienced leadership of Mary Humphrey and Florence Steward, founding members who understood the value of maintaining a high public profile. As president and vice president, respectively, they were assisted by Jane V. D. Wright, as secretary, and Charlotte Lawrence, as treasurer.

Foremost on the agenda was the reinstatement of an exhibition under the club's own name at the Art Institute of Chicago. This they accomplished: the Atlan Club opened its twelfth annual exhibition at the Art Institute on November 14, 1905 (apparently the 1904 Arts and Crafts entry, numerically the twelfth, did not count).

The exhibition included 115 pieces, including teapots, cups and saucers, and steins; bowls for berries, oatmeal, and cream soup; and covered boxes. There were lots of plates for serving bonbons, fruit, relish, sandwiches, bread and butter, ice cream, or salad, or for use as service plates. Prices ranged from $1 (about $34) for Mary Alden's cold cream box to $40 (now $1,360) for Helen Frazee's vase ornamented with asters.

An Atlan Club exhibition was once again worthy of coverage by the press, garnering positive publicity once more. "China painting of unusual artistic merit is being shown," reported New York–based *American Art News*, "and the exhibition is regarded as one of the chief events of the winter."[1] A week later, the magazine added, "The exhibition of the Atlan Ceramic Art Club in the Art Institute is the most successful in the twelve years' history of the organization. The standard of merit fixed by the jury is so high that this china painting display is one of dignity and importance."[2]

The reviewer for the Chicago journal *Brick* agreed: "The visitor is surprised to find real masterpieces, both in regard to shape and decoration, as well as rich harmony in the beautiful glazes with which the

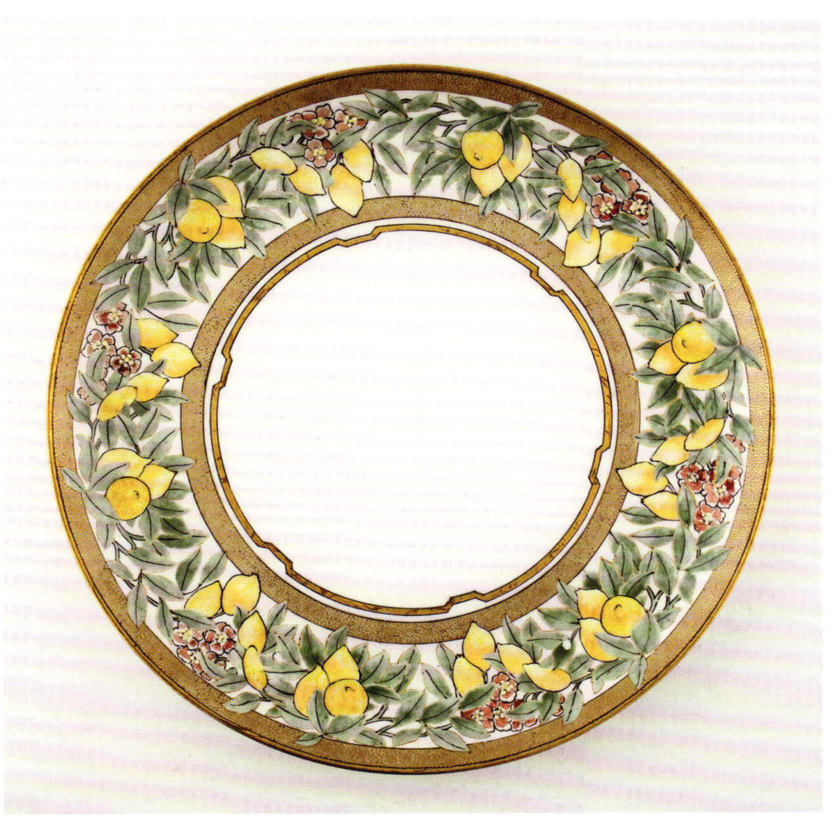

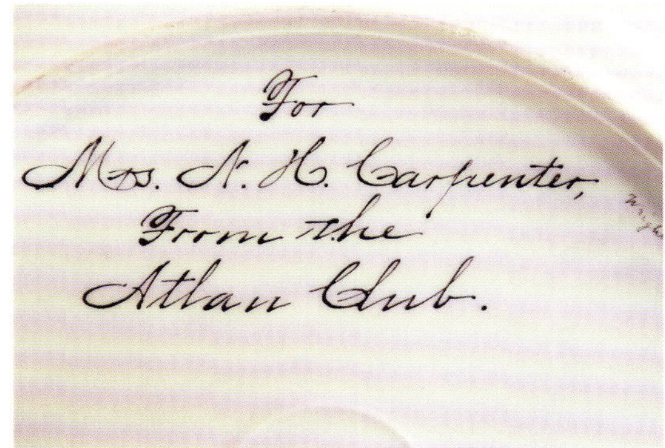

12.1A AND B Luncheon plate decorated with conventionalized clusters of lemons from a set of twelve presented to Harriet Lewis Carpenter, wife of Newton Henry Carpenter, secretary of the Art Institute of Chicago. Each plate was signed, "For Mrs. N. H. Carpenter From the Atlan Club" on the reverse. Only one bears an artist's signature, "Wright," for Jane V. D. Wright, who exhibited between 1905 and 1912 and was club president in 1911. Signed: Wright. Blank: GDA/France. (d: 8½") *Photos*: Robert W. Switzer; Ronald Bry Collection.

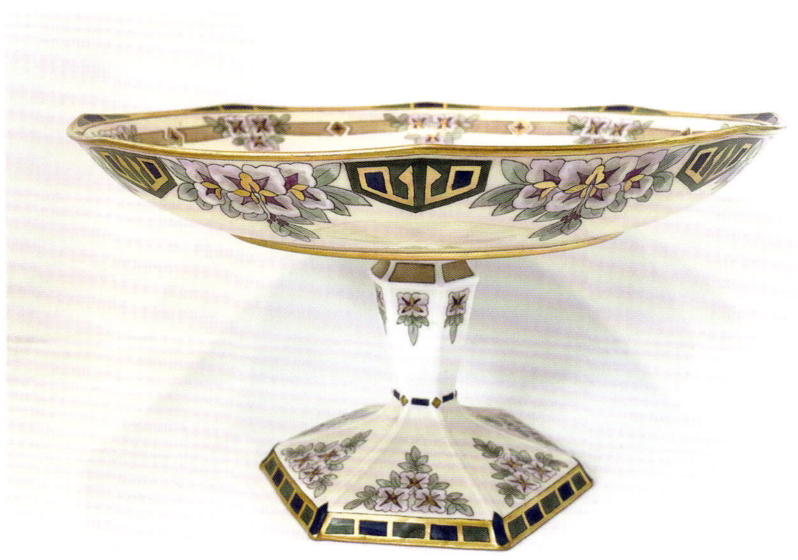

12.2 Compote, Stella Rintoul, ca. 1905. This may be the "open bonbon" Rintoul exhibited in 1905. Signed: ST cipher [Stella Rintoul]/Atlan. (9¾" × 5¾") *Photo*: Private collection.

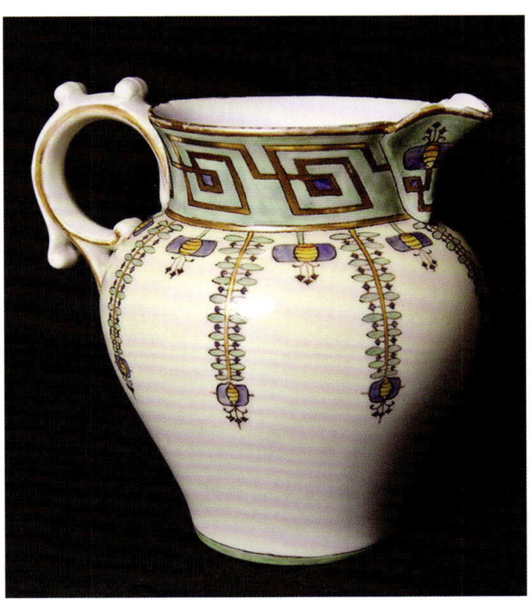

12.3 Cream pitcher with geometric motifs, Mary Humphrey, 1905. It was offered for $4 ($139) in the twelfth Atlan Club exhibition in 1905. Signed: M. Humphrey/'05/PPP/Atlan. Blank: MR/France. (h: 4½") *Photo*: Tim Blackburn.

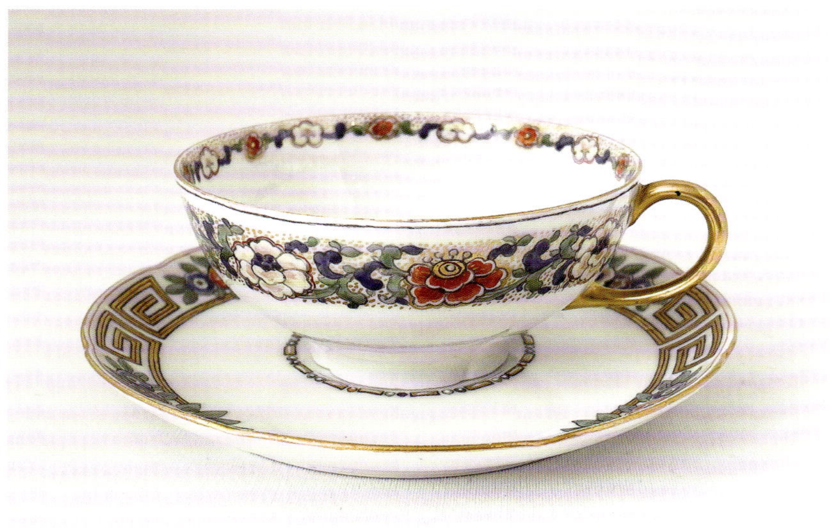

12.4 Cup and saucer with Chinese-inspired floral bands, Lillie E. Cole, 1905. Although Cole's final exhibition with the Atlan Club was in 1904, she continued painting in the Atlan style. Signed: LECole cipher/1905. Blank: Limoges/W. G. & Co./France. (saucer, d: 4⅝"; cup, h: 2¼") *Photo*: Private collection.

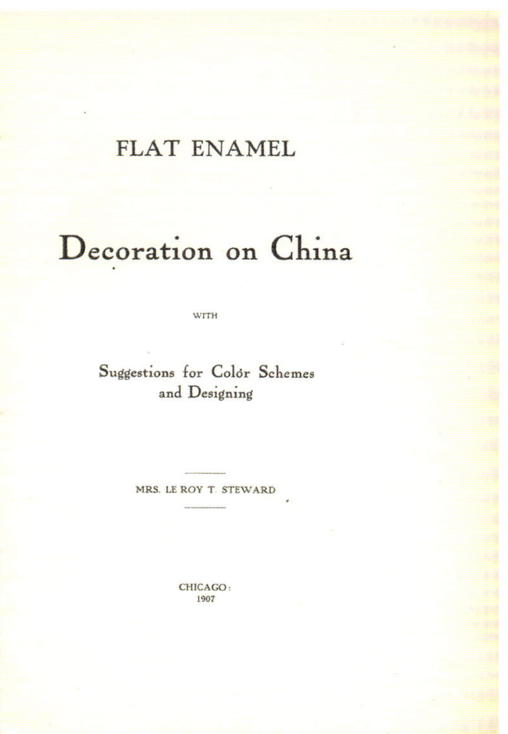

FLAT ENAMEL

Decoration on China

WITH

Suggestions for Color Schemes
and Designing

MRS. LE ROY T. STEWARD

CHICAGO:
1907

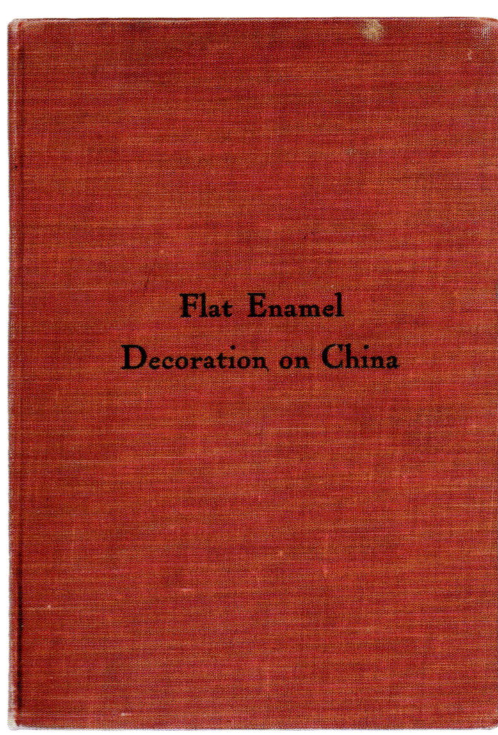

12.5A AND B Florence Steward used her booklet *Flat Enamel Decoration on China* in the study classes she conducted for associate members from 1907 through 1921. The hardcover version was sold for $1. *Photo*: (A) Author's collection; (B) Tim Ingram.

pottery is covered. The prices marked are far from high, making it possible for almost anybody to possess at least one or two pieces of art for the enrichment and decoration of the home."[3]

The journal's somewhat exaggerated claim echoed sentiment among city boosters like investment banker and philanthropist John Farson, who considered Chicago the "capital of the New West" in art as well as industry. The most notable thing about the city's development in art, according to Farson, was its democratic appeal to the masses. This was evidenced by the fact that, in 1904, the Art Institute of Chicago claimed an attendance of more than half a million visitors, more than that of any other art museum in America. "China decoration of the highest art is conserved and fostered by the well-known Atlan Club," he reported, a nod to the widespread appeal of china painting among the city's residents and its acceptance as art.[4] Two days after the Atlan exhibition closed at the Art Institute, the fourth Arts and Crafts exhibition opened with an Atlan Club entry of fifteen items decorated by eight members. Porcelain decorated overglaze was also shown by former members Lillie E. Cole, May McCrystle, Matilda Middleton, Grace H. Peck, and Helen M. Topping. An interesting addition was nine vases of "hand turned pottery" with a variety of green glazes made by former member Nellie A. Cross and her son Richard, who launched Crossware Pottery in the city's Rogers Park neighborhood.[5]

In the club's 1906 election, Florence Steward was elevated to the office of president and Jane V. D. Wright became vice president;

newcomers Teresa Naper and Laura Nye were supporting officers for two-year terms. Steward injected new life into the club by revitalizing the annual winter study course, allowing women holding associate membership to benefit from practical instruction as well as critiques on their work from its councilors. Beginning each January, she offered associate members a free three-month course, meeting one day a week, in the epochs of historical ornament, the study of appropriate ornament as it related to ceramic shapes, the study of conventionalization from nature, and the application of enamel. In 1907, as an aid in instruction, she wrote and published *Flat Enamel Decoration on China with Suggestions for Color Schemes and Designing*, which she "affectionately dedicated to all of the co-workers in the Atlan Ceramic Art Club but brought out at the earnest request of and for the special use of the associate members." An enthusiastic speaker and untiring club promoter, Steward also entertained members of the city's women's clubs with a talk on "Conventional Decorations on Porcelain Surfaces," accompanied by a small ceramic exhibit.

In June, Atlan members sent a selection of their work to the 1906

Mary Helen Stevens Humphrey, 1893–1922

Mary Helen Stevens Humphrey (1857–1935) was a loyal member of the Atlan Club from its founding in 1893 through 1922. An officer every year between 1894 and 1915, she served as president, 1898–1900, and, at various times, held every other office. She was president in 1900, when the club sent its exhibition to the Paris Exposition.

Born in Fall River, Massachusetts, Mary arrived in Chicago in 1861, when she was four years old. Her father, a jeweler and watchmaker, operated his own shop until 1872, when he joined Giles Bros. & Co., one of the city's largest jewelry retailers. She married Edward L. Humphrey, a salesman for Hyman & Berg, a large wholesale jewelry firm, in June 1889.

Mary's education and art training are unknown; however, she was already a talented artist when invited to join the Atlan Club in 1893. She participated in annual exhibitions sponsored by Western China Decorating Works and was active in the Chicago Ceramic Art Association. She exhibited with the Atlan Club in Arts and Crafts exhibitions at Chicago's Art Institute, 1904–1910, and the Richmond, Indiana, Art Association, 1906, 1907.

When her husband retired in 1910, the couple moved to Pasadena, California, hoping that his health would benefit from the milder climate; while there, during the winter of 1911, Mary taught a class in china painting. After his death in 1912, she returned to Chicago, where she resumed her activities with the Atlan Club.

In January 1915, Mary began teaching classes in conventional design in the Auditorium Tower studio of Helen Frazee, a fellow Atlan Club member. From 1915 through 1919, she conducted study courses in design and color, based on the method of California artist Ralph Helm Johonnot, for the Chicago Ceramic Art Association.

After her aged mother, who lived with her, died in November 1918, Mary split her time between Chicago and Pasadena. She was elected a Life Member of the Atlan Club in 1922. She died in April 1935, at age seventy-seven, in Los Angeles, California.

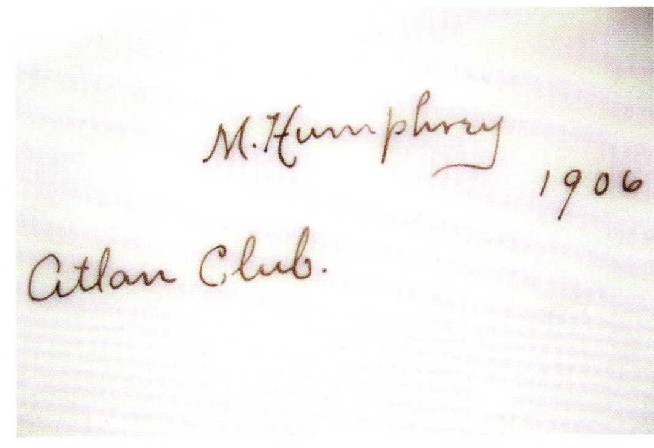

Maker's mark: Mary Helen Stevens Humphrey. *Photo:* Private collection.

art exhibition in Richmond, Indiana. Ceramics on display represented the work of many of the most progressive china painters in the country, ranging from Marshall Fry of New York to local artist H. O. Punsch. Despite such celebrities, the local *Richmond Item* did not hesitate to write, "The exhibit sent by the Atlan ceramic club, of Chicago is the most beautiful conventional work ever seen here. Each piece discloses remarkable skill in design, color and technique."[6]

Among those touring the Richmond exhibition were members of the Indiana Keramic Association, based in Indianapolis. While enthusiastic in their praise of the "exquisite" work of Fry, Punsch, and the Atlan Club, the ladies also admired the excellent porcelain decorated by one of their club members, Margaret Overbeck, art instructor at DePauw University in Greencastle, Indiana.[7] Margaret and her sister, Hannah, a local art teacher, were frequent contributors of conventionalized designs to *Keramic Studio*; in 1911, Hannah joined sisters Mary Frances and Elizabeth in establishing Overbeck Pottery in their hometown of Cambridge City, Indiana.[8]

Indiana Keramic Association, founded in 1897 by Mrs. T. E. Hadley, its president for many years, was one of many American china painting clubs that adopted several of the tenets established by the Atlan Club: membership was limited to women whose artwork met the standards set by a committee; pieces could be exhibited only once; exhibition pieces had to be produced within the year exhibited. Like Atlan, they experimented with making their own pottery forms to decorate in 1903.[9] Similarly, the group exhibited annually at the John Herron Art Institute for several years and sponsored study courses and lectures.

On the national level, the superlative skills of longtime Atlan member Mabel C. Dibble were receiving well-earned recognition. *Keramic Studio* devoted almost its entire October 1906 issue to the work of Dibble, considered "one of the leading disciples of the Conventional school."[10] The issue, which featured Dibble's punch bowl with peacock decoration as its color supplement, was in a series featuring the country's most prominent conventional style decorators.

The Atlans' thirteenth annual exhibition, in November 1906, featured 126 examples of plates, pitchers, serving pieces, and boxes , along with various bowls and vases on Satsuma ware. Florence Steward alone showed more than twenty examples of her work, including a fernery and a nut bowl of "pottery," perhaps made by her; Frances Barothy and Mary Humphrey had almost as many pieces.[11] The 1907 exhibition, with twenty-one exhibitors, had a similar mix of items.[12]

Their fifteenth exhibition, in November 1908, was even larger, with 24 exhibitors and 208 entries. The most unusual entry was Florence Steward's set of framed National Anthem tiles, on which, according to the catalog, "The forms following each note are those produced by the Soprano Voice in an Eidophone, after lycopodium dust has been place on the disc, i.e., the vibrations of the Voice in singing 'My Country 'tis

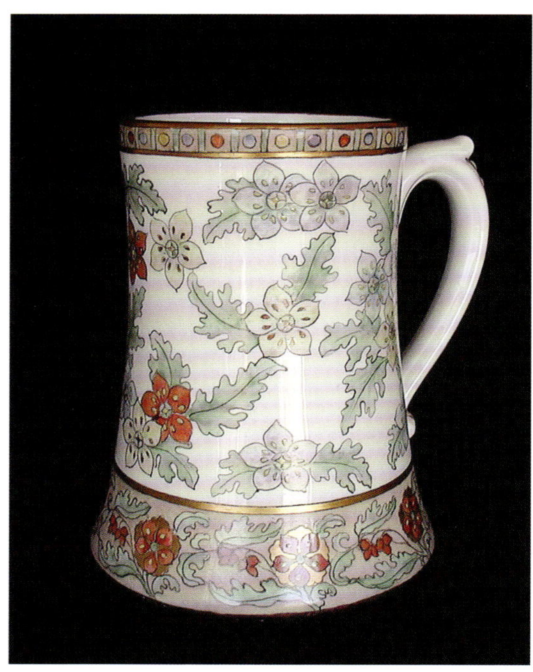

12.6 Mug, Florence Steward, 1906. Signed: For Dr. Archard with best luck wishes for 1906/F. Steward. (h: 5½") *Photo*: Private collection.

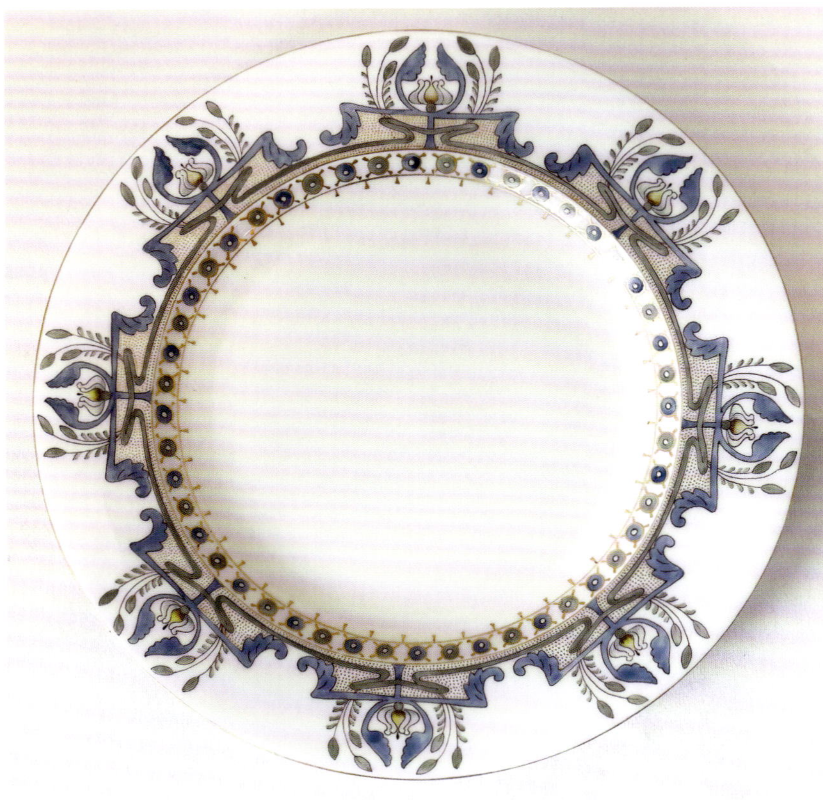

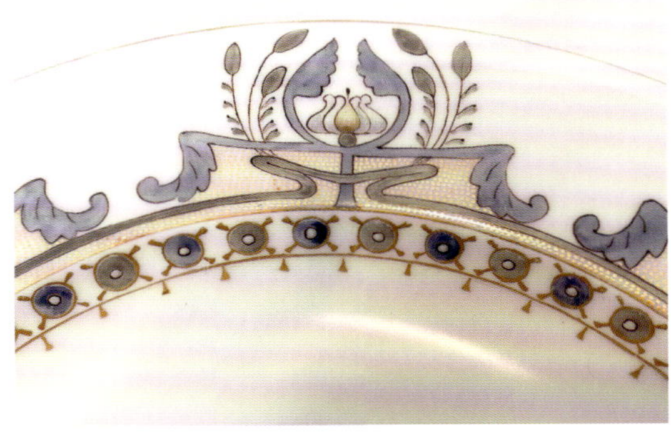

12.7A AND B Plate with conventional tulips, Mary S. Humphrey, 1906. In the 1906 Atlan Club exhibition, Humphrey showed several items from a table service commissioned for Belle T. Hall, who wed Walter L. Hudson on June 6, 1906, in Chicago. Signed: M. Humphrey/Atlan Club/1906. Blank: Haviland. (d: 8¾″) *Photo*: Private collection.

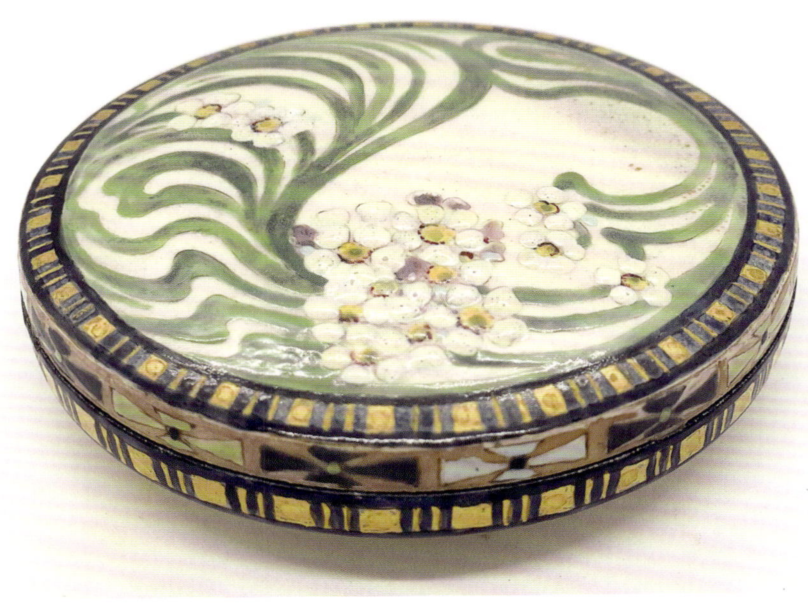

12.8 Powder box with floral motif, Mary S. Humphrey, ca. 1907. Humphrey offered a small box for $4 ($136) in the 1906 Atlan exhibition; it may also have been shown in the Richmond, Indiana, exhibition in June 1907. Signed: Mary S. Humphrey/PPP/Atlan Club/1907 (date in different paint). (1″ × 3½″) *Photo*: Grant Smith.

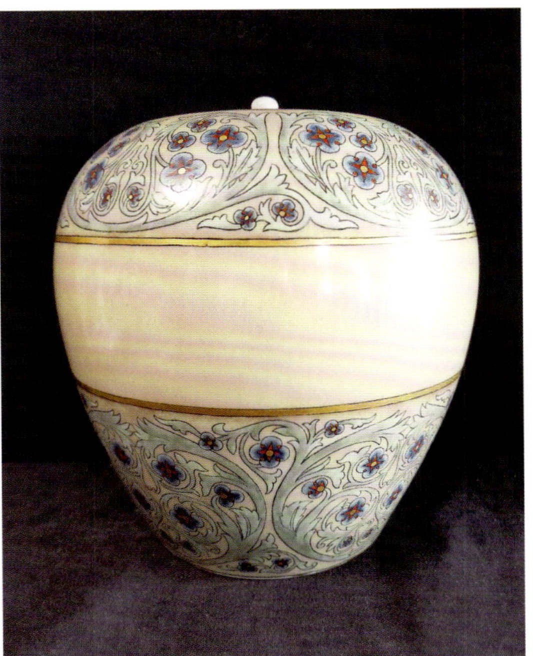

12.9 Tobacco jar, Anna Hays Abercrombie, 1907. Abercrombie showed her work in annual exhibitions and with the club in Chicago Arts and Crafts exhibitions between 1907 and 1911. Signed: PPP/Atlan/Anna H. Abercrombie/1907. Blank: Belleek/Willets. (7¾″ × 6¾″) *Photo*: Ian Lawler, Estate Fresh Austin.

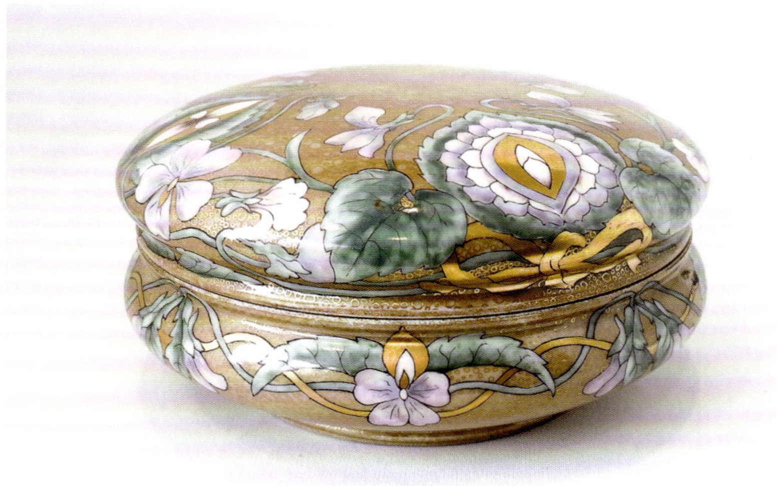

12.10 Powder box, Lylian Root Hulbert, ca. 1908–1911. Hulbert exhibited a variety of porcelain boxes along with tableware in the Atlan Club exhibitions. Signed: L. Root Hulbert/PPP/Atlan. Blank: T&V/Limoges/France. (7″ × 3¾″) *Photo*: Private collection.

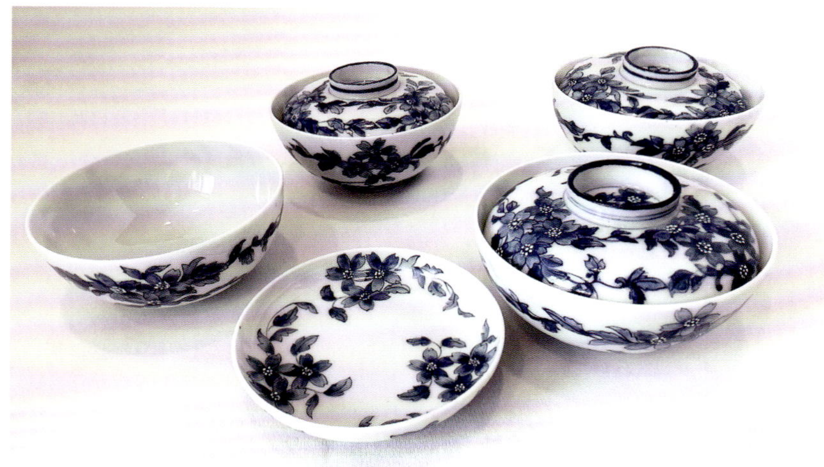

12.11 Covered bowls, Florence Steward, 1908. Described as "Covered Tea, Buillon [sic] or Rice Bowls (9 ea.)" in the 1908 Atlan Club exhibition, Steward painted blue Japanese-style blossoms on white porcelain blanks with blue lines on the lid and base. Signed: F. Steward/PPP/Atlan over blue Japanese marks. (2¼″ × 4″) *Photo*: Private collection.

of Thee,' arranged this series of geometrical figures."[13] It appears that she was experimenting with "voice figures," or visible sound, created by singing a note into a wide-mouthed tube, or resonator, with an elastic membrane (creating a eidophone) stretched over its circular opening (the disk). The musical note sent the membrane, dusted with lycopodium powder mixed with water or milk, into vibration, creating a sound wave that caused a unique floral or geometrical form to appear on the disk.[14] (To date, no examples have been located.)

Shown for the first time were examples of art jewelry, with hand-painted porcelain medallions offering an alternative to both manufactured and "fine" jewelry. Mai Fare Williams, one of the club's younger members, offered a variety of gold-mounted oval medallions with conventional decoration suitable for brooches, pendants, or belt pins. "Miss Mai Fare Williams' work indicates most painstaking care

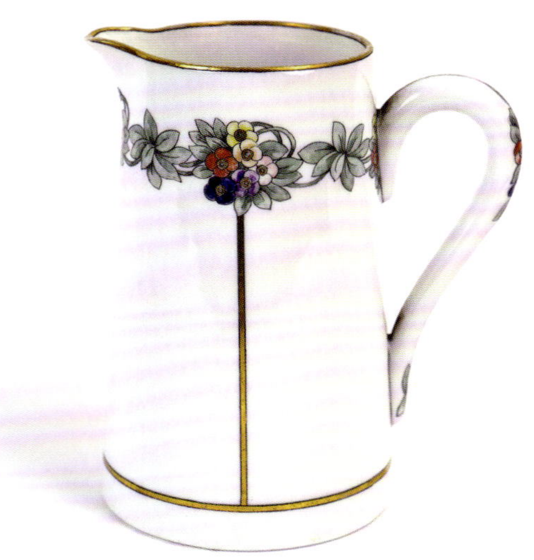

12.12 Pitcher, Linda C. Dunne, 1908–1913 This may have been the pitcher Dunne offered for $5.50 ($184) in the 1909 Atlan Club exhibition. She exhibited three other pitchers between 1908 and 1913, each on loan or already sold. Signed: L. C. D./PPP/Atlan. Blank: Favorite/Bavaria. (h: 6½″) *Photo*: Marvin Venis Benjamin.

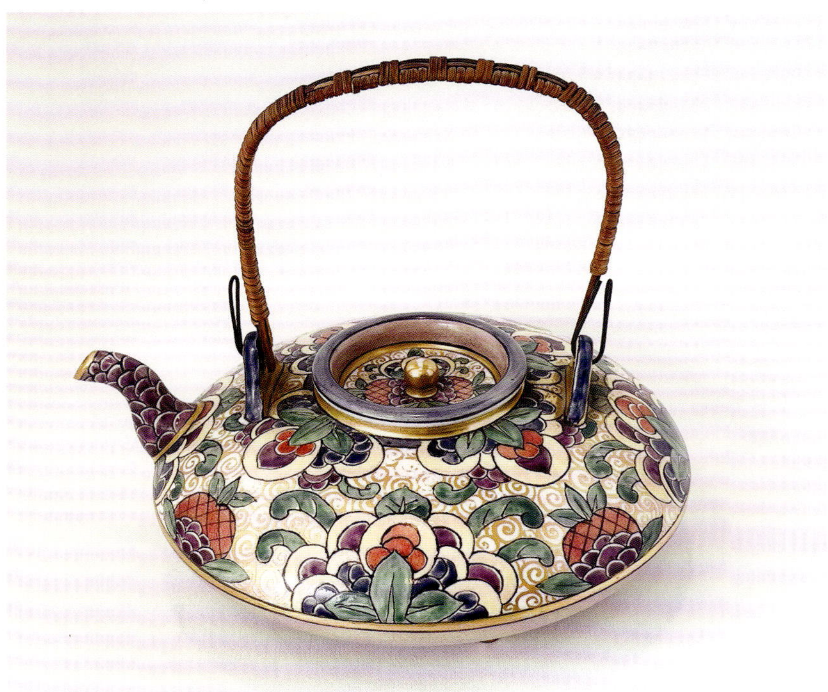

12.13 Satsuma tea pot, Frances Barothy, ca. 1908. Barothy exhibited three Satsuma teapots, priced at $4, $6, and $10 ($133, $198, $332), in the 1908 Atlan Club exhibition. Signed: FAB. (3″ × 7″) *Photo*: Private collection.

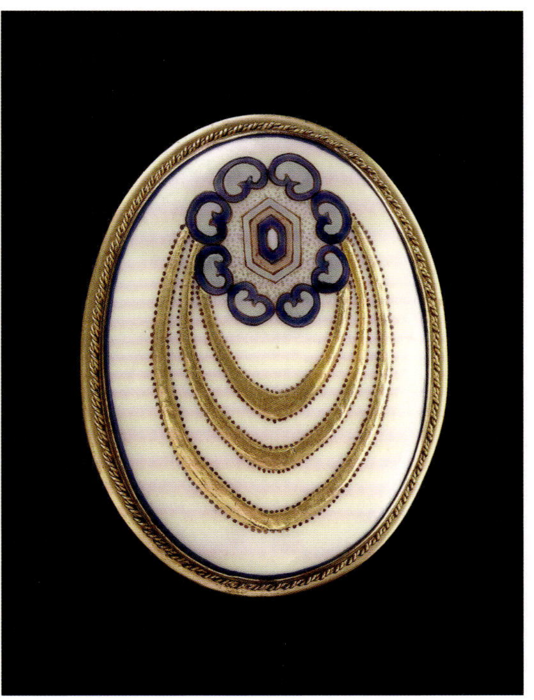

12.14 Brooch, Mai Fare Williams, ca. 1908. Signed: M. F. Williams/Atlan Club/PPP/1908. Williams exhibited several "medallions" in the 1908 exhibition, including three for belt pins, five for pendants, and one for brooch and pendant or pin, priced from $3 ($99) to $6 ($198). Signed: M. F. Williams/Atlan Club/[mark]1908. *Photograph:* John A. Faier, 2014, courtesy of the Richard H. Driehaus Museum.

in her elaborate designs," one reviewer remarked, "Some of the smaller pieces particularly are so intricate as to suggest the use of a magnifying glass."[15] Williams exhibited only three years, 1907 through 1909; like many young members, she resigned when she married.

In 1908, on the club's fifteenth anniversary, members created the Atlan Ceramic Art Club Prize, a ten-dollar gold piece, for the best original design in conventional ornament executed on porcelain displayed during the annual Arts and Crafts exhibition at the Art Institute. Atlan Club members would not compete, and the prize would not be awarded more than once to a competitor.[16] Its first recipient was former Atlan member Matilda Middleton for her overglaze conventional plate design.[17]

In that year's Arts and Crafts exhibition, the Atlan Club entry included a select group of their overglaze decorated porcelain, along with Florence Steward's "My Country 'Tis of Thee" tiles. Describing the Atlan Club's Art Institute showing, *Palette and Bench* observed, "Beyond a doubt, delicate and careful work, simple and strictly conventional motifs, much white porcelain showing makes the most refined and charming decoration for tableware, and the ceramic workers of Chicago certainly excel in this style."[18] By then, only three founding members—Mabel C. Dibble, Mary Humphrey, and Florence Steward—remained active in the club.

Chapter Thirteen

"This Brand of Ecstasy"

This club is composed of the leading creators and admirers of decorative china and pottery. They are the inner circle of the painted china cult, the seventh heaven of this brand of ecstasy.

—"When the Poor Barbarian Visited the Exhibition of Ceramic Art," *Chicago Daily Tribune*, November 21, 1909, 13

"Yes, it was a big day for Satsuma," declared the Poor Barbarian assigned by the *Chicago Daily Tribune* to review the Atlan Club's sixteenth annual exhibition of ceramic art in November 1909. "This delicate, tender coloring of Japanese blue held sway from the first parting of the curtains to the last tinkle of a teacup. Satsumatics came in large numbers. They swished gracefully toward the cases, glimpsed, clasped hands, closed eyes, sighed softly, and stole away." "This club is composed of the leading creators and admirers of decorative china and pottery," the recalcitrant no-doubt male reviewer continued, "They are the inner circle of the painted china cult, the seventh heaven of this brand of ecstasy. Mrs. Le Roy T. Steward, wife of the chief of police, is president and one of the most enthusiastic members."[1]

By 1909, decorated Satsuma ware imported from Japan was a predominant feature in Atlan Club exhibitions. Produced by a variety of small potteries in the Japanese province of Satsuma, mainly for export to the West, the ware had become popular with Atlan decorators because of its simple shapes, wide range of colors, and adaptability to enamel paints fusible at low temperature. Because the Japanese ware was less durable than French or German porcelain, it was best suited for vases and ornamental pieces, rather than tableware that received routine washing and frequent use. Sedji ware, with its delicate green glaze, was another Japanese import that frequently appeared in Atlan exhibitions.

At least two Atlan members—Mabel C. Dibble and Florence Steward—imported Satsuma ware in shapes made according to their own designs, which they offered for sale along with the appropriate enamel paints. Florence Steward's *Flat Enamel Decoration on China* was a popular booklet used in training Atlan associates. Dibble also authored a practical treatise, *How to Use Enamels on China*, which paid special

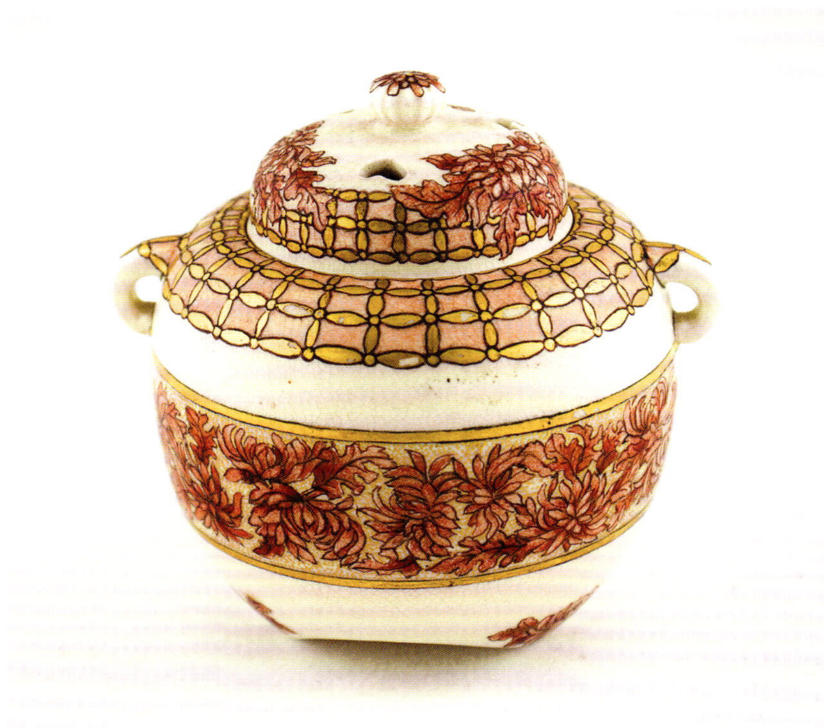

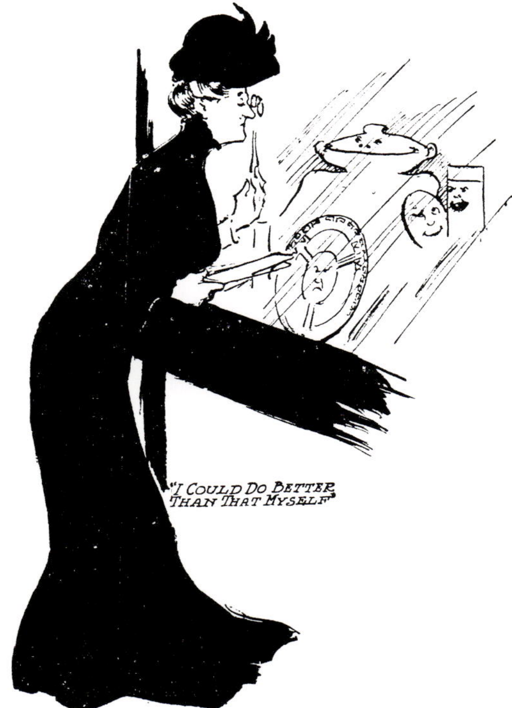

13.1 Satsuma incense jar, Florence Pratt Steward, 1909. Priced at $3.50 ($117), the "small incense jar" was one of "a group of Satsuma pieces selected in Japan by Miss Katherine Irons for this exhibition," according to the 1909 Atlan Club catalog. Noting the group of twenty-one pieces, the *Chicago Tribune* commented "the shapes are decidedly different from any former importations." Signed: F. Steward/PPP/Atlan, 09. (3¾" × 3¾") *Photo*: Robert W. Switzer.

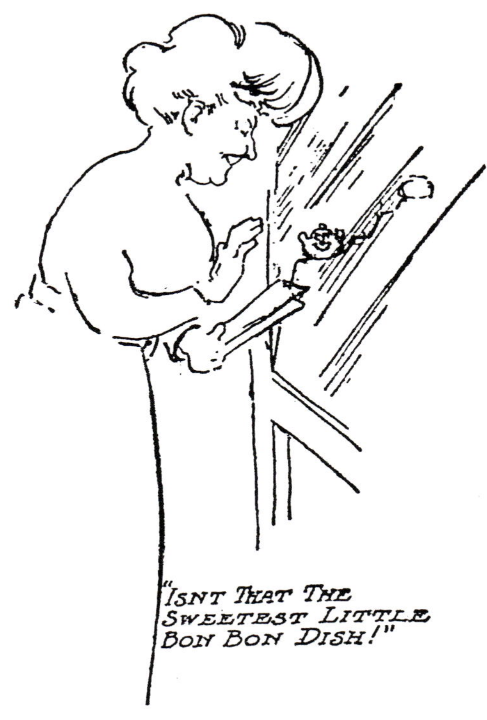

13.2A AND B A cartoonist's view of visitors judging hand-painted china featured in the Atlan Club's 1909 exhibition at the Art Institute of Chicago. *Source*: "When the Poor Barbarian Visited the Exhibition of Ceramic Art," *Chicago Tribune*, November 21, 1909, 73.

attention to the decoration of Satsuma ware.[2] A few years later, the Anglo-French Art Co. of Chicago issued a series of albums for "enamel workers," each of which contained ten to twenty original studies designed by Florence Steward, Mary Humphrey, or Helen Frazee "of the Atlan Club." Advertised in the club's exhibition catalog, the albums were $1 each ($23).[3] The Anglo-French Art Co. also offered *Enamel Work Lessons*, a sheet explaining Florence Steward's method of mixing, applying, and firing enamels, that was accompanied by a full-size design and enough Steward Enamels to paint the design on a plate, all for 75 cents ($17.50).[4]

In the 1909 Atlan Club exhibition, Florence Steward showed, in a separate case, a group of twenty-one pieces of Satsuma selected for her in Japan by Atlan associate member Katherine R. Irons. "Their shapes are decidedly different from any former importations," commented Marie Kingston in the *Chicago Tribune*. "The decoration shows her thorough knowledge of ornament suitable to the forms. The underglaze blue is a rare combination of a smooth glaze applied to a surface where the glaze laid over the [unglazed] biscuit with an intervening color gives the typical crackle, which marks this ware and is a Japanese secret."[5]

"A number of the exhibitors show boxes, bowls, tea sets, etc. of creamy Satsuma ware in fine shapes, which they have adorned with delicately conventionalized flowery patterns," wrote journalist Harriet Monroe, reviewing the same exhibition. "It requires a singularly true instinct for form to use and not misuse these Japanese shapes, as Mrs. Steward, Mrs. Barothy, Miss Dibble and others have done."[6]

The following month, when nineteen Atlans exhibited as a group in the 1909 Chicago Arts and Crafts exhibition, *Keramic Studio*'s editors also found the quantity and unique shapes of Satsuma ware of great interest, suggesting that "Eastern workers would do well to imitate Chicago in this respect as well, and find some Japanese importer to secure for them these quaint little shapes in Satsuma, Sedj[i] and Oribe ware."[7] They also noted that while the Atlan Club continued to follow the principles of decoration learned from the study of Asian art and historic ornament, the designs were becoming "more modern in motif."

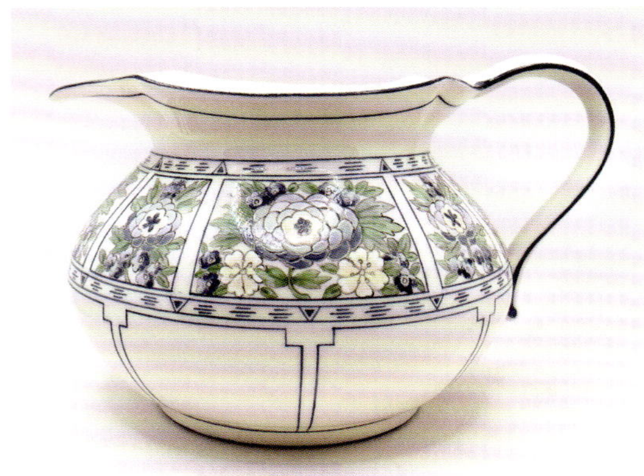

13.3 Pitcher with floral band, Anna O. Senge, 1909. This Willets' Belleek pitcher may have been painted while Senge was an associate of the Atlan Club, before becoming an exhibiting member in 1911. Signed: AS cipher/09. Mark: Belleek/Willets. (5½" × 8") *Photo*: Mikell C. Darling.

Helga Mae Peterson, 1907–1922

Helga Mae Peterson (1873–1934) was an award-winning teacher of china painting who exhibited with the Atlan Club every year from 1907 through 1922.

Born in Chicago, Helga was the daughter of Swedish immigrants who arrived in Illinois around 1868. She was less than seven years old when her father died, leaving her widowed mother to raise three young children.

Helga's early education and art training are unknown. In 1900, at age twenty-six, she was working as a bookkeeper, an occupation she followed until at least 1906.[1] It seems likely that she was self-taught, acquiring her skills in design and painting through study courses with the Chicago Ceramic Art Association, of which she was an active member and exhibitor. In 1909, in addition to being treasurer of the Chicago association, she was secretary to the president of the National League of Mineral Painters.[2]

By 1910, Helga was an established teacher of "arts and crafts" with a studio in the Auditorium Tower.[3] That year, in the Burley & Co. exhibition, her chop platter combining dandelion flowers with geometrical forms won first prize in the conventional class (fig. 14.5).[4] The next year, she took the prize again, this time for a chocolate pot with sugar and creamer (fig. 14.16).[5] Her work was selected for exhibit in the 1915 Panama-Pacific Exposition in San Francisco and won the highest awards in their class at the Illinois State Fair, 1913–1917.

Helga's talents extended beyond china painting. In 1913, she received a patent for a Device for Decorating Chinaware to be used to hold a pen steady when marking lines.[6] By 1915 she had added leathercraft to the techniques offered in her studio.[7]

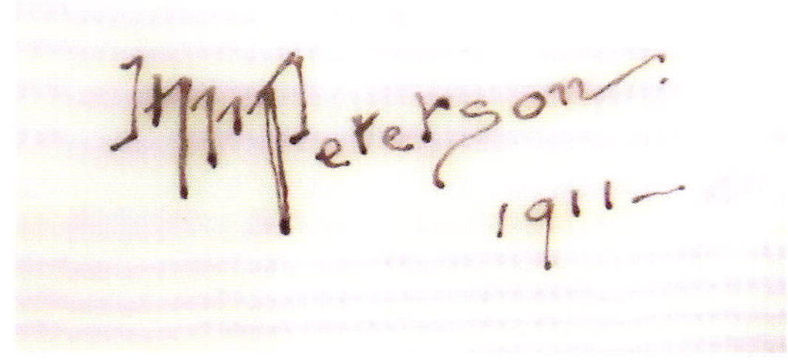

Maker's mark: Helga Mae Peterson. *Photo*: Private collection.

In December 1915, Helga moved her studio from the Auditorium Building to her home on Winona Avenue. There she gave lessons and sold her booklet, *How to Mix Enamels,* along with her own line of Helga M. Peterson China Colors.[8]

In 1923, Helga joined the staff of Wesley Memorial Hospital as its director of occupational therapy, a new field focusing on the rehabilitation of veterans of World War I. She was still working in this position in 1930. She died, age sixty-one, in Chicago on May 17, 1934.

Chapter Fourteen

Director for Life

Go to nature—to plant forms to get life and breadth in your work. You will never become more than a commonplace designer if you do not go to nature for your inspiration.
—Florence Steward, *Flat Enamel Decoration on China*, 1907, 31

The year 1910 proved to be a watershed year for the Atlan Ceramic Art Club, the Chicago Ceramic Association, and the local china painting community. In June, Atlan Club members elected Florence Steward director general for life. Members had attempted during the last few years of her continuous presidency to persuade her to accept the presidency for life, but she had refused, so the new office was created instead.[1] She did agree to be elected president for the coming year; Mary Humphrey, another founding member, was named vice president. Except for 1911, when Jane V. D. Wright was president, Steward went on to hold both offices—president and director—over the next decade.

A few months earlier, Mabel C. Dibble, the third remaining cofounder, resigned. One of Chicago's most popular teachers, Dibble juggled a heavy schedule of classes following the sudden death in 1907 of Helen M. Topping, who shared her studio; at the end of 1909, Eva E. Adams, another lapsed Atlan member, joined her in the Marshall Field Building. In 1910, Dibble became the first midwestern women to be named a Master Craftsman by the Society of Arts and Crafts, Boston, the oldest and one of the most exclusive crafts societies in the country. The previous year, she had been invited to join London's Royal Society of Arts.[2] One can only speculate: was Dibble's resignation prompted by her hectic schedule, Adams' partnership, or Steward's appointment as director general? Did she perhaps feel that the Atlan Club had plateaued and she, at age forty-seven, was ready to enjoy the final phase of her career? There was a hint of this in her 1906 correspondence with Allen Whiting, secretary of the Boston Arts and Crafts Society, regarding membership when she wrote, "I do not suppose you care for the names of china painters unless you wish those who were first in the Arts and Crafts movement in ceramics that really started in Chicago in our Atlan Club. . . . I was obliged to earn

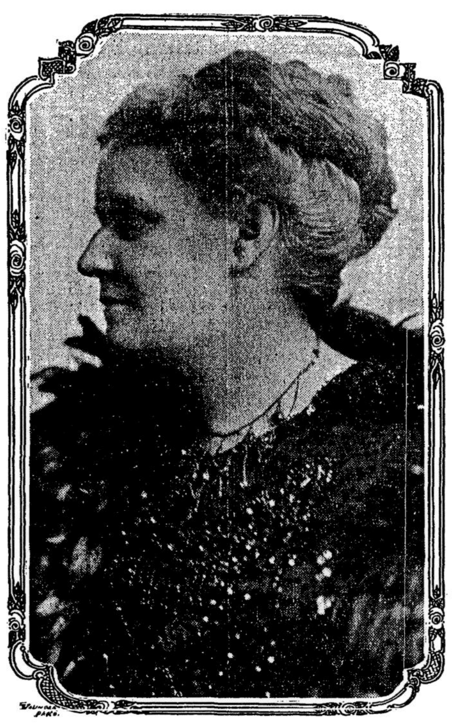

14.1 Florence Pratt Steward was elected director general for life in January 1910. "I am proud and appreciative of the club's act," she told readers of the *Chicago Daily Tribune*, "and will do my best to keep the club what it now is, the foremost society of its sort in the United States." "Ceramic Club Creates Life Post for Wife of Police Chief Steward," *Chicago Daily Tribune*, June 12, 1910, 7.

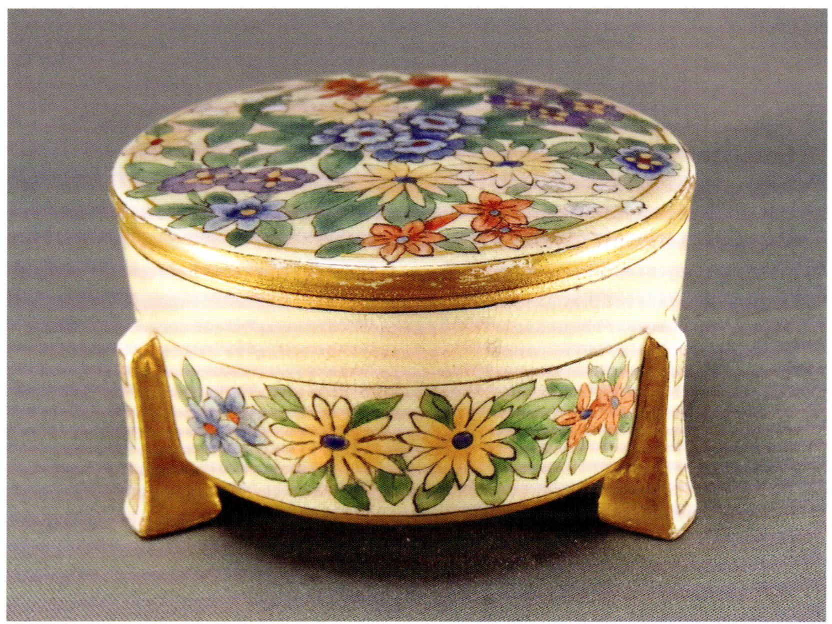

14.2 Satsuma box, Eleanor Rose Benson Daily, 1910. The box was one of Daily's six unpriced entries in the 1910 Atlan Club exhibition. Signed: E. R. Daily/PPP/Atlan/10. (1½" × 2½") *Photo*: Courtesy of Dark Flowers Antiques.

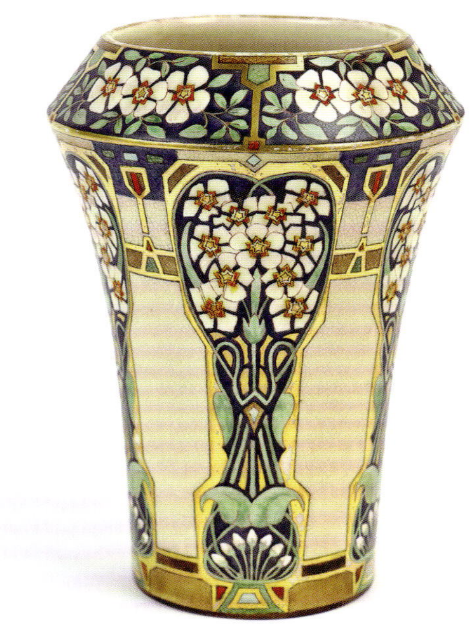

14.3 Satsuma vase, Stella Rintoul, ca. 1910. This vase with conventionalized apple blossoms may have been the "Vase, Satsuma, Old Chinese Ornament" that Rintoul exhibited in the 1910 Atlan Club exhibition. Inscription: SR cipher/PPP/Atlan. (h: 8½") *Photo*: Marvin Venis Benjamin.

money, and instead of working in the line in which I could make the most, I selected conventional designing and painting on china, and have had the pleasure of seeing this work grow until now it stands at the head of ceramic work, and those of us who have grown with this movement, are rewarded."[3]

In May 1910, the National League of Mineral Painters disbanded. Apparently, the various clubs had lost interest in participating in exhibitions and were unwilling to share management responsibilities. For the previous six years, the work of the league had been performed by officers of the Chicago Ceramic Association, who were not eligible for reelection; no others stepped forward to take their places. The overworked officers claimed that increased interest in the league's study course, which provided six free professional criticisms on each member's designs, had essentially turned the league into a correspondence school. While the result had been a great improvement in ceramic decoration throughout the country, it had deprived the Chicago club of the work of many of its best designers. Additionally, the formation of regional Arts and Crafts societies, which gave china decorators opportunities to exhibit with other craftspeople, had lessened the interest of ceramic clubs in the league's annual exhibitions, which had become "small and unimportant."[4] The league held its final meeting at the Art Institute of Chicago on May 10, during which it presented the gold medal won at the Paris Exposition to the museum's collection. Freed from league duties, the Chicago association,

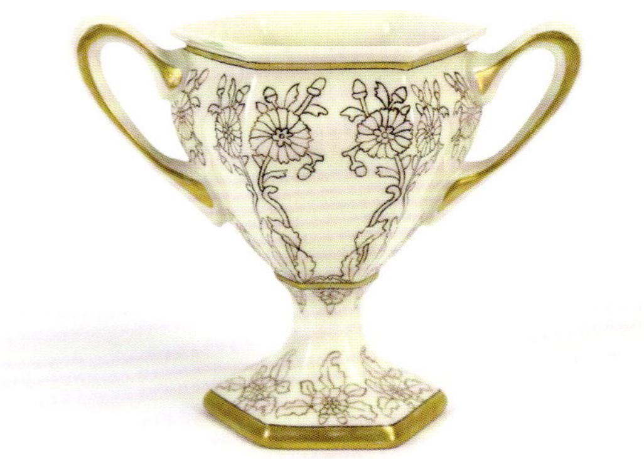

14.4 Sugar bowl with gold tracery, Mai Fare Williams, 1910. Williams, who married in November 1910, the same month as the Atlan Club exhibition, did not exhibit that year. The decoration may be unfinished. Signed: M. F. Williams Atlan Club PPP Chicago 1910. (3¼" × 4½") *Photo*: Marvin Venis Benjamin.

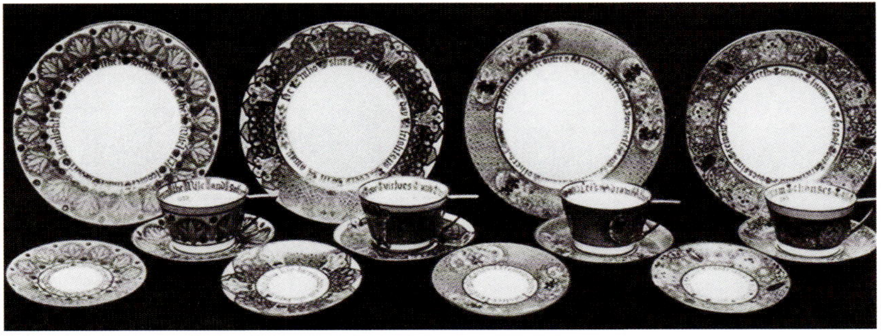

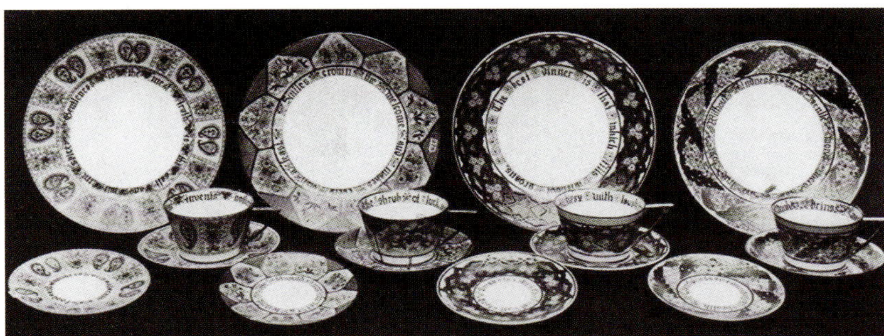

14.5A AND B Florence Pratt Steward's 1910 "Conversational Set" based on epochs in historic ornament included eight place settings, each consisting of a plate, bread and butter plate, cup, and saucer. Egypt, China, Japan, India, Arabia, Moorish Spain, Persia, and the Renaissance (seventeenth century) were represented, with typical motifs and quotations representing each epoch. Mira Burr Edson, "Ceramic Work of Mrs. Steward: Methods of the President of the Atlan Club," *Arts & Decoration*, 1, no. 7 (May 1911): 308.

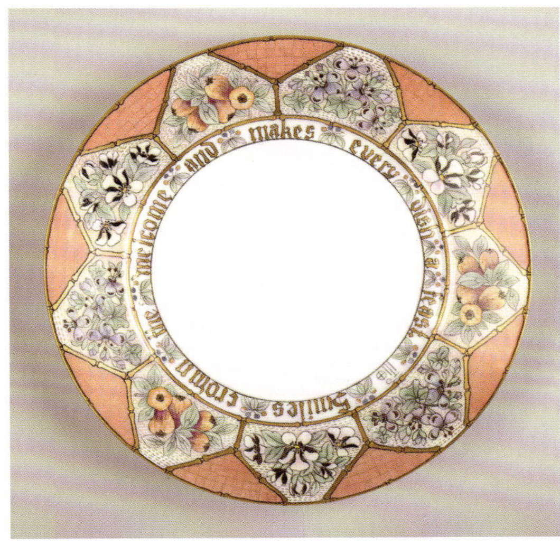

14.6 "Japanese" plate inscribed "Smiles crown the welcome and makes [*sic*] every dish a feast." (d: 8⅝")
Photo: Chicago History Museum _i174200-pm.

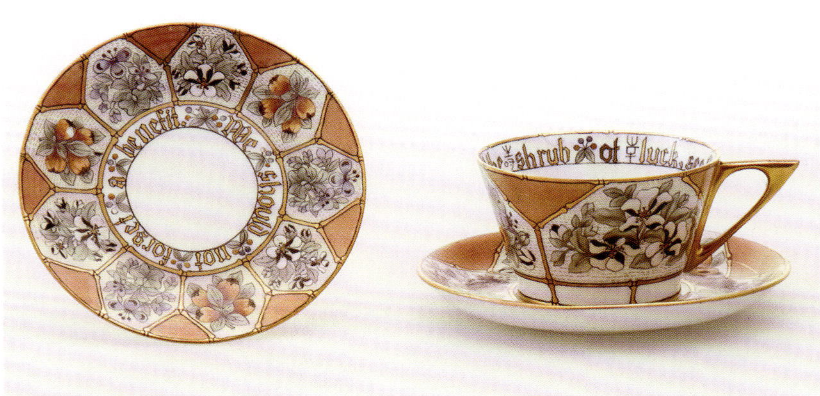

14.7 "Japanese" inspired bread and butter plate, cup, and saucer from the Conversational Set in Historic Ornament, Florence Pratt Steward, 1910. The inscription on the plate reads "We should not forget a benefit;" on the cup, "Tea is the Shrub of luck, see its symbols." Signed: F. Steward/Atlan/logo. (Plate: d: 5⅛") *Photo*: Chicago History Museum.

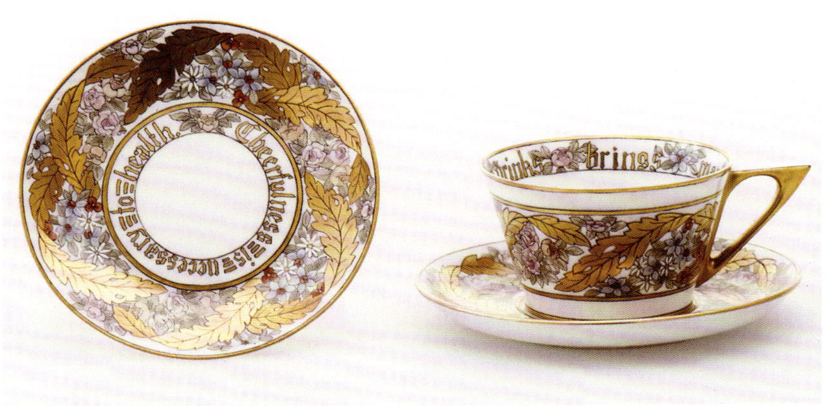

14.8 "Renaissance (17th Century)" inspired bread and butter plate, cup, and saucer from the "Conversational Set" in historic ornament, Florence Pratt Steward, 1910. "Cheerfulness is necessary to health" is painted on the plate; the cup is inscribed "Many drinks bring many diseases." Signed: F. Steward/Atlan/Renaissance/17th Cent. (Plate: d: 5⅛") *Photo*: Chicago History Museum.

with the word "Art" permanently in its name, continued its annual exhibitions at the Art Institute.

By then, many league members had expanded their skills beyond china painting to include pottery, leatherwork, jewelry, or other crafts, in keeping with the Arts and Crafts philosophy of producing handcrafted objects. Even the league's organizer, ceramist Susan S. Frackelton, a Chicago resident since 1902, replaced her ceramic activity with book illumination in 1910 and joined the Arts and Crafts lecture circuit.[5] Florence Koehler, too, gave up painting china to fabricate unique, intricately detailed jewelry for affluent clients.[6] Several Atlan members also expanded their scope, with Augusta Baron McCarn and Helga M. Peterson advertising lessons in jewelry and leatherwork as well as ceramics in the club's exhibition catalogs.

In contrast, the Atlan Ceramic Art Club was thriving. In November 1910, the opening reception for its seventeenth exhibition drew fully 2,000 persons. The display was large, with 313 entries contributed by 24 members. All, however, were overshadowed by Florence Steward's "Conversational Set" with decorations based on various epochs in historic ornament. Priced at $500 ($15,746), the set consisted of eight

Florence Jane Donovan Wilcox Pratt Steward, 1893–1921

After launching the Atlan Ceramic Art Club in 1893, Florence Pratt Steward remained its indefatigable guiding force until her death in 1921. The club survived her by only one year.

Florence Jane Donovan (1851–1921) was born in Auburn, Cayuga County, New York, in 1851. Around 1855, her parents, Mary and John E. Donovan, moved to Sauk County, Wisconsin, where her father served as sheriff for several years. Florence remained behind, perhaps to attend school; in 1865, according to the New York state census, she was living with a Donovan uncle in Cayuga County. In 1866, her parents divorced, with her mother moving to Waukesha, Wisconsin, and her father to Chicago. Florence joined her mother, who operated a successful millinery shop.

While living in Waukesha, Florence married John Newton Wilcox in July 1871 and moved to Chicago, where John was employed as a bookkeeper. In May 1891, Florence divorced Wilcox, claiming desertion. Seven months later, on December 26, 1891, she married Chicago realtor Ezra Huntington Pratt.

Florence had training in drawing and painting before taking up china decoration, having studied at the Chicago Art Institute, although details remain unknown.[1] By 1893, her superior china painting skills made her a prominent member of the Chicago Ceramic Art Association, treasurer of the National League of Mineral Painters,[2] and organizer of the Atlan Club.

After divorcing Pratt in 1895, Florence exhibited as "Mrs. Florence Pratt" until marrying Le Roy T. Steward in 1897. At the time, Steward was superintendent of the Chicago Post Office. He took a leave of absence to serve as the city's chief of police, 1909–1911, before returning to the Post Office for the remainder of his professional career. It is possible that they met during the 1893 Chicago World's Fair, where she coordinated all the exhibits from the various clubs in

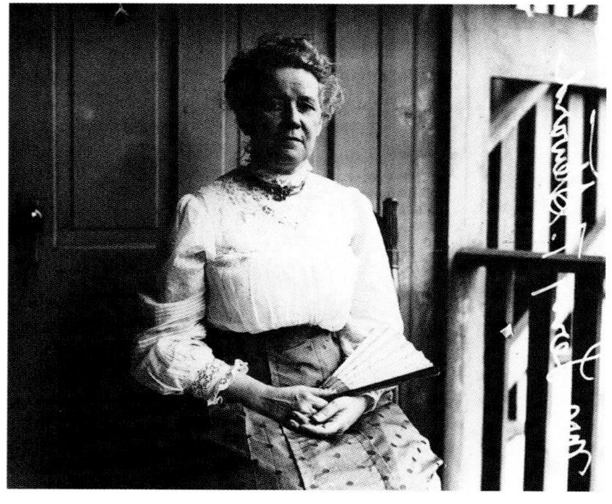

Florence Steward, 1909. Courtesy of the Chicago History Museum, Daily News Collection DN-0054878_pm.

four-piece place settings—plate, cup and saucer, and bread plate—each with ornament representing an epoch, including Egyptian, Chinese, Japanese, East Indian, Persian, Arabic, Moorish, and Renaissance.

Each of the set's pieces also bore a proverb or saying from the literature of the people.[7] "Curiosity impels the reading or spelling out of each of these, which are placed within the rim of the cups and form an inner ring upon the saucers and plates," wrote Mira Burr Edson in a feature article, "Ceramic Work of Mrs. Steward: Methods of the President of the Atlan Club of Chicago," published in *Arts and Decoration*, a New York–based magazine on art and interior decoration. "While the conversation sets may be looked upon as a *tour de force* they are eminently successful as such and show clearly the ability of the artist."[8]

Columnist H. Effa Webster, who covered the Atlan Club exhibition as a quasi-society event for the *Chicago Examiner*, was impressed by the sheer quantity of objects, mentioning Helen Frazee's thirty-seven "sumptuous pieces," along with those by Frances Barothy, who showed twenty-six, and Elva Secreste Harner, with twenty-two.[9]

Fred W. Sandberg, art critic for the *Chicago Daily Tribune*, complimented Steward's ambitious "Conversational Set" and paid homage

---

the National League of Mineral Painters and Steward chaired the committee on public information.[3]

In 1902, Florence, as club historian, wrote "The History of the Atlan Ceramic Art Club of Chicago, Ill., 1893–1901," covering its first decade, upon invitation from the Chicago Historical Society (now the Chicago History Museum).[4] That year, having been elected a life member, she finally agreed to hold office. She served as vice president until 1907, when she was elected president, an office she then held every year through 1921, except 1911. In June 1910 she was elected director general for life. Announcing the honor, the *Chicago Tribune* acknowledged Florence as the "guiding spirit and conscientious guide" of the Atlan Club and described her personally as "earnestly enthusiastic, cultured of a rare intelligence and sympathetic perception," but modest regarding credit for the club's enviable reputation.[5]

A firm believer in art education, Florence lectured on ceramic art to local women's clubs and various art organizations, in addition to providing ongoing art history lessons to Atlan members and associates. In 1907, she published *Flat Enamel Decoration on China with Suggestions for Color Schemes and Designing*, primarily for use in the Atlan Club's annual winter study courses for associate members. Beginning in 1910, she advertised her booklet and private lessons in Atlan exhibition catalogs. The "Ceramic Work of Mrs. Steward; Methods of the President of the Atlan Club of Chicago" was featured in *Arts and Decoration* in May 1911.[6]

In addition to organizing and participating in Atlan Club exhibitions, Florence actively promoted the club while exhibiting at Burley & Co. and in various regional exhibitions. She occasionally served on the jury selecting the recipient of the Atlan Ceramic Art Club Prize awarded at Arts and Crafts exhibitions sponsored by the Art Institute of Chicago. After joining the Chicago Woman's Club in May 1914, she served on numerous philanthropic committees.[7]

Florence died unexpectedly, at age seventy, following an operation on November 29, 1921. Under the terms of her will, her "valuable collection of ceramics was left to the Art Institute, consisting of specimens of Satsuma and others."[8] Ironically, the *Chicago Daily Tribune*'s brief obituary mistakenly credited her as "being for years the president of the Chicago Ceramic club, which makes annual exhibits at the Art Institute."[9] Fortunately her local newspaper got it right, noting that she was "well known in artists' circles, was president and life director of the Atlan Ceramic Club, which she had organized in 1893."[10]

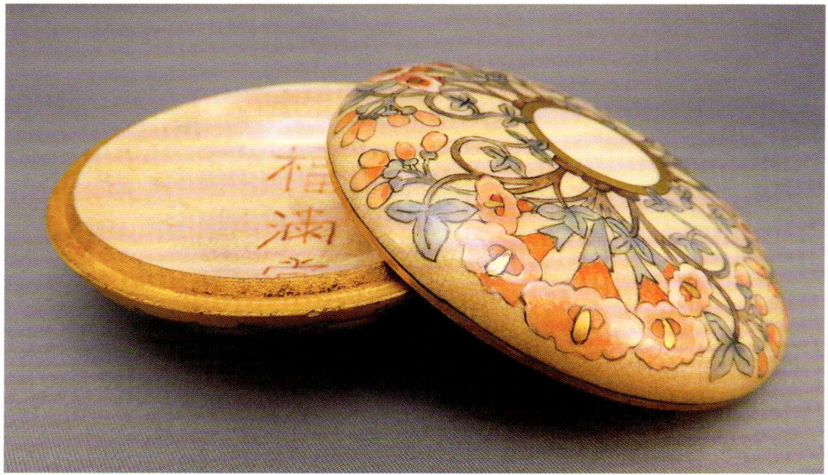

14.9 Japanese pottery box, Florence Steward, ca. 1911. Decorated with conventional decoration and the phrase "Prosperity will follow you" on its base, it may be the Japanese pottery box exhibited in the Atlan Club's exhibition in 1911. Signed: "Prosperity will follow you"/F. Steward/PPP/Atlan. (1½″ × 3″) *Photo*: Dark Flowers Antiques.

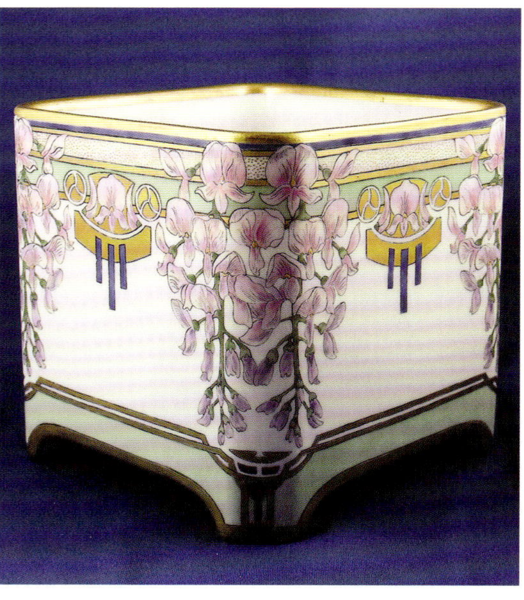

14.10 Square fernery with sweet peas, Ruth Anna Blomquist, 1911. Blomquist was living in Berwyn, a new Chicago suburb, when she exhibited the fernery in the 1911 Atlan Club exhibition. Signed: R. Blomquist/Berwyn/Ill./ACAC in swastika. Mark: D & C/France. (5½″ × 5½″) *Photo*: Dark Flowers Antiques.

to the club's guiding spirit. "Earnestly enthusiastic, cultured of a rare intelligence and sympathetic perception, she has mastered all the difficulties and brought about a most gratifying result," he wrote, noting Steward "modestly disclaims any particular amount of credit, insisting that all members, through their loyalty and interest in their art have gained the club its enviable reputation." The club enjoyed "the distinction of being the most important one of its kind in the United States and its works have been shown at several prominent European installations, receiving the highest awards accorded to nonprofessional workers in this branch of industrial art."[10]

That said, Sandberg gave his honest critique of the exhibition. It contained "some exceptionally good bits" as to design and execution but suffered from monotony; the cases were too crowded; there was too much Satsuma. "There is a notable lack of independent conception, versatility, and originality of design; if the club, most of the members of which are well grounded in technique, must needs consult a designer, it ought to choose a person possessing some creative ability," he wrote. "The prevailing designs are, barring the native or epochal ones, but slightly modified adaptions of what has been seen for many years."[11] (Was Sandberg the "Poor Barbarian" overwhelmed by Satsuma in 1909?)

In December, most of the Atlan Club members who participated in the club's exhibition showed work under the club's banner in the 1910 Arts and Crafts exhibition, a large show with 1,448 entries filling four large Art Institute rooms. Exhibiting under their own names were Helen Frazee, who had seventeen pieces of tableware, and Florence

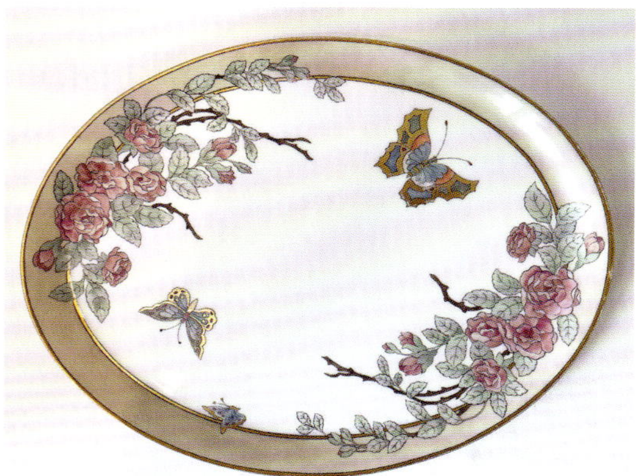

14.11 Platter with butterflies, Carrie Ethel Frame Killham, 1911. This piece was likely commissioned as a duplicate of one shown in the Atlan Club's November 1911 exhibition, in which Killham showed various examples of tableware. Signed: E. Killham/PPP/Atlan/12-22-11. (10½″ × 8⅛″) *Photo*: Private collection.

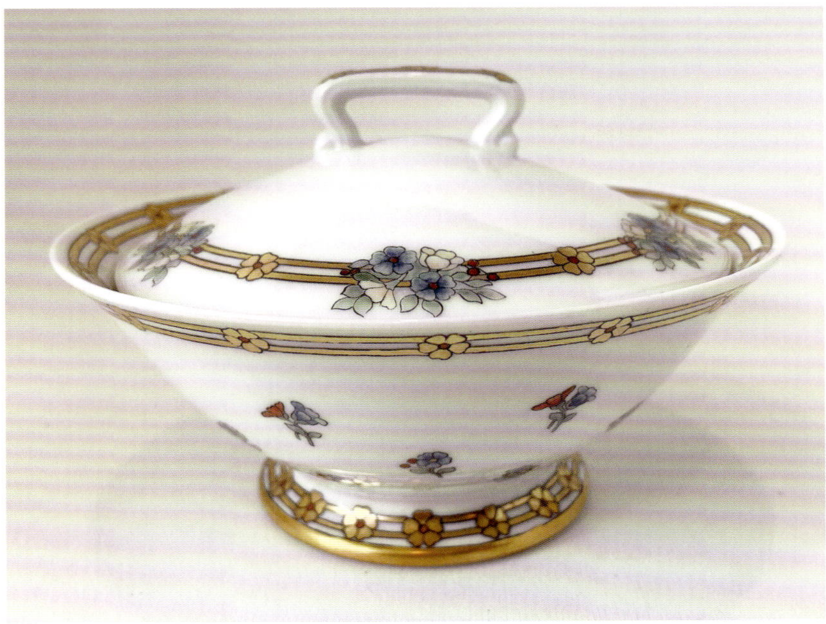

14.12 Mayonnaise bowl, Florence Steward, 1911. Offered in the 1911 Atlan Club catalog for $5 ($160), it was shown alongside a radish bowl priced at $4 ($128). Signed: F. Steward/PPP/Atlan. (4¾" × 6") *Photo*: Private collection.

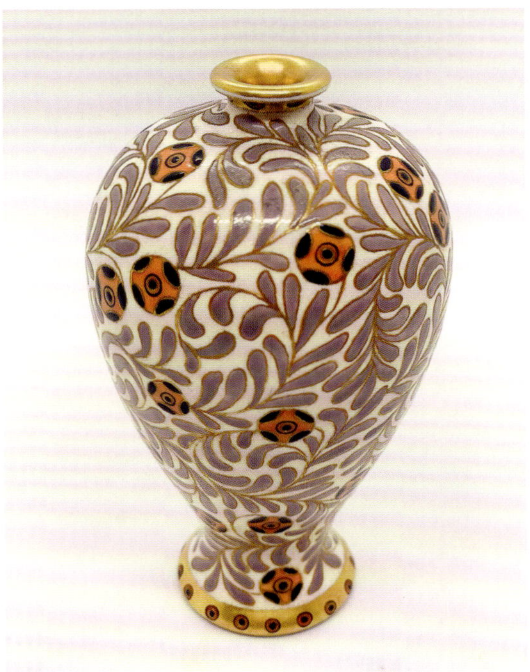

14.13 Satsuma vase, Alma F. Ludwig, 1911. One of two vases (the other was on Belleek) among nine objects listed "not for sale" exhibited by Ludwig in the 1911 Atlan exhibition. An Art Institute graduate, she advertised lessons in watercolor and ceramics in the club's catalog. Signed: Alma F. Ludwig, Atlan mark obscured. (h: 4¾") *Photo*: Grant Smith.

Steward, who displayed her "Conversational Set" and a few Satsuma vases. Non-Chicagoans exhibiting overglaze decorated porcelains included former Atlan member Henrietta Zeublin, residing in Massachusetts, and Kathryn E. Cherry and students from the ceramic school at People's University at University City, St. Louis. The formidable display of art pottery included work from the Acoma Pueblo, Marblehead Pottery, Markham Pottery, Handicraft Guild of Minneapolis, Newcomb Pottery, Paul Revere Pottery, Rookwood Pottery, and University City.[12] The jury of selection for ceramics, composed of Helen Frazee, Florence Steward, and local designer Carleta P. Ashcraft, awarded the 1910 Atlan Club Prize for overglaze decorated porcelain to Kathryn E. Cherry, the talented St. Louis china painter and teacher on the faculty of the short-lived People's University, operated by St. Louis publisher Edward G. Lewis in conjunction with the American Woman's League, 1909–1912.[13]

When the Club's nineteenth annual exhibit opened in November 1911, the *Chicago Daily News* art critic quoted Florence Steward (despite Jane V. D. Wright being president), who was inordinately proud of the Atlan Club having "taken the initiative in exclusive conventional American ideas," claiming "ceramic artists of New York, Boston, Philadelphia and other large eastern cities have adopted our American ideas and hailed us as the originators of an art superior to anything in this line shown in the east."[14] *Chicago Tribune* art critic Harriet Monroe had her own opinion, deeming the club's display "extremely fine," but formulaic. "If one were to criticize the present array of beautiful

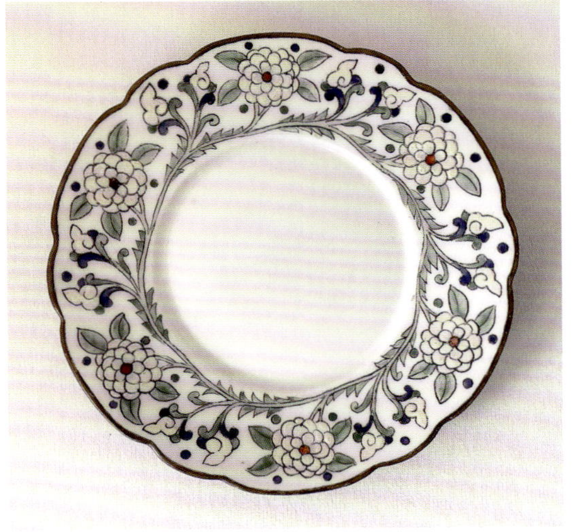

14.14 Bread and butter plate, Florence Steward, ca. 1911. This small plate with floral border may have been from one of two sets Steward exhibited in 1911. Signed: Florence Steward/PPP/Atlan. (d: 5") *Photo*: Private collection.

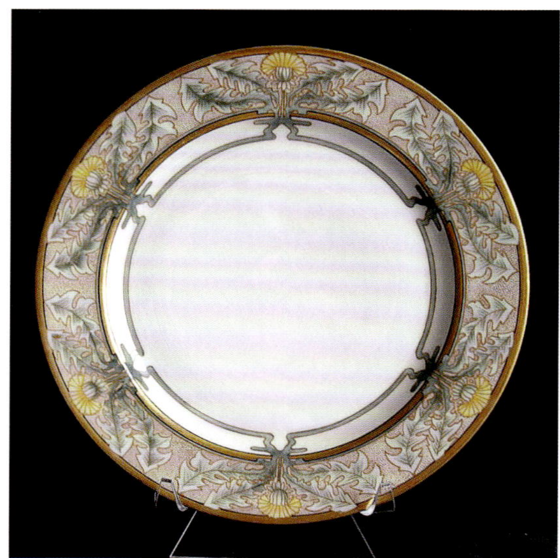
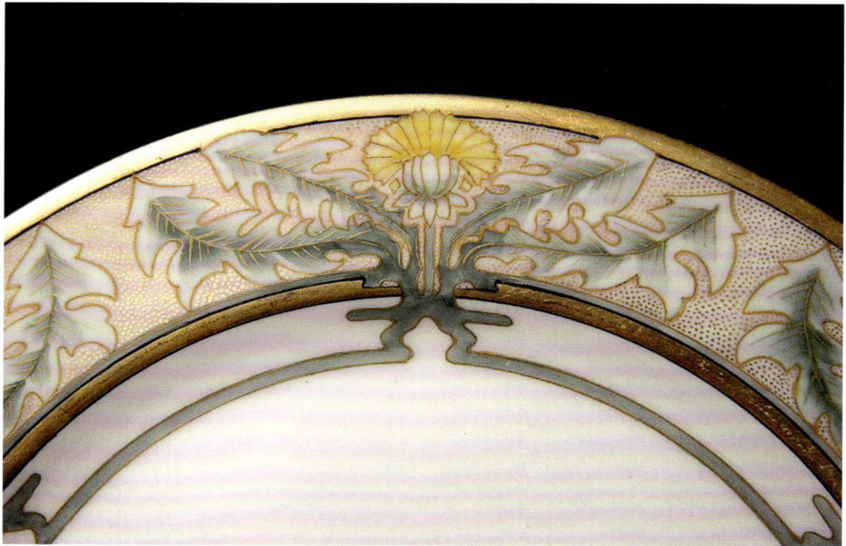

14.15A AND B Chop platter with dandelion motif, Helga M. Peterson, 1910. This platter was awarded first prize in the conventional class at the 1910 Burley & Co. exhibition in Chicago. On September 11, 1910, the *Chicago Tribune* art critic explained, "In designing for a round space the result of the placing of masses is almost as important as the main decoration and this is a splendid example of this construction. The soft colors are accentuated by the snap of the drawing of the outlines. The richness necessary to so important a piece is secured partly by the use of gold bands contrasted with the dotted background upon which is used the dandelion flowers and leaves in natural colors." When the platter was exhibited in the 1910 Atlan Club exhibition, the catalog noted that it could be duplicated for $50 ($1,606); it was also among the club's entries in the 1910 Arts and Crafts exhibition at the Chicago Art Institute. (d: 9¾") *Photo*: Private collection.

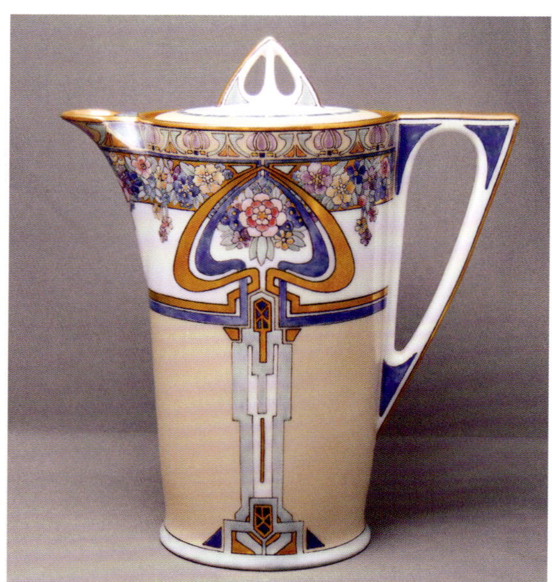
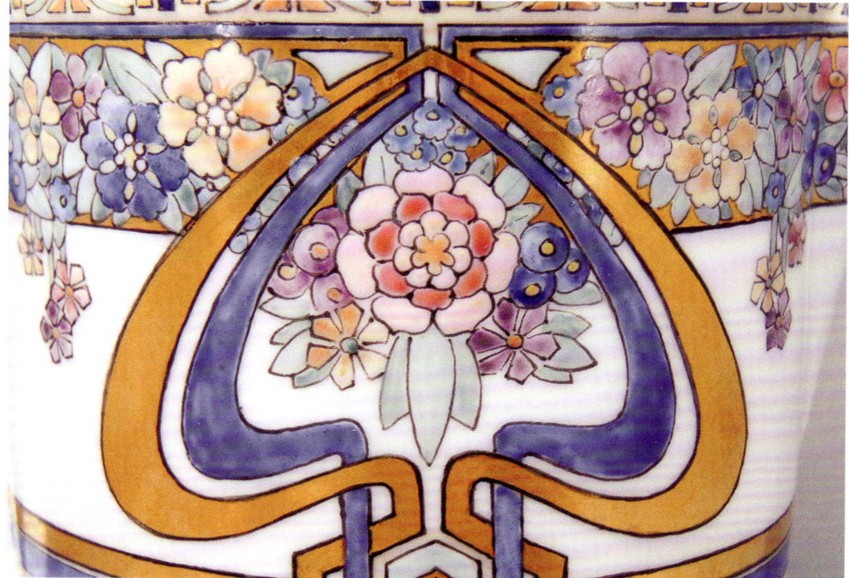

14.16A AND B Chocolate pot, Helga M. Peterson, 1911. Part of a set that included sugar and creamer, her chocolate pot won first prize for conventional work in the Burley & Co. exhibition in 1911. It was exhibited but "not for sale" in the 1911 Atlan Club exhibition. "The geometrical forms were well drawn and the floral parts were artistically adapted to enclosures of the decoration and the form of the china," wrote *Keramic Studio* in February 1912 ("Burley Exhibit," 13, no. 9, 201, illus. p. 203). Signed: H. M. Peterson/1911. Mark: Favorite/Bavaria. (h: 8½") *Photo*: Dark Flowers Antiques.

14.17 Dresser tray, Florence Hubbard, 1912. Part of a five-piece dresser set, the original of which was on loan in the 1912 Atlan Club exhibition but could be duplicated for $25. Signed: Florence Hubbard/5961 West End Ave/Chicago/PPP/Atlan/1912. (7¾″×¼″) *Photo*: Marvin Venis Benjamin.

dishes the only complaint would be of too much reserve, too close obedience to good taste, too much harmonious paleness of color. One longs for more richness, more daring, more originality. These ladies have worked together so long, pursued the same ideals so intently, that their personalities begin to be lost in their association."[15]

Atlan members also participated in the annual exhibition at Burley & Co., the city's largest importer of porcelain blanks and glassware. In 1910, Burley had resumed sponsoring, and heavily promoting, annual exhibitions of overglaze decorated china, most likely to stimulate a flagging business. Although no article was for sale, prizes were awarded by popular vote, with conventional and naturalistic designs receiving the same consideration. In 1911, Atlan member Helga M. Peterson won the first prize of $25 (approximately $787) for conventional work (as she had in 1910), while pieces by Frances Barothy, Edna Jack, and Florence Hubbard received favorable mention. Florence Steward displayed her "Conversational Set" in "a class by itself," not in competition.[16]

The exhibitions, which drew a large gathering of the best work from china painters in Chicago and the western states, attracted thousands of visitors eager to see the latest designs in porcelain decoration and examine up close the work of eminent ceramic painters. The work of Atlan members was not only widely admired but inspired imitations. For example, the local Pickard China Company proudly introduced a pattern called "Atlan Enamel" in 1911; "The Chinese Border" pattern, based on a motif at an Atlan exhibition, followed a few years later.[17]

Steward's "Conversational Set" was also illustrated in an article in *International Studio*, which affirmed that the Atlan Club under Steward had established the use of conventional ornament on porcelain and queried, "Why not help to make its style of decoration known as 'American'?"[18] But was the conventional style really a distinctive

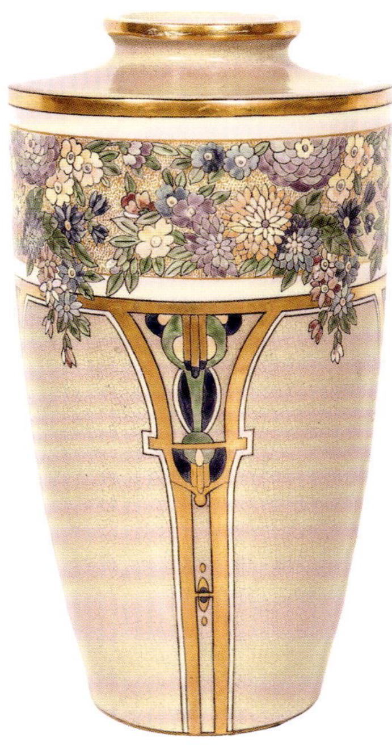

14.18 Vase, Anna Senge, 1912. One of two Satsuma vases Senge displayed in the 1912 Atlan Club exhibition. One was priced $60 ($1,887), the other $50 ($1,573). Signed: Anna Senge/Chicago, Ill/1912. (11¾″× 6¼″) *Photo*: Ahlers & Ogletree Auction Gallery.

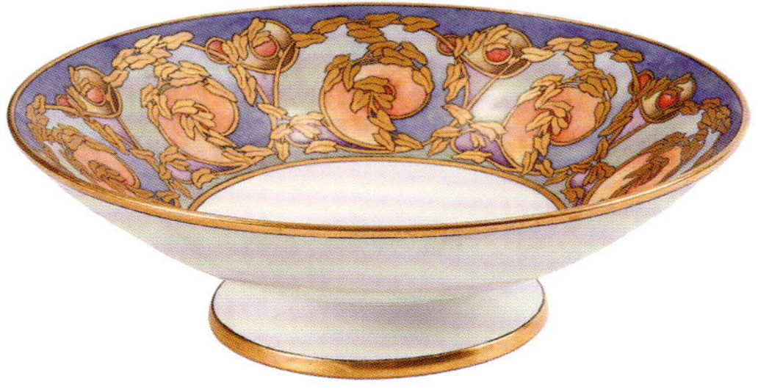

14.19 Footed bowl, Florence Steward, ca. 1910–1921. The border of this small bowl features a stylized nautilus and vine decoration. Signed: Steward Mark: Titanic/Austria. (3″× 8¾″) *Photo*: Treadway Toomey Auctions.

American form of decoration for china? That was not clear, not even to *Keramic Studio* editors, who wrote, "To-day [*sic*] we are evolving a new style, one derived from the inspiration of grandmother's china and the study of historic styles, together with the modern thought in design inspired by the Japanese."[19]

The editors of *Keramic Studio*, staunch proponents of the conventional style, used the Burley & Co.'s exhibitions to confirm the widespread acceptance of conventional decoration, and as an object lesson, comparing the effect of the same forms decorated in both schools. "We feel that even the most devoted lover of the naturalistic must see how much more refined and suitable the conventionally decorated pieces seem," they pointed out in 1912.[20] A year later, the journal was pleased to note that three-fourths of the exhibition pieces were decorated in the conventional style, whereas, four years earlier, three-fourths had featured naturalistic decoration.[21] "A revolution in the style of china decoration has taken place in the last few years," confirmed the *Indianapolis News*. "The inappropriateness of eating food placed on top of a naturalistic painting has been overruled by a more conventional treatment in better taste."[22]

While most sophisticated American china painters adopted the conventional style, there were regional differences regarding its interpretation and application, occasionally sparking friction between major ceramic clubs. This was evident in February 1911, when "two distinct styles" were evident in the New York Society of Keramic Art exhibition, in which the Atlan Club was a guest exhibitor. Reviewing the exhibition for *Keramic Studio*, Maud M. Mason, a member of the New York society, described the Atlan exhibit, which filled three cases, as being, overall, very beautiful in color and tone, with designs well adapted to the Satsuma shapes, and showing remarkable skill in execution. There were, however, areas for improvement: some motifs used in a single decoration were sometimes unrelated; others lacked contrast of light and dark. "Our chief regret," she rather cattily concluded, "is that it embodies so little of the modern spirit and is not distinctly national in character."[23]

On that issue's editorial page, *Keramic Studio* diplomatically pointed out that it was "provincial" for workers to think there was only one good style of designing. "Each might probably gain from the other: the Atlan Club, by a bigger way of treating large pieces and a greater simplicity in the small objects; the New York Society, by a daintier touch on small objects and a directing of attention to a closer study of appropriateness of design in the treatment of table service."[24] Comparing the limited number of black-and-white illustrations, the only difference between the work of the two clubs appears to be larger, flatter, bolder motifs and greater use of repetitive diaper patterns by members of the New York society. Both relied upon geometrical placement of conventionalized floral forms.

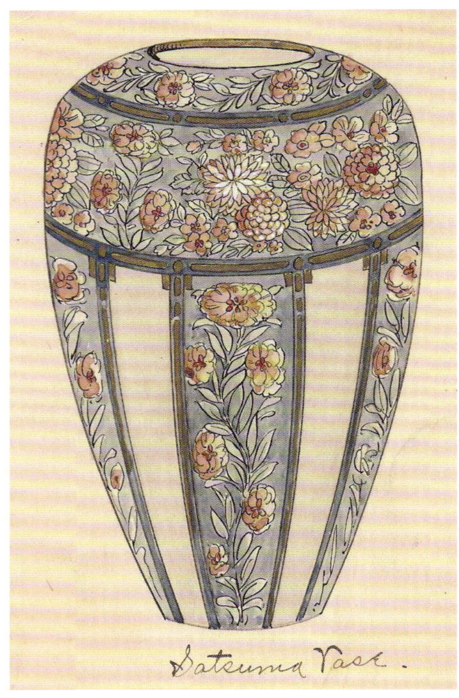

14.20 Sketch for Satsuma vase, Anna Senge, 1913. The final floral motif on the vase is a slight variation of that in the sketch. *Photo:* Private collection.

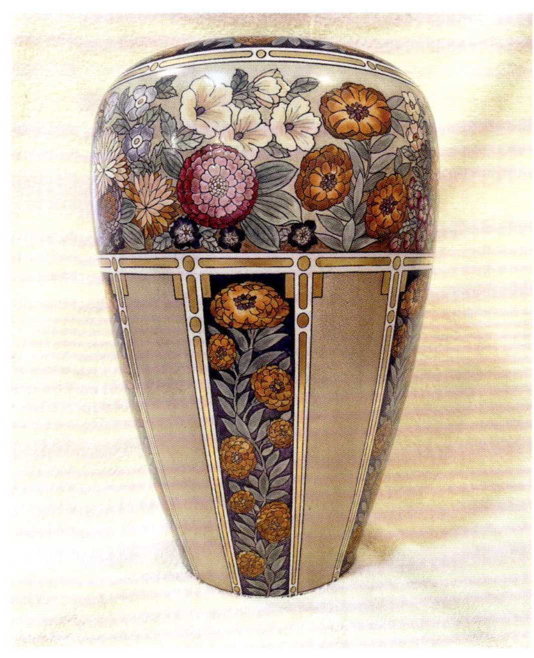

14.21 Satsuma vase, Anna Senge, 1913. The large vase was offered for sale at $100 ($3,082) in the 1913 Atlan Club exhibition. Signed: Anna Senge/Atlan Club/1913. (h: 15½") *Photo*: Mikell C. Darling.

Members of the New York Society of Keramic Art, founded as a branch of the National League of Mineral Painters in 1893, were often referred to as "disciples" of Arthur Wesley Dow, because so many of its members, including Maud M. Mason, had been his students at Pratt Institute or Columbia Teachers College. A year later, in 1912, when the Keramic Art Society was absorbed by the National Society of Craftsmen, several of its key members, including Dorothea Warren O'Hara and Marshall Fry formed the Keramic Society of Greater New York to focus on decorative ceramics.[25]

In 1912, the Atlan Club celebrated its twentieth anniversary. Honoring its long relationship with the Art Institute of Chicago, it donated $1,000 to the museum to establish the Atlan Ceramic Art Club Fund to be used to purchase ceramics for the museum's permanent collection.[26] The institute responded by offering the club a permanent exhibition case on the first floor of the museum. Each year, when its annual exhibition closed, representative examples were selected for display in the case.[27]

The club also developed a traveling exhibition of members' work, accompanied by an "interpretative paper" written by Florence Steward, that was available for loan to regional art and ceramic clubs through the Illinois Federation of Women's Clubs.[28] When the Amateur Art Club of Springfield, Illinois, displayed the Atlan exhibit in November, concurrent with the club's exhibition at the Chicago Art Institute, the local *Daily Illinois State Journal* called it "the most remarkable exhibit of decorated china ever given in Springfield."[29]

One member of the Springfield club, Georgia Watson Miner, had studied enamel work under Mabel C. Dibble, design under Helen Frazee, and "ceramics" (perhaps pottery) under Matilda Middleton.[30] In a local Art Association exhibition, Miner proudly showed a jelly jar she decorated "after the Frazee style of decoration" and a chop plate "after Matilda Middleton."[31] Like many china decorators in smaller midwestern towns, Miner admired, studied, and tried to emulate the work of leading members of the Atlan Club.

In 1912, when debate over women's suffrage dominated local, state, and national politics, the Atlan Club, which espoused no political agenda, was even mentioned by some advocates as a prime example of women who were advancing the goal of political equality. "The work of the Atlan club, of Chicago, in overglaze decoration of china has changed the standard in this much abused effort of women," wrote suffragist Clara E. Dyer in a newspaper column promoting "Art and Suffrage" in the *Detroit Times*. While noting that all women artists may not be suffragists, Dyer argued that all women successfully asserting their "distinct individuality" through the applied arts, despite restrictions favoring men, could only benefit from the greater artistic freedom and social status that the ballot would give.[32]

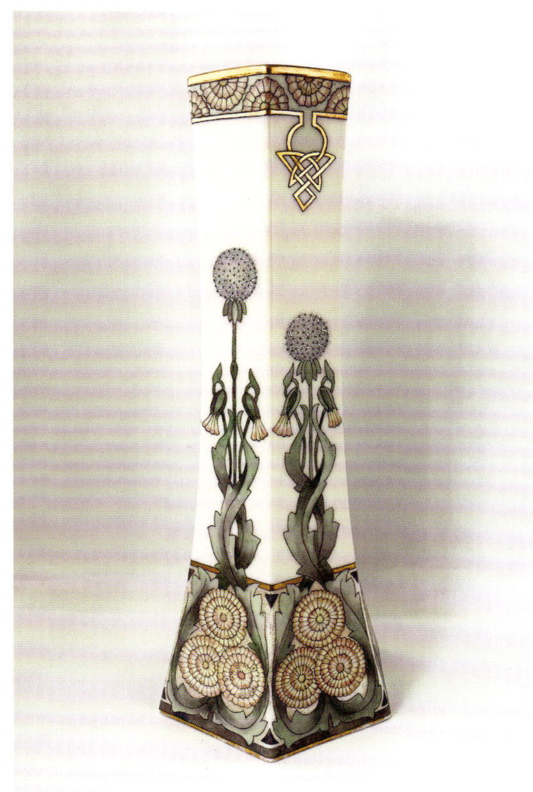

14.22 Vase with dandelion motif, attributed to Lillian G. Farr, 1913. Farr, a teacher of china painting, exhibited a Belleek vase in the 1913 Atlan Club exhibition. Signed: Illegible/PPP/Atlan. Mark: Belleek/Willets. (h: 12⅜") *Photo*: Private collection.

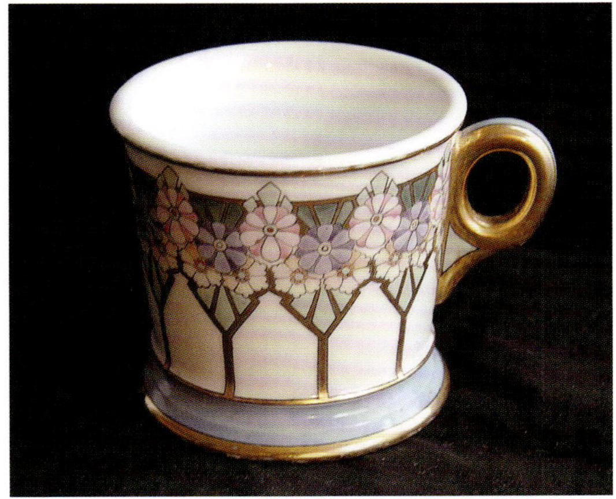

14.23 Mug, Ruth Anna Blomquist, ca. 1911. Although signed Atlan, the mug is not dated. Blomquist exhibited her work in Atlan Club exhibitions in 1911 and 1912. Signed: R. Blomquist/Berwyn, Ill./ACAC in swastika. (h: 5½") *Photo*: Private collection.

Chapter Fifteen

Unfazed by World War

The mind must have refuge from the horrors [of war] which prevail in order to preserve its balance, and this it finds in Museums and art galleries and in the individual possession of beautiful things.
—Henrietta Barclay Paist, *Keramic Studio* 20, no. 5 (September 1918): 51

The outbreak of World War I in Europe in July 1914, brought about many changes in art crafts, some of which were particularly noticeable among ceramics workers. Exports of porcelain from France and Germany ceased, and only blanks made in America and Japan were readily available. American potteries, large and small, were profiting from the war, with particularly fine work being produced at the Belleek factory at Trenton, New Jersey, and factories in Illinois, Ohio, and New York. China decorators willing to use American-made ceramics were still busy turning out all sorts of lovely, decorated china for the housewife who wanted individual pieces, reported New York ceramist Dorothea Warren O'Hara in *Housewives Magazine*.[1]

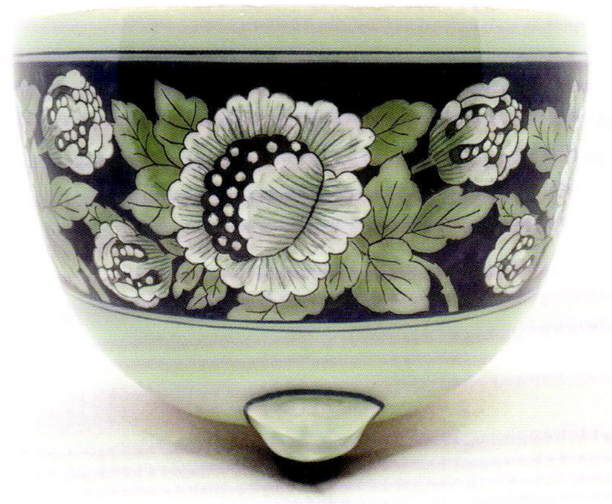

15.1 Sedji flowerpot, Anna Senge,1914. Senge's flowerpot of Japanese Sedji ware was "not for sale" in the 1914 Atlan Club exhibition. The March 1912 *House Beautiful* noted that Sedji ware came in a number of solid colors. The most popular imitated Chinese celadon, in a "lovely light green, not unlike the palest jade." Signed: Anna Senge/1914. (4¾" × 6⅛"). *Photo*: Mikell C. Darling.

Given that Atlan members preferred Japanese blanks—and that Chicago retailers held sizable stocks of plain white European china—the club's Art Institute exhibitions continued without interruption during the war years. In 1914, the club's exhibition was enhanced by the work of six members of the Twin City Keramic Club of Minneapolis–St. Paul, Minnesota, who also entered pieces in the annual Arts and Crafts exhibitions that followed; Twin City painters carried off the Atlan Club Prize, "one of the coveted yearly prizes of the Keramic art world," each year from 1914 through 1917.[2]

Modeled after the Atlan Club, the Minneapolis club was organized in 1912 by fourteen of the city's professional china painters; its membership was restricted to women whose work passed a jury review and shared a commitment to "appropriate" conventionalized floral ornament. During the winter months, the women studied design with Mary Moulton Cheney (1871–1957), head of the decorative design department at the Minneapolis Institute School of Art, or Henrietta Barclay Paist (1868–1930), the club's president in 1916. Paist, who achieved a national reputation for her oil and china painting, was a

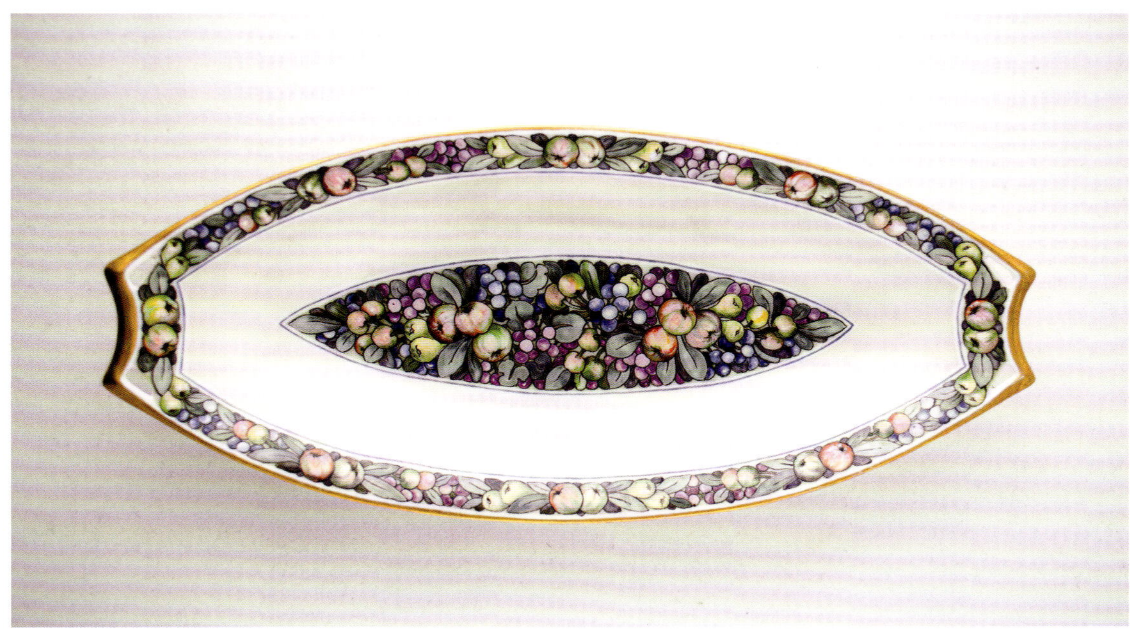

15.2 Serving tray, Emma Hutchinson, 1914. A resident of Michigan City, Indiana, Hutchinson decorated the tray in a semi-conventional style, with the arrangement not strictly conventionalized but following the rules of design. Signed: E. Hutchinson/ PPP/Atlan/1914. Mark: Favorite/ Hutschenreuther/ Bavaria. (5½″ × 12½″) *Photo*: Robert W. Switzer.

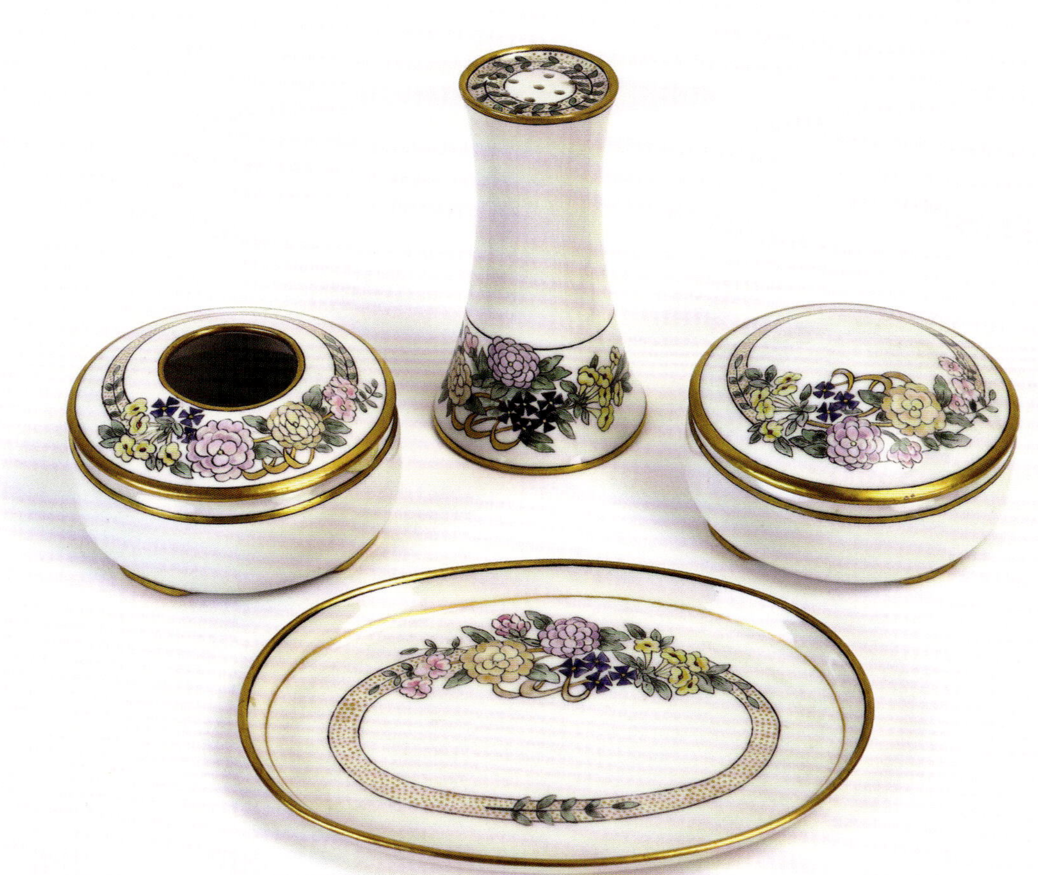

15.3 Child's dresser set, Linda C. Dunne, ca. 1914. Dunne, a china painting instructor in LaGrange, Illinois, exhibited an adult-sized dresser set consisting of two candlesticks, tray, powder box, and jewel box in the Atlan Club exhibition in 1914. Hatpin, tray signed: LCD/PPP/Atlan; O&E G Austria. (hatpin: 4¼″; tray: 6″ × 4″ × ¼″; jars: 2″ × 3½″) *Photo*: Marvin Venis Benjamin.

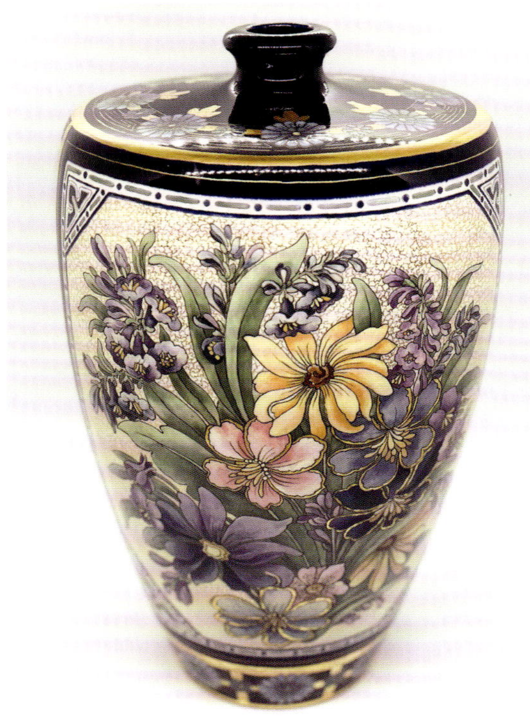

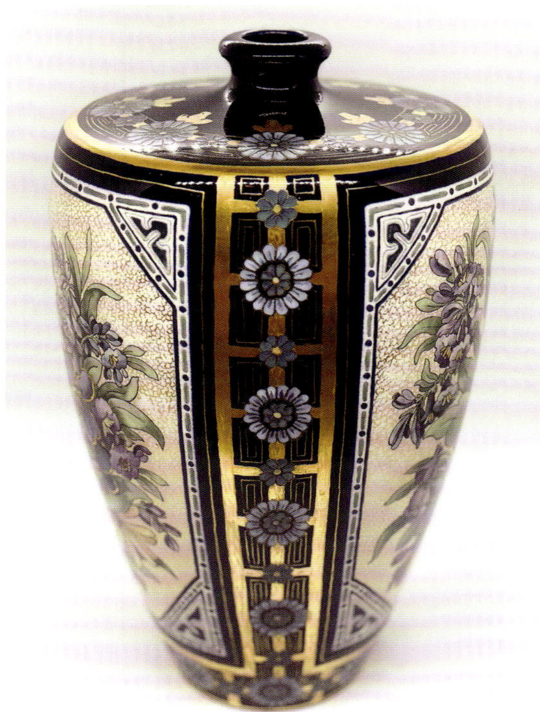

15.4A AND B Vase, Emma Hutchinson, 1915. The vase, "with heavy gold geometrics forming oblong medallions that are inlaid with delicate blue gray daisy-like color forms with smaller flowers that are in lighter accents," was awarded Honorable Mention in the Satsuma Class at the 1915 Burley & Co. exhibition, according to *Keramic Studio*. Signed: E. Hutchinson/PPP/Atlan/1915. (11") *Photo*: Grant Smith.

frequent contributor to *Keramic Studio* and, later, assistant editor. Both women had been key members of the Handicraft Guild of Minneapolis, an organization of craftworkers active between 1904 and 1911.[3]

In 1914, the Atlan Club's annual exhibition catalog was the first to contain a brief organizational history entitled "Its Objects." It noted that members had launched the use of conventional ornament on porcelain, "convinced that it was the correct form of decoration for china," with the goal of raising "the standard of china painting to what might properly be termed *legitimate* ornamentation." In this they had succeeded, according to an eminent, but unnamed, art authority, who claimed, "Your Club has certainly succeeded in presenting a new and beautiful form of ornament, and the public has *accepted* it; I see no reason why it should not become an established American style of decoration for china."[4]

This sentiment was echoed in a review in the *Christian Science Monitor*, in which Florence Steward stressed the club's claim of establishing a unique style of ornament. "We have sought a legitimate ornamentation, a conventional ornament arranged on an underlying geometrical idea. The influence of our work has been felt in nearly all the big cities of the country. Another thing on which the Atlan Ceramic Art Club prides itself," she continued, "is that it started to popularize the overglaze, which is distinctively American, and has been spoken of as the "American coloring."[5]

Steward's concept of the club's "American style" of china decoration

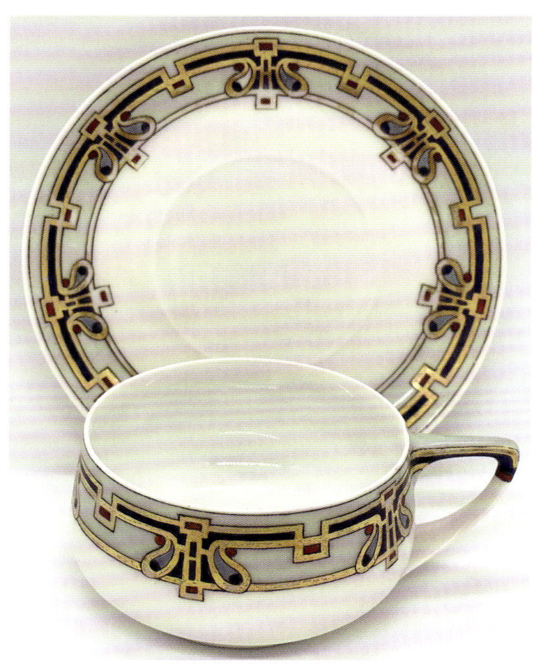

15.5 Cup and saucer, Ethel B. Jones, 1915. Jones was secretary of the Atlan Club when she offered this cup and saucer for $7 ($211) in the 1915 exhibition. Signed: E. B. Jones/PPP/Atlan. Mark: Rosenthal/Selb Bavaria/Donatello. (cup 2" × 3½"; saucer 5½") *Photo*: Grant Smith.

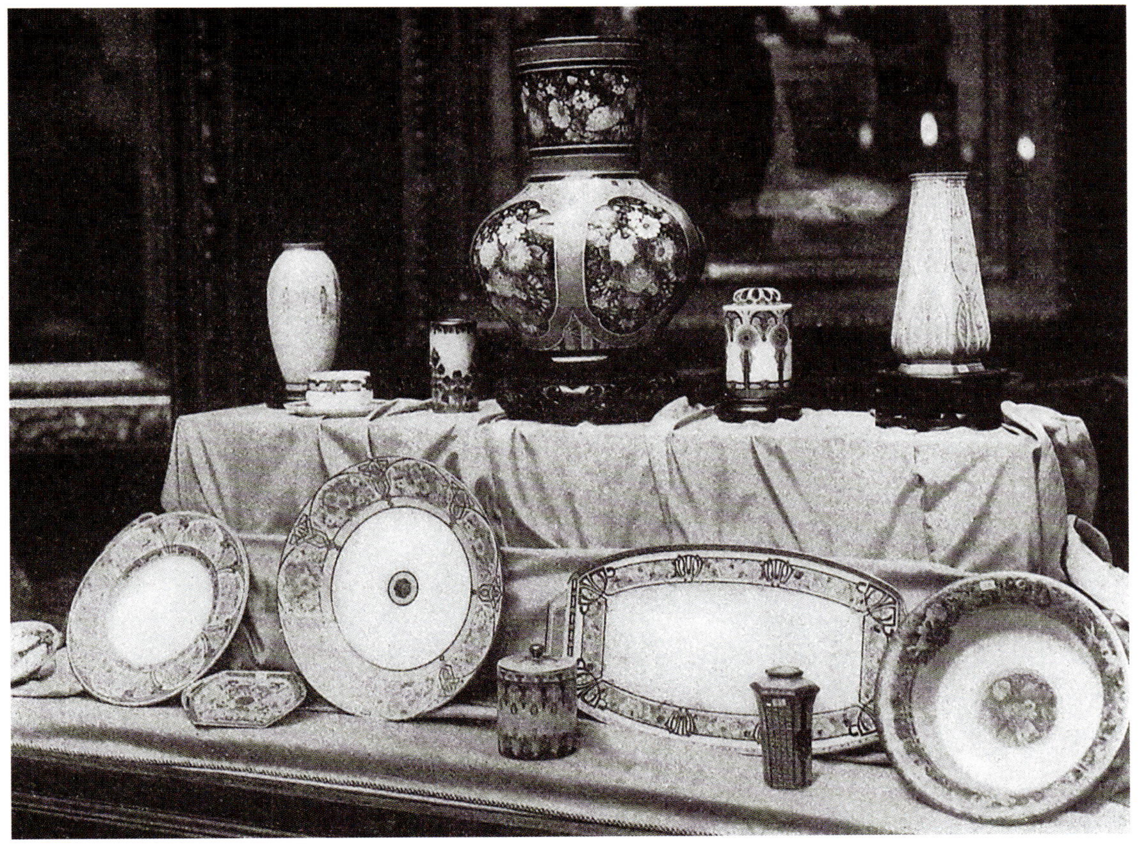

15.6 One of the display cases in the 1915 Atlan Club exhibition at the Art institute of Chicago. Ellen Lovgren's serving tray (fig. 15.7) is visible on the lower right. A Satsuma fruit bowl by Frances A. Barothy is on the far right on the lower row; a large vase by Emma Hutchinson stands in the center of the upper row. *Source*: Agnes Gertrude Richards, "An Exhibition of Keramics," *Fine Arts Journal* 34, no. 1 (January 1916): 41.

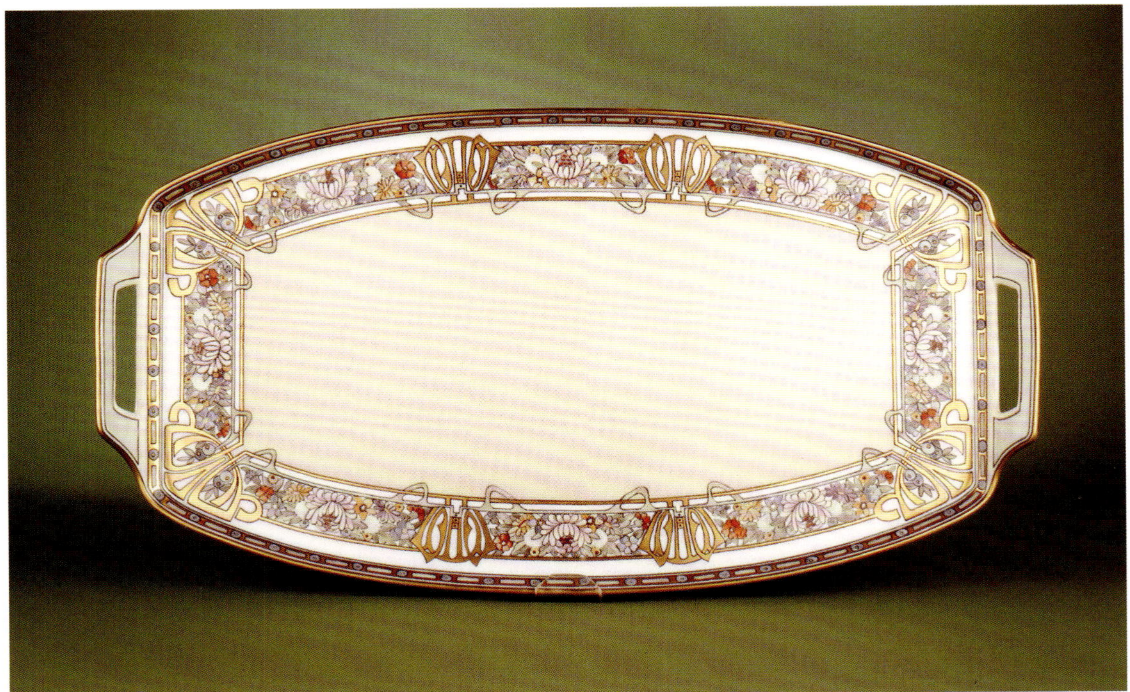

15.7 Serving tray, Ellen Lovgren, 1915. This large tray with open handles was available for $25 ($755) in the 1915 Atlan exhibition. It was also illustrated in the May 1915 *Keramic Studio* review of Burley & Co.'s exhibition. Signed: E. Lovgren. (l: 17¼") *Photo*: Private collection.

is difficult to define; in fact, Atlan members were unclear about the definition themselves. Their claim seems to mean the geometrical abstraction of nature (i.e., fruits and flowers) or non-Western historic motifs (whose origins, they claimed, were also nature based) arranged symmetrically to create a unique work of art; the cautious use of color; and a design "appropriate" for the size and shape of the object being decorated. Equally, the high level of artistic and technical skill evidenced in their decorated china elevated it to "legitimate" fine art. Undisputed was the Atlans' pioneering commitment to conventional style decoration, which by this time had been adopted by America's most progressive china painters. Like many nineteenth-century groups and individuals concerned with developing a unique national style, it appears that the Atlan Club was hoping that their form of porcelain overglaze decoration, which merged past and present, would be the one adopted as the one capable of expressing modern American identity.

Despite the Atlan Club's pioneering leadership in promoting the conventional style as a unique and modern approach to china decoration, and the adoption of this style by leading ceramics clubs, the naturalistic approach remained popular with American decorators and their customers. In fact, in 1914, half of the patterns offered in *Keramic Studio* depicted naturalistic fruits and flowers, despite the magazine

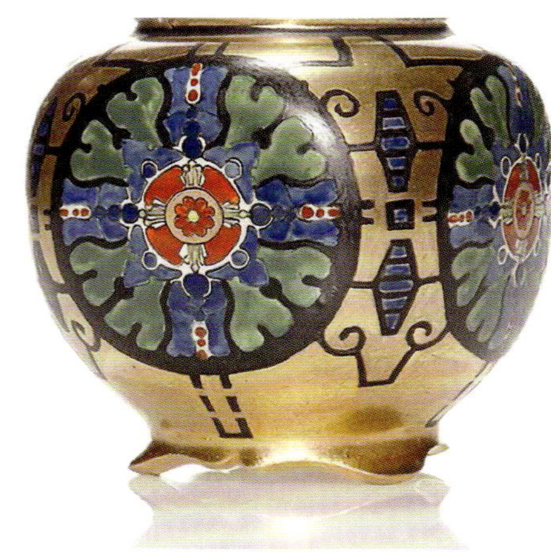

15.8 Satsuma vase, Adelaide M. Liebolt, 1915. The large Satsuma vase was priced at $25 ($755) in the 1915 Atlan Club exhibition; two much smaller vases were $3 ($90) each. Signed: A. M. Liebolt/Atlan Club/1915. (h: 4¼") *Photo*: Humler & Nolan.

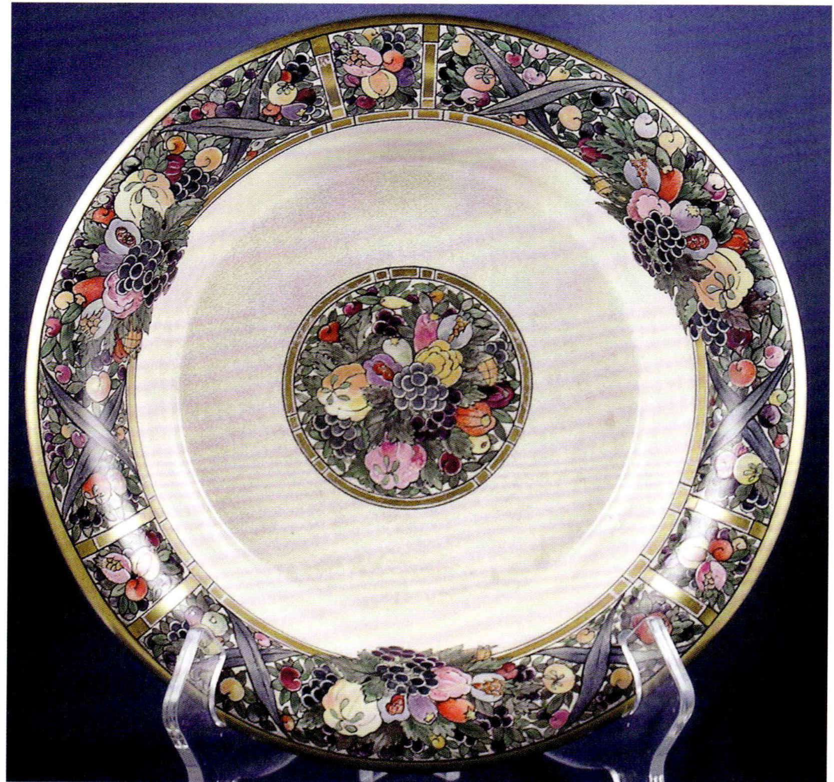

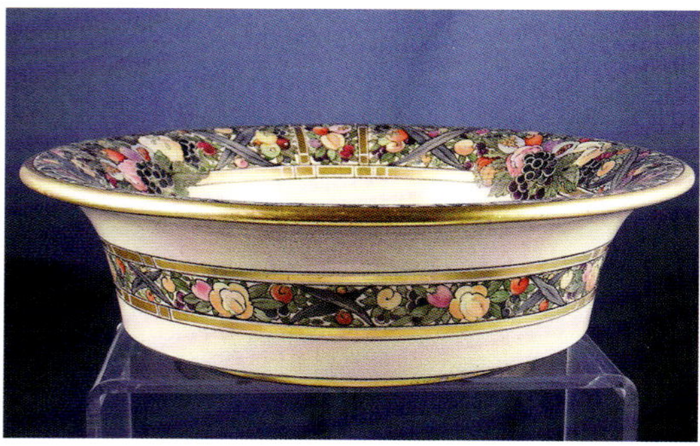

15.9A AND B Satsuma fruit bowl, Frances A. Barothy, ca. 1915. This bowl is very similar to the one, priced at $20 ($604), pictured in the 1915 Atlan exhibition (fig. 15.6). Barothy exhibited Satsuma bowls in various sizes, pricing large bowls between $15 and $40 ($508 to $705), between 1906 and 1919. Signed: F.A. Barothy. (3¾" × 12⅛") *Photo*: Dark Flowers Antiques.

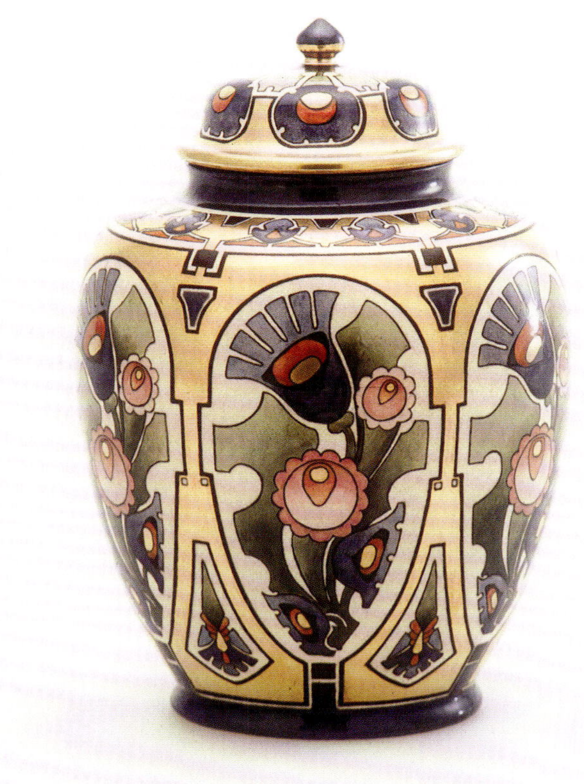

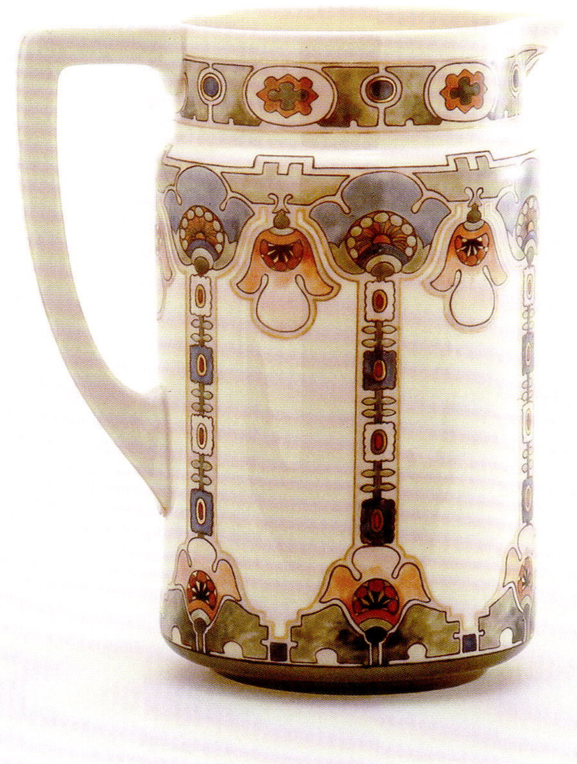

15.10 Rose jar, Ellen Lovgren, ca. 1916. Rose jars were often filled with a potpourri of dried rose petals, herbs, and spices. This jar with bold conventionalized flowers may be the one listed, but unpriced, in the 1916 Atlan club exhibition. Signed: Ellen Lovgren. (h: 7½") *Photo*: Private collection.

15.11 Pitcher, Ellen Lovgren, ca. 1916. Several items, including this pitcher, were listed without purchase prices in the Atlan Club's 1916 exhibition. Signed: Ellen Lovgren. (h: 7¾") *Photo*: Private collection.

constantly deriding the style. By way of apology, its editors explained, "We have been convinced that our teachers and workers really need it for bread and butter while they are striving to educate themselves and the public to better things; the great mass as yet have not learned to appreciate the refinement of decoration." In the meantime, they would do their utmost to give their readers "the best and least offensive of this style of work as long as the necessity of catering to the public exists."[6] For those unwilling to commit to one style, the magazine offered patterns for semi-conventional designs, which combined naturalistic and conventional motifs.

Despite rumblings of war, Burley & Co.'s annual National Exhibition of Decorated China, the city's most important ceramics event after those sponsored by the Art Institute of Chicago, took place in 1914 and 1915. In the fall of 1914, Atlan member Bertha Park was awarded first prize in the Conventional Class; Helen Frazee's entire entry was pictured in *Keramic Studio*.[7]

Florence Steward, by invitation, showed her "Conversational Set" in Historic Ornament and was also the featured lecturer in 1915. Atlan members, as usual, carried off major prizes: Helen Frazee placed first

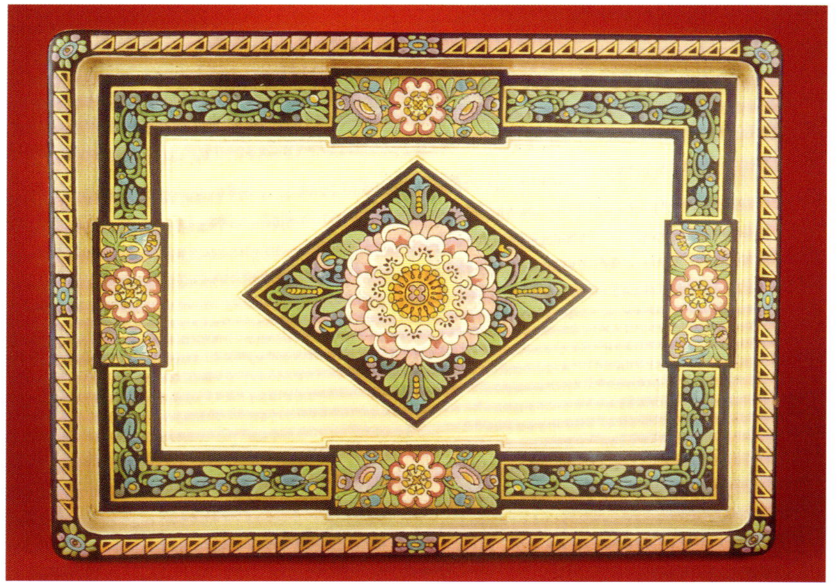

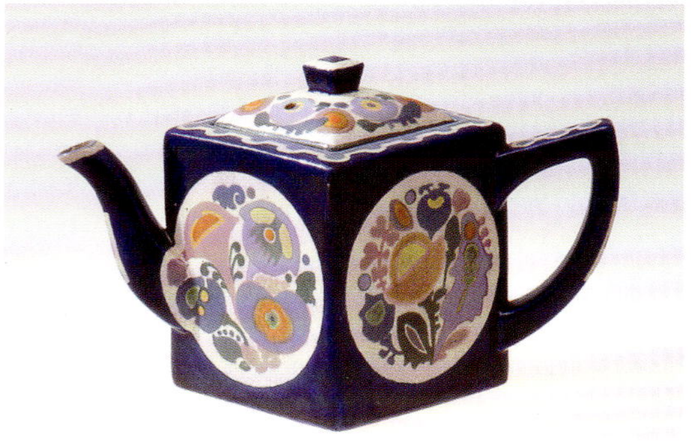

15.12 Satsuma teapot, Helen Frazee, 1917–1922. A small teapot with a bold floral design. Signed: Frazee. (4″) *Photo*: Chicago History Museum.

15.13 Chop plate, Amanda Berglund, 1916. One of ten items, all unpriced, displayed by Berglund in the Atlan Club exhibition in 1916. Signed: Berglund. (8⅞″ × 12″) *Photo*: Private collection.

in the Satsuma Class; Anna Senge won second; Emma Hutchinson and Helga M. Peterson received honorable mentions. In the Conventional Class, Lydia Hadden took second prize, and Amanda Berglund obtained an honorable mention. Attracting comment was the set of six tea plates decorated with simple Dutch scenery by Anna Senge's husband Frank, a commercial illustrator, who occasionally entered "his clever ideas expressed on porcelain surfaces" in Burley's exhibitions.[8]

The Atlan Club was also well represented in the American Arts and Crafts section in the Palace of Varied Industries at the Panama-Pacific International Exposition, a celebration of the completion of the Panama Canal, held in San Francisco from February to December in 1915. The exhibition must have been quite sizable, given that Mollie Sparks alone sent twelve pieces.[9] The club's exhibition received a silver medal, as did Helga M. Peterson.[10]

"The war," Florence Steward told a *Christian Science Monitor* reporter in 1915, "is making women realize that we must rely on developing our own country potteries for table and ornamental ware, or else upon the Japanese manufacturers. The Japanese wares up to date have a soft glaze and are extremely easy to decorate and refire, but are somewhat brittle for service . . . The Belleek wares of New Jersey have shown us that we have both class of clay and soft glaze, which takes flat colors and enamel in a very easy and attractive manner. This is, however, too expensive and too brittle to be used for tableware in general."[11] One company receiving a production impetus was the Haeger Potteries in Dundee, fifty miles northwest of Chicago, which could supply simple pottery shapes suitable for decorating in unlimited quantities. While pottery shapes were occasionally mentioned in the club's exhibition catalogs, makers were usually unidentified; sources

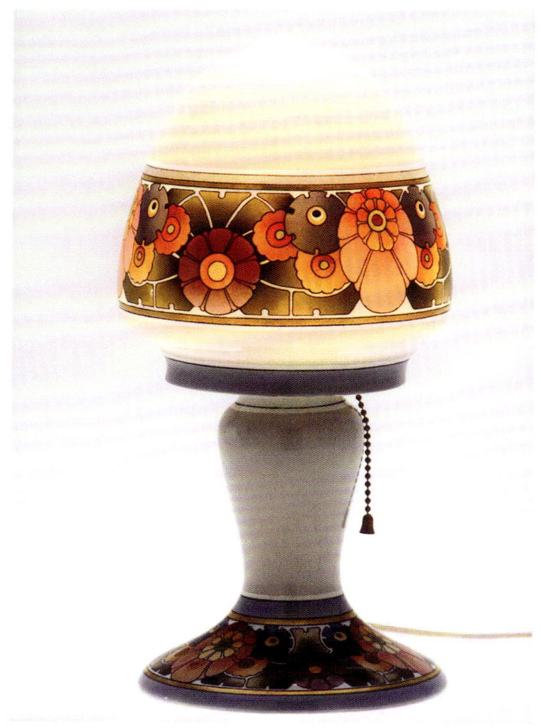

15.14 Lamp and shade of frosted glass with bands of enameled flowers, Ellen Lovgren, 1917. Offered for sale for $50 ($1,192) in the 1917 Atlan Club exhibition, the lamp's glass was manufactured by the Morimura Company of Japan. Unsigned, family provenance identifies Ellen Lovgren as the artist. (h: 13¾″) *Photo*: Private collection.

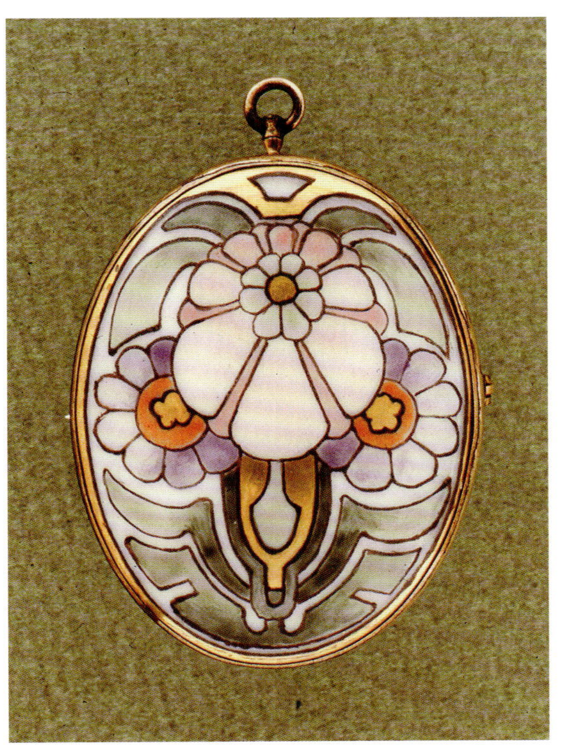

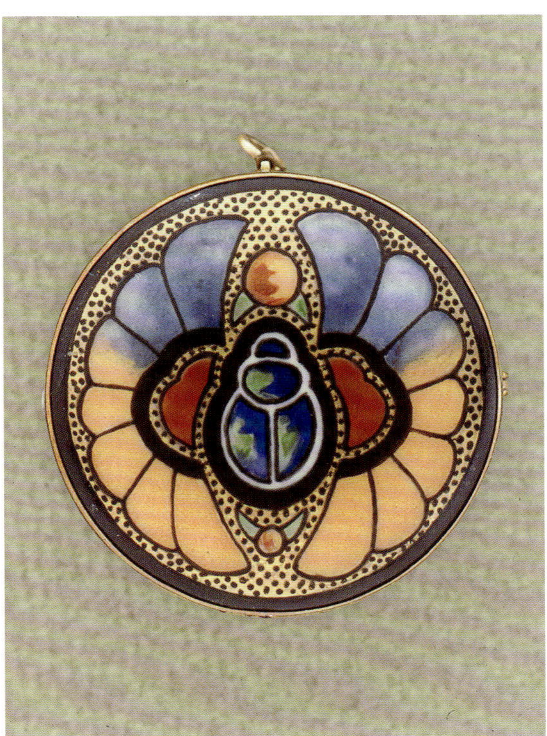

15.15A AND B Medallions, Ellen Lovgren, 1915–1917. Lovgren displayed gold-mounted porcelain brooch/pins, identified as "medallions," each priced $5 (about $125), which she would also duplicate, if sold, in Atlan Club exhibitions in 1915, 1916, and 1917. (h: 1.7") *Photo*: Private collection.

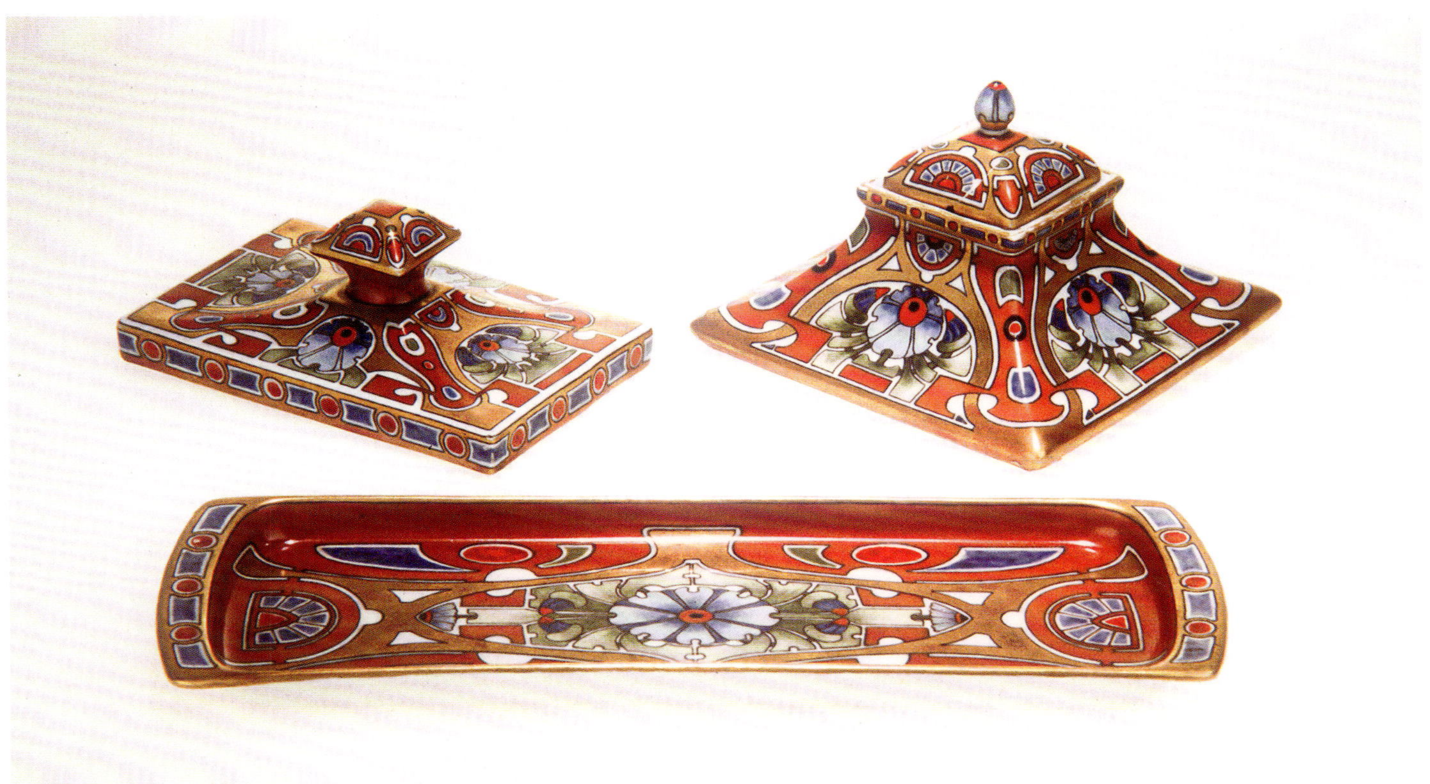

15.16 Inkwell, blotter, and pen tray, Ellen Lovgren, 1917. Part of a six-piece porcelain desk set with conventionalized blue flowers priced at $75 ($1,788) in the Atlan Club's 1917 catalog. Signed: E. Lovgren. *Photo*: Private collection.

of porcelain blanks, except for Belleek, also remained anonymous. It seems unlikely that Florence Steward used brittle American porcelain for the elaborate "Meat Course Set" that she displayed in the 1916 Atlan Club exhibition. Its forty-eight pieces featured decoration representing twelve eras in the history of art, ranging from Egyptian to seventeenth-century French, available for $1,000 (about $27,447). Steward's display "has excited much admiration," commented the reviewer from the *Chicago Daily Tribune*, "It has been secured to the east and will leave Chicago at the close of the exhibition."[12] Although it may have been purchased, it seems more likely that it was sent for display in an unnamed exhibition.

Amid grim battlefield news delivered via telegram and newspaper, or perhaps to dispel it, the club's twenty-fifth anniversary exhibition in 1917 was large, with 334 pieces, mostly Japanese Satsuma, displayed at the Art Institute. Rather than sets of tableware, there were lots of boxes, vases, tea sets, and smoking accessories, with many items priced under $10 ($234), reflecting the austerity of the wartime economy. In its review, the *Chicago Daily Tribune* mentioned an enameled glass lamp decorated by Ellen E. Lovgren as being particularly attractive (fig. 15.14).[13] Given the scarcity of porcelain blanks, many china painters were experimenting with the decoration of glass, which was readily available, and ornamenting useful household items like electric boudoir and table lamps. Although firing glass was a more delicate operation than firing china, it was easily learned, with tips and instructions readily offered in *Keramic Studio* and art publications.

In honor of the club's silver anniversary, members added an additional $500 to the Atlan Ceramic Art Club Fund established in 1912 at the Art Institute of Chicago.[14] Among the museum's first purchases using interest from the fund were four pieces of stoneware made by studio potter and educator Charles Fergus Binns, who established the first college-level ceramics program at the New York State School of Clay-Working and Ceramics (now New York State College of Ceramics) at Alfred University in Albany, New York.[15]

During the war years, and particularly after the United States entry in 1917, some Atlan members dropped out to devote time to war work, particularly with the Red Cross. Many Chicago china painters and teachers, including several Atlan members, gave up expensive downtown studios to work at home, cutting expenses to a minimum and effectively dismantling what had long been known as the china painting district. In 1915, Helga M. Peterson moved her studio from the Auditorium Tower to her home on Winona Avenue. The following year, Helen Frazee, one of the tower's pioneer tenants, transferred to the Fine Arts Building (S. S. Beman, 1898), on Michigan Avenue near the Art Institute, where she shared a studio with her daughter Hazel Inez Frazee (1889–1972), a recent Art Institute graduate working as a commercial illustrator.

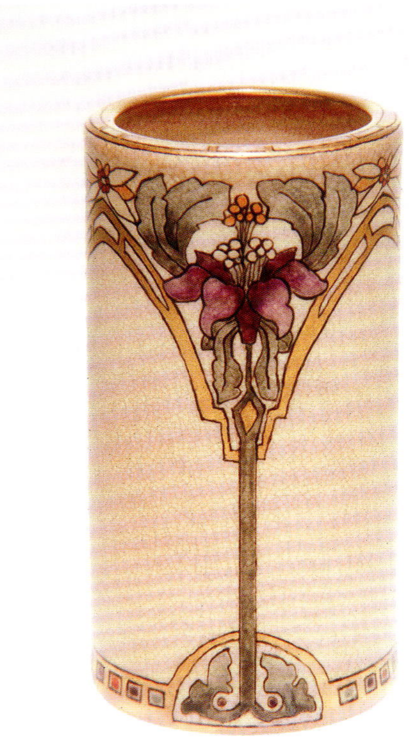

15.17 Vase, Ellen Lovgren, 1917. Lovgren priced this Satsuma "cylinder vase" with conventionalized purple iris panels at $20 ($477) in the 1917 Atlan Club exhibition. Unsigned, family provenance identifies Ellen Lovgren as the artist. (h: 4¾") *Photo*: Private collection.

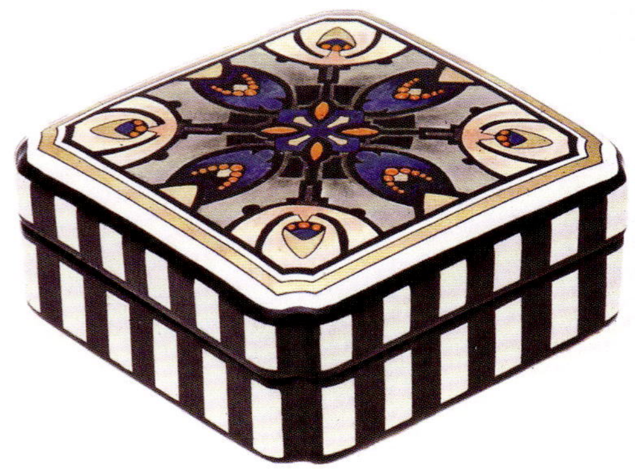

15.18 Box, Ellen Lovgren, 1917. Lovgren offered this "square box" with bold black-and-white striped border for $10 ($238) in the Atlan Club's 1917 exhibition. Signed: Ellen Lovgren. (4¾" × 4¾") *Photo*: Private collection.

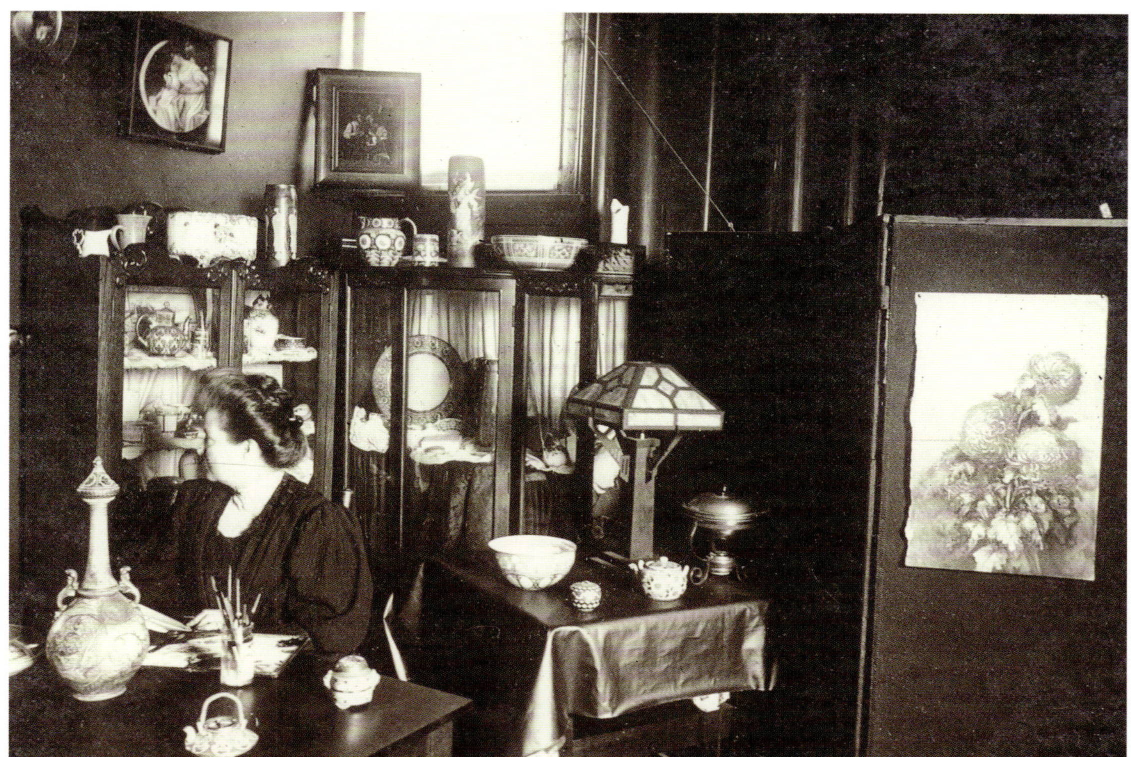

15.19 Helen Fenton Frazee in her studio in the Auditorium Tower, 1895–1915. She moved to the Fine Arts Building on Michigan Avenue in 1916. *Photo*: Chicago History Museum.

Helen Inez Fenton Frazee, 1893–1922

After joining the Atlan Club in August 1893, Helen Inez Fenton Frazee (1858–1923) exhibited with the club through 1922. She frequently served as a club councilor and was vice president in 1916. She was also an active member of the Chicago Ceramic Art Association. For decades, she was one of the most admired china painting teachers in Chicago.

Born in Perinton, Monroe County, New York, in 1858, Helen was the daughter of a "mechanic" who died when she was four years old. Helen and her mother had relocated to Chicago by April 1887, when Helen married grain broker Abraham A. Frazee. A graduate of the Chicago Art Institute, Helen was a skilled china painter by 1893, when she received a medal for a vase decorated with a peacock motif at the Chicago World's Fair.[1] In 1895, she and fellow Atlan member Nellie Cross opened a studio in the Auditorium Tower. A versatile artist, she excelled at portraits, pencil sketches, watercolor effects on porcelain, and floral motifs. In 1895, for example, her exhibit at Western China Decorating Works included "a fern jardinière with cupids, head of Rembrandt, cup and saucer with clusters of roses, and a rose bowl with apple blossoms."[2] In 1896 she was awarded a gold medal by *Arts for America* for her work, with the judges praising her wide subject range, excellent drawing skills, and "ability to decorate a form instead of painting it."[3]

After 1898, Helen limited her painting to conventional design and figure work. "The greatest charm of Mrs. Frazee's work lies in the extreme simplicity of its lines and the rich combination of colors," wrote the *Ceramic Monthly* in 1898, praising her "honest study of ornament and design." It went on to note that she was "one of the Chicago painters who have achieved success by appealing to popular taste."[4]

Maker's mark: Helen Inez Fenton Frazee. *Photo*: Dark Flowers Antiques.

In 1900, critics singled out her large "Peacock Vase (Persian)" as the most imposing and important article in the Atlan Club's selection for the Paris Exposition.[5] She went on to exhibit at the 1901 Pan-American Exposition; 1904 St. Louis World's Fair; 1915 Panama-Pacific

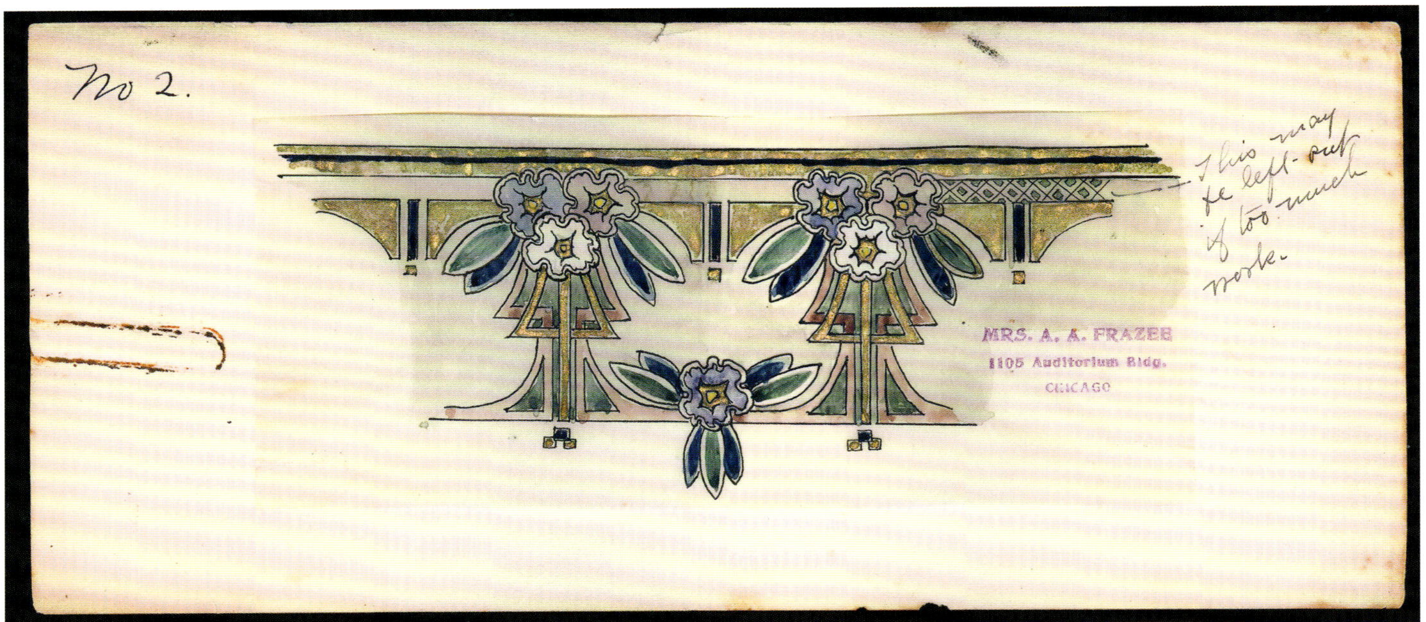

Exposition; local Arts and Crafts exhibitions; and with the Chicago Ceramic Association and the New York Society of Keramic Art.

In 1916, Helen moved to the Fine Arts Building, where she joined the Artists' Guild and exhibited in its gallery. She shared the studio with her daughter Hazel, an Art Institute graduate working as a commercial illustrator. In addition to teaching, Helen sold her own line of "tested, hard and Satsuma enamel," imported Royal Satsuma blanks for decorating, and sold and rented original conventional designs. Her reputation as an outstanding teacher drew students from almost every state and Canada, with many women teaching college-level china painting in addition to those heading individual studios crediting her as their instructor. She also served as guest instructor for various ceramic clubs, among them Pittsburgh's Duquesne Ceramic Club in 1913, and judged ceramics at various Arts and Crafts exhibitions and state fairs.

Helen's conventional designs frequently appeared in *Keramic Studio*, 1900–1920. Her work was also included in the "studies" for enamel workers published by the Anglo-French Art Co. in 1911.[6] She received first prize for a vase in the Satsuma class at Burley & Co.'s 1915 exhibition;[7] the Artists' Guild Prize in 1916;[8] the A. H. Abbott & Co. Prize for Best Individual Exhibit in 1918; and the D. M. Campana prize for best individual piece, an incense jar, in the Chicago Ceramic Art Association's 1919 exhibition.[9] After participating in the Atlan Club's last exhibition in 1922, Helen joined the Technic Arts League, according to notes taken during meetings held at the Art Institute.[10]

Helen died at age sixty-four on March 11, 1923. Her husband Abraham, bookkeeper for the art studio, continued the business, including the renting of her designs, through 1924.[11] After her daughter Hazel died in 1972, her executor donated a collection of Helen's ceramics and designs to the Chicago History Museum.

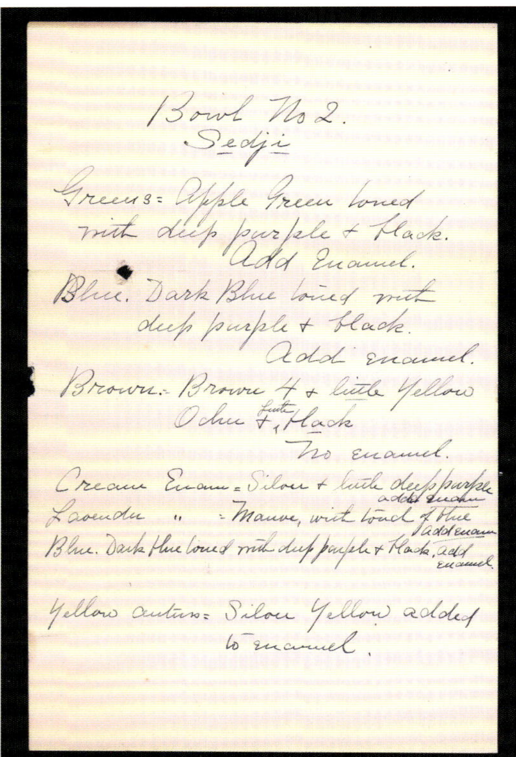
Bowl No 2.
Sedji

Greens = Apple Green toned with deep purple + black. Add Enamel.

Blue. Dark Blue toned with deep purple + black. Add enamel.

Brown - Brown 4 + little Yellow Ochre + little Black. No enamel.

Cream Enamel = Silver + little deep purple

Lavender " = Mauve, with touch of blue add enamel

Blue. Dark blue toned with deep purple + black. add enamel

Yellow centers = Silver Yellow added to enamel.

Watercolor cartoon and treatment, Helen Frazee, 1913. A notated sketch and treatment for a Sedji bowl were among designs Frazee mailed to Rudolph Eyerdam (1888–1942) in Cleveland, Ohio, in 1913. Frazee sold and rented designs for amateur china painters to copy. Stamped: Mrs. A. A. Frazee, 919 Fine Arts Bldg., Chicago. *Photo*: Tim Ingram.

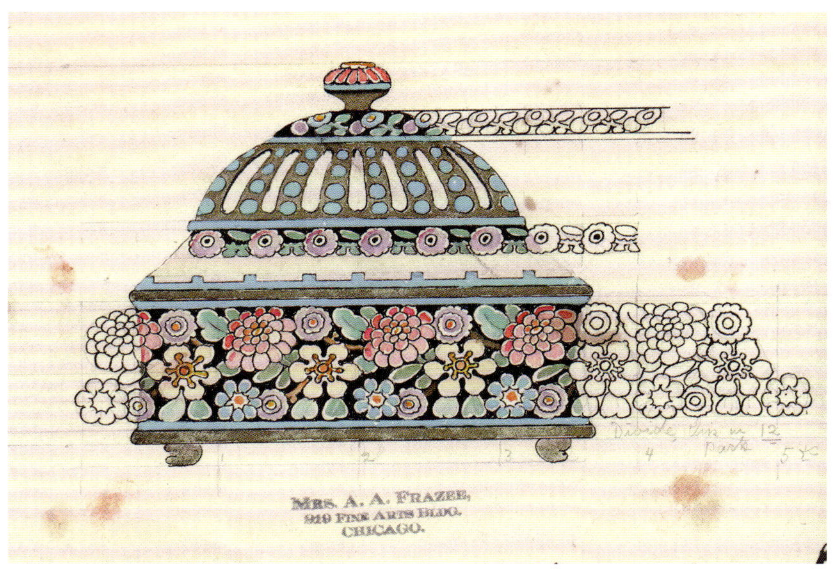

15.21 Watercolor cartoon, Helen Frazee, 1916–1922. One of the designs sent to Edna Woodard (1889–1988), a china painter with a home studio in Oskaloosa, Iowa. Woodard won first prize in the conventional class when Frazee judged the hand-painted china at the Southern Iowa Fair and Exposition in 1918. Stamped: "Mrs. A. A. Frazee, 919 Fine Arts Bldg., Chicago; handwritten Miss Woodard/Oskaluza [*sic*]. *Photo*: Tim Ingram.

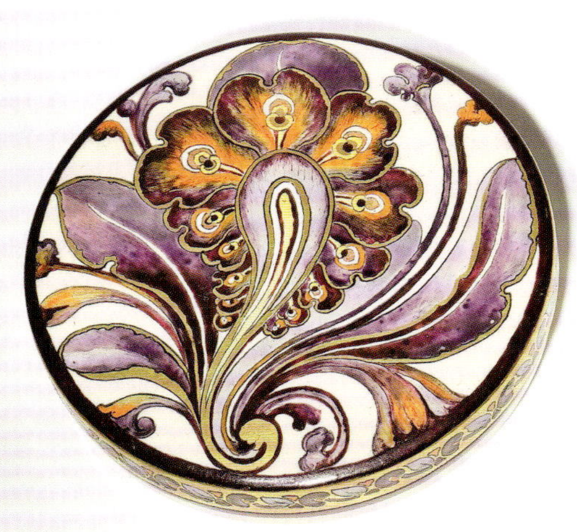

15.22 Satsuma box with orchid motif, Helen Frazee, ca. 1914. Signed: Frazee; red border sticker with note, "Exhibited Paris France 1914 or 1915." (d: 4¼") *Photo*: Private collection.

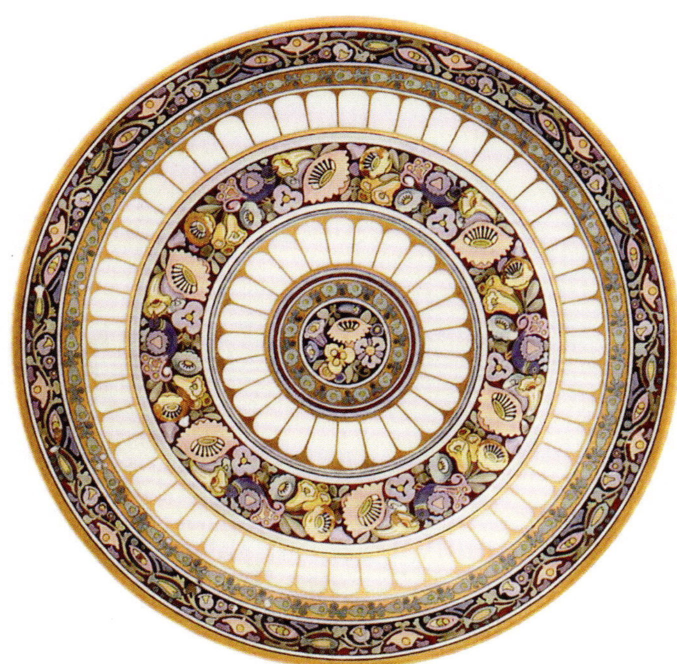

15.23 Helen Frazee, ca. 1900. One of the complex plates Frazee kept in her studio as a sample of her work. (d: 10¼") *Photo*: Chicago History Museum.

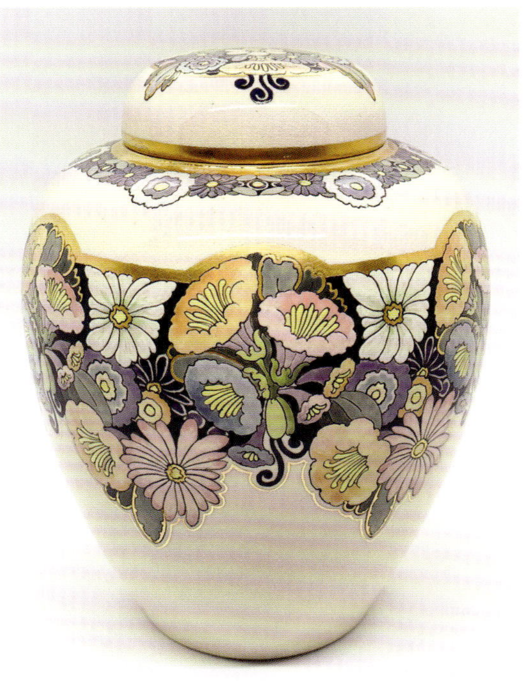

15.24 Satsuma covered jar, Helen Frazee, ca. 1916. Frazee showed Satsuma jars in the 1916 and 1917 Atlan Club exhibitions. Signed: Frazee, 919 Fine Arts Building. (h: 8") *Photo*: Grant Smith.

Chapter Sixteen

Nurturing New Members

We study historic ornament to gain an appreciation of form. The forms used in historic ornament were originally suggested by nature, but nature was modified and adapted to surface decoration by omitting details and accidents of growth. This adaption we term conventional ornament.
—Florence Steward, *Flat Enamel Decoration on China*, 1907, 30

After 1912, when Florence Steward was president and director for life, Atlan Ceramic Art Club activities fell into a predictable pattern, with a focus on the winter study course and preparation for the annual exhibition. Monthly meetings were still held at the Art Institute, where decorative arts curator Bessie B. Bennett critiqued member's designs, which they had sketched on the ceramic forms with colors indicated. Each part of the design was discussed, with either a commendation or a correction, along with the reason why the ornament was appropriate or flawed. Bennett's criticism was often followed by a lecture by Florence Steward, who had developed a series of talks on Arabian and East Indian art.

The club now claimed an associate membership of one hundred women "who may or may not paint," whose work was not yet up to the standard required by the club, but who were eligible for membership when it was.[1] Free training classes were taught by Florence Steward one day each week, January through March, at the Chicago Public Library. In addition to explaining the evolution of historic ornament and design, Steward often provided a watercolor lesson or a short tutorial in French; her booklet *Flat Enamel Decoration on China* was the textbook. At the close of each season, there was practice work in pottery, not for its own sake but so the decorator could learn to know the forms she decorated.[2] When an associate member was discovered to have talent coupled with ambition, she was invited into active membership.

Between 1914 and 1918, at least forty women joined the club, which had increased its exhibiting membership from twenty-five to thirty. Several of the new members were already teaching china painting or art in the public schools; others were academically trained artists; most were hobbyists or painting to supplement their income, rather than pursuing china painting as a career. The new members were younger

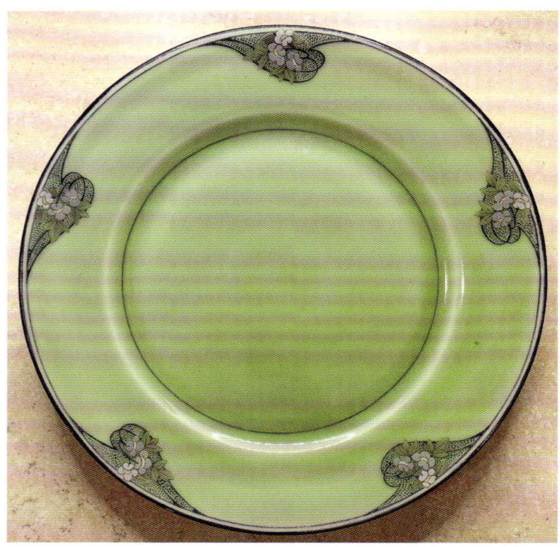

16.1 Green Sedji plate with floral clusters, Anna Senge, 1915. One of three plates of Japanese Sedji ware, commonly known as "green ware," priced $3.50 to $4.00 ($106 to $121), shown in the 1915 Atlan exhibition. Signed: Anna Senge/1915/Atlan Club. (d: 8⅝") *Photo*: Mikell C. Darling.

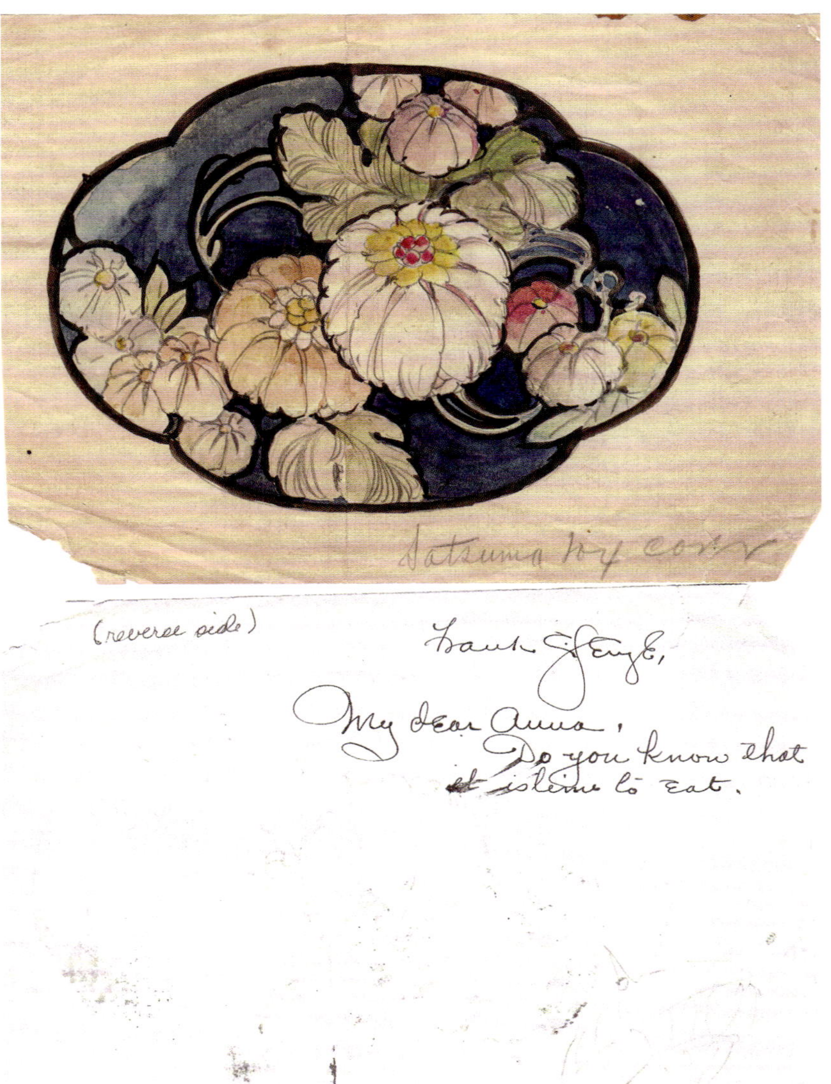

16.2 Watercolor sketch for a Satsuma box cover, Anna Senge, 1911–1922. The reverse carried a note from her husband Frank, "My dear Anna, Do you know that it is time to eat." Frank C. Senge, a commercial artist, occasionally exhibited his own hand-painted china in local exhibitions. *Photo*: Private collection.

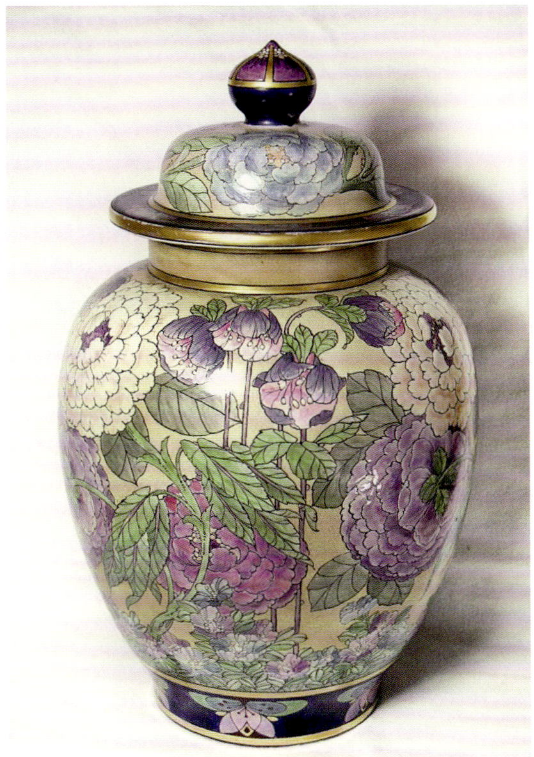

16.3 Satsuma rose jar with peonies and hellebore, Anna Senge, 1917–1921. Senge displayed Satsuma rose jars in two Atlan Club exhibitions. This may have been the one offered for $20 in 1917. Six small swatches of test colors appear on the base. Signed: Anna O. Senge/Atlan Club + six test colors (h: 15″) *Photo*: Private collection.

in age, ranging from nineteen years to their early fifties, with the majority in their thirties and forties. There was almost an equal mix of married and unmarried women.

The women came from a wider geographic area than earlier members, nearly all of whom had lived in Chicago. Although many still lived in the city, others commuted to club affairs from surrounding suburbs—Aurora, Evanston, Des Plaines, La Grange, Oak Park, Winnetka, and Wheaton—using Chicago's highly developed regional railroad system. Emma Hutchinson, who lived in Michigan City, and Rita Letz, Belle Lund, and Sheila Banner, of Hammond, traveled from Indiana via the South Shore Line, which had stations in each of their cities. Chicago teacher Miriam M. Gleason offered lessons in Atlan-style painting in the Hammond area, as well as in Buffalo and East Aurora, New York.[3]

Membership was also more inclusive and ethnically diverse. Unlike its founding mothers—many of whose parentage qualified them for membership in Daughters of the American Revolution (DAR)—an impressive number of new members were daughters of first-generation immigrants, primarily from Ireland, Germany, or Sweden; one was an Illinois-born mixed-race woman whom colleagues assumed to be white. While older Atlans were predominantly Protestant, this younger group included Catholics, Jews, and Christian Scientists. Technical skill and commitment to high artistic standards, rather than wealth or social status, remained the criteria for membership, at a time when many private clubs and societies in Chicago barred people of specific ethnic origins and religions from membership.

As in earlier years, some of the new members exhibited only one year; others dropped out after three or four, due, perhaps, to the time commitment required, changing personal or family circumstances, or to volunteer for war work as the nation mobilized. Although still relegated to "female occupations," middle- and upper-class women were finding a greater variety of job types available, not just in artwork.

During the winter, one of the Chicago Ceramic Art Association instructors was Mary Humphrey (the other Atlan Club founding member still active). In 1917, Humphrey began teaching a study course in design and color harmony based on the method of California-based art instructor Ralph Helm Johonnot (1880–1940), who lectured to the association during the winter of 1915–1916 and included his work in their exhibition the following year.[4] A former pupil of Arthur Wesley

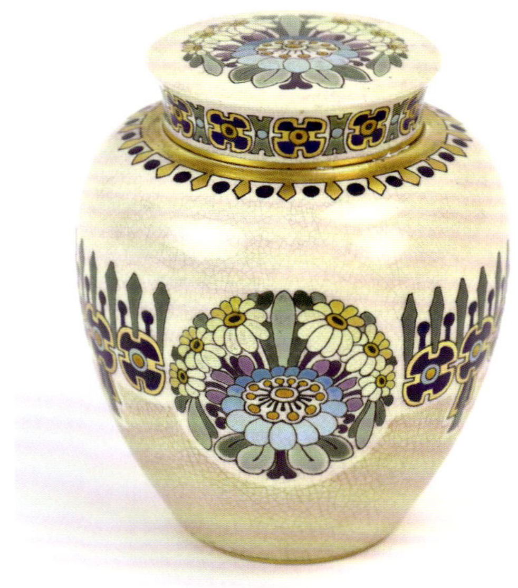

16.4 Satsuma rose jar, Amanda Berglund, 1917. Rose jars were often filled with a potpourri of dried rose petals, herbs, and spices. Berglund exhibited three rose jars, two on loan and one for sale, in the Atlan Club's twenty-fifth annual exhibition in 1917. Signed: E.A.L. Berglund 17/PPP. (h: 5") *Photo*: Marvin Venis Benjamin.

Anna Obermaier Senge, 1911–1922

After joining the Atlan Club in 1911, Anna Obermaier Senge (1872–1959) exhibited annually through 1922. She held numerous offices, including one term as secretary; two terms each as vice president and councilor; and three terms as treasurer.

Born in Chicago of German-American parents, Anna married commercial artist Frank Charles Senge (1872–1943) in 1896. Anna's training as a china painter is unknown, although she was listed as an artist, working "at home," by the 1910 U.S. federal census. By then, Frank was well established as an illustrator with the Floricultural Illustrating Co., where he specialized in drawing flowers for the *American Florist* and similar publications.[1] Formally trained in Chicago and Munich, Germany, Frank also painted landscapes, which he exhibited with the Palette & Chisel Club and Commercial Artists' Association of Chicago.

Beginning with her first Atlan Club entry, Anna's exquisite decorated porcelain drew praise, with critics consistently singling out her Satsuma pieces as among the handsomest in every exhibition. "An especially rich

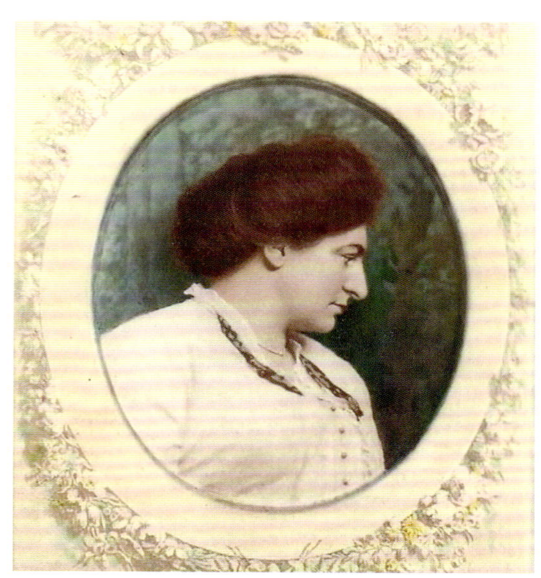

Anna Obermaier Senge. *Photo*: Private collection.

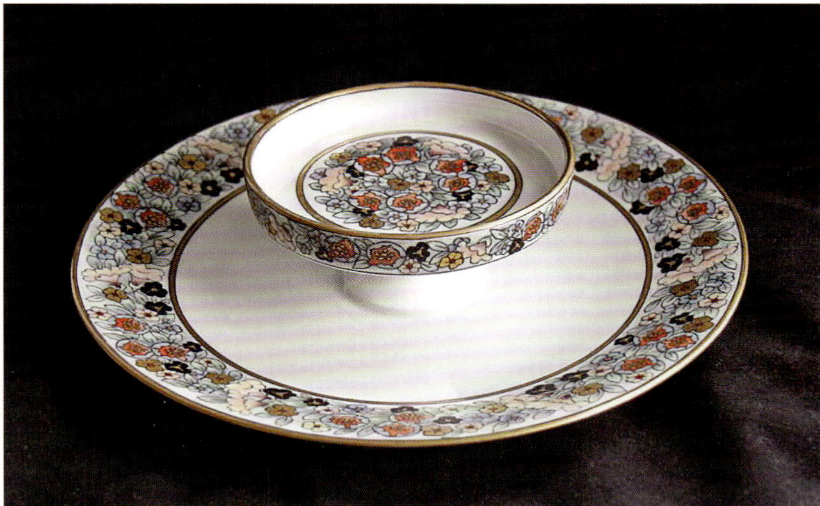

16.5 Combination cracker and cheese plate, Melina Millar Maxson, 1917. Decorated with floral bands, this service piece was available for $8 ($190) in the 1917 Atlan Club exhibition. Maxon was a student of Florence Steward. Signed: Melina Maxson/1917/PPP. (d: 9½"). *Photo*: Private collection.

Dow, Johonnot had been head of the design department at the Pratt Institute in Brooklyn, New York, from 1909 until 1912, when he moved to California.

The 1917 study course, the first in which Humphrey employed Johonnot's theory, was "in the opinion of all, the best the club has ever had," according to the association's correspondent to *Keramic Studio*.[5] The Chicago Ceramic Art Association, which exhibited at the same time as the Arts and Crafts exhibitions each spring, had also adopted conventional ornament as the "correct" form of decoration on china,

and graceful design in this ware was the bowl done by Mrs. Frank C. Senge," noted the *Inter Ocean* in 1911, "Mrs. Senge's work, twelve examples of which are in the present exhibit, shows wonderful beauty of design and execution."[2]

Ann also exhibited her work in Chicago Arts and Crafts exhibitions, and at the Illinois State Fair, where she won top premiums. In 1915, her rose jar with conventionalized peony flowers won second prize in the Satsuma category at Burley & Co.'s national exhibition. In that same exhibition, Frank entered a set of six tea plates with Dutch scenery, causing *Keramic Studio* to comment, "It is not quite usual to find a gentleman exhibitor who is in no sense identified with ceramics, but in the case of Mr. F. C. Senge, we have an illustrator who sometimes gives us the advantage of his clever ideas expressed on porcelain surfaces."[3] Anna and Frank, who shared a love of art and flowers, may have critiqued each other's designs.

In the Atlan Club's final exhibition in 1922, Anna's eighteen entries included service plates, Satsuma boxes, and a Kay-Bee China lemonade pitcher. At the back of the catalog was an advertisement for "Designs" available at her home studio in Rogers Park; as the club's conscientious treasurer, she had also convinced Frank and his office mate to purchase ads for their advertising art studio.[4]

In 1924, Anna and Frank traveled to Germany to visit relatives and study art.[5] A 1920 census listing for the couple has not been located; however, in 1930 and 1940, Frank is listed as a commercial artist working in advertising, with no occupation given for Anna.

Anna's professional career appears to have ended with the Atlan Club; however, she continued to decorate porcelain in her home studio, filling orders for place settings and tableware for customers. According to the granddaughters of a family friend, she maintained a kiln in her Chicago home until her death, at age eighty-seven, on April 19, 1959.[6]

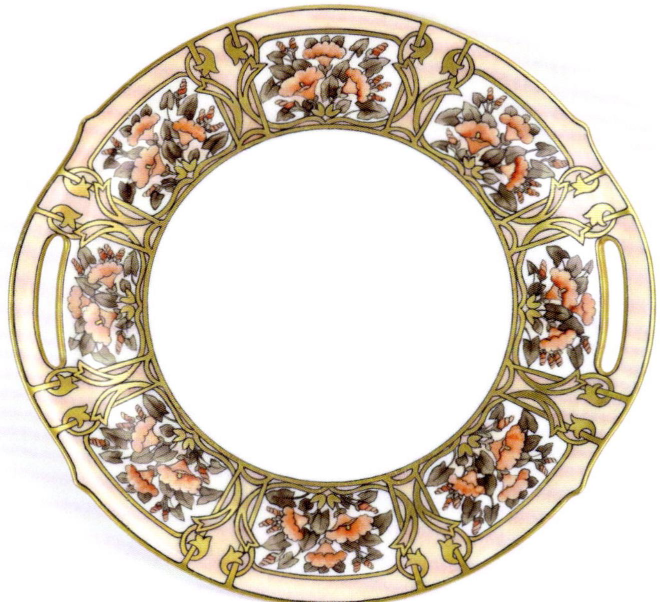

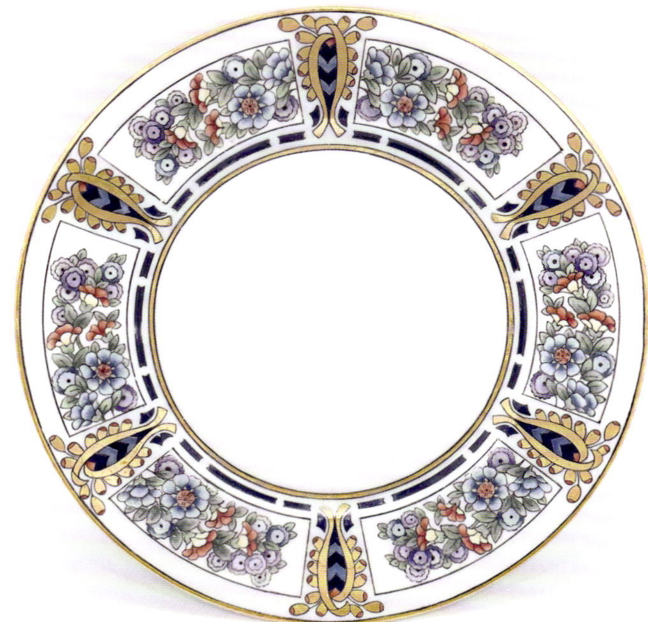

16.6 (left) Cake plate, Grace Cosgrove Gale, 1917. Gale offered this cake plate for $5 ($119) in the 1917 Atlan Club exhibition. Signed: G. C. Gale/PPP/AL. (w: 10½") *Photo*: Marvin Venis Benjamin.

16.7 (right) Luncheon plate, Rita Letz, 1917. Letz, who operated a china painting studio in Hammond, Indiana, exhibited a luncheon set that included a chop platter and set of plates, in 1917. Signed: Rita Letz/PPP/Atlan. (d: 8½") Photo: Grant Smith.

although its members adhered to a less strict interpretation than the Atlan Club.The study of "design" as the basic principle governing all creative work, not just china painting, facilitated work in other crafts, allowing women to take advantage of radical changes taking place in home furnishings, as represented in the new field of "interior design." In a 1917 editorial encouraging this progression, *Keramic Studio*'s editor acknowledged the Atlan Club's pioneering work as "the enthusiastic group that commenced this work many years ago," noting that the New York Keramic Society, "with Mr. Dow as their prophet," had followed a similar course for fifteen years, during which time "most of the other Ceramic Clubs have fallen in line."[6] By this time, the original New York Society of Keramic Art had been absorbed by the National Society of Craftsmen. Its successor, the Keramic Society of Greater New York, was guided by former Kansas City artist Dorothea Warren O'Hara, who served three terms as president.[7] Work by its members had begun shifting to vivid hues and highly abstract designs inspired by the Incas of Peru or similar "primitive" cultures represented in the collections at the American Museum of Natural History, where the society maintained its headquarters. Discussing their recent exhibition in a 1917 issue of the *Art World*, art critic Charles de Kay conceded that the group, in introducing such bold designs, was "doing a work for the public which is hardly appreciated as yet in all its bearings."[8]

After the 1910 dissolution of the National League of Mineral Painters, in which Chicago women played such a dominant role, New York replaced Chicago as the primary place to which aspiring porcelain painters looked for inspiration. In this dynamic East Coast state, one could find *Keramic Studio* copublishers Adelaide A. Robineau in Syracuse and Anna B. Leonard in New York City; Charles Fergus Binns at Alfred University; Arthur Wesley Dow at the Pratt Institute in Brooklyn; and high-profile decorators and teachers like Marshall Fry and Dorothea Warren O'Hara, with their private art schools, in New York City. While the best-known Chicago teachers and their studios remained busy, their clientele was drawn primarily from midwestern and southwestern states.

Nationwide, membership in strictly ceramic clubs was stagnant or declining, particularly in major cities. In 1916, the *American Art Directory* listed the Indiana Keramic Club as having 50 members; Jersey City Keramic Art Club, 22; Kansas City Keramic Club, 45; Keramic Society of Greater New York, 55; and Minneapolis's Twin City Keramic Club, 18. The Chicago Ceramic Art Association had 50 members, a far cry from its 250 men and women in 1893. Oddly, the Atlan Ceramic Club was not listed in the directory, although it appeared in some earlier editions. Organizations that included ceramists but embraced a broader artistic range fared better: the Chicago Artists' Guild, founded in 1910, had a membership of 250; the National Society of Craftsmen, organized in Manhattan in 1906, counted 300; and the venerable Boston Society of Arts and Crafts, founded in 1897, claimed 900.[9]

Ellen Elizabeth Lovgren, 1915–1918

Ellen Elizabeth Lovgren (1885–1952) served as an Atlan Club councilor in 1917 and as second vice president in 1918.

Ellen's parents migrated from Sweden a year or two before her birth in Chicago in 1885. She was only four years old when her father died. According to the 1900 U.S. federal census, Ellen's widowed mother operated a boardinghouse while her seventeen-year-old brother Carl Hjalmar Lovgren worked as a clerk. Carl, who became a successful business executive, supported his mother and younger sisters, Ellen and Edith, until their deaths.

Ellen's early art training is unknown; however, it is likely that she was an associate member of the Atlan Club before being invited to full membership in 1915. By 1916, the *Chicago Daily Tribune*'s art reviewer considered Ellen's work among "the most notable" in the Atlan Club exhibition.[1] She participated in Burley & Co.'s annual exhibitions and won several first premiums for entries at the Illinois State Fair in 1916 and 1917. Despite such success, Ellen dropped her membership after the 1918 exhibition, perhaps choosing to sell her work through the Artists' Guild of Chicago. In 1920 she was among Chicago ceramics artists listed as guild members in the *American Art Annual*.[2] Her studio address was her home at 5240 Kenmore Avenue.

After brother Carl married in the early 1920s, Ellen and her sister moved to an apartment in Evanston, Illinois. Following Ellen's death at age sixty-six in 1952, her sister Edith kept the collection of Atlan Club ceramics intact. When Edith died in 1967, it was inherited and preserved by their niece. Most pieces in the family collection were signed with her name but undated; some, signed only with her name, match descriptions in Atlan Club exhibition catalogs; others may have been intended for sale through the Artists' Guild.

Maker's mark: Ellen Elizabeth Lovgren. *Source*: Author's collection.

Chapter Seventeen

The Beginning of the End

The gallery where this [Atlan Ceramic Art] work is ensconced has an exceeding gay and festive appearance. There is something appealing to every one in the warm tones of beautiful luster and in graceful forms of pottery. There are seen here about 230 pieces of porcelain, decorated in various designs and treated in various ways to further their purposes of ornament.

—Eleanor Jewett, Art, *Chicago Daily Tribune*, November 7, 1920, 112

The Atlan Club's postwar exhibitions bore a strong physical resemblance to those mounted before and during the world conflict, although its catalogs included the names of many newcomers. Its twenty-seventh annual exhibition in 1919 included a variety of Satsuma pieces decorated by senior members Frances Barothy, Helen Frazee, and Florence Steward, three women who never missed an exhibition. As usual, Florence Steward came up with something unique: a set of twelve tiles with borders inspired by historic ornament framing flowers, suitable for incorporation in a mantel or a wall mural, priced at $600 (about $10,376).[1] Given the similarly high prices on many of the 233 items, it appears that many had been created specifically for exhibition drama; indeed, Helen Frazee advertised "special designs for exhibition pieces" in Atlan catalogs. Rather than write a detailed on-site review, Eleanor Jewett, the *Chicago Tribune*'s art critic, quoted from the club overview in the Atlan catalog, mentioning Steward's "fascinating series of twelves tiles" and naming a few of the local exhibitors.[2]

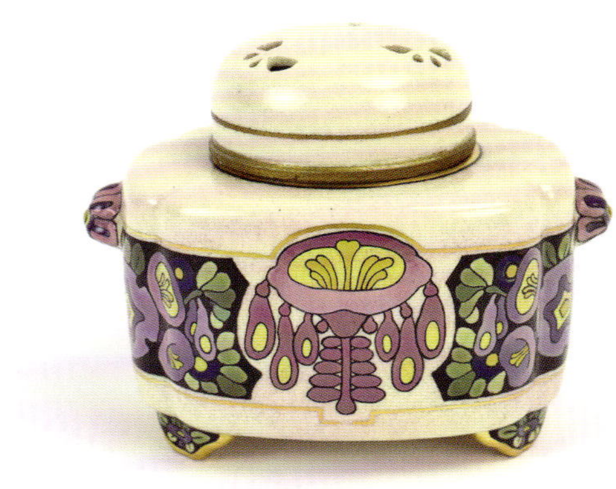

17.1 Satsuma incense burner, Amanda Berglund, 1918. One of eleven Satsuma articles, all unpriced, displayed by Berglund in the 1918 Atlan exhibition. Signed: A. Berglund/PPP/Atlan/'18. (w: 5″) *Photo*: Marvin Venis Benjamin.

Florence Steward's entry in the 1920 exhibition hinted that she and the Atlan painters were aware of changes taking place in the postwar American household. Unique not only in design, but in purpose, her "maidless" luncheon set featured multiple trays, which rested one upon another, with a cover of teakwood and jade, forming a handsome as well as useful centerpiece.[3] Continuing a trend started during the war, exhibition items were predominantly practical: boxes, tea sets, dresser accessories, trays, and various serving pieces that might appeal to modern homemakers seeking a more casual lifestyle.

Resisting, or perhaps denying, the trend toward casual living, Helen Frazee showed an imposing breakfast set—which included a coffee set, cups and saucers, cereal bowls, candlesticks, even a fernery—for $150 ($2,507) in the 1921 exhibition. Also offered for the top price

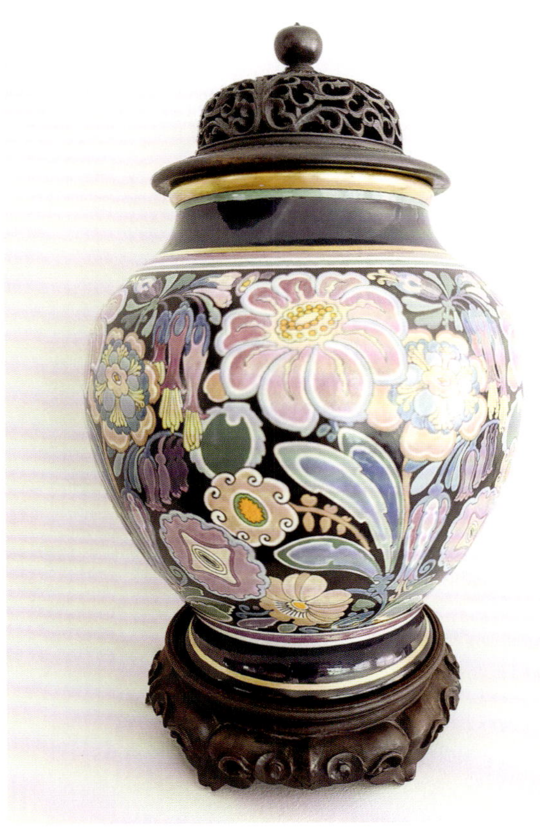

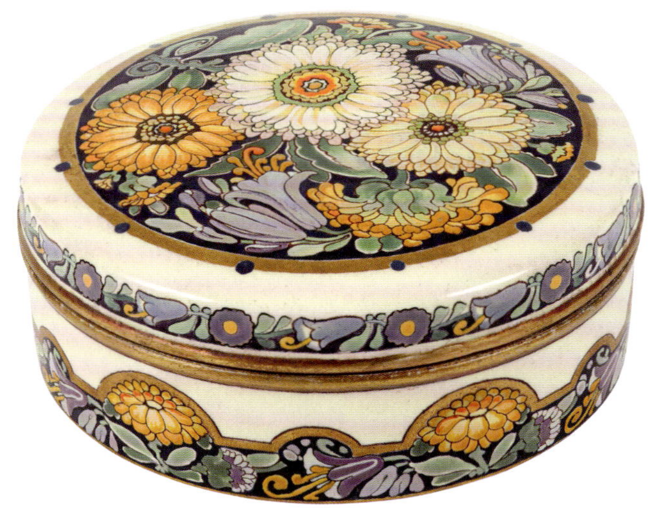

17.2 Satsuma box, Helen F. Frazee, 1919. Featuring conventionalized zinnias, this may have been one of the two bonbon boxes displayed by Frazee in the 1919 Atlan Club exhibition. Signed: Frazee/1919/Fine Arts. (2½″ × 6″) *Photo*: Toomey & Co. Auctioneers.

17.3 "Rose jar with teakwood stand and cover," Amanda Berglund, 1919. This rose jar with "modern" decorative motif was priced at $65 ($1,146) in the 1919 Atlan Club exhibition. Signed: A. Berglund/PPP/Atlan. (h: 15½″) *Photo*: Tim Blackburn.

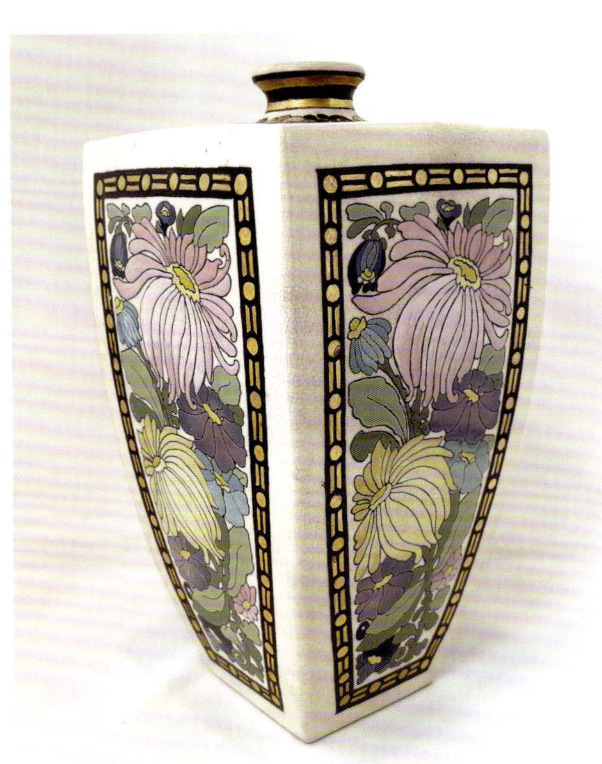

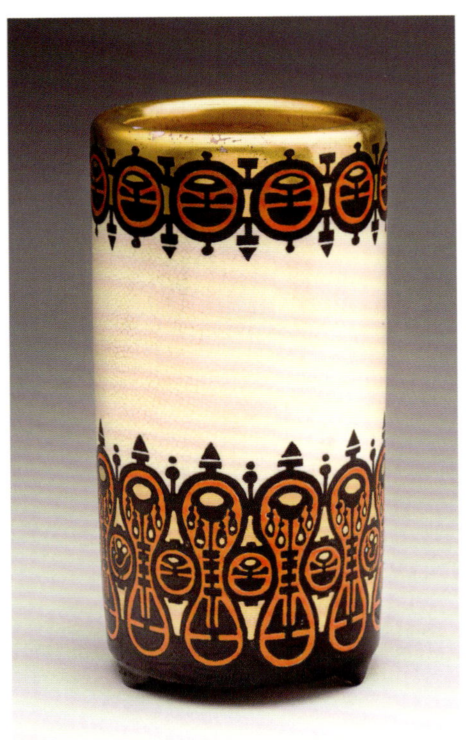

17.4 Satsuma lamp vase, Ida Ma Whinney, 1919. This "Lamp Vase, Square" was exhibited unpriced in the 1919 Atlan Club exhibition. Signed: Ma Whinney. (9⅝″ × 4″) *Photo*: Private collection.

17.5 Vase, Ida Ma Whinney, 1920. This cylindrical vase with a bold geometric motif was featured in the Atlan Club exhibition in 1920. Signed: Ma Whinney/ Exhibite [*sic*]/Art Inst/1920. (7½″ × 3⅝″) *Photo*: Art Institute of Chicago/Art Resource, New York.

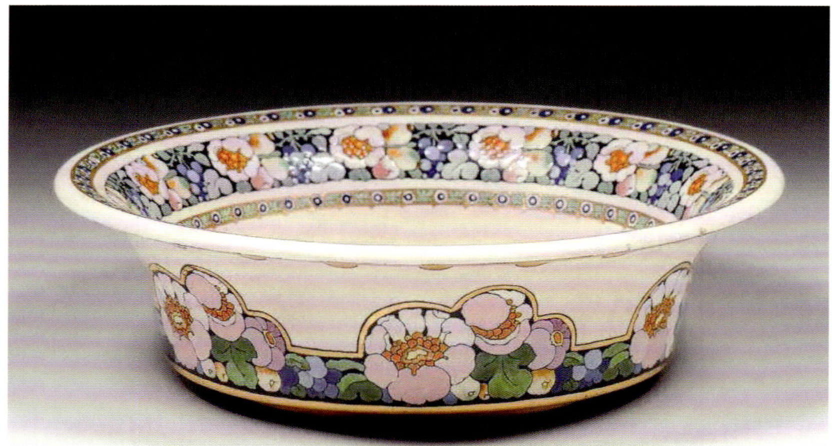

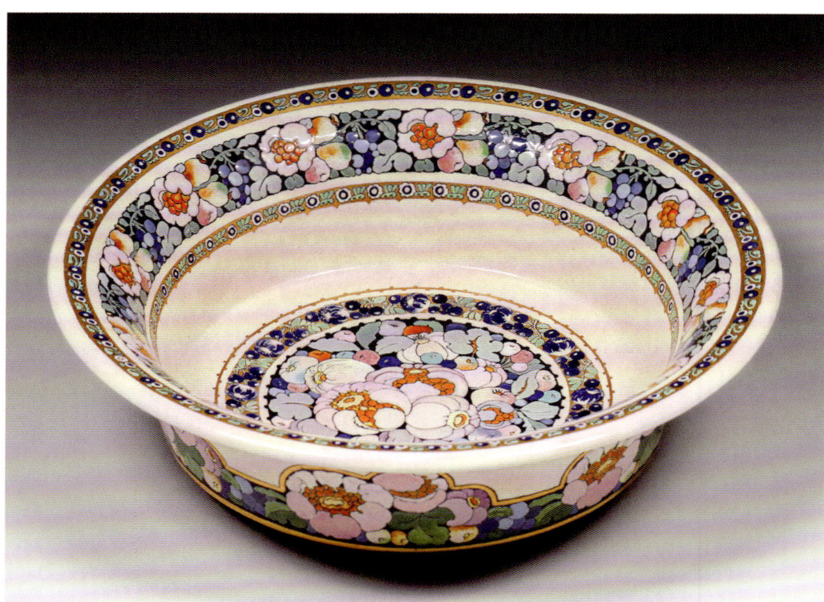

17.6A AND B Satsuma fruit bowl, Ida Ma Whinney, 1920. Colorful floral bands decorate the interior and exterior of the bowl Ma Whinney displayed in the 1920 Atlan Club exhibition. Signed: Ma Whinney/1920/Atlan/Exhibite Art Inst. (3¾" × 12⅛"). *Photo*: Gus Bostrom, California Historical Design.

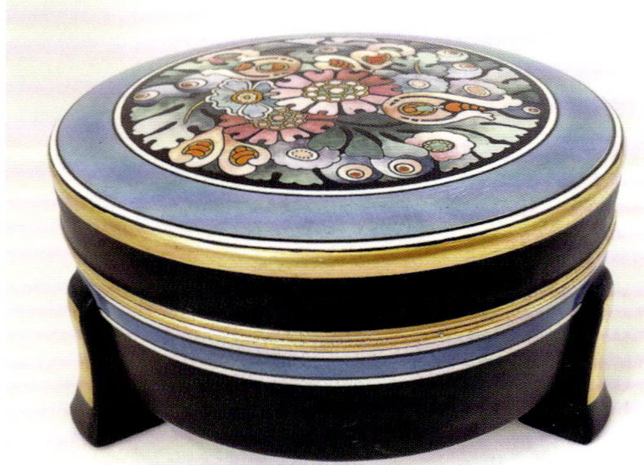

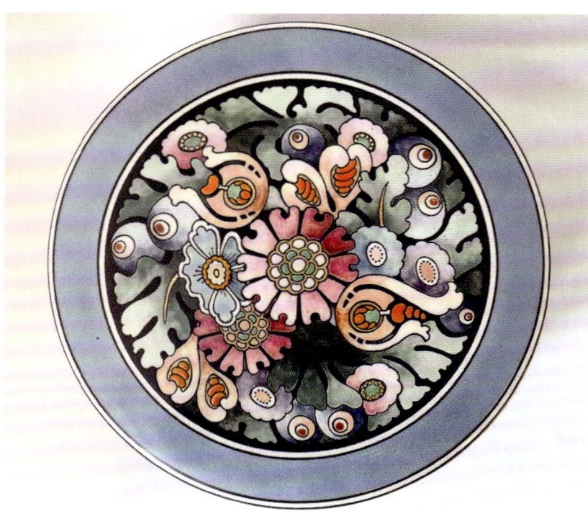

17.7A AND B Satsuma powder box, Helga M. Peterson, 1920. The box features a pomegranate motif. Signed: HMP/1920. (4" × 7¼") *Photo*: Private collection.

of $150 were Katherine Mosser's large Satsuma fruit bowl and Anna Senge's remarkable Satsuma vase. In contrast, Florence Steward had an assortment of nine small "Friendship Gifts," each bearing a quotation, priced from $3 to $20 ($50 to $334). No images of the exhibition have been found; however, "among the decorated objects displayed this year are a number of large bowls, vases, and lamp bases, which are strong in color and vigorously painted, and suggest a new development in the artistic career of this club," observed the editor of the Art Institute's *Bulletin*, which recorded the affairs of its museum, school, and library.[4] Indeed, the few pieces attributed to members—especially younger women—during this period, indicate a greater use of bright colors, larger and bolder motifs, use of translucent luster glazes, and more visible white space on the ceramic forms.

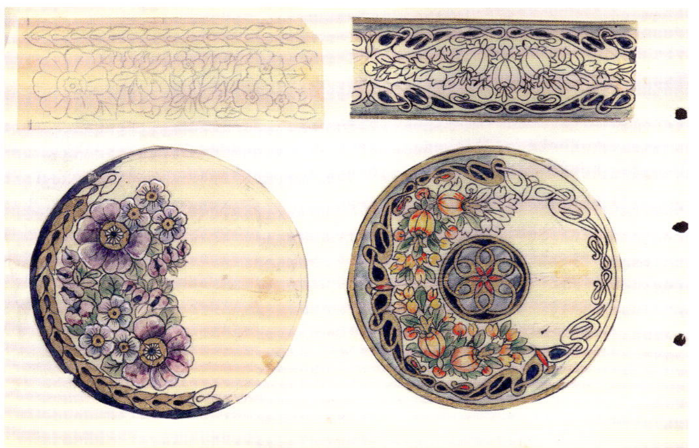

17.8 Watercolor patterns for box covers and borders painted on tissue paper from the album of associate member Elva B. Eichling, 1916–1922. *Photo*: Author's collection.

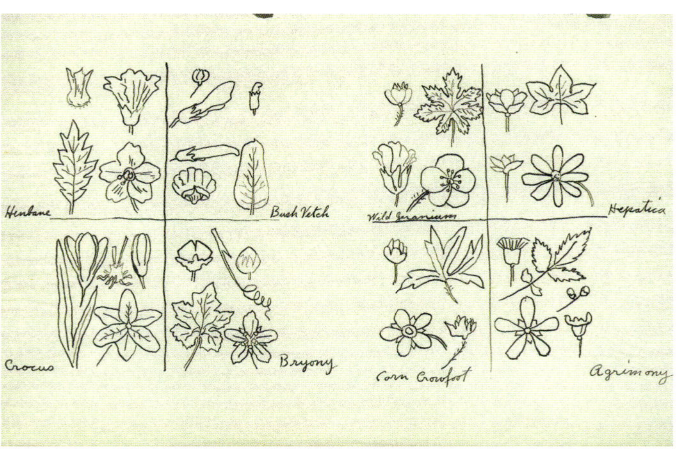

17.9 Exercises in the conventionalization of flowers were drawn on tissue paper by associate member Elva B. Eichling, 1916–1922. *Photo*: Author's collection.

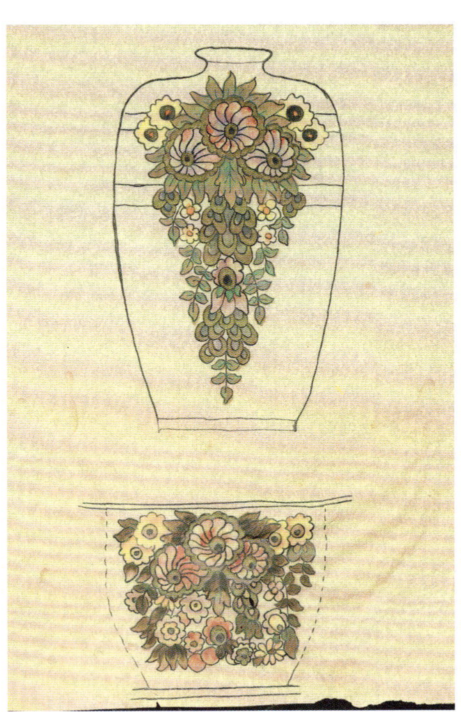

17.10 Floral designs for a vase and a bowl from the design notebook of Elva B. Eichling, 1916–1922. *Photo*: Author's collection.

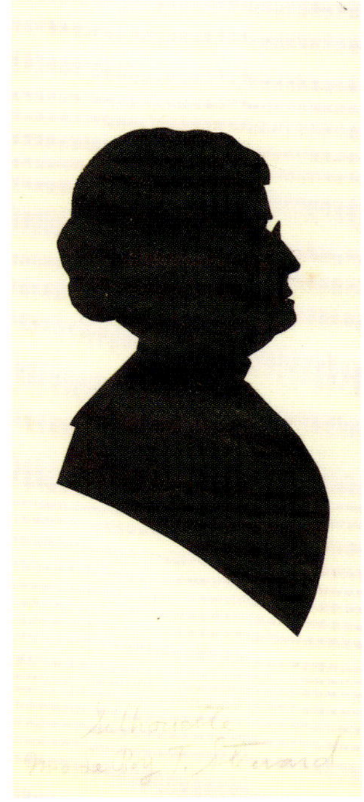

17.11 Paper silhouette of Atlan Club founder Florence Pratt Steward cut by Elva B. Eichling during an Atlan Club winter study course, ca. 1917. Steward exhibited a pottery bowl with a "silhouette border-our critic and some of her students" in the 1917 Atlan Club exhibition. *Photo*: Author's collection.

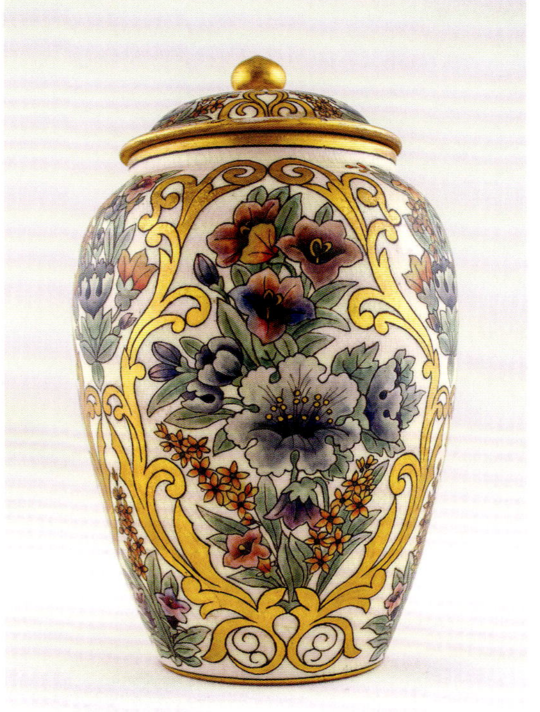

17.12 Satsuma rose jar, Elva B. Eichling, 1921. One of nine items, all unpriced, displayed by Eichling in the twenty-ninth Atlan exhibition in 1921. Signed: E. B. Eichling/Oct. 1921/PPP/Atlan. Mark: Japan. (h: 7½") *Photo*: Robert W. Switzer.

Among the new members exhibiting for the first time was Elva Eichling, wife of an Evanston florist, who had been an eager student in Steward's associate classes. Like neophytes in previous years, she studied Steward's booklet on technique, kept a sketchbook of her watercolor designs, and sketched pencil motifs on tissue paper for transferring to porcelain bodies. One of the study classes must have included a lesson on cutting silhouettes from black paper, as Eichling included a profile of instructor Steward in her portfolio (see fig. 17.11). Also showing her work in 1921 was Marcia Ruth Simons, wife of a wealthy oil producer in the small town of Okmulgee, Oklahoma, who had recently spent two months in Chicago studying china painting under Helen Frazee. Upon her return to Okmulgee, she had her own one-woman show of 300 pieces she decorated within the year, including a monumental three-foot-tall vase, "a copy of one of Mrs. Frazee's prize winners," that was decorated with conventional floral motifs.[5]

Although the 1921 Atlan Club exhibition varied little from previous years, the setting in which it took place had changed considerably. Opening and closing dates were still mentioned in the press, but Atlan exhibitions no longer received detailed reviews by the city's art critics or society columnists; at most, they generated a few generic sentences and a listing of some of the better-known exhibitors' names. Its opening receptions were no longer events thronged by socialites and art aficionados.

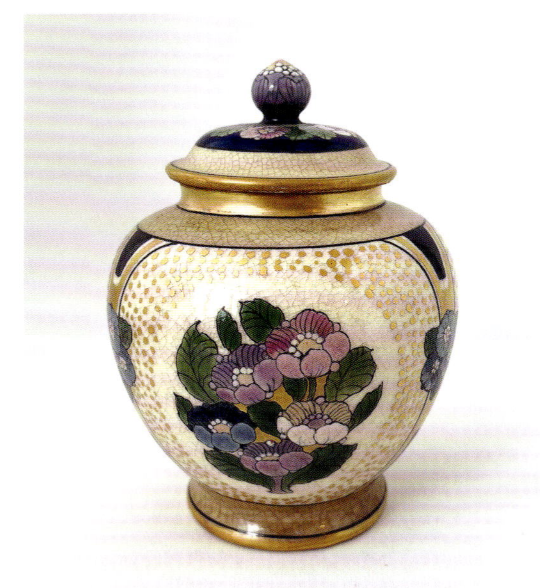

17.13 Satsuma rose jar, Anna Senge, ca. 1921. This may have been the rose jar "loaned by Miss E. Wahl" in the 1921 exhibition. Ella E. Wahl was a commercial artist in Chicago. Signed: Anna O. Senge/Atlan Club. (h: 5") *Photo*: Private collection.

Emma Amanda Lindquist Berglund, 1914–1922

Born in Stockholm, Sweden, Emma Amanda Lindquist Berglund (1879 to after 1964) was only a few months old when she arrived in the United States with her parents in 1880. The daughter of a blacksmith, Amanda worked as a seamstress in Chicago before marrying Axel Arvid Berglund, a tailor, on June 22, 1901.

Amanda attended public and private schools in Chicago; however, her art training is unknown. In addition to exhibiting with the Atlan Club, Amanda showed her work at Burley & Co., where, in 1915, she received Honorable Mention for a card tray decorated with geometrical lines enclosing a conventionalized floral pattern. She was listed as an "artist," working on her own account, in the 1920 U.S. federal census.

The Berglunds moved to Evanston, Illinois, around 1927, then to neighboring Skokie ten years later. In 1945, she was "known in Evanston and North Shore art circles as Amanda Berglund," according to her husband's obituary. In 1945, she was listed in *Who's Who in Chicago and Illinois* as a "painter in oils and teacher of ceramics" who had been awarded numerous prizes and was a member of the American Federation of Arts.[1] The same biography appeared in *Who's Who in Michigan* and *Who's Who in Indiana* in 1947.[2] She was also listed in *Who's Who of American Women* in 1958.[3]

Amanda was still living in November 1964, when she was mentioned in the obituary of her son LeRoy Roger Berglund.

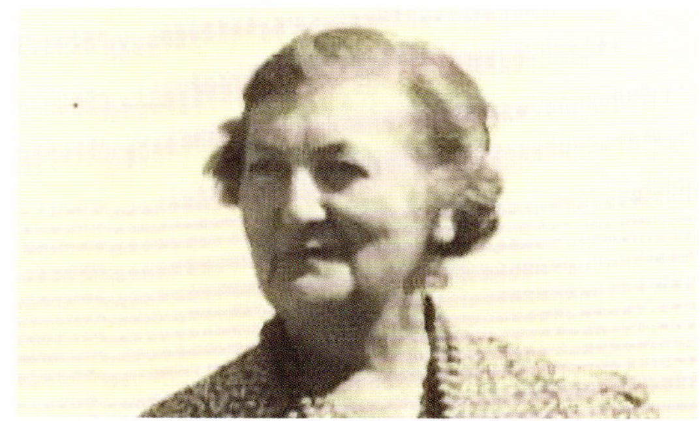

Emma Amanda Lindquist Berglund. *Photo*: Bridget A. Berglund.

Chicago's once vibrant china painting community had become a shadow of itself. Gone were the large annual china painting exhibitions sponsored by Burley & Co., which closed its doors in 1919.[6] On a national level, *Keramic Studio* was evolving into a magazine of general design, its editors noting that many china decorators felt the need to supplement their work in ceramics with other crafts to make a living wage.[7] Faced with a small and declining membership, even the venerable Chicago Ceramic Art Association had merged with the Technic Arts League, a newly formed association of workers in the various applied arts, and assumed its name in February 1921.[8]

Although many considered china painting a fad whose time had passed, it remained a popular art form in many parts of the country throughout the 1920s. "Even today the decoration of dishes is one of the fields for artistic expression that women still cherish [and] those who are still loyal to their art after the fad stage has passed are serious craft workers with high ideals," wrote newspaper journalist Marguerite B. Williams. "In their work they aspire to the standards of good design set by applied art workers in all fields. The clientele of the china decorator is, of course, not as large as it once was, but those who do buy are people of discrimination and good taste and to whom the quality of the workmanship is of more importance than the price."[9] In 1930, china painting classes were still being advertised by the Y.W.C.A., women's clubs, vocational services, art schools, and private art studios from coast to coast.

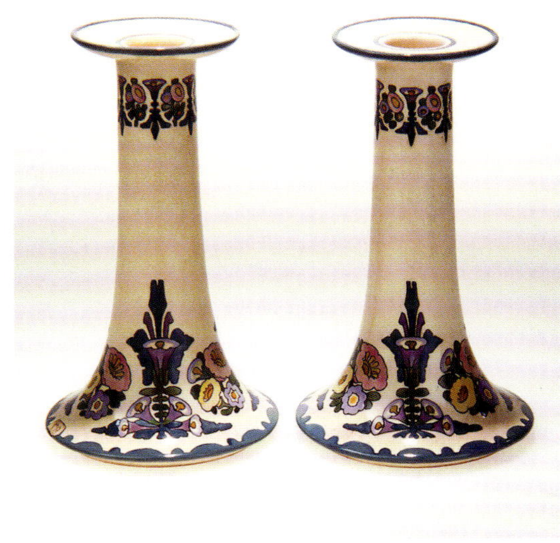

17.14 Pair of candlesticks, Helen Frazee, ca. 1921. Frazee exhibited two candlesticks as part of a large breakfast set priced at $150 ($2,557) in the 1921 Atlan Club exhibition. Signed: Frazee. (h: 7¼") *Photo*: Chicago History Museum.

Elva Johanna Bryant Eichling, 1921–1922

While raising three children, Elva Johanna Bryant Eichling enjoyed painting as a hobby. She was an associate member of the Atlan Club before being invited to exhibit in 1921. She took careful notes during the study courses taught by Florence Steward and maintained an album of her designs for hand-painted china. When the club ceased in 1923, she completed a correspondence course in drawing and composition with the Washington School of Art in Washington, DC. During the 1920s, Elva showed her artwork in annual exhibitions of the Works of Artists of Evanston and the North Shore sponsored by the Evanston Woman's Club.

Born in St. Louis, Missouri, Elva Johanna Bryant (1889–1978) was a toddler when her father, a cabinetmaker and upholsterer, moved the family to Chicago in the early 1890s. By 1900, the family had settled in Evanston, Illinois, where Elva graduated from high school.

In 1909, at age nineteen, Elva married florist Philip H. Eichling, future owner of Eichling's Flowers in Evanston and, later, Skokie. In addition to operating a retail shop, the family maintained a flower farm with eight acres of peonies and lilacs in Des Plaines, Illinois.[1] Over the years, Elva presented numerous programs on floral design to Chicago-area garden clubs and women's groups.

After her husband's death in 1967, Elva went to live with a son in Naples, Florida, where she died, age eighty-eight, in 1978.[2]

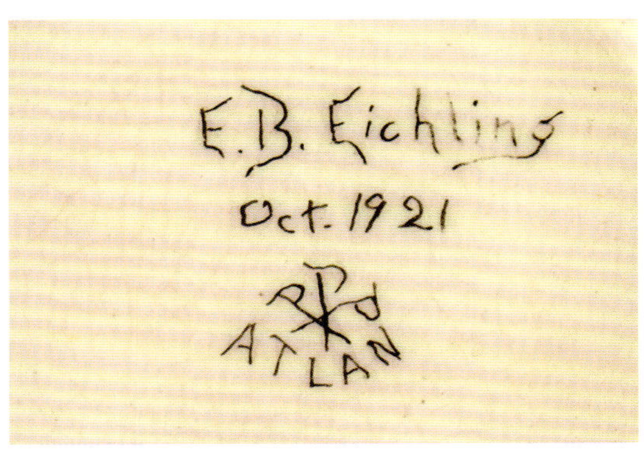

Maker's mark: Elva Bryant Eichling. *Source*: Author's collection.

Chapter Eighteen

A Grand Finale

Artists should not be narrow minded and imagine that because they have already developed some skill in some craft, say china painting, they cannot do anything but decorate china. If, as a foundation to their art work, they have a good understanding of the laws of design and color harmony, they will rapidly, in case of necessity, shift to a new and better paying line of work, or at least add to their favorite craft some other work which may, temporarily or permanently, pay better.

—Editorial, *Keramic Studio* 23, nos. 3–4 (July–August 1921): 45

On November 29, 1921, two days after the close of the Atlan Club's twenty-ninth exhibition, Florence Pratt Steward, its founder and indefatigable leader for thirty years, died at age sixty-five after undergoing an operation at a South Shore hospital.[1] A few weeks later, the Art Institute of Chicago published a gracious tribute to Steward in its *Bulletin*: "With the passing away of Mrs. Le Roy T. Steward, president of the Atlan Ceramic Club, the Art Institute has lost a loyal friend. Mrs. Steward founded the Atlan Club at the time of the World's Fair and ever since has been its leader in raising the standard of decoration on porcelain. During this period the Atlan Club and the Institute have been closely associated, each cooperating with the other in the attainment of its ambitions and ideals."[2] In her will, Steward bequeathed a collection of her ceramics to the Art Institute of Chicago.[3] Among the forty-two items were her 1910 "Conversational Set" place settings, a silver medal from the 1915 Panama-Pacific exposition, and various Satsuma items shown in Atlan Club exhibitions. However, the museum's Decorative Arts Committee voted not to accept the items for inclusion in the collection.[4] One wonders how Bessie B. Bennett, the museum's curator of decorative arts—and Atlan advisor and honorary member—would have voted, had she been a member of the three-person trustee-level committee in October 1922.

Upon Steward's death, Atlan members promoted Claire Van Doren, who joined in 1918, from vice president to president and appointed Frances Barothy as vice president; Frances Lowes, second vice president; Melina Maxon, secretary, and Anna Senge, treasurer. Grace Gale and Sheila Banner were councilors. Mary Humphrey, the last surviving founding member, and Helen Frazee, who joined in August 1893, were made Life Members. Honorary members included Bessie B. Bennett, the Art Institute curator who advised the club; St. Louis

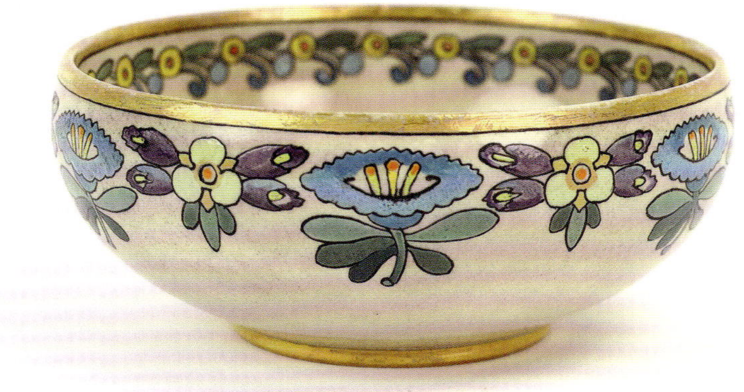

18.1 Satsuma mayonnaise bowl, June Hibbard Kern, 1922. One of two Satsuma bowls included in the dozen items Kern exhibited in 1922. Signed: June Hibbard Kern/PPP. Mark: Japan. (2¼″ × 5″) *Photo*: Alan Reed Family.

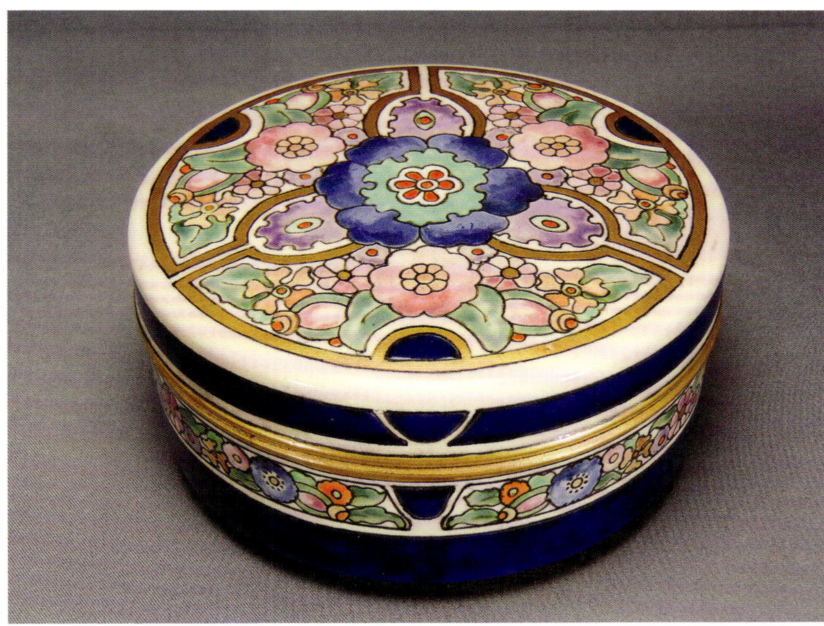

18.2 Satsuma box, Sadie Hall Lowes, ca. 1922. Lowes entered five Satsuma boxes, ranging in price from $5 to $10 ($90 to $182), in the 1922 Atlan Club exhibition. Signed: S. H. Lowes. Mark: Made in Japan/62. (2¼″ × 5¼″) *Photo*: Dark Flowers Antiques.

ceramic artist Kathryn E. Cherry; and Dorothea Warren O'Hara, president of the Keramic Society of Greater New York.[5]

A special feature of the club's thirtieth exhibition, which opened in November 1922, was the work of out-of-town members. Among the thirty-eight exhibitors were four women from Cleveland, Ohio; three from Hammond, Indiana; and one from Minneapolis. Except for one of the Hammond women, none had previously exhibited with the club; thus, it seems likely they were invited to join based on their reputations within the national china painting community. Fifteen members had exhibited the previous year, including veterans Helen Frazee and Anna Senge; Helga Peterson, who last showed her work

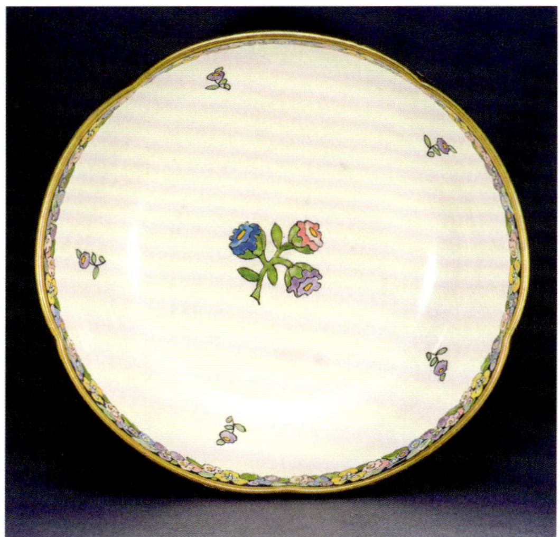

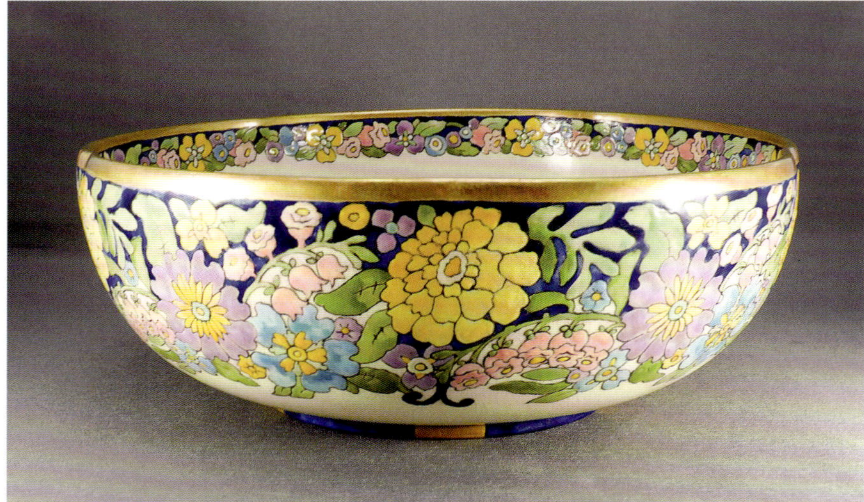

18.3A AND B Bowl, Bertha Shoop Odgers, ca. 1922. Conventionalized floral motifs decorate this Satsuma bowl by Odgers, a first-time exhibitor in the final Atlan exhibition in 1922. Signed: Bertha S. Odgers. (3″× 7½″) *Photo*: Dark Flowers Antiques.

in 1916, also took part. Frances Barothy, who had not missed an exhibition since 1901, had recently returned from a summer in Europe and did not participate.[6] Sixteen members were new, exhibiting for the first time. The large number of new members, recently elevated from associates, and out-of-towners suggests that the club was insecure about its future and eager to have an impressive turnout. Without Florence Steward's leadership and tireless commitment was the club's thirtieth exhibition a celebration of its resilience or a grand finale?

As in previous exhibitions, most of the entries were Satsuma ware decorated with colorful enamels, along with examples of American and European porcelain; many were unpriced, making it unclear whether the pieces were for sale or just being shown as proud examples of the women's work. Shown for the first time were bowls, vases, and a lemonade pitcher—decorated by local members Minnie Band, Elva Eichling, Anna Senge, and June Hibbard Kern—made by Kay-Bee China Works in Chicago's Norwood Park neighborhood. A new company, Kay-Bee had begun making fine highly glazed china for decorating, etching, and flat enamel decoration, along with underglazed blue "Bavarian" china, all in new modern shapes, according to its advertisement in the Atlan Club catalog.[7]

In her brief *Chicago Daily Tribune* review, Eleanor Jewett expended little effort, remarking, "The collection in the glass cases is fascinating. It is difficult to pass many of the articles by without special mention, but, as so many are beautiful, probably it is wiser to lump them all as being of particular charm rather than risk comparisons, odious always, by selecting special jars or plates for elaborated praise."[8]

In contrast, the *Christian Science Monitor*, courtesy of its Chicago bureau, published a substantial article that paid homage to the Atlan Club's founding by Florence Steward, its long relationship with the Art Institute of Chicago, and its influential role in the widespread

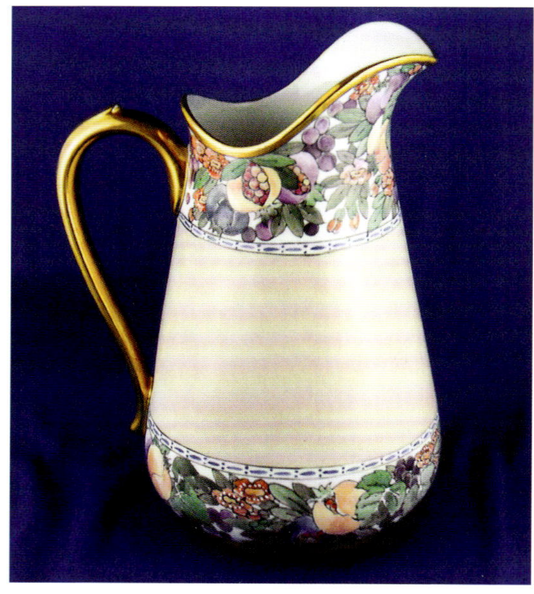

18.4 Pitcher with pomegranates, Frances A. Barothy, undated. Although Barothy rarely dated her work, it was included in Atlan exhibitions. Signed: F.A.B. Mark: PL/Limoges/France. (9¾″× 6½″) *Photo*: Dark Flowers Antiques.

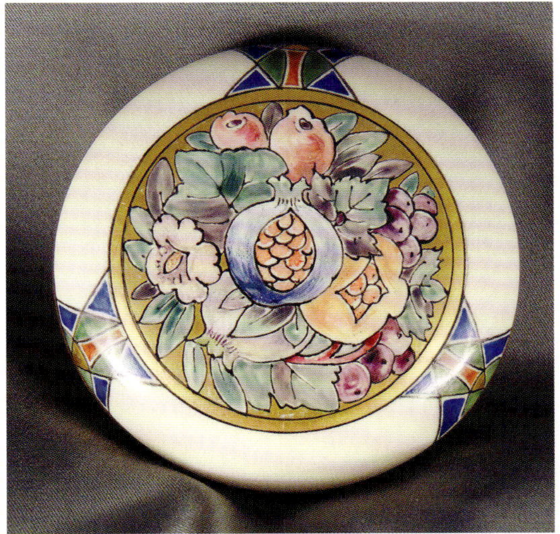
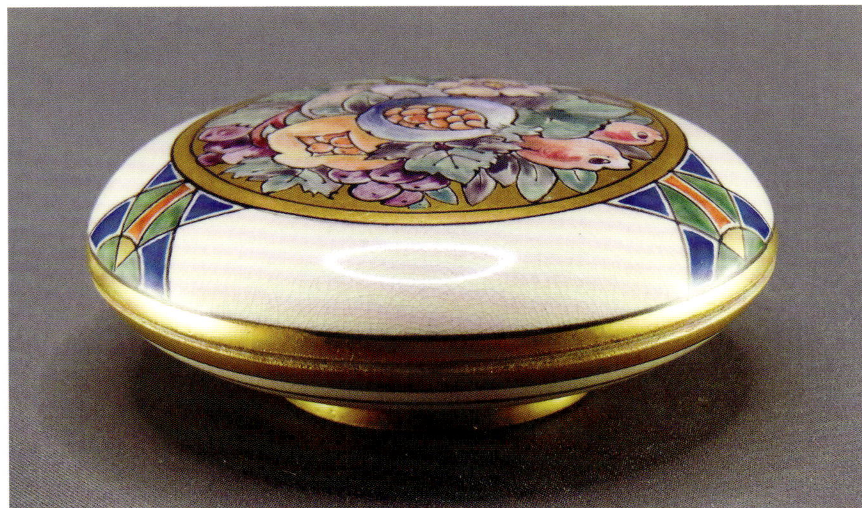

18.5A AND B Satsuma powder box with pomegranates, Frances A. Barothy, undated. Barothy exhibited sixty-nine Satsuma boxes in Atlan Club exhibitions between 1906 and 1921, including eleven in 1913 and seventeen in 1917. Prices ranged from $4.50 to $15.00 ($152 to $256). Signed: F.A. Barothy. (1¼" × 3" × ½") *Photo*: Dark Flowers Antiques.

adoption of conventional design. "The exclusive feeling in borders and the elaboration of small motifs to grace bowls, boxes, vases, trays, and pitchers, where the shape of the object demands special consideration, have been worked with an expert sense," noted the reviewer, "The combinations of color on the ivory-toned surfaces have indescribable charm."[9] It was a fitting swan song for the club's final exhibition.

Seven months later, in June 1923, Atlan Club members agreed to a merger with the Technic Arts League, formed when the Chicago Ceramic Art Association merged with the group and assumed its name in 1921.[10] Announcing the Atlan merger, a columnist for the suburban *Oak Parker* optimistically suggested, "The joining of forces and efforts cannot fail to be of great benefit to all concerned, and it is hoped to the cause for which all are working." Exhibitions hosted by the united organization, with about 200 members, would include many crafts in addition to ceramics.[11] The Technic Arts League did exhibit craftwork at the Artists' Guild salesrooms in the Fine Arts Building in November 1923.[12] But it never thrived. Artist Frances Barothy, a longtime Atlan member, dutifully served as president of the league between 1931 and 1943, when it claimed to be the oldest organization of craftworkers in Chicago.[13] The last reference to the league was in 1949, mentioning a meeting held in the Fine Arts Building.[14]

In the 1923 Applied Arts exhibition, the final Atlan Ceramic Art Club Prize was awarded to multi-talented Chicago artist and Art Institute student J. Edgar Miller (1899–1993) for a bowl decorated overglaze with an abstract modernist design. Miller, who showed three bowls, was the sole exhibitor of ceramics with overglaze decoration.[15] Miller would go on to become one of Chicago's most prominent and versatile artists, creating graphics, murals, stained glass, and ceramics.[16]

Oddly, a thirty-first exhibition of the Atlan Club appears in the Art Institute of Chicago's online archive of past exhibitions for February 1 through March 11, 1924.[17] There was no exhibition catalog and no mention appeared in the press. Most likely it was scheduled months before the merger and still on the calendar in its *Bulletin*. Still viable is the Atlan Ceramic Art Club Fund, created by the club in 1912, which has been the source of many additions to the museum's ceramics collection.

Mary Humphrey, who had spent several winters teaching china painting in Pasadena, retired to California. The highly regarded Helen Frazee, who had shown her work annually since 1893, died in March 1923. Her husband Abraham, bookkeeper for her china painting studio, tried to maintain the business by renting out her original designs, but this lasted only a year or so.[18]

With the demise of the Atlan and Chicago ceramic clubs, many of Chicago's independent china decorators continued working, but on a small scale, with a few veteran painters exhibiting with the Artists' Guild and in local art shows. A few, like Helga M. Peterson, leveraged her diverse art-craft skills to become an occupational therapist, a new field that emerged to rehabilitate soldiers disabled during World War I. Some, like Anna Senge, continued to fill the occasional orders for place settings and tableware from former clients. Others, like former Atlan member Francis Barothy, turned to painting on canvas; she was still giving art lessons in her Rogers Park studio in 1957, when she was eighty-six.[19] Many, including former Atlan president Jane V. D. Wright,

---

Frances Alice Nessling Barothy, 1901–1921

After joining in October 1901, Frances Alice Nessling Barothy (1873–1961) exhibited in every annual Atlan Club exhibition from 1901 through 1921. She held various offices, including three terms as secretary; two terms each as second vice president and vice president; and four terms as a councilor. After the Atlan Club merged with the Technic Arts League, she served as the league president, 1931–1943.[1]

Frances was born in Oshkosh, Wisconsin, of English-Canadian parentage, in 1873; her father was employed as a railroad conductor in Wisconsin and in Chicago. While living in Chicago, she graduated from the Art Institute in the 1890s.[2]

In 1901 she married Dr. Arpad M. Barothy, a young neurosurgeon who graduated from Rush Medical College in 1894. Barothy, who had migrated from Hungary to Nebraska in 1884, was an avid cyclist who rode his "wheel" from Omaha to Chicago; in 1891, the "able, enterprising young man" rode to New York, then bicycled from Hamburg across Europe to visit his old home in Austria-Hungary.[3] A pioneer in the development of electrical therapy, he became one of Chicago's best-known doctors. He served as president of the Hungarian-American Federation. While his mother was alive, he regularly visited Hungary accompanied by Frances, who took advantage of the opportunity to study painting in Europe and collect art.

Frances joined the Atlan Club four months after her June 1901 marriage; in addition to Atlan Club exhibitions, she participated in those sponsored by the Chicago Ceramic Art Association, Burley & Co., and the Art Institute of Chicago. Her work was frequently complimented for its distinct individuality, characterized by rich color and original style.

In 1914, Frances served on the jury of selection for ceramics for the Art Institute's Arts and Crafts exhibition, which included a selection of Hungarian handicrafts.[4] In 1921, when the Ceramic Art Association merged with the Technic Arts League, she exhibited under the league's banner in that year's Arts and Crafts exhibition.[5] In 1925, she exhibited her

continued to paint for pleasure. In 1933, writing from a hotel in Paris, where she had spent the winter, Wright, age ninety, told a relative that she still found "delight" in decorating china: "My hand is still steady and I do beautiful work which I give away. Ash trays, bonbon boxes, dozens of plates, etc."[20]

One noteworthy Chicago survivor was Pickard China, the large commercial studio devoted to volume production. After 1922, it focused on all-over-gold etched ware and patterns that required minimal hand painting in its complex in the city's Ravenswood neighborhood. In 1937, the company opened a manufacturing facility in Antioch, Illinois, where it produced its first Illinois-made ware under the name Pickard, Inc.; it continues in business today.[21]

Changes in direction were also evident on the East Coast. When the Keramic Society of Greater New York resumed postwar exhibitions in 1923, it broadened its scope to include various decorative artists and designers, not just ceramic workers. By 1930, renamed the Keramic Society and Design Guild, its exhibitions featured textiles and model dining room setups, as well as ceramics "with a contemporary twist, the modernistic trend apparent in the clay and porcelain pieces."[22] Former china painter superstars Dorothea Warren O'Hara and Marshall Fry, now honorary members, accepted its invitation to show some of their work, providing a nostalgic historical component.[23] By then, O'Hara was developing colorful glazes for commercial potteries

---

hand-painted china in the Works of Artists of Evanston and the North Shore sponsored by the Evanston Woman's Club.

In the 1920s, working in her home studio, Frances turned to painting on canvas and became known for her treatment of flowers. She served as art director of the Rogers Park Woman's Club; lectured frequently on art and travel before the Municipal Art League and various women's clubs; and was active in the Arts Club, the Chicago Galleries Association, and Association of Chicago Painters and Sculptors. In 1957, at age eighty-six, she was still teaching art classes while painting landscapes in summer and still life in winter. "I like beauty with emphasis on color," she told a *Chicago Tribune* reporter. "Art is my first love. After 50 years, I'm still very happy with it."[6]

In 1930, Dr. Barothy built a cottage on the banks of the Pere Marquette River in Walhalla, Michigan, where he planned to establish a health resort.[7] Instead, the venue became Barothy Lodge, a fishing camp managed by their sons, Victor and Frederick.[8] In the 1940s, Victor operated a sport fishing lodge in the Florida Keys before moving the enterprise to Cuba. When Castro confiscated the property, he set up a new lodge in Belize, capital of British Honduras. In October 1961, Florence was visiting Victor when a hurricane destroyed the fishing camp; soon after, she died of shock at age eighty-eight. She is buried at Barothy's Caribbean Lodge, now known as Belize River Lodge, in British Honduras.[9] Frances is listed in the second edition of *Who Was Who in American Art 1564–1975: 400 Years of Artists in America*.[10]

Maker's mark: Frances Alice Nessling Barothy. *Photo*: Dark Flowers Antiques.

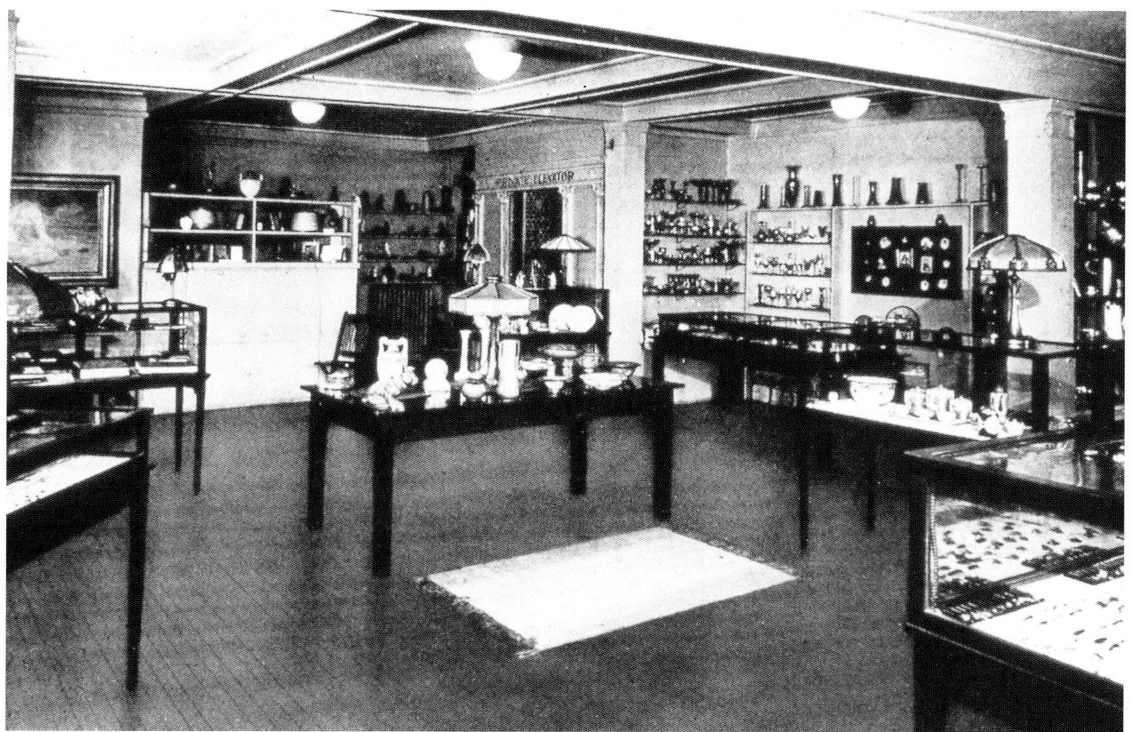

18.6 Salesroom for Hand Wrought Objects of the Artists' Guild, Fine Arts Building, Chicago, in 1917. The success of the Artists' Guild led to the formation of the Arts Club of Chicago in 1916. *Source*: Edward M. Ericson, *A National Association of Artists and Craft Workers* (Chicago: Artists' Guild, 1917).

at her studio-house in Darien, Connecticut;[24] Fry was a Brooklyn-based interior designer of table linens summering in Southampton, Long Island.[25]

By the mid-1930s, Chicago's once vibrant china-painting community and its practitioners were forgotten or considered "old-fashioned" by the between-the-wars generation. "Where, may I ask, is Aunt Clara, the maiden aunt who wrote poetry or did china painting, or sang for her nieces and nephews?" lamented a *Chicago Tribune* journalist concerned by the effect of the loss of multigenerational families on modern children, only to concede that, in 1935, "Aunt Clara is now the independent woman, well groomed, with a job and an apartment or room of her own."[26] A few years later, former Chicago china painter Dominic M. Campana (1871–1956) shared his memories of the days "When Grandma Painted China" with *Tribune* readers in 1941, when the Auditorium Building was being converted into the Chicago Service Men's Center during World War II. Recounting the "china painting fad" of the 1890s, when the Auditorium Tower's entire tenth, eleventh, and twelfth floors were occupied by china painting studios, including his, Campana noted, "Almost every woman in the city, the state, and perhaps the nation took up the hobby, and households that did not contain hand-painted china were rare. . . . China painting grew into a business whose proceeds were many million dollars a year." Campana spoke from personal experience; he was the founder of the D. M. Campana Art Co., selling his own line of mineral paints and china painting supplies, and publishing more than fifty instruction booklets.[27]

Despite the demise of the Atlan Ceramic Art Club, along with other formal clubs and societies in major American cities, china painting remained a popular hobby, particularly among women in small towns, where the naturalistic style of decoration still prevailed in hobby shows and county fairs. In many circles, attitudes had not changed much since 1905, when one *Keramic Studio* reader proclaimed conventional work "a god-send to people who are not capable of making an interesting and artistic arrangement of flowers, fruits, & c., in the naturalistic."[28] Conventional designs continued to appear on porcelain, with designs becoming increasingly simplified and stylized, moving toward the totally abstract, geometrical motifs that complemented Modernistic and Art Deco–style home furnishings. Naturalistic motifs, which required far less planning, precision, time, and skill—less *patience* and *persistence* in Atlan Club parlance—were preferred by hobbyists, who soon outnumbered professionals working in commercial studios. Many carry on the tradition of painters like Franz B. Aulich and Franz A. Bischoff, who maintained studios in Chicago at the turn of the century.[29]

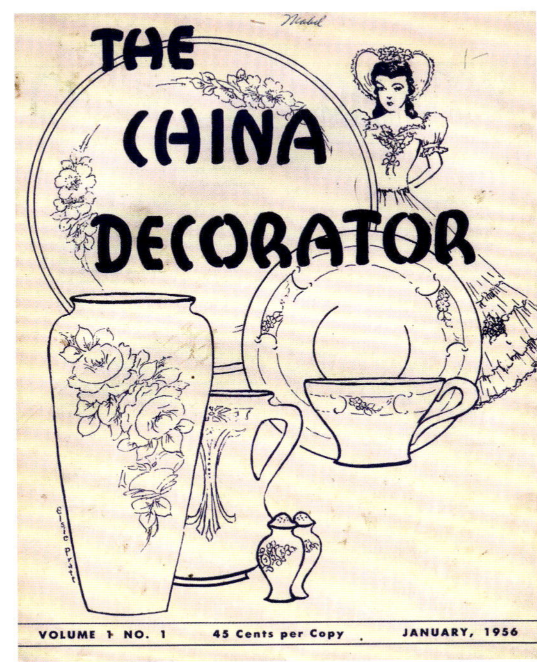

18.7 The first monthly issue of the *China Decorator* was published in January 1956 by Nettie E. Pillét of Pasadena, California. Purchased by Gladys Burbank Nelson and her husband in the 1960s, the magazine was last issued in 2018. *China Decorator* 1, no. 1 (January 1956). *Photo*: Author's collection.

After World War II, china painting experienced a renaissance in the United States, particularly in the 1960s and 1970s. Nettie E. Pillét, who had worked as a decorator in a California pottery, played an instrumental role in revitalizing china painting when she published *China Painting*, an updated instruction manual for painting overglaze, in 1954. She was a youthful seventy-nine when she began publishing the *China Decorator* in 1956.[30] Modeled after the *China Decorator* of the Victorian era, the monthly magazine offered studies and articles for the beginning china painter as well as the seasoned artist. In 1959, the National China Painting Teachers Organization was formed in Dallas, Texas; this group later became the International Porcelain Artists and Teachers (IPAT).[31] Oklahoman Pauline Salyer, who took up china painting as a hobby in the 1940s, wrote and published her first book, *The Great Artists of China Decoration*, in 1967, the same year that she founded the World Organization of China Painters and began publishing the *China Painter*.[32]

National attention peaked in 1979 when Judy Chicago's multimedia exhibition "The Dinner Party" toured the United States; its massive ceremonial banquet, featuring thirty-nine china-painted porcelain plates, each commemorating a notable woman, became an important icon of feminist art.[33] After persistent lobbying from American china painters, President Jimmy Carter signed a proclamation declaring china painting a fine art in January 1980. The 96th Congress also designated July as "National Porcelain Art Month."[34]

Today, porcelain painters and clubs remain active in the United States, as well as internationally, where, ironically, the naturalistic style of overglaze decoration is called "the American style" by many contemporary china painters. The nonprofit World Organization of China Painters, whose membership includes artists and clubs in the United States and Japan, maintains a museum of porcelain art in Oklahoma City, Oklahoma, and publishes the *China Painter*, a quarterly magazine.[35] Similarly, IPAT (International Porcelain Arts and Teachers, Inc.), founded in 1958, operates a museum at its headquarters in Grapevine, Texas; sponsors conventions; publishes *Porcelain Artist*; and offers virtual lessons via home computer.[36]

Virtual lessons and workshops are available through Porcelain Painters International Online and numerous self-made YouTube videos. Colorful images of porcelain with overglaze decoration, antique as well as modern, are featured on "pinboards" in Pinterest, an image-sharing social media service; some even feature work, colloquially called "American Satsuma," decorated by members of the Atlan Ceramic Art Club.

As one of the county's premier china painting enterprises, the Atlan Ceramic Art Club acquired a national reputation and maintained its high standards for thirty years. Under Florence Steward's tireless leadership, the club never wavered from its commitment to raising the overall artistic standards of china painting and succeeded in introducing and promoting a new form of conventionalized overglaze porcelain decoration in America.

Atlan Club women also served as role models for aspiring china painters. Their skillful application of historic ornament to modern porcelain shapes—radical and "modern" at the time—encouraged experimentation, while their insistence upon technical excellence demonstrated the value and rewards inherent in perfecting one's proficiency in painting and design.

For many women, china painting provided the artistic and management skills needed to become successful ceramists and businesswomen; for others, it was a bridge to work as interior decorators in the 1920s and 1930s, when European-influenced modernism prevailed, or to participate in the studio ceramics movement in America in the early 1940s.

Although the Atlan Ceramic Art Club's utopian dream that conventional ornament would be adopted as a national style was never realized, its members succeeded in establishing the style and its appropriateness on ceramic forms as a new art medium for the American Arts and Crafts movement.

The women achieved their goal, recorded by Florence Steward in 1902, "to win a first place, as a Club among associated Artists, and deserving to be named as pioneers who blazed the path and painted the way for recognition, and as American Ceramic Painters, to attain the coveted place where artists who use mineral color and enamel shall be given an important place in American history of ornament."[37]

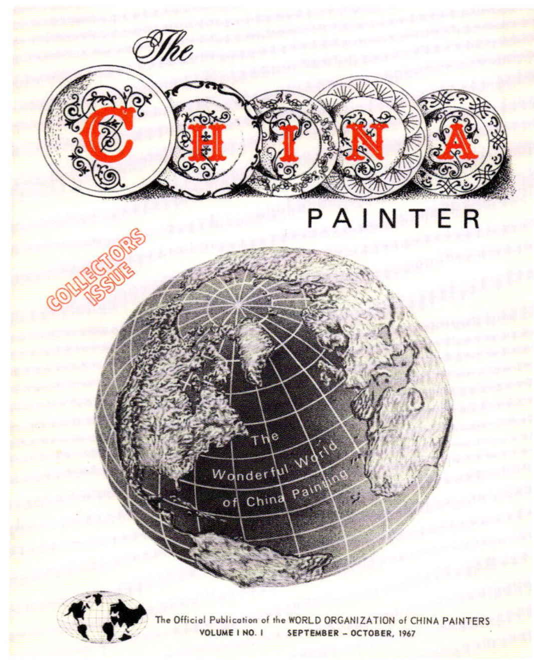

18.8 *The China Painter*, the official publication of the World Organization of China Painters, was edited by Pauline Salyer when first issued in September 1967. She remained editor and publisher until her death in 1991. It is now a quarterly publication. *China Painter* 1, no. 1 (September–October 1967). *Photo*: Author's collection.

Appendix 1

Members of the Atlan Ceramic Art Club, 1893–1922

Abercrombie, Anna M. Hays, 1907–1911
Kentucky-born Anna M. Hays (1863–1924) married jeweler and watchmaker Charles B. Abercrombie in Denver, Colorado, in 1890. In 1897, the couple moved to Chicago, where Charles operated a retail jewelry store. In addition to annual Atlan Club exhibitions, she participated with the club in Arts and Crafts exhibitions, 1907–1910. She was still listed among "active" members contributing to the Art Institute's Atlan Fund in 1912. It appears that Anna dropped out of the Atlan Club shortly after her father, widowed brother, and his three children came to live with the family around 1910. She was also a member of the Chicago Ceramic Art Association.

Adams, Eva E.: *see* Eva Eliza Adams biography, p. 16.

Alden, Mary Emmons, 1901–1907
Mary Emmons Alden (1858–1934) came to Chicago with her widowed mother in the 1890s from Little Falls, New York. After joining the Atlan Club in December 1900, she exhibited with the club, 1901–1907, as well as in the 1902, 1906, and 1907 Chicago Arts and Crafts exhibitions. She was also a member of the National League of Mineral Painters and the Chicago Ceramic Art Association, serving as historian of the latter, 1900–1901. After 1908, Mary lived with the family of her sister, who had married a wealthy Chicago businessman, and spent summers at the family farm in Oneonta, New York. She was still listed among "active" members contributing to the Art Institute's Atlan Fund in 1912.

Allfree, Esther L., 1916–1918
Esther L. Allfree (1876–1958) accompanied her parents to Chicago from Indianapolis, Indiana, in 1905. She operated a china painting studio in New Orleans, Louisiana, between 1912 and 1915, winning third prize for Conventional Ornament in Burley & Co.'s 1913 Chicago exhibition (*Keramic Studio*, 15 [December 1913]). Returning to Chicago in 1916, she joined the Atlan Club. She married widower Franz A. Berger, a mechanical engineering professor at Washington University in St. Louis, Missouri, in the mid-1920s. The couple maintained "a hospitable artistic home" in suburban University City (Hazel May M, Kendall, *Descendants of William Gregg* [Anderson, IN: self-published 1944], 202). https://archive.org/details/thisbookrecordsdookend. She is listed in *Who Was Who in American Art 1564–1975: 400 Years of Artists in America* (1999).

Alschuler, Mae B. Beckenheimer, 1922
Daughter of a wealthy Pana, Illinois, coal operator, Mae B. Beckenheimer (1883–1965), "a leading social belle of Pana," studied at the Art Institute of Chicago and was also a proficient musician. In 1906, she married Waukegan clothing manufacturer Clarence S. Alschuler. Mae exhibited her paintings in the Lake County Art League (1939), All-Illinois exhibition of Artist Members (1946), and the Chicago No-Jury Art Society of Artists (1951).

Anderson, Louise Compton, 1893–1896
A founding member, Louise Compton Anderson (1858–1925) left Oconomowoc, Wisconsin, with her sister, Emma Anderson Kittredge, in 1891 to open a china decorating studio in Chicago's Auditorium Building. In 1893, her work was exhibited in the Woman's and Illinois Buildings at the Chicago World's Fair. By 1894, Anderson was manufacturing her own enamels and gold paint; by 1895, she was making unique items of wood and leather "decorated with fire etching" (i.e., pyrography). In 1897, she was a charter member of the Chicago Arts and Crafts Society. After 1898, she worked in the Tree Studio Building, sharing a studio with her niece, craftworker Jeannette Kittredge. Her work was exhibited in Arts and Crafts exhibitions in Rockford and Boston, as well as in Chicago.

Anderson, M. Teresa: *see* Naper, Teresa Margaret Anderson.

Atchison, Grace Relyea Abeel, 1904
Born in Ft. Scott, Kansas, Grace Relyea Abeel (1871–1930) was an 1895 graduate of the Chicago Art Institute. She married Chicago architect John Danley Atchison in 1900. In 1905, the couple moved to Winnipeg, where John introduced innovative Chicago School of Architecture

ideas to the architecture of western Canada. They moved to Pasadena, California, in 1924, where Grace was active in the First Presbyterian Church, Shakespeare club, and Browning Society.

Ayer, Winnona North Whitaker, 1917–1922
Winnona North Whitaker (1887–1977), daughter of a Chicago livestock buyer, married salesman Alvin Clarence Ayer in 1914. She served as second vice president of the Atlan Club in 1919. Divorced in the mid-1920s, she resumed her maiden name. In the 1930s, as art chairperson of the Morgan Park Woman's Club, Whitaker organized its annual exhibitions. In January 1947, she moved to Woodstock, Vermont, where she lived until her death at age 90.

Baird, Marie "Nannie" B. Northcutt, 1902–1903
A nonresident member, Marie "Nannie" B. Northcutt (1857–1930) was a founder and the first president of the Kansas City Keramic Club in 1899; she was elected to a third term in 1901. She exhibited with the Atlan Club in the 1902 and 1903 Chicago Arts and Crafts exhibitions. Born in Kentucky, Nannie moved to Kansas City, Missouri, around 1880 with her husband, William G. Baird, a successful real estate dealer. Baird's china painting studio was located on Troost Avenue (*Kansas City Star*, October 3, 1911).

Band, Minna "Minnie" Katharina Henriette, 1918–1922
Chicagoan Minna "Minnie" Katharina Henriette Band (1881–1962) lived with her parents before keeping house for her unmarried siblings in Chicago and later in Evanston, Illinois.

Banner, Sheila Little, 1922
Sheila Little Banner (1888–1980), a resident of Hammond, Indiana, was an Atlan Club councilor when she exhibited with the club in 1922. Married to William J. Banner Jr., a salesman for meatpacker Swift & Co., she was active in the Hammond Woman's Club, 1921–1923, before the family moved to Los Angeles, California.

Barothy, Frances Alice Nessling: *see* Frances Alice Nessling Barothy biography, p. 108.

Berglund, Emma Amanda Lindquist: *see* Emma Amanda Lindquist Berglund biography, p. 102.

Bidwell, Alice Lorena Phoenix, 1921–1922
Chicagoan Alice Lorena Phoenix (1882–1950) married Charles W. Bidwell, manager of Favor, Ruhl & Co., an art supply company, in 1918. She exhibited paintings with the Illinois Women's Painters, Artists of Chicago and Vicinity, and South Side Arts Association in the 1920s and 1930s. She was employed as a Christian Science Practitioner in 1950, according to the federal census.

Bigelow, Madge Lualyce Secreste, 1908
A graduate of the Chicago Art Institute, Madge Lualyce Secreste (1879–1966) had a studio in the Auditorium Tower by 1904. She married William Frederick Bigelow at the Berwyn, Illinois, home of her sister, Elva Bell Secreste Harner, in June 1908. The couple was living in Minneapolis, Minnesota, when she exhibited with the Atlan Club in the 1908 Chicago Arts and Crafts exhibition. An avid golfer, Bigelow served as president of the Women's Golf Association of Minnesota from 1920 to 1924; in 1921, she was reportedly the first woman golfer in Minnesota to score a hole-in-one. Her final years were spent in Indianapolis, Indiana.

Blair, Margaret, 1922
Margaret Blair was a resident of Cleveland, Ohio, when she exhibited three vases in the 1922 exhibition.

Blodgett, Caroline Wygant, 1908–1911
Missouri-born Caroline Wygant Blodgett (1874–1959) was brought to Chicago, where her father became a merchant and Street Railway official, in 1880. She was listed as an artist in the Atheneum Building in Chicago city directories in 1909 and as a china decorator in the 1910 census. In 1912, Caroline, her mother, and three sisters spent the summer in England and France. Around 1915, she relocated to Duxbury, Massachusetts, where, in 1921, she married James W. Hastings; divorced by 1933, she resumed her maiden name.

Blomquist, Ruth Anna, 1911–1912
Born in Chicago of Swedish parents, Ruth Anna Blomquist (1889–1980) lived with her parents in Chicago, Berwyn, and then St. Charles, Illinois, where she exhibited her work in the "Made in St. Charles" exhibition in 1916. After marrying Frank Reuben Johnson in 1917, she lived in Geneva, Illinois, where her husband owned the Globe Music Company, a manufacturer of guitars and other string instruments. Later, they moved to St. Charles, where he was employed by the Howell Co., a manufacturer of furniture and kitchen cabinets. She lived in St. Charles until her death at age ninety-one.

Brunemeyer, May E., 1907–1919
Born in Aurora, Illinois, May E. Brunemeyer (1884–1936) was a graduate of the Art Institute of Chicago. After marrying salesman Paul Gus Hoelscher in 1909, she taught china painting in a home studio in Elgin, Illinois. As May Hoelscher, at least fifteen of her designs were published in *Keramic Studio* between 1913 and 1918. After moving to Aurora around 1917, May continued working as an artist and served as an Atlan councilor in 1918; she was operating an art shop in downtown Aurora in 1932. Her *Chicago Tribune* obituary described her as a "well known artist" who was a member of the American Federation of Artists, Rocky Mountain Art club, and Smoky Hill Art Club of Kansas. She is listed as May B. Hoelscher, painter of landscapes and flowers, in Chris Petteys, *Dictionary of Women Artists. An International Directory of Women Artists Born Before 1900* (Boston, MA: G. K. Hall, 1985), 342.

Butler, Maud Franklin Daggett, 1907–1914
Born in Chicago, Maud Franklin Daggett (1880–1948) married insurance executive John F. Butler in 1908. While living in suburban Wheaton, she served as its city treasurer and was active in the Wheaton Woman's Club, DAR, and First Presbyterian Church. In 1918, she applied for a passport to travel to France to serve with the American Red Cross. She was sixty-seven when she died in Wheaton, Illinois.

Clarke, Maud Cathleen Powers, 1909–1911
Wisconsin-born Maud Cathleen Powers (1872–1938) married Chicago salesman Harry Hale Clarke in 1902. In addition to exhibiting her work in the Atlan Club's annual exhibitions, she exhibited pieces painted by her, but designed by Florence Steward, in the Chicago Arts and Crafts exhibitions, 1909–1911. The couple lived in Chicago until the early 1930s, when they retired to St. Petersburg, Florida.

Coffman, Genevieve Virginia Southard, 1903
A nonresident member, Genevieve Virginia Southard (1866–1958), one of the founders of the Kansas City Keramic Club, exhibited with the Atlan Club in 1903. Born in Knox County, Illinois, she married Kansas rancher Charles A. Coffman, head cattle buyer for Swift & Co., in 1885.

Cole, Lucy "Lillie" Elizabeth: *see* Lucy "Lillie" Elizabeth Cole biography, p. 23.

Cooper, Helen Gertrude, 1908–1910
Chicagoan Helen Gertrude Cooper (1887–1967) was listed as a china decorator in the 1910 federal census. She also exhibited her work in Chicago Arts & Crafts exhibitions, 1908–1910. After marrying George Washington Clark in June 1911, she raised her family in River Forest, Illinois.

Coulter, Mary Jenks, 1905–1908
Born in Kentucky, Mary Jenks (1882–1966) attended the Cincinnati Art Academy and graduated from the School of the Art Institute of Chicago. After marrying Frederick J. Coulter in Newport, Kentucky, in 1901, she moved to Evanston, Illinois, where she taught china painting. In 1904–1905, she was the president of the Chicago Ceramic Art Association and often exhibited with the National League of Mineral Painters. She won a silver medal for pottery and overglaze at the Lewis and Clark Exposition, Portland, Oregon, in 1905, and the Atlan Club Prize at the Chicago Arts and Crafts exhibition in 1909. She advertised classes in metalworking as well as porcelain in the 1906 Atlan Club exhibition catalog. Around 1915, the Coulters moved to San Francisco, California; she served as chairperson of the American Arts and Crafts jury for the Panama-Pacific International Exposition, where she exhibited porcelain, jewelry, and textiles. Divorced from Coulter in the 1920s, she lived in Santa Barbara until marrying Amherst professor Orton L. Clark in 1953. She then divided her time between California and New England.

Crane, Anna Barnes, 1897–1900
Daughter of a Laporte, Indiana, dry goods merchant, Anna Barnes (1861–1932) married William J. Crane in in 1882. When she exhibited her decorated china in 1891, the *South Bend Tribune* (September 22) claimed Anna "studied in the best schools of this country, in New York City, Buffalo and elsewhere, and since following the profession has kept up with the latest styles in decoration." Widowed in 1892, she moved to Chicago, where she taught china painting in the Auditorium Tower. The *Chicago Chronicle* (December 7, 1897) noted, "Mrs. Anna Barnes Crane has some beautiful specimens of original glazed work in the dark green and browns. It is called "Annaswood" by her studio friends." The *Art Interchange* (December 1899) called her the best china painter in Chicago in "the handling of dark color, Rookwood and monotone, fruit studies and designs of flowers." She was also an active member of the Chicago Ceramic Association. In 1910 she taught china painting in LaPorte but returned to Chicago by 1914. Anna and a daughter moved to California in 1926.

Cremer, Adelaide Belle Mark, 1911
Born in Iowa, Adelaide "Ada" Belle Mark (1869 to after 1910) married salesman Harry L. Cremer in Ringgold, Iowa, in 1892 and moved to Chicago in 1896. The 1910 federal census shows Adelaide and her husband living in Chicago; however, only her husband, listed as a married lodger, appeared in records thereafter through 1951.

Cross, Nellie Agnes Maguire, 1894–1900
Daughter of an Irish plumber, Nellie Agnes Maguire (1858–1923) was listed as an artist in the *Chicago City Directory*, 1878–1882, and after she married salesman Richard Watson Cross in 1883. In 1893–1896, when she shared a studio in the Auditorium Tower with the Anderson sisters (Louise and Emma Kittredge), followed by Helen F. Frazee, she was known for enameling glassware "marvelously like the imported ware from France and Germany" as well as decorated porcelain. Her glassware was exhibited in the Woman's Building at the 1893 World's Fair. Her decorated china was included in the Atlan Club's 1900 Paris exhibition. She was the president of the Chicago Ceramic Art Association in 1899 and 1902 and served as exhibition chairperson for the National League of Mineral Painters. By 1905, she and her sons were exhibiting Crossware Pottery, featuring hand-turned pottery and tiles with semi-matte glazes, made at their home in the Rogers Park neighborhood.

Daily, Eleanor Rose Benson, 1908–1911
Born in Cincinnati, Ohio, Eleanor Rose Benson (1875–1960) married advertising executive Charles Thomas Daily in 1895 in San Francisco, California, where her father was an olive grower, and moved to Chicago by 1900. Daily was also active in the Arché Club and the Colonial Club, social clubs for women on Chicago's South Side. In 1935, the couple moved to Wilmette, Illinois, where she lived until her death in 1960.

Dibble, Mabel C.: *see* Mabel Caroline Dibble biography, p. 47.

Dickson, Elizabeth Grieve Oliver, 1922
Elizabeth Grieve Oliver (1866–1950) married Scottish physician William Ferguson Dickson in Ontario, Canada, in 1890. In 1893 they moved to Chicago, where Dr. Dickson practiced medicine for fifty years. The family was living on Kimbark Avenue in 1922.

Dunham, Edna Alice Dunbar Jack: *see* Jack, Edna Alice Dunbar.

Dunne, Linda Chase Fox, 1907–1922
Chicagoan Linda Chase Fox (1865–1943) graduated from St. Mary's Academy in South Bend, Indiana, in 1883. She married railroad agent George R. Dunne, a widower with two children, in 1899 and moved to suburban LaGrange. After Dunne's death in 1903, she was a self-employed ceramic artist; she served as an Atlan councilor in 1910. In October 1914, the *Idaho Daily Statesman* reported that she gave a lecture

explaining the Atlan Club's conventional design techniques while visiting her stepdaughter Georgina Dunne in Boise, Idaho. After marrying widower Frank E. Sanford, former superintendent of La Grange public schools, in 1917, she moved to Chicago, where Sanford was an editor and publisher.

Dutcher, Anna Mary Hopkins, 1910–1911
A nonresident member, Anna Mary Hopkins (1851–1924) was born in New York but raised in St. Louis, Missouri. After graduating from Webster College in Oxford, Ohio, she was a schoolteacher in St. Louis in 1883, when she married grain inspector Clinton O. Dutcher. Described as a "wonderfully skillful artist" by the *St. Louis Post-Dispatch*, she exhibited portraits on porcelain and glassware at St. Louis expositions in the 1890s. In 1897, she received honorable mention for notable gold and raised paste work at a national china decorating contest held in Buffalo, New York. She was listed as an artist, working in a home studio, in the St. Louis city directories, 1899–1904. After her husband's death in 1903, she moved to New York City, where she was living when she exhibited with the Atlan Club in 1910 and 1911. In 1916, while living in Lincoln, Nebraska, she won third prize at the Burley & Co. exhibition. She died in White Plains, New York.

Eichling, Elva Johanna Bryant: *see* Elva Johanna Bryant Eichling biography, p. 103.

Emmons, Lulu Belle Elliott, 1907–1914
Born in LaGrange, Indiana, Lulu Belle Elliott (1868–1956) moved to Chicago after marrying salesman George Elwood Emmons in 1903. In 1914, she was an Atlan Club councilor. She was also active in the Chicago Ceramic Art Association, serving as corresponding secretary in 1917; in 1919, she won the association's prize for best individual exhibit; she also exhibited work in Burley & Co. exhibitions. Around 1923, Lulu moved to Lakeland, Florida, where she became chairperson of the fine arts department for the local women's club. She died in Florida, age eighty-eight.

Farr, Lillian G., 1911–1917
Born in Canada, Lillian G. Farr (ca. 1883 to after 1934) arrived in Chicago in 1902. In 1910, she was teaching china painting in Chicago while living with her mother, who kept a lodging house. In November 1911, Harriet Monroe, reviewing the Atlan Club exhibition for the *Chicago Tribune*, called Lillian's entries—a Satsuma teapot, gray-blue salad bowl, and relish dishes—"quite original in design." In 1913, Lillian visited England, returning via Canada. She was still considered a member in 1917, when her work was included in the Alan Club's twentieth anniversary traveling exhibition. By 1927, Lillian was a field worker for the Georgia Children's Home in Atlanta; in 1930, she was teaching in the Atlanta, Georgia, public schools. Returning to Canada, Farr was on the staff of the Vancouver Day Nursery until July 1934, when the *Vancouver Sun* announced that she was leaving "for New York where she will continue her social service research."

Foster, Marie Belle, 1893
A founding member, Marie Belle Foster (1873–1954) married salesman

Phone 437

MRS. GEORGE R. DUNNE

CERAMICS

329 South 7th Avenue

La Grange, Ill.

Exclusively Conventional Decorations

Class Days Tuesdays and Thursdays

Source: *Catalog of the Twenty-Third Annual Exhibition of the Atlan Ceramic Art Club* (Chicago: Art Institute of Chicago, 1915).

MRS. B. L. FRAZER

1344 Jackson Boulevard

Classes in China Painting
and Water Colors
Conventional Work a Specialty

CLASSES
TUESDAY and FRIDAYS

Source: *Catalogue of the Eight Exhibition of the Atlan Ceramic Art Club* (Chicago: Art Institute of Chicago, 1900).

Albert Lincoln Tucker in November 1893. The couple was living in Oak Park, Illinois, in 1896.

Frazee, Helen Inez Fenton: *see* Helen Inez Fenton Frazee biography, p. 89.

Frazer, Beulah Louise Wolcott, 1898–1908
Born in Galena, Illinois, Beulah Louise Wolcott (1859–1938) married railroad rate clerk William Edward Frazer in Chicago in 1878. Her work was included in the Atlan Club's exhibition with the Chicago Arts and Crafts Society in 1898. Widowed in 1899, she was listed as an "artist" in census records, 1900–1920. Frazer advertised china painting lessons in Atlan catalogs beginning in 1900; she served as a club councilor in 1905–1907. She exhibited with the Atlan Club in Chicago Arts and Crafts exhibitions in 1902, 1906, and 1907; at the St. Louis World's Fair, 1904; and in Richmond, Indiana, 1907. Her design for a plate (misattributed to Helen Frazee) was published in *Keramic Studio* in April 1901. She was an active member of the Chicago Ceramic Art Association.

Freytag, Henrietta Marie Metz, 1918–1922
Henrietta Marie Metz (1898 to after 1931) moved to Chicago after marrying stockbroker Harry Charles Freytag at her parents' home in Kansas City, Missouri, in 1916. She served as the Atlan Club's secretary in 1919. Divorced by 1923, she married Chicago auto salesman Julius Dean Browning in 1924. She was a Chicago resident when widowed in 1931.

Fuller, Lura Ward, 1902–1903
A nonresident member, Lura Ward (1878–1943), a graduate of the

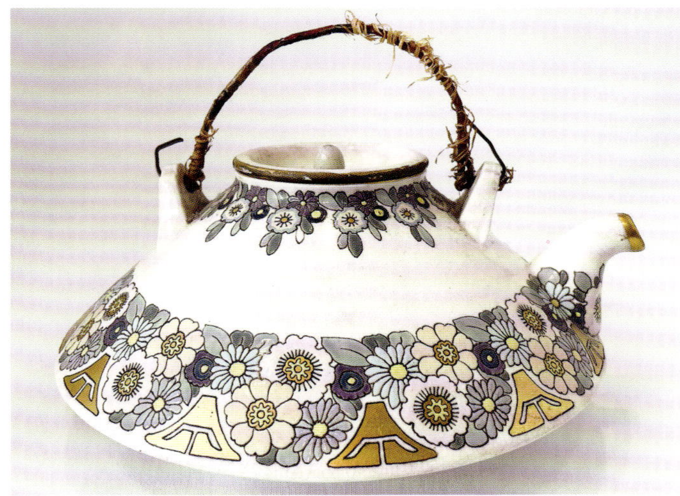

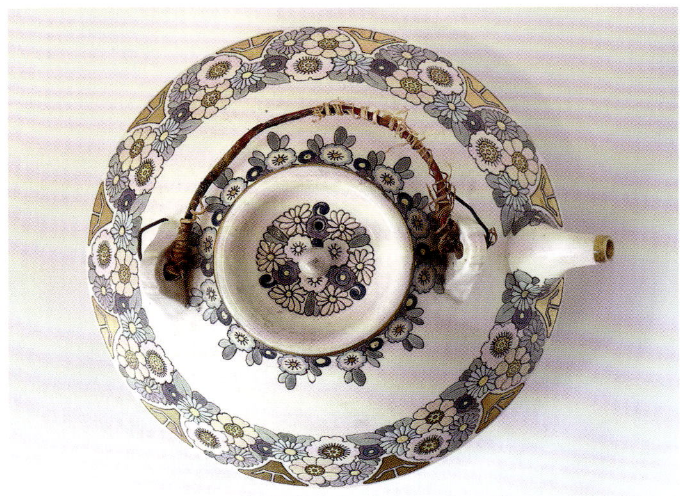

Satsuma teapot painted by associate member Henrietta M. Freytag, 1916. Signed: Henrietta M. Freytag/'16. (6¼" × 4½") *Photo*: Private collection.

Kansas City Art Institute and School of Design, was teaching ceramic art in 1901 when she married wholesale jeweler Noble R. Fuller. In 1902, as a member of the Kansas City Porcelain and Pottery Club, she studied with Florence Koehler. She exhibited with the Atlan Club in the Arts and Crafts exhibition at the Chicago Art Institute in 1902 and 1903. After 1904, she exhibited with the Arts and Crafts Society of Kansas City and in various regional exhibitions, showing jewelry in 1908. By 1933, she was showing work in three mediums, including batik, in Kansas City Society of Artists and Boston Society of Arts and Crafts exhibitions.

Gale, Grace Anna Cosgrove, 1914–1922

After attending the University of Minnesota and studying two years at the Pratt Institute, Grace Anna Cosgrove (1876–1960) was a teacher when she married Chicago railroad accountant Charles Albert Gale at her parent's home in Le Sueur, Minnesota, in 1903. The couple lived in Evanston, Illinois, from 1904 until 1949, when they moved to Jackson, Tennessee. Grace was an Atlan councilor in 1922. In September

Mrs. Miriam M. Gleason

115 East Aurora, New York

TEACHER and DECORATOR

All Styles of Conventional designs Executed in flat-enamels and colored golds.

BUFFALO and EAST AURORA, N. Y.

Source: *Catalog of the Twenty-Ninth Annual Exhibition of the Atlan Ceramic Art Club* (Chicago: Art Institute of Chicago, 1921).

1914, she exhibited "some very good decorations" in the Burley's annual exhibition, according to the *Evanston Index*. In the 1920s, she showed hand-painted china in exhibitions sponsored by the Evanston Woman's Club.

Gerard, Laura S. Simonson, 1902–1903

Laura S. Simonson (1866–1954), a resident of Kansas City, Missouri, married grocer Mark E. Gerard in 1888. As a member of the Kansas City Porcelain and Pottery Club, she exhibited with the Atlan Club in the Chicago Arts and Crafts exhibitions in 1902 and 1903.

Gleason, Miriam Mendenhall Baker, 1918–1922

Miriam Mendenhall Baker (1867–1955) married U.S. Army captain Willard E. Gleason in Van Wert, Ohio, in 1892. Widowed in 1903, she moved to Chicago, where she taught china painting. She joined the Buffalo Society of Mineral Painters in 1921, while living with her daughter in East Aurora, New York. That year, she included a hammered copper bowl made in East Aurora at the Roycroft Shops as an exhibition entry. In 1922, she was teaching china painting in Chicago and Hammond, Indiana, as well as in East Aurora and Buffalo, New York. She later lived in Erie, New York, and Butler, Pennsylvania, where she died, age eighty-seven.

Gray, Nellie J. Johnson, 1922

Nellie J. Johnson (1877–1946), a resident of Minneapolis, Minnesota, married Roland Alexander Gray in 1902. She was the vice president of the Minneapolis Keramic Art Club in 1919 and was considered a "distinguished" china artist in the 1920s. The Grays moved to Oakland, California, around 1939.

Greenleaf, Nellie Louise DeGolyer, 1893–1896

A founding member, Nellie Louise DeGolyer (1864–1900), daughter of a prominent varnish manufacturer, grew up in Riverside, Illinois. She attended Lake Forest University before studying at Smith College in 1884; she studied art in Europe between 1887 and 1889. Nellie married musician Walter Gregory Greenleaf in 1891. A talented artist who excelled in "figure work" and portrait painting, she had a studio in Chicago's Venetian Building in 1892; her porcelain was exhibited

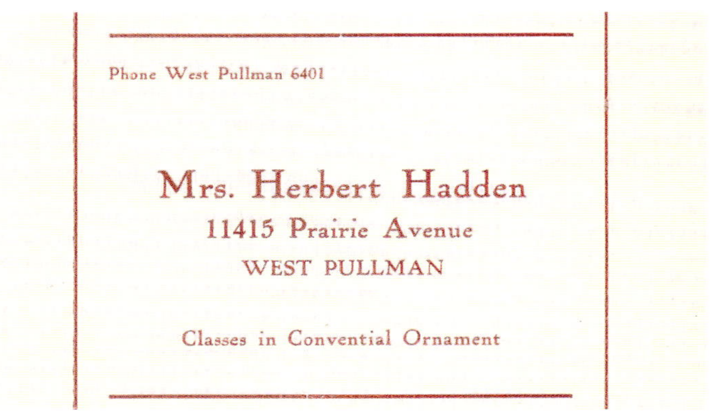
Phone West Pullman 6401

Mrs. Herbert Hadden
11415 Prairie Avenue
WEST PULLMAN

Classes in Convential Ornament

Source: *Catalog of the Twenty-First Annual Exhibition of the Atlan Ceramic Art Club Catalog* (Chicago: Art Institute of Chicago, 1913).

in the Illinois and Woman's Buildings at the Chicago World's Fair in 1893. In 1897, when her husband was appointed the manager of the Montezuma Hotel at a hot springs resort, the family moved to Las Vegas, New Mexico. In 1900, she became ill and died there, leaving two small children.

Hadden, Lydia Mary Erffmeyer, 1907–1916
Born in Schenectady, New York, of German parents, Lydia Mary Erffmeyer (1875–1954) married Herbert D. Hadden in Chicago in 1893. She was an Atlan councilor in 1912 and treasurer in 1916. She advertised classes in conventional ornament in her West Pullman home in the club's 1913 catalog. Her cake plate won second prize in the conventional class in the 1915 Burley & Co. exhibition. In 1916, the *Chicago Daily Tribune* critic reviewing the Atlan Club's exhibition, remarked: "Mrs. Herbert Hadden's list is so diversified and so delightfully handled that it is quite difficu t to select the best." During the 1920s, she worked as an interior decorator from her studio in the Fine Arts Building.

Hall, Mrs. S. N., 1915
Mrs. S. N. Hall was a resident of Oak Park, Illinois, in 1915.

Harner, Elva Bell Secreste, 1904, 1907–1917
Born in Ohio, Elva Bell Secreste (1873–1958) married George Warde Harner in Baltimore, Maryland, in 1900. The couple moved to Chicago, where they lived in the Woodlawn district, before moving to Berwyn, Illinois, in 1904. There, Elva taught classes in ceramics and leather work in "The Cottage Studio" she maintained in her home. She served as an Atlan councilor in 1909, 1911, and 1915 and exhibited in Chicago Arts and Crafts exhibitions between 1907 and 1915. The couple moved to Minneapolis, Minnesota, around 1918 but returned to Berwyn by 1930. According to the 1930 census, she was employed as a Christian Science Practitioner. She was the sister of Madge Secreste Bigelow.

Hewen, Sarah Celestia, 1912–1917
Sarah Celestia Hewen (1889–1974) was the club's second vice president in 1915. Born in Milwaukee, Wisconsin, she came to Chicago with her parents in the 1890s. In 1912, the Chicago *Inter Ocean* called out her work as "worthy of attention" in the Atlan Club exhibition; in 1913, she

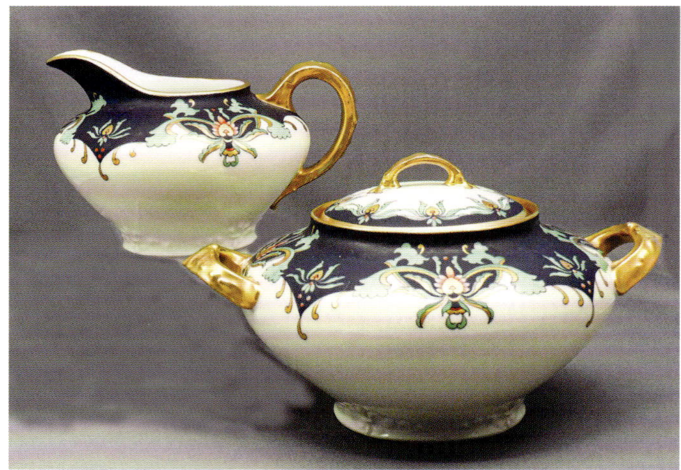

Creamer and sugar bowl, Elva Bell Secreste Harner, 1904–1917. The motif for this set was inspired by a design by Edith H. Loucks published in the December 1902 issue of *Keramic Studio*. Harner operated "The Cottage Studio" in her home in Berwyn, Illinois, 1904–1917. Signed: "The Cottage Studio/Berwyn, Ill." Mark: GDA/Limoges. (sugar bowl: 4¼" × 6¾"; creamer: 4¼" × 5¼") *Photo*: Dark Flowers Antiques.

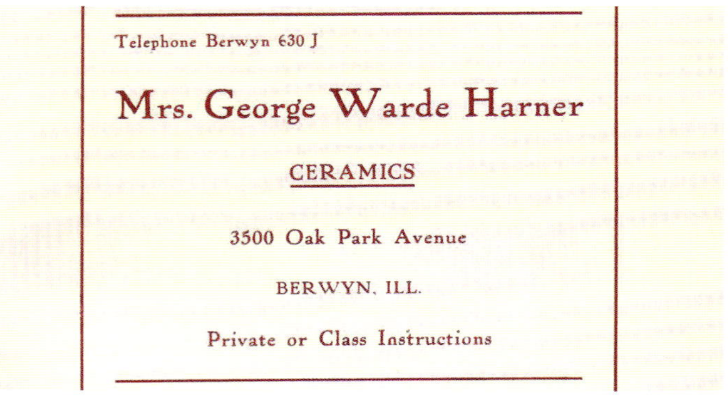
Telephone Berwyn 630 J

Mrs. George Warde Harner

CERAMICS

3500 Oak Park Avenue

BERWYN, ILL.

Private or Class Instructions

Source: *Catalog of the Twenty-Third Annual Exhibition of the Atlan Ceramic Art Club* (Chicago: Art Institute of Chicago, 1915).

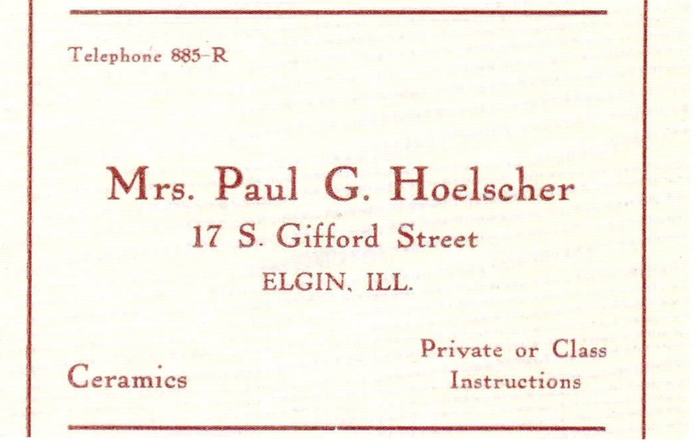
Telephone 885-R

Mrs. Paul G. Hoelscher
17 S. Gifford Street
ELGIN, ILL.

Ceramics

Private or Class Instructions

Source: *Catalog of the Twenty-First Annual exhibition of the Atlan Ceramic Art Club Catalog* (Chicago: Art Institute of Chicago, 1913).

won second prize for conventional china at Burley & Co.'s exhibition. She married wholesale grocer Grover Cleveland Wilson in September 1916; as Mrs. Grover C. Wilson, she was the Atlan Club's vice president in 1917. The couple moved to Evanston, Illinois, in the 1920s.

Hoelscher, May E. Brunemeyer: *see* Brunemeyer, May E.

Holtgreve, Fay T. Titchner, 1916–1917
The name of Fay T. Titchner (1884–1951) was misspelled "Tichenor" in the 1916 catalog. Fay was living in Chicago in 1916 when she married electrical engineer Charles Augustus Holtgreve. In 1920, they were living in Walla Walla, Washington. Daughter of a Bushnell, Illinois, barber, Fay was identified as Black in the 1900 federal census and as Mulatto in 1910. In 1930, she was a music teacher, listed in that year's census as White. She was working as an accountant in Portland, Oregon, when she died in 1951.

Hoyt, Josephine Dora Mitchell, 1893
Josephine Dora Mitchell (1844–1920) left her home in Bradford, New York, to marry Chicago fire insurance agent and banker Lucius Hoyt Jr. in 1870. Widowed in 1885, she lived with her son Thatcher, a steel and iron broker, and two servants in Chicago until her death in 1920.

Hubbard, Florence Gertrude Hill, 1910–1913
Born in Richmond, Indiana, Florence Gertrude Hill (1878–1977) married Chicago optician Dr. Charles Fayette Hubbard in 1897. A teacher of china painting, she served as secretary of the Atlan Club in 1911 and 1912. In the 1920s, she worked as an interior designer and lecturer and was active in a club that promoted the creation of a national park in the Indiana Dunes. She was working as a saleswoman in a Chicago department store in 1948 when she won the Walking Man contest on NBC's *Truth or Consequences* radio program; the plethora of prizes included a sedan, diamond jewelry, fur coat, kitchen appliances, furniture, a piano, a boat, and a trip to Hollywood. In November 1950, she was quoted in the *Chicago Tribune* as saying the contest publicity changed her life, driving her into seclusion. She was ninety-nine when she died in Dallas, Texas, in 1977.

Hulbert, Lylian Root, 1907–1912
Lylian Root Hulbert (1872–1959) was the second vice president of Atlan Club in 1911. That year, the *Chicago Tribune* (November 7, 1911) reviewer of the club's exhibition observed, "The most beautiful boxes are from Lillian [*sic*] Root Hulbert." A bowl and plate of her design were featured in the March 1911 *Keramic Studio*. Born in Kent, Ohio, Lylian taught painting classes in Waterloo, Iowa, before entering the Art Institute of Chicago in 1899 and graduating with a decorative design degree in 1914. She was listed among "active" members contributing to the Art Institute's Atlan Fund in 1912. The 1920 federal census lists her occupation as artist and decorative designer. When she applied for a passport in 1920, Hulbert gave her occupation as decorative designer and the reason for travel as art study in Italy, France, and England, 1920–1925. In 1942, returning from Scotland, she listed her home as Chicago. She was living with her widowed brother, a retired university teacher, in Fayetteville, Arkansas, when she died, age eighty-six, in 1959.

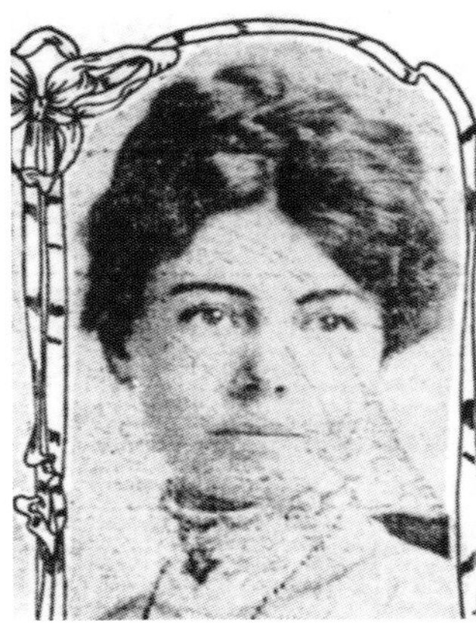

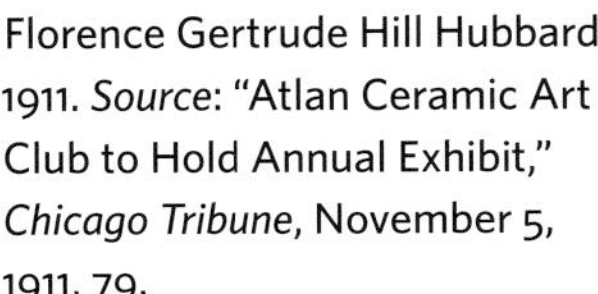

Florence Gertrude Hill Hubbard, 1911. *Source*: "Atlan Ceramic Art Club to Hold Annual Exhibit," *Chicago Tribune*, November 5, 1911, 79.

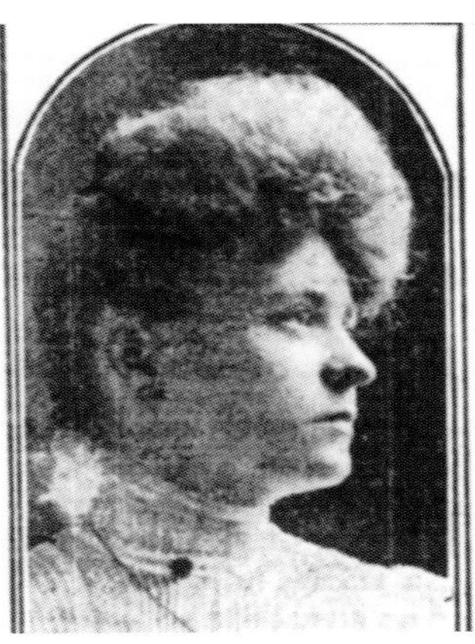

Edna Alice Dunbar Jack, 1905. *Source*: "Mrs. Harry T. Jack," *Chicago Tribune*, November 27, 1905, 5.

Humphrey, Mary H. Stevens: *see* Mary Helen Stevens Humphrey biography, p. 61.

Hutchcraft, Alma Belle Colson, 1916
Alma Belle Colson (1879–1965) married surgical instrument salesman Edward F. Hutchcraft in Indianapolis, Indiana, in 1903. They were residents of Wheaton, Illinois, when she exhibited with the Atlan Club.

Hutchinson, Emma Snyder, 1912–1921
Born in Ohio of Swiss parents, Emma Snyder (1856–1933) accompanied her family to Michigan City, Indiana, at age fourteen. In 1874, after studying music in Indianapolis, she married William B. Hutchinson, founder and president of Citizens Bank of Michigan City; he was elected an Indiana state senator in 1880. In 1886, the Hutchinson family spent a year in Europe, where she did considerable painting; in 1898, the family made a trip around the world. Widowed in 1908, she remained active in the arts and charitable causes in Michigan City. Her July 18, 1933, *Michigan City News* obituary noted that "besides having been a pianist of exceptional ability, she was an artist of note, her painting of china winning the admiration of many art critics and others. . . . The Atlan club and Colonial Coverlet guild of Chicago, of which she was a member, held some of their meetings at the Hutchinson home, and, whenever they met in Chicago, she was usually in attendance, for she was a life member of the Chicago Art Institute." Emma served as an Atlan Club councilor in 1916. She was a loyal member of the First Church of Christ, Scientist, in Michigan City.

Irons, Katharine R., 1904
Although her name does not appear in any extant exhibition catalogs, Katherine R. Irons (1875–1958) was a member in 1904, when she decorated a plate for the 12th annual exhibition, which did not take place. In 1909, Florence Steward's entry included a collection of Satsuma ware "selected in Japan by Miss Katherine Irons for this exhibition." Born in Deerpark, Orange County, New York, Katharine was the daughter

of a Scottish shoemaker who fought in the American Civil War. The family moved to Chicago in the 1890s. Katherine was a bookkeeper, 1900–1930, according to federal censuses. In 1911, Bessie B. Bennett exhibited three rings made for Katherine in the Art Craft Exhibition at the Art Institute of Chicago, alongside one made for Florence Steward. Katherine lived with family members in Oak Park in the 1930s and in Chicago after 1940.

Jack, Edna Alice Dunbar, 1907–1913
In 1900, at age nineteen, Michigan-born Edna Alice Dunbar (1880–1952) was "at school" in Chicago. She married optometrist Harry Tibbetts Jack in 1904, but the marriage was brief. Exhibiting as Mrs. Edna Dunbar Jack, she was the Atlan Club's secretary in 1910 and vice president in 1911. After marrying Chicago chemical engineer Frank S. Dunham in 1912, she served as Atlan treasurer in 1913. She also exhibited with the club in Arts and Crafts exhibitions sponsored by the Art Institute of Chicago.

Jones, Anna Louise Holmes, 1894–1908
Annie Louise Holmes (1866–1914) came to Chicago from St. Louis, Missouri, following her 1887 marriage to Edmund H. Jones, a dealer in building materials. She was active in social and charitable activities in the Hyde Park neighborhood of Chicago. She died at age forty-seven in 1914.

Jones, Ethel Clara Burgesser, 1913–1922
Chicagoan Ethel Clara Burgesser (1878–1926), an Art Institute of Chicago graduate, was listed as an "artist-painting" living with her parents in the 1900 federal census. No occupation was listed after she married furniture salesman Raymond A. Jones in 1904. She was the Atlan Club's secretary in 1914 and 1915. She was forty-seven when she died in Chicago.

Kelley, Beulah Madge Scott, 1922
Born in Ligonier, Indiana, Beulah Madge Scott (1885–1972) attended college in South Bend, Indiana, and worked as bookkeeper before marrying hometown sweetheart William Thomas Kelley in Chicago in 1913. She was a homemaker, while her husband was a shoe buyer, in 1920. The couple returned to Ligonier in the 1960s.

Kern, June Mabelle Hibbard, 1922
June Mabelle Hibbard (1897–1965) taught drawing in her hometown of Galesburg, Illinois, before marrying railroad locomotive engineer Frederick Milton Kern in 1912. In Chicago by 1920, she was an artist on her "own account" before teaching art in the Chicago public schools in the 1930s and 1940s. Back in Galesburg, Illinois, by 1950, June participated in exhibitions sponsored by the Civic Art League and was active in the garden club and horticultural society.

Killham, Carrie Ethel Frame, 1910–1911
Chicagoan Carrie Ethel Frame (1885–1968) married Benjamin J. Killham in 1906. She was the Atlan Club's treasurer in 1911. After her husband graduated from veterinary college in 1912, the couple moved to Kansas, where Dr. Killham was state veterinarian, and then to Michigan, where he was associated with Michigan State College for twenty years. She died in East Lansing, Michigan, at age eighty-two.

Kirchner, Alma Florence Pfau, 1910–1911
In 1905, Alma Florence Pfau (1880–1966), daughter of a Chicago realtor, married printer Julius C. Kirchner, later president of Kirchner-Meckel Co., commercial printers. The couple lived in the Belden-Stratford Hotel on Sheridan Road in the 1930s and 1940s. When her husband died in 1945, she became a wealthy widow, inheriting half of his $910,000 ($15 million today) estate. She died in Chicago at age eighty-five.

Kittredge, Emma Anderson, 1893
A founding member, Emma Anderson Kittredge (1851–1909) was the vice president of the Atlan Club in 1893 and secretary-treasurer in 1894. She was a divorcee with three daughters in 1889 when she left Oconomowoc, Wisconsin, to teach china painting in a Chicago studio shared with her sister Louise Anderson. She was among the founders of the Chicago Ceramic Association in 1892. Her work was exhibited in the Woman's Building at the 1893 Chicago World's Fair. By 1895, she had begun making "unique things of wood and leather decorated with fire etching" in addition to decorating china; in 1897, she was among the founders of the Chicago Arts and Crafts Society. Emma married Chicago paving contractor Duncan S. McBean in 1894; following his death, she married millionaire lumberman Charles Adams Goodyear in 1906. She was fifty-eight when she died in Chicago in 1909.

Krueger, Rose Belle Schmohl, 1913
The daughter of German parents who settled in St. Joseph, Missouri, Rose Belle Schmohl (1877–1954) was a milliner in Chicago in 1901 when she married dentist George Eugene Krueger. She was a homemaker in 1910. She and her husband died in Chicago within four days of each other in September 1954.

Kulp, Eolah A. Germain, 1917–1918
Eolah A. Germain (1885–1971) was living in Topeka, Kansas, when she married realtor Harley D. Kulp in 1912. The couple was living with Eolah's parents in Chicago in 1917–1918, when Eolah served as an Atlan Club councilor. When World War I ended, the couple moved to Ocean Springs, Mississippi; they moved back to Topeka around 1925.

LaBryn, Harriett May, 1915–1917
Harriet May LaBryn (1883–1957), daughter of a Dutch carpenter, was employed as a clerk in various Chicago offices after 1900. She moved to Evanston with her parents in 1927, where she lived until the late 1940s, when she moved to an apartment in Chicago.

Lathrop, Alice Laura Hinds, 1917–1921
Aurora, Illinois, homemaker Alice Laura Hinds (1875–1946) married William Brown Lathrop, a certified public accountant, in 1899. She lived in Aurora until her death in 1946.

Lawrence, Charlotte J. Wyllis, 1904–1906
Daughter of a prominent Marshalltown, Iowa, attorney, Charlotte J. Wyllis (1861–1923) took lessons in painting before she married James Averell Lawrence in 1883. While living in Evanston, Illinois, she divorced her unfaithful husband, a wealthy member of the Chicago Board of Trade, in 1903. Listed as an artist in the Evanston city directory in 1905,

MRS. ADELE V. LAWSON
No. 110 53rd Street
Class Days, Monday and Friday.

Source: *Catalogue of the Seventh Exhibition of the Atlan Ceramic Art Club* (Chicago: Art Institute of Chicago, 1899).

Lawrence served as an Atlan Club councilor in 1905 and 1906. She lived in Rockford, Illinois, from 1908 through 1916, when she moved to Pasadena, California.

Lawry, Mabel Irene Gordon, 1912–1916
Chicagoan Mable Irene Gordon (1884–1963) married civil engineer Raymond George Lawry in 1908. She lived in Chicago until widowed in 1949; she then lived with her son John's family in Boulder, Colorado, and later in Washington, DC.

Lawson, Adele M. Vestey, 1897–1899
Wisconsin-born Adele M. Vestey (1860–1952) married Norman Bryn Lawson in Muskegon, Michigan, in 1885. After moving to Chicago in the 1890s, she and her husband ran a photography studio. Adele also exhibited her work in Western Decorating Works exhibitions and with the Chicago Ceramic Association and National League of Mineral Painters. She advertised china painting lessons in Atlan Club catalogs in 1898 and 1899. Her work was included in the Atlan Club's Paris exhibition in 1900; by then, however, the couple had returned to Muskegon, Michigan. Adele died, age ninety-one, in Muskegon in 1952.

Letz, Rita Mull, 1917–1922
Rita Mull (1888–1969), daughter of a Hammond, Indiana, banker and labor leader, married railroad engineer Francis C. "Frank" Letz in 1908. She operated a china painting studio in Hammond from 1915 through 1929 and frequently lectured on china painting to local clubs; she served as an Atlan Club councilor in 1921. She had given up her studio by 1935, when she was appointed an old-age pension examiner for the Lake County Department of Public Welfare; during the 1940s, she was a well-known Hammond social worker. Active in the Hammond Woman's Club, she headed its art department in the 1950s.

Levedahl, Edith R., 1915–1919
Born in Illinois, Edith R. Levedahl (1884–1966) lived with her Swedish parents and later with a sister in Aurora, Illinois. Her father, an inventor and toolmaker, was one of the founders of the Independent Pneumatic Machinery Co. In 1904, she was an officer in the Epworth League, the youth organization of the Swedish Methodist Church. She died in Aurora at age eighty-one.

Liebolt, Adelaide Melinda, 1911–1917
The eighth of nine children of German parents (surname Liebold), Adelaide Melinda Liebolt (1883–1947) left Bellevue, Ohio, to attend the Art Institute of Chicago. In 1914, while serving as an Atlan Club councilor, she was listed as an artist in the *Chicago City Directory*; in

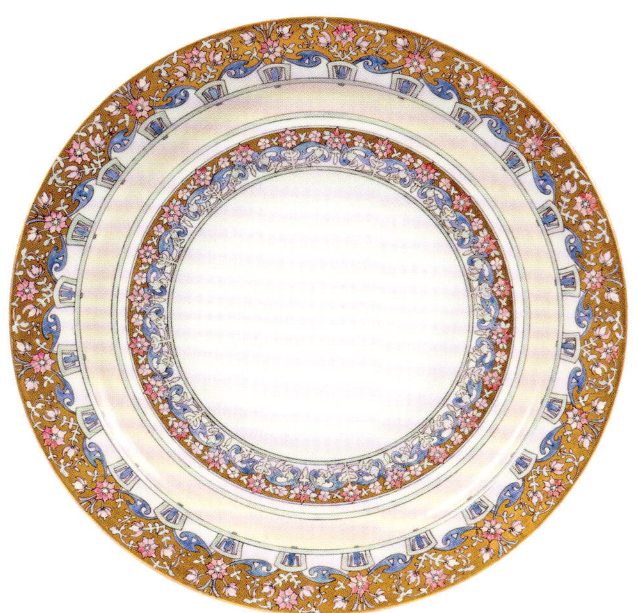

Platter, Adelaide Liebolt, undated. Liebolt exhibited a variety of plates in Atlan exhibitions, 1911–1916. Signed: Liebolt. Mark: Haviland/France. (1¼″ × 12½″) *Photo*: Treadway Toomey Auctions.

Miss Adelaide Liebolt
1101 Auditorium Tower, Chicago, Ill.
Teacher of Conventional Design on China.
Designs for rent for enamel work.
Formula for enamel work given by mail.
Work started or finished for out of town students.

Source: Teachers' Directory, *Keramic Studio*, 19 (1917–1918): viii.

1917, working from a studio in the Auditorium Tower, she advertised as a teacher of conventional design on china who offered lessons, designs for rent, and "work started or finished for out-of-town students" in *Keramic Studio* (vol. 19). After 1920, she worked as a bank clerk until her 1944 marriage, at age sixty, to widower William J. Newberry. Their happiness was brief; he died in 1946, she in 1947.

Linsted, Cornelia Burns, 1893
A founding member and councilor in 1893, Cornelia Burns (1846–1916) married Chicago steamship agent and Civil War veteran Daniel B. Linsted in 1887. A pioneer Wisconsin settler, Cornelia's father was the sheriff of Mineral Point when she was born and lieutenant governor of Wisconsin in 1853 when he died. Cornelia lived with relatives in Minnesota and Dakota Territory before settling in Chicago. Widowed in 1892, she married Charles Otis Shannon of Edgerton, Wisconsin, in 1907. In 1912, once again a widow, she and a niece homesteaded in St. Maries, Idaho. They were spending the winter in Tacoma, Washington, when Cornelia died in 1916.

Lovgren, Ellen Elizabeth: *see* Ellen Elizabeth Lovgren biography, p. 97.

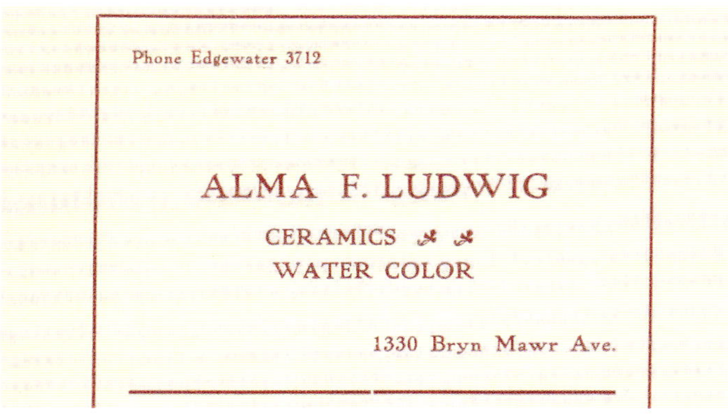

Phone Edgewater 3712

ALMA F. LUDWIG

CERAMICS
WATER COLOR

1330 Bryn Mawr Ave.

Source: *Catalog of the Twenty-First Annual exhibition of the Atlan Ceramic Art Club Catalog* (Chicago: Art Institute of Chicago, 1913).

Lowes, Sadie H. Hall, 1917–1922

Born into a family of pioneer Indiana settlers, Sadie H. Hall (1867–1945) was a court reporter and private secretary in Indianapolis before marrying Chicago attorney Francis M. Lowes in 1894. She was the second vice president of the Atlan Club in 1922. According to a profile in the *Chicago Tribune* (March 17, 1940), Sadie's only creative outlet was painting china until she began taking formal art lessons in middle age. She exhibited still life paintings at the Chicago Artists' shows in 1935 and 1937 and the All-Illinois Artists Society. After joining the Ravenswood Woman's Club in 1906, she initiated the club's annual "view day" when members toured the Art Institute. She was also a member of the Technic Art League, Artists' Guild, Municipal Art Society, Chicago Woman's Club, Cordon Society, Indiana Artists Club, and the Hoosier Salon.

Ludwig, Alma Frances, 1911–1913

Atlan Club treasurer in 1912, Alma Frances Ludwig (1886–1931) studied ceramics, oil, and watercolor painting at the Art Institute of Chicago. The daughter of a talented Chicago engraver, Alma was skilled in oil and water colors, as well as china decoration. After marrying business college manager Roy H. Puterbaugh in 1915, she moved to Lafayette, Indiana, where she continued to decorate china. She is mentioned in Jacob Piatt Dunn's *Indiana and Indianans* (American Historical Society, 1919, p. 1951).

Luman, Grace Alberta Price, 1922

A resident of Cleveland Heights, Ohio, in 1922, Grace Alberta Price (1879–1958) married John Roy Luman in Mansfield, Ohio, in 1905. She was a homemaker in Cleveland Heights, Ohio, 1914–1958.

Lund, Belle Whitford Jenks, 1922

A resident of Hammond, Indiana, in 1922, Belle Whitford Jenks (1879–1956) was born in South Dakota, where she married Norwegian building contractor Erick Lund in 1895. The couple moved to Indiana in 1901. According to her *Lake Geneva (Wisconsin) Regional News* obituary, she "produced and painted a quantity of ceramics, operating her own kiln." An active artist all her life, she studied at the Art Institute of Chicago and participated in exhibitions sponsored by the Art Students' League of Chicago and the South Side Art Association. During the 1920s, she spent summers at the Oxbow Artists' Colony in Saugatuck, Michigan.

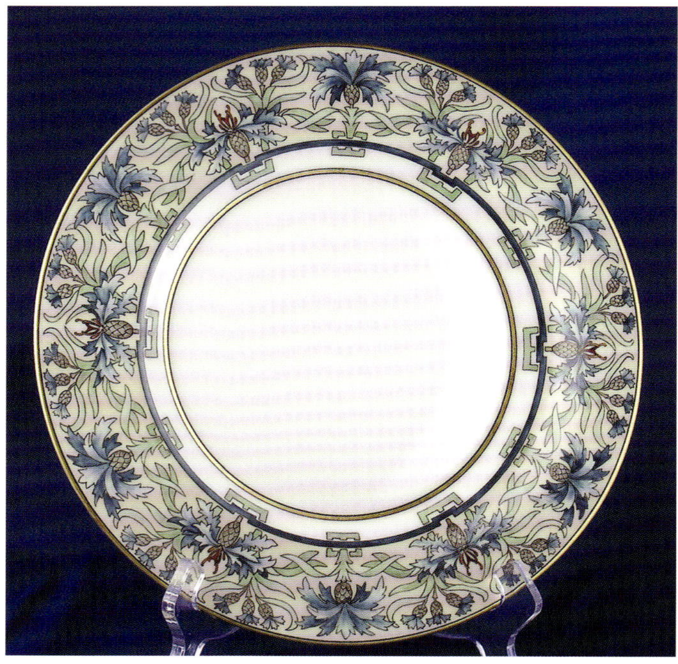

Plate, pineapple motif, Alma Frances Ludwig, 1911–1915. Signed: Alma F. Ludwig. Mark: PL/Limoges/France. *Photo*: Dark Flowers Antiques.

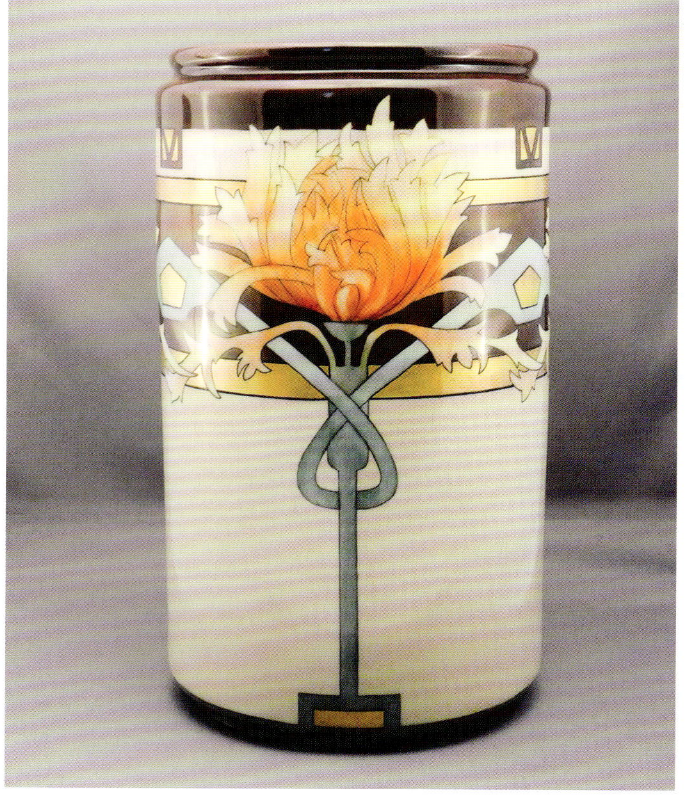

Vase, Alma Frances Ludwig, 1910–1914. Signed: Alma F. Ludwig. Mark: D & Co. [Delinieres & Co]/France. (10" × 6") *Photo*: Dark Flowers Antiques.

After 1931, she taught drawing and painting classes in her Hammond studio. She continued to paint and exhibit her work after moving to Williams Bay, Wisconsin, around 1940.

Lytle, Jennie A. Merriam, 1912
Born in Lake Geneva, Wisconsin, Jennie A. Merriam (1862–1947) married Chicago grain merchant George Alfred Lytle in 1880. Widowed in 1915, she married Chicago attorney James R. Howe in 1923. She was eighty-four when she died in Manteno, Illinois, in 1947.

Mahony, Margaret L., 1911–1917
Born in Chicago of Irish parents, Margaret L. Mahony (1874–1954) was living with her mother, stepfather, and siblings on Woodlawn Avenue in 1910. In 1920, according to census records, she was a stenographer in a bank; from 1930 on, she kept house for her unmarried siblings until her death at age eighty in 1954.

Mancl, Ottilie Klenovec, 1912
Born in Chicago of Austrian parents, Ottilie Klenovec (1888–1966) was listed as an artist and teacher in the 1910 federal census. The following year, she married attorney Frank John Mancl. In the mid-1920s, the couple moved to Riverside, Illinois, where Ottilie became known for her impressive garden. She spent the last two years of her life near a son in Madison, Wisconsin, where she died in 1966.

Mann, Cornelia Hooker: *see* Cornelia Hooker Mann biography, p. 6.

Marsh, Annie Silsby Porter, 1895
Vermont-born Annie Silsby Porter (1851–1925) came to Chicago in 1872, following her marriage to attorney John Worthington Marsh. By 1891, she was teaching ceramics in her elegant home on Aldine Square, where she held receptions and sales of her pupils' work. She was the first president of the Chicago Ceramic Association in 1892 and remained active in its affairs until 1907, when she returned to her hometown of Springfield, Vermont.

Ma Whinney, Ida Lorraine Specht, 1919–1921
Ida Lorraine Specht (1874–1937) was the second vice president of the Atlan Club in 1921. Born in Illinois, she grew up in Morgan Park, a village annexed to Chicago in 1914. Little is known about Ida's early years, other than her marriages: she wed twice, in 1892 and 1904, before marrying widower Dr. Elgin A. Ma Whinney, a Chicago dentist and Northwestern University Dental School professor, in 1916. In 1925, the couple retired to Phoenix, Arizona, where they built a handsome residence in the midst of a citrus grove. Ida became a prominent member of the community, serving as president of the Arizona Artists Guild, chairing the art department of the Woman's Club, and hosting events for the Garden Club. She exhibited landscape paintings and was widely known for her watercolors, according to her *Arizona Republic* obituary.

Maxson, Melina Marie Millar, 1917–1922
Melina Marie Millar (1864–1950) left Ontario, Canada, for Michigan in 1889 when she married railroad engineer Clarence M. Maxson. The couple moved from Leslie, Michigan, to Oak Park in 1915. In 1917, while visiting Michigan, she gave an address on "Conventional and Realistic Art Painting of Chinaware" to the End of the Century Club in Leslie. Melina was a graduate of the London (Canada) Art and Design School and, in Chicago, studied under Atlan Club founder Florence Steward. She was the secretary of the Atlan Club in 1918, 1921, and 1922. In October 1920, the Oak Park *Oak Leaves* noted that "her pieces are in

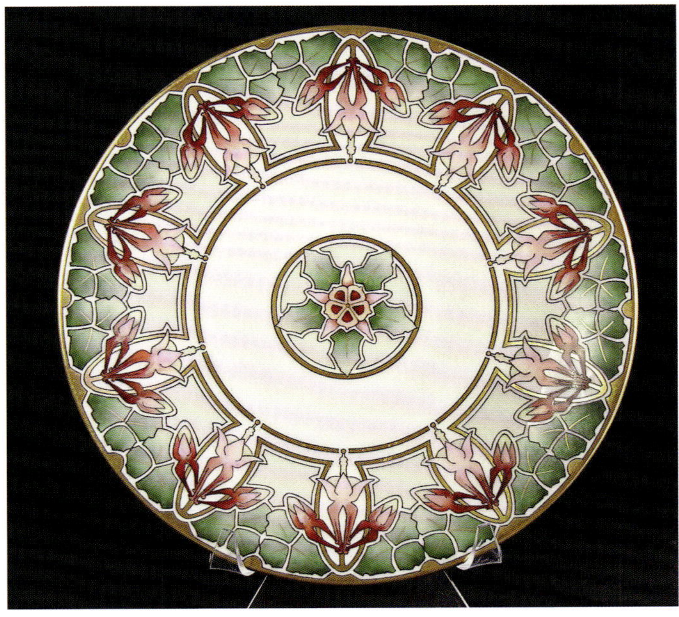

Plate with fuchsia motif, Ottilie Mancl, undated. Mancl exhibited a serving plate and a set of dessert plates in 1912, the only year she participated in an Atlan exhibition. Signed: O. Mancl. Mark: Bavaria. (d: 9½") *Photo*: Private collection.

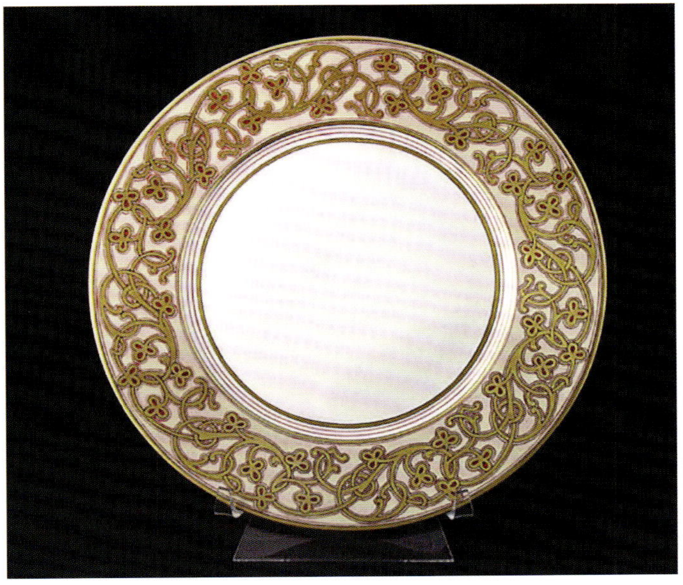

Plate with Celtic or Arabesque design, Ottilie Mancl, undated. Signed: Mancl. Mark: Hutschenreuther Selb/Bavaria/Favorite. (d: 7¾") *Photo*: Private collection.

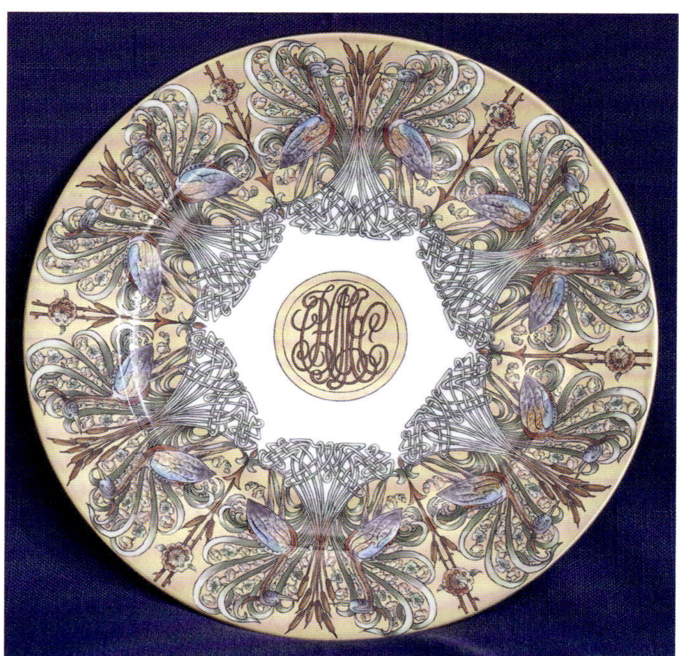

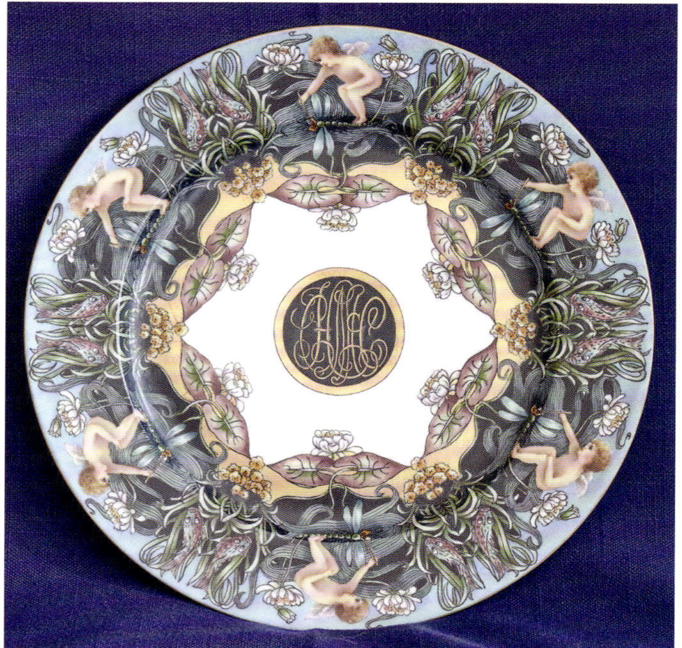

Service plates, Rhoda Marie Baldwin McCreery, ca. 1902. Bearing the central monogram of Chicago druggist Charles H. McConnell, the plates were likely part of the set shown in McCreery's studio in 1902. On December 21, 1902, the *Inter Ocean* reported, "One of the latest and most beautiful conceptions in porcelain work shown by Mrs. McCreery is represented in the handsome serving plates. These are the flat, flanged Haviland plates. Each plate represents an exclusive design in fruit, flower, and the renaissance, overlaid in gold. Some of the designs shown in this collection are among the most beautiful ever exhibited in this particular line of work." Signed: Rhoda M. Baldwin McCreery; Designed and copyrighted by Rhoda Marie Baldwin McCreery. Mark: Limoges/France. (1″× 10½″) *Photo*: Marx Broszio.

the main satsuma done in enamels and include plates, bonbon dishes, boxes and cups and saucers." Around 1942, Melina and her husband moved to Dallas, Texas.

McCarn, Sarah Augusta Barton, 1908–1911

Born in Fort Wayne, Indiana, Sarah Augusta Barton (1864–1954) moved to Chicago after marrying salesman Burtis D. McCarn in 1887. She was a graduate of the School of the Art Institute of Chicago. Listed as "A. B. McCarn" in the Chicago city directories, she operated an art studio between 1909 and 1920. She toured Europe and the Baltic in 1922 and lived in Paris, France, in the mid-1930s. Widowed in 1939, she later lived with a son's family in Illinois and New Jersey.

McConnell, Sarah Crosby, 1904

Daughter of a Chicago publisher, Sarah Crosby McConnell (1874–1955) was listed as an artist in 1898 and operated a studio for china painting in 1900–1905 in Evanston, Illinois, according to city directories. Advertising in the *Evanston Index*, she offered classes, private lessons, designing, and firing in her studio in the Rood Building. In 1920, she was working as an artist for a mail-order house in New York City. By 1945, she was living in Boston, Massachusetts, where she died in 1955.

McCreery, Rhoda Marie Baldwin, 1894–1900

Boston-born artist Rhoda Marie Baldwin (1859–1926) married businessman Charles W. McCreery in New York in 1885 and moved to South

MRS. R. M. McCREERY
902 Marshall Field Annex
Daily Instruction in Painting

Source: *Catalogue of the Seventh Exhibition of the Atlan Ceramic Art Club* (Chicago: Art Institute of Chicago, 1899).

Carolina. Two years later, she escaped an unhappy marriage by moving to Chicago, where she was granted a divorce in 1891. After joining the Atlan Club in 1894, she served as a councilor (1896–1899) and exhibited with the club at the 1900 Paris Exposition. She was an active member of the Chicago Ceramic Association (second vice president, 1899; secretary, 1900–1901; recording secretary, 1901–1903; vice president, 1903; exhibiting at the Pan-American Exposition, 1901), as well as the National League of Mineral Painters and Central Art Association. She maintained a studio in the Marshall Field Building until 1904, when she moved to New York City, where she worked as an artist. She was living in Cambridge, Massachusetts (as Mrs. Baldwin McCreery) in 1920 and in San Diego, California, in 1922. She died, age sixty-six, in Portland, Maine, in 1926.

McCrystle, Gertrude May Farnham, 1900–1906

Born on a farm in Libertyville, Illinois, Gertrude May Farnham (1864–1944), called May, married merchant tailor James B. McCrystle in

1888 in Minneapolis, Minnesota; they moved to Chicago in 1890 after a fire destroyed his tailoring business. She maintained a studio in the Athenaeum Building, while her husband operated a tailor shop. She was the Atlan Club's vice president in 1900 and 1901. In 1908, the family moved to Libertyville, Illinois, where she maintained a home studio. She showed work in exhibitions in Minneapolis, 1905; Boston, 1905–1909; Richmond, Indiana, 1907; and New York, 1908. Her designs were illustrated in *Keramic Studio* in February 1909. The 1910 census listed May as an art teacher with her own studio, living with her family in Libertyville, Illinois. In 1920, May's husband worked as a tailor while she managed a large boardinghouse in Highland Park; in 1940, as a widow, she operated a "poorhouse" in the city.

McDonald, Minna Myrtle Kenyon, 1902–1903
One of the founders of the Kansas City Porcelain and Pottery Club in 1902, Minna Myrtle Kenyon (1866–1960) married dentist Arthur J. McDonald in 1891. She exhibited with the Atlan Club in the Chicago Arts and Crafts exhibitions, 1902 and 1903. After her husband's death in 1948, she moved to Mishawaka, Indiana.

McDonald, Mary Theresa O'Shaughnessy, 1915–1917
Mary Theresa O'Shaughnessy (1866–1951) married brewing company executive Harley C. McDonald in Chicago in 1887 and soon moved to suburban LaGrange, Illinois. Widowed in 1905, she lived in La Grange until 1921, when she moved to Los Angeles, California.

McGilvray, Flora, 1921–1922
Born in Canada, Flora McGilvray (1886–1974) was living on her parents' fruit farm in South Haven, Michigan, when she was listed as an artist painting china in the 1910 census. In Chicago by 1920, she worked as an artist at various companies; in 1930 and 1940, she was employed decorating lampshades.

McIntyre, Letitia, 1893
A founding member in 1893, Letitia "Lettie" McIntyre exhibited her work in the Atlan Club's second exhibition at Eva E. Adams home in December 1893. She became an associate member in March 1894.

Mettenet, Martha Helena Sparrow: *see* Sparrow, Martha Helena.

Middleton, Matilda: *see* Matilda Middleton biography, p. 55.

Milliken, Callie C. Thacker, 1894
A nonresident member, Callie C. Thacker (1858–1924) was a schoolteacher in Traverse City, Michigan, when she married dry goods merchant James Wheelock Milliken in 1881. The *Inter Ocean,* reviewing the Atlan Club's 1894 exhibition, noted that "Mrs. J. W. Milliken, of Traverse City, contributes a uniformly excellent exhibit." Milliken's husband was elected a Michigan state senator in 1897 and served through 1900. After his 1908 death, she was the secretary-treasurer of J. W. Milliken, Inc.

Miner, Florence Hart, 1893–1909
Artist Florence Hart Miner (1866–1909) was the daughter of Cyrus Miner, a prominent Janesville, Wisconsin, merchant, and member of the 1889 state legislature. In 1891, she won eight awards at Wisconsin State Fair for her paintings and decorated china. She joined the Atlan Club in 1893 while living in Chicago and served as a councilor in 1895. When she exhibited with the club in 1898, she was living in Boston. In 1900–1903, she was in Madison, Wisconsin, where, in addition to painting china, she crafted silver and enamel jewelry while serving as chaperone for a sorority house at the University of Wisconsin. In 1904, she married Chicago architect John Henry Wagner, widower of former Atlan member Anne Frances Brown Wagner, and moved to his home in Elmhurst, Illinois.

Mitchell, Helen, 1893
Assumed to be Helen Mitchell (1868–1953), who married Chicago attorney James Todd in June 1894. They moved to Oak Park, Illinois, in the 1920s. Widowed in 1944, Helen lived with her son's family in Nantucket, Massachusetts.

Mosley, Glennie, 1917–1919
Born in Georgia, Glena "Glennie" Mosley (1876–1972) studied art at the Georgia State College for Women. Between 1904 and 1910, while maintaining a studio in Birmingham, Alabama, she spent summers in Chicago studying at the Art Institute, under china decorator Franz Aulich, and with Atlan members Helen Frazee and Helga M. Peterson. Moving to Chicago in 1911, she had a studio in the Hood Building until 1921, when she took charge of the art department of the Woman's College, Hattiesburg, Mississippi, through 1924. Returning to Illinois, she lived with a sister's family in Winnetka until 1931, when she became head of the art department of Jones County Junior College, Ellisville, Mississippi; during summers, she taught at the Institute of Fine Arts at Monteagle, Tennessee. She was a longtime resident of Laurel, Mississippi.

Mosser, Katherine E. Newell, 1921–1922
Atlan Club treasurer in 1921, Katherine "Kate" E. Newell (1865–1944) married Abingdon, Illinois, manufacturer and banker Samuel T. Mosser in 1887. When the couple moved to Chicago in 1912, her husband chaired a stockbrokerage firm. Widowed in 1927, she lived in Chicago and St. Petersburg, Florida.

Naper, Teresa Margaret Anderson, 1905–1912
Chicagoan Teresa Margaret Anderson (1876–1960) was a schoolteacher in 1906 when she married architect and engineer Herbert John Naper. She was the secretary of the Atlan Club in 1907–1908 and exhibited with the club in Arts and Crafts exhibitions at the Chicago Art Institute 1906–1908. She was still listed among "active" members contributing to the Art Institute's Atlan Fund in 1912. After 1920, the family resided in Wilmette, Illinois.

Nye, Laura Marie Norton Starr, 1905–1908
An 1895 graduate of Chicago's Hyde Park High School, Laura Marie Norton (1876–1958) married John Monroe Starr in March 1902 but was widowed one month later. As Laura Norton Starr, she showed a punch bowl in the Chicago Ceramic Art Association exhibition, illustrated in

the *Chicago Tribune* (December 4, 1902). In 1906, she married salesman Edward Carlton Lawrence Nye and moved to suburban Oak Park, Illinois, in 1909. As Mrs. Nye, she was the treasurer of the Atlan Club in 1907–1908. The Nye family lived in Oak Park until moving to Los Angeles, California, around 1918.

Odgers, Bertha Shoop, 1922
The daughter of a Polo, Illinois, dry goods merchant, Bertha Shoop (1865–1955) was in Chicago taking painting lessons in 1885 when she eloped with salesman George Clark Odgers. As recounted in the press, detectives hired by the bride's aunt, pioneer Chicago physician Sarah Hackett Stevenson, surprised the newly wedded couple at the Palmer House and convinced them to take a voluntary separation; two months later, the young couple reunited. In Chicago, Bertha was active in the Norwood Park Woman's Club, where she gave an illustrated talk on pottery in 1934. She died in Chicago at age ninety in 1955.

Oliver, Edna Antoinette Baltic, 1922
Born in Wisconsin, Edna Antoinette Baltic (1880–1962) was raised in Minneapolis, Minnesota, where she studied china painting and worked as a receptionist in an art gallery, 1900–1903. She moved to Chicago after marrying sales manager Nelson H. Oliver in Colorado in 1908. By 1917, the couple were residing in Oak Park, Illinois. In 1926, she divorced her husband due to his infidelity. In 1930, she managed an apartment building in Chicago, before moving to New York City to be near her daughter.

Park, Bertha Jane Alexander, 1914–1922
Bertha Jane Alexander (1871–1961) was a schoolteacher in Springfield, Ohio, 1900–1903. After marrying Chicagoan Ralph Raymond Park in 1906, she maintained a ceramics studio in her Chicago home. She was the treasurer of the Atlan Club in 1915, 1917, and 1918 and vice president in 1919. In 1915, her round fruit platter and matching set of small plates won first prize in the conventional class in Burley & Tyrrell Co.'s national exhibition. In 1930, she was designing embroidery, an occupation she continued through 1950, while living in Evanston, Illinois.

Parker, Edythe Stoddard, 1904
Edythe Stoddard Parker (1876–1974), a resident of Winnetka, Illinois, graduated with a degree in sculpture from the Art Institute of Chicago in June 1901; she taught a summer class at the institute in 1902. After her 1909 marriage to Charles Neville Beard, she lived in Lower Merion, Pennsylvania, where she died, age ninety-seven, in 1974.

Peck, Grace Harriet: *see* Grace Harriet Peck biography, p. 49.

Peterson, Helga Mae: *see* Helga Mae Peterson biography, p. 68.

Phillips, Mary Agnes, 1895–1905
Atlan Club treasurer, 1898–1899, and councilor in 1900, Mary Agnes Phillips (1869–1907) was the daughter of prominent Chicago portrait painter John Phillips, an original member of the Academy of Design. Born in New York, she was brought to Chicago as a baby; by 1880, she was with her parents in Denver, Colorado, where her father

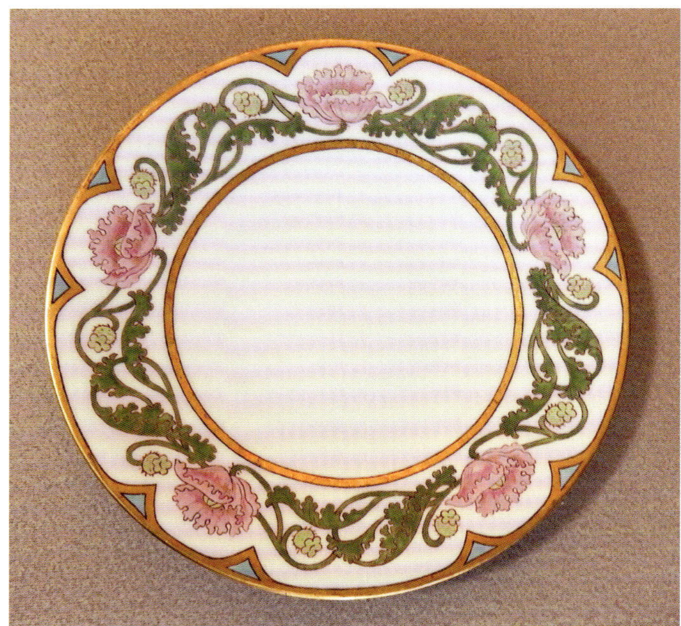

Plate, Mary A. Phillips, 1903. Signed: Mary A. Phillips/1903. (d: 8⅜")
Photo: Ronald Bry collection.

unsuccessfully engaged in gold mining. While living in Helena, Montana, 1888–1893, she won numerous awards for her decorated china and paintings at state fairs. She and her widowed mother moved back to Chicago in 1893. Known for portraits on porcelain plaques, Mary participated in Western Decorating Works exhibitions in the 1890s. Also active in the Chicago Ceramic Art Association, she received a gold medal for the finest collection of decorated china in 1896 and first prize in 1897; she was the association's vice president in 1900. A popular teacher, she was listed as an artist working in a home studio on Indiana Avenue in the 1904 *Chicago City Directory*. Mary was thirty-seven years old when she died on January 1, 1907.

Porter, Alice S., 1906
Daughter of a Presbyterian minister, Alice S. Porter (1872–1916) graduated from the Presbyterian Girl's School in Oswego, Illinois, before studying at the Art Institute of Chicago. She operated a china decorating studio in Chicago, 1901–1907. She returned to her hometown of Fort Scott, Kansas, where she served as art supervisor of the public schools from 1908 through March 1916, when she died of Bright's disease at age forty-three.

Pratt, Florence: *see* Florence Jane Donovan Wilcox Pratt Steward biography, p. 72.

Preuszner, Roxana Foote Beecher, 1893
One of the founders of the Atlan Club, Roxana Foote Beecher (1840–1924) was born in New York, the daughter of Rev. William Henry Beecher, a Congregational minister who held various pastorates in Ohio and Massachusetts. He was a brother of author Harriet Beecher Stowe and Katherine Beecher, founder of domestic science. After studying at

Abbott Female Academy in Andover, Massachusetts, Roxana married Civil War veteran Carl F. W. A. Preuszner in 1867. Rev. Beecher and his family accompanied the newlyweds to Chicago in 1868. Widowed in 1872, Roxana took art lessons at the Academy of Design, where she was hired to teach its china painting class in 1878. By 1881 she had opened a studio in her home and paid for a kiln to be installed at Phillips & Co., so that porcelain and pottery pieces could be fired in Chicago. In addition to giving china painting and art lessons, Roxana was a noted Sunday School teacher of "rare talent." In 1895, when she was appointed the state superintendent of primary Sunday schools for Kansas, she moved to Lawrence, Kansas, where she lived until her death at age eighty-three.

Pruden, Elizabeth Marie Kniessel, 1916–1918
Born in Chicago of German parents, Elizabeth Marie Kniessel (1872–1936) married broker Alfred J. Pruden in 1896. In 1910, they were living in LaGrange, Illinois. In 1920, Elizabeth was boarding with a sister's family in Chicago, while her husband established a citrus farm in Winter Haven, Florida, where they were operating when Elizabeth died in 1936.

Pyott, Mary V. De Luce, 1895–1896
When Chicagoan Mary V. De Luce (1862–1927), a student of Eva E. Adams, married David Alexander Pyott in 1886, the young couple moved into a completely furnished new house, a wedding gift from the groom's industrialist father. That marriage ended before 1898, when Mary married grain dealer Archibald D. Wright. In 1909, the couple lived in Kansas City, Missouri; they moved to Santa Barbara, California, in 1921, where Mary died in 1927.

Randall, Cora A. Chandler Kenney, 1908
A Chicago Art Institute graduate, Cora A. Chandler Kenney (1862–1925) married auditor Gilbert B. Randall in LaPorte, Indiana, in 1894. Moving to Chicago, she exhibited in Western Decorating Works exhibitions, 1895–1897, and with the National League of Mineral Painters in 1899. Active in the Chicago Ceramic Art Association, she served as vice president in 1902 and secretary, 1908–1909. She was listed as an artist, working at home, in the 1910 federal census. Widowed in 1914, she married Chicago insurance broker Frederick Guy Gale in 1917; divorced in 1920, she spent her final years in LaPorte.

Ransom, Katharine L., 1893–1895
Born in Missouri, Katharine L. Ransom (1868–1937) came to Chicago with her parents from New York in the 1880s. She participated in the Atlan Club's second exhibition held at Eva E. Adams' home in December 1893. She became an associate member in March 1894, when she moved to Burlington, Wisconsin. Back in Chicago by 1900, she accompanied her parents when they moved to Pasadena, California, in 1915.

Reece, Amelia Gimmell Dilworth, 1910–1911
Born into a Quaker family in Ohio, Amelia Gimmell Dilworth (1859–1954) married telegraph operator Oliver H. Reece in Richmond, Indiana, in 1879. Widowed in 1903, she moved to Chicago, where she shared studio space in the Auditorium Tower with Atlan member Helen Frazee. Between 1910 and 1930, she maintained a home studio where she gave lessons in oil, watercolor, pastel, and ceramic decoration. In 1941, she

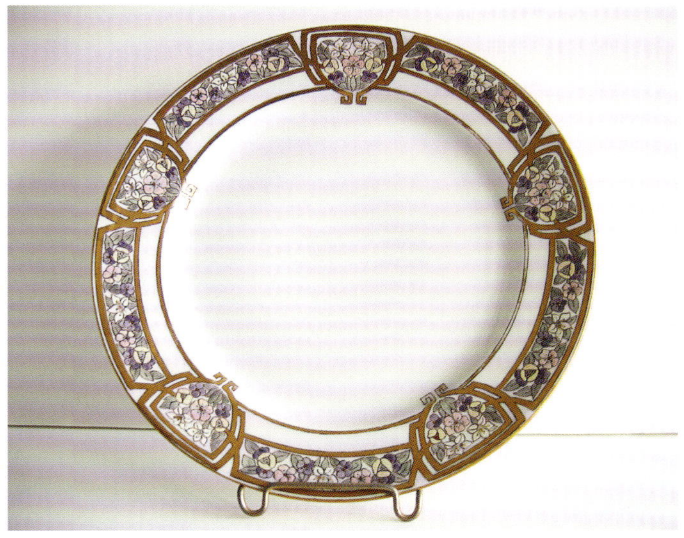

Plate, Cora A. Randall, 1910–1916. A well-known Chicago artist, Randall served as an officer in the Chicago Ceramic Art Association before joining the Atlan Club in 1908. Signed: C. A. Randall. (d: 8½") *Photo*: Private collection.

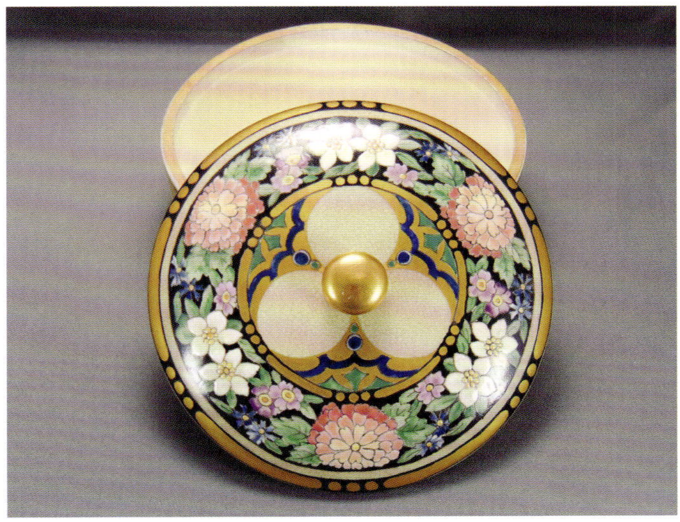

Satsuma box, Stella Gordon Rintoul, 1915. Signed: S/G/Rintoul/12/15. (3½" × 5¼") *Photo*: Dark Flowers Antiques.

received the president's award for "Peonies" from the All-Illinois Society of the Fine Arts. She was ninety-five when she died in Chicago.

Riecks, Anna Marie, 1916–1917
Anna Marie Riecks (1891–1989), daughter of an Anchor, Illinois, hardware dealer, attended school in Chicago, where she later worked as a stenographer for meatpacker Armour & Co. While working for the company in Denver, Colorado, she married Michael George Marrin, an oil company accountant, in 1921. They moved to Tulsa, Oklahoma, from Casper, Wyoming, in 1930. Widowed in 1951, she spent her final years in Colfax, Illinois, where she died at age ninety-eight.

Rintoul, Stella Gordon Grace Drainie, 1905–1912
Stella Gordon Grace Drainie (1874–1945) offered china painting lessons in a studio above her father's art store in Vancouver, Canada, from 1897 until 1902, when she married Scottish banker Robert Rintoul. The couple moved to Chicago, where Robert Rintoul was the manager of the Bank of Montreal for eleven years. She was an Atlan Club councilor in 1905 and second vice president in 1909. She also participated in Arts and Crafts exhibitions, 1906–1910. She was still listed among "active" members contributing to the Art Institute's Atlan Fund in 1912. Widowed in 1917, she donated a sunroom to a Vancouver soldier's hospital in Robert Rintoul's memory in 1918. She married Chicago banker and stockman John Clay in London, England, in 1925. After his death in 1934, she lived in Carmel, California, until her death in 1945.

Sanford, Linda Chase Fox: *see* Dunne, Linda Chase Fox.

Semple, Bertha Marguerite Hulsebus, 1911
Bertha Marguerite Hulsebus (1882–1957) married electrical engineer Francis H. Semple Jr., in Burlington, Iowa, and moved to Chicago in 1904. Widowed in 1920, she moved from Park Ridge, Illinois, to Chicago in 1935, before retiring to Santa Barbara, California, around 1955.

Senge, Anna Obermaier: *see* Anna Obermaier Senge biography, p. 94.

Sessions, Anna May Orton, 1895–1919
Anna May Orton (1857–1947) accompanied her husband Frank M. Sessions from Rome, New York, to Chicago in the 1880s. She was the secretary of the Atlan Club in 1899 and a councilor in 1901. She exhibited in Chicago Arts and Crafts exhibitions, 1907–1910. In 1900 and 1910 census records, she was listed as an artist, while her husband headed a furniture company. She lived on 54th Place in Chicago until her death at age ninety in 1947.

Sexton, Marie Antionette Rodman, 1906–1922
Missouri-born Marie Antionette Rodman (1870–1948) married retail merchant Stephen William Sexton in Chicago in 1892. She was an Atlan Club councilor in 1909. In November 1912, the *Inter Ocean* found Marie's work in the Atlan exhibition "worthy of attention." She also exhibited in Arts and Crafts exhibitions at the Chicago Art Institute, 1907–1910, and in Burley & Co. exhibitions. The family lived in suburban Wheaton, Illinois, before moving to Chicago around 1920, where Marie taught music in the city's public schools until her retirement in 1936.

Seymour, Minnie N., 1922
Minnie N. Seymour was living on St. James Place in Chicago when she exhibited in 1922.

Simons, Marcia Ruth Syfert, 1921
Iowa-born Marcia Ruth Syfert (1891–1974) was working as a bookkeeper in Oklahoma City when she married pioneer oil operator George A. Simons in 1910; they moved to Okmulgee, Oklahoma, in 1914. In 1921, she spent two months in Chicago studying china painting with Helen Frazee and joined the Atlan Club. Returning to Okmulgee, she completed more than 300 pieces, including two complete dinner sets, examples of Satsuma, lamps, and vases, which a local art shop exhibited in 1926, according to the *Okmulgee Daily Times*. After a contentious 1928 divorce, in which her mental competency was an issue, she remained in Oklahoma with a sister as her guardian. She married farmer George Casper Boes of Raymond, Kansas, in the late 1940s.

Smith, Lavena "Vena" Lautzenhiser, 1915–1917
Lavena "Vena" Lautzenhiser (1868–1957) moved to Chicago from Indiana following her 1896 marriage to leather novelties salesman Charles Courtland Smith. Widowed in 1926, she moved to Midland, Michigan, in the 1930s.

Sparks, Mollie Effie Carter Dolson, 1912–1917
Iowa-born Mary "Mollie" Effie Carter Dolson (1864–1931) studied at the Art institute of Chicago before joining the faculty of Valparaiso University as head of the Fine Arts department in 1898. She taught painting and drawing at the Indiana university for twenty years. In 1911, she married her drawing assistant, George Alden Sparks. She also exhibited with the Atlan Club in the 1915 Panama-Pacific Exposition and the 1917 Amateur Art Club exhibition in Springfield, Illinois. In the 1920s, the family moved to Los Angeles, California, where she died in 1931.

Sparrow, Martha Helena, 1912–1917
Daughter of a Chicago jeweler, Martha Helena Sparrow (1889–1956) married civil engineer and utility executive Francis X. Mettenet in April 1914. The family lived in Indianapolis, Indiana, 1929–1935, before returning to Chicago. Their daughter Ardith attended the School of the Art Institute of Chicago, 1935–1938. Martha died in Chicago at age fifty-seven in 1956.

Starr, Laura N.: *see* Nye, Laura Marie Norton Starr.

Steele, Ella Amanda Pratt, 1896–1900
Born in New York, Ella Amanda Pratt (1849–1930) arrived in Chicago with her parents in the 1850s. She married Chicago industrialist and railroad baron Frederick Morgan Steele in 1883. She was one of the women exhibiting "original designs most worthy of notice" at the Western Decorating Works in 1891; her work was selected for display in the Woman's Building at the 1893 Chicago World's Fair. She was the vice president of the Atlan Club in 1898, when she exhibited in the Chicago Arts and Crafts Society exhibition. A biography of her husband in J. Seymour Curry's *Chicago: Its History and Its Builders* (1918) noted that "his wife possesses notable artistic talent as manifest in ceramic work which appeared at the Paris Exposition in 1900 and the World's Columbian Exposition in 1893." The family moved to Highland Park, Illinois, around 1903, and to Los Angeles, California, by 1920.

Steward, Florence Pratt (Mrs. LeRoy T.): *see* Florence Jane Donovan Wilcox Pratt Steward biography, p. 72.

Stubbs, Minerva "Minnie" Gray, 1911
Minerva "Minnie" Gray (1868–1949) was a daughter of well-known electrical inventor Elisha Gray, cofounder of the Western Electric Manufacturing Company. Minnie married commission merchant

William Chisholm Stubbs in 1893 at her parents' residence in Highland Park, Illinois. In 1901, the couple moved to Cleveland, Ohio, where William died in 1903, leaving Minnie a widow with three young children. The Stubbs family returned to Highland Park, where, in 1916, a jury hearing declared her sane after undergoing treatment in a private sanitarium. She lived in Highland Park and Waukegan, Illinois, until moving to Laguna Beach, California, around 1944.

Tichenor [Titchner], Fay T.: *see* Holtgreve, Fay T. Titchner.

Topping, Helen Maria: *see* Helen Maria Topping biography, p. 36.

Umbach, Mary Edna Good, 1922
Born in Kansas of Canadian parents, Mary Edna Good (1882–1924) married Edward Milton Umbach, a Presbyterian minister, in Chicago in June 1907. A talented soprano, she had graduated from the music school at Kansas State Normal School in Emporia, Kansas, in 1903. In July 1920, after living in Kansas, the couple settled in Evanston, Illinois, where Rev. Umbach was the assistant minister of the First Presbyterian Church. Edna died, age forty-two, in Evanston in June 1924.

Van Doren, Claire Blanchard Stillman, 1918–1922
The last president of the Atlan Club in 1922, after serving as vice president in 1921, Claire Blanchard Stillman (1875–1950) married musician William E. Van Doren in Toledo, Ohio, in 1900. In 1911, the couple moved to Chicago, where her husband played in small orchestras and theaters and taught trumpet. They were living in Oak Park, Illinois, in 1930, when her husband was killed in an auto crash. Her occupation was listed as craft worker in an art studio in the 1940 federal census.

Von Oven, Johanna M., 1906–1907
Johanna M. Von Oven (1868–1909), an 1897 graduate of the Art Institute of Chicago, was born in Naperville, Illinois. When she died at the age of 41 in 1909, her obituary in the October 13 *Naperville Clarion* noted that "her only vocation in life seemed to be Art, for which she was highly talented, teaching at times at Chicago University and other institutions. With a studio in the Fine Arts Building, her productions there were of the highest quality and received especial mention." She was a member of the Chicago Arts and Crafts Society and the Art Institute's Alumni Association of Decorative Designers.

Wagner, Ann Francis Brown, 1893–1894
Ann Francis Brown (1846–1897) married prominent Chicago architect and engineer John H. Wagner in 1886. After joining the Atlan Club in 1893, she entertained club members with a Russian tea at her Chicago home in 1894. She was a founding member of the Chicago Ceramic Art Association in 1892; in 1895, she hosted association members at her new home in suburban Elmhurst, Illinois. She died, age fifty-one, in 1897. Her widower married Atlan member Florence Hart Miner in 1904.

Wagner, Florence Hart Miner: *see* Miner, Florence Hart.

Ward, Ada Holland, 1917–1922
Born in Michigan of Irish parents, Ada Holland (1863–1939) married

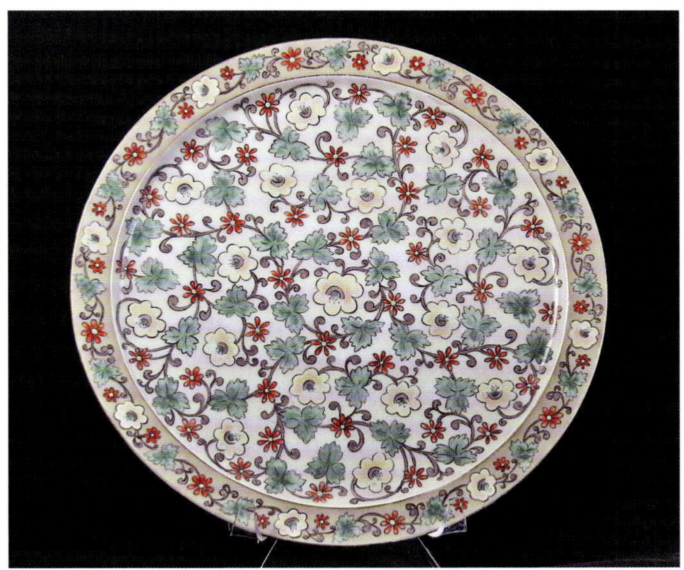

Chop plate, Mary Edna Good Umbach, ca. 1922. This may have been the "chop plate" exhibited by Umbach in 1922. Unsigned, family provenance identifies Mary Edna Good Umbach as the artist. (d: 11") *Photo*: Private collection.

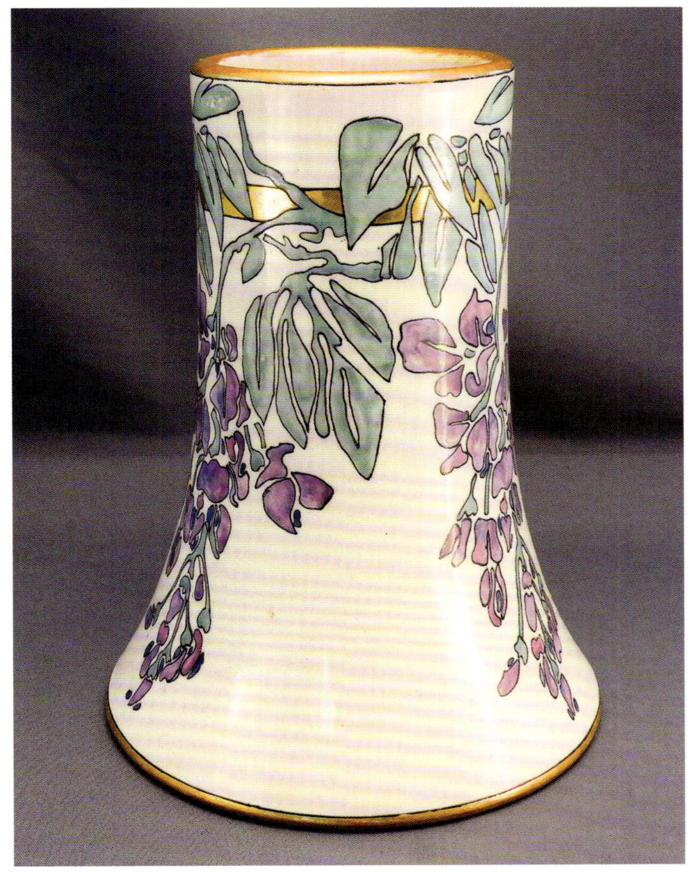

Vase, Mearle Beatrice Warner, 1923. Signed: Mearle Beatrice Warner/To Mabelle/From Mearle/1923. (7"× 5 ½") *Photo*: Dark Flowers Antiques.

salesman James Clark Ward in Port Sanilac, Michigan, in 1888. In Chicago before 1900, they lived in suburban Des Plaines for several years. In 1929, they returned to Port Sanilac, where their son Donald was the village president.

Warner, Mearle Beatrice Hagar, 1917–1921
Mearle Beatrice Hagar (1884–1954), a lifelong resident of Aurora, Illinois, was employed as a bookkeeper in 1911 when she married local attorney George Raymond Warner. The daughter of a miller, Mearle was "a popular and attractive girl," according to the *Aurora Beacon*, April 1911.

Weaver, Martha Elmina Tibbals, 1922
Martha Elmina Tibbals (1859–1944), a resident of Cleveland, Ohio, was a member of the first graduating class of the Cleveland School of Art in 1886. She was instructor of painting at Western Reserve School of Design for Women, Cleveland, before marrying Arthur Frank Weaver in 1892. She was widowed in 1901. According to her obituary in the *Cleveland Plain Dealer* (January 19, 1944), "She went to New York in 1905 to study overglazed decorations and ceramics and, on her return to Cleveland, founded the Weaver School of Ceramics. Her school was absorbed by the Cleveland School of Art in 1909, and she headed the department of ceramics for 19 years before her retirement in 1928." While in New York, she studied with Marshall Fry and Charles Fergus Binns. In 1924, Martha spent a summer in Europe, studying art in Greece, France, Italy, and the British Isles. She died in Cleveland at age eighty-four.

Webster, Cora Maud, 1915
Chicagoan Cora Maud Webster (1898–1985) graduated from the two-year vocational course at John Marshall High School in June 1914. She was employed as a nurse in 1920, when she married Walter William Wilson. The couple lived in Oak Park, Illinois.

Wells, Mrs. Julia 1893
Mrs. Julia Wells was a founding member of the Atlan Club in 1893. She may have been Julia Amanda Hitchcock Wells (1852–1925), a widow operating a boardinghouse on 62nd Street in 1900.

Wiese, Eleanor Harriet, 1918–1919
Daughter of a Chicago pharmacist, Eleanor Harriet Wiese (1894–1972) lived with her parents in the Lincoln Park neighborhood. She traveled to Europe in 1922, 1924, and 1926. In 1940, she lived in suburban Berwyn, Illinois, where she served as the secretary of the Ladies Aid of the Bohemian Orphanage, organized by her mother May. After her mother's death in 1952, Eleanor lived in Los Angeles, California, before moving to St. Petersburg, Florida.

Williams, Caroline Roselle Greene, 1922
Cleveland, Ohio, artist Caroline Roselle Greene Williams (1855–1931), aka Mrs. Caroline G. Williams, was best known for oil and watercolor paintings. The daughter of pioneer Cleveland photographer Jeremiah M. Greene, Caroline married accountant Charles Fitch Williams in 1879; divorced by 1900, she and her five children lived with her parents. An 1892 graduate of the Cleveland School of Art, Caroline maintained a

Phone Kedzie 3824

Cora M Webster

STUDIO

3009 W POLK STREET CHICAGO

Lesson Days
Tuesday and Thursday

CHINA
PAINTING

Source: Catalog of the Twenty-Third Annual Exhibition of the Atlan Ceramic Art Club (Chicago: Art Institute of Chicago, 1915).

studio in the Pythian Temple as early as 1897 and was listed as an artist in city directories through 1926. One of the organizers of the Women Artists of Cleveland in 1913, she was also a member of the Water Color Society and the Woman's Art Club of Cleveland.

Williams, Mai Fare, 1907–1909
Daughter of a prosperous Chicago manufacturer, Mai Fare Williams (1881–1959) exhibited china designed by Atlan member Mary H. Stevens Humphrey in the 1906 Chicago Arts and Crafts exhibition before exhibiting with the Atlan Club. She married sales manager Hugh Moore Clopton in November 1910; divorced by 1914, she resumed her maiden name. In July 1920, she married French war hero and perfume importer Alfred Soriano. Widowed in 1935, she moved to Los Angeles, California.

Wilson, Sarah Celestia Hewen: *see* Hewen, Sarah Celestia.

Wolf, Helen K. Bauer, 1915–1922
Born in Chicago of German parents, Helen K. Bauer (1875–1964) married Otto O. Wolf, a musician with the Chicago Symphony orchestra, in June 1900. Widowed in 1916, she opened a beauty salon where she worked as a hairdresser. As Mrs. Helen Wolf, she advertised her salon in Atlan Club exhibition catalogues between 1917 and 1922.

Wright, Jane Remson Van Doren, 1905–1912
Atlan Club president in 1911, Jane "Jennie" Remson Van Doren (1843–ca. 1935) moved to Chicago from Indianapolis, Indiana, in 1885, following the death of her husband, Dr. Mansur H. Wright. Daughter of a New York clergyman, she was the aunt of prominent Chicago architect Howard Van Doren Shaw. Jennie held several other Atlan Club offices, including secretary, 1905–1906; vice president, 1907; treasurer, 1909; and councilor in 1910 and 1912. She was listed among "active" members contributing to the Art Institute's Atlan Fund in 1912.
Jennie also exhibited with the Chicago Ceramic Art Association and in Arts and Crafts exhibitions, 1907–1910. In the 1920s, she spent

winters in Florida or Europe; she lived in France between 1930 and 1935. In May 1933, at age ninety, Jennie was still decorating china while living in a Paris hotel, according to correspondence with her nephew's wife, Frances Wells (Mrs. Howard Van Doren) Shaw, on May 20, 1933 (Chicago History Museum). It is assumed that she died in Paris around 1935.

Wyeth, Lucy Snow, 1914–1916
Lucy Snow Wyeth (1879–1956) taught music and china painting in her hometown of Newark, Ohio, before moving to Chicago to open an art studio in the Auditorium Tower around 1912. In 1917, at the outbreak of World War I, she accepted the position of supervising clerk in the U.S. Motor Transportation Corps in Washington, DC, where she managed nearly 100 clerks for four years. In 1923, Lucy moved to San Diego, California, where she engaged in hand-tinted landscape photography. She married San Diego realtor Simon Burget Stonerook in 1930; as a widow, she moved to Fort Worth, Texas, in 1946.

Yeoman, Marguerite Mills, 1897–1899
Moving to Chicago from Columbus, Ohio, in 1894, Marguerite Mills Yeoman (1867–1950) exhibited her decorated china in exhibitions sponsored by the Western Decorating Works, Chicago Ceramic Art Association, and National League of Mineral Painters. In September 1897, the Chicago *Inter Ocean,* reviewing the Western Decorating Works exhibition, claimed, "An oval slab decorated with pansies by Miss M. M. Yeomans is one of the gems of the exhibition." Her work was also included in the 1898 Chicago Arts and Crafts Society exhibition. She maintained a studio in the Auditorium Tower, where, according to her 1915 advertisement in *Keramic Studio*, she specialized in "naturalistic painting on china, after the method of F. B. Aulich." She won first prize, naturalistic class, in the Burley & Co.'s 1915 exhibition. After 1940, Marguerite returned to Ohio, where she died in 1950.

Young, Corabelle Beers Rugar, 1908
Corabelle Beers Rugar (1863–1934) was a student at the Art Institute of Chicago in 1886 when she won a prize for her drawing and painting

Marguerite M. Yeoman
STUDIO
1101 AUDITORIUM TOWER
CHICAGO

CLASSES IN
CHINA PAINTING AND WATER COLOR

Source: *Catalogue of Eighth Annual Exhibition of the Chicago Ceramic Art Association* (Chicago: Art Institute of Chicago, 1900).

skills. Returning to her hometown of Galesburg, Illinois, she married attorney George Warner Young in 1889. The couple lived in Joliet, Illinois, where she was listed as an artist in the 1900 federal census. She also exhibited in the 1908 Arts and Crafts exhibition.

Zeublin, Henrietta Columbia Follett, 1893–1904
Henrietta Columbia Follett (1845–1921), a daughter of Judge Charles H. Follett of Newark, Ohio, married John Evans Zeublin in 1864. Moving to Chicago in the mid-1880s, she took up china painting at the age of forty-five. Excelling in "figure work," according to newspaper reviews, she exhibited in Western Decorating Works exhibitions and joined the Chicago Ceramic Art Association in 1892. Elected to the Atlan Club in March 1893, she served as a councilor, 1894, 1898; vice president, 1895, 1899; and president, 1896, 1897. President again in 1900, she resigned in July when her husband, chief executive of the Chicago Telephone Co. (later Illinois Bell), was killed in a train accident. She was the mother of Charles Zueblin (her son spelled his surname "Zueblin" rather than "Zeublin"), a pioneering University of Chicago sociology professor who, with his wife Rho Fisk, was a strong proponent of the American Arts and Crafts movement. In 1904, Henrietta returned to Newark, where she lived until 1909, when she joined her son's family in Winchester, Massachusetts, and became a member of the Boston Society of Arts and Crafts. In 1914, she was again in Newark, where she lived with a niece's family until her death in 1921.

Appendix 2

1918 Atlan Catalog

CATALOG

OF THE

TWENTY-SIXTH ANNUAL EXHIBITION OF THE ATLAN CERAMIC ART CLUB

OFFICERS

DIRECTOR AND PRESIDENT

MRS. LE ROY T. STEWARD

VICE-PRESIDENT

MRS. FRANK SENGE

2ND VICE-PRESIDENT

MISS ELLEN LOVGREN

SECRETARY

MRS. MELINA MAXSON

TREASURER

MRS. RALPH A. PARK

COUNCILORS

MRS. PAUL HOELSCHER

MRS. EOLAH KULP

ART INSTITUTE

FROM NOVEMBER 7TH TO DECEMBER 1ST, 1918

ATTENTION IS INVITED TO THIS PAGE

The Atlan Ceramic Art Club

ITS OBJECTS

Many years ago this Club, following the suggestion of the Art Institute of Chicago, started the use of conventional ornament on porcelain surfaces, convinced that it was the correct form of decoration for china.

This effort was made, not as individuals seeking a novelty for their work, but as a Club unit to raise the standard of china painting to what might properly be termed *legitimate* ornamentation.

To quote an eminent eastern art authority, will briefly state our present standing: "The Atlan Club has certainly established a new form of china decoration for the United States; their work is far ahead of anything I have ever seen done here and compares favorably with the best of Europe."

Another authority, who had watched our progressive work said, ten years ago: "Your Club has certainly succeeded in presenting a new and beautiful form of ornament, and the public has *accepted* it; I see no reason why it should not become an established American style of decoration for china.

To preserve this high standard, the *exhibiting* membership has been limited to a comparatively small number, with an art critic at each meeting.

There is also a large Associate membership who may or may not paint; they have equal opportunities for assistance in design and color, and the additional benefit of a winter class in the study of Historic and Miscellaneous ornament one day each week.

The object of this free class is to extend the educational influence of the Club to all who are not already identified with the study. The ladies in attendance at this exhibition will be glad to give such other information as may be desired relative to the Club work or its interests during our twenty-six years of earnest study and work.

CATALOG

MRS. A. C. AYER

6837 Cornell Ave.

1	Satsuma Box	$7 00
2	Satsuma Trinket Box	4 00
3	Satsuma Hot Water Pot	10 00
4	Satsuma Box	6 00
5	Satsuma Lamp Vase	15 00
6	Satsuma Open Bonbon	10 00
7	Satsuma Powder Box	7 00
8	Belleek Bowl	25 00
9	Bonbon Plate	3 50
10	Bonbon Plate	3 50
11	Salt and Peppers	5 00
12	Salt and Peppers	5 00
13	Candelabra, Faience	25 00

MISS ESTHER L. ALLFREE

5433 Kenmore Avenue

14	Tea Set	
15	Six Bread and Butter Plates	
16	Bonbon Dish, Faience	
17	Satsuma Tea Caddy	
18	Small Satsuma Box	
19	Small Satsuma Plate	
20	Belleek Vase	

MRS. A. M. BAROTHY

7619 Eastlake Terrace

21	Satsuma Bowl	$15 00
22	Satsuma Box	10 00
23	Bowl	10 00
24	Satsuma Box	7 00
25	Box	10 00
26	Bonbon Box	15 00
27	Bonbon Box	15 00
28	Bonbon Box	12 50

3

MRS. A. M. BAROTHY—*Continued*

29	Satsuma Bowl	20 00
30	Satsuma Bowl	18 00
31	Satsuma Box	8 00
32	Satsuma Box	6 00
33	Satsuma Box	6 00
34	Satsuma Box	3 00
35	Satsuma Box	3 00
36	Satsuma Box	10 00

MRS. A. BERGLUND

4117 N. Crawford Ave

37	Satsuma Bonbon	
38	Satsuma Open Bonbon	
39	Satsuma Button Box	
40	Satsuma Bowl	
41	Satsuma Box	
42	Satsuma Box	
43	Satsuma Box	
44	Satsuma Rose Jar	
45	Satsuma Incense	
46	Satsuma Small Lamp Vase	
47	Satsuma Small Vase	
48	Ink Well (French)	

MINNIE C. BAND

1324 Greenleaf Avenue

49	Plate	$ 4 50
50	Fruit Bowl	12 00
51	Satsuma Box	5 00
52	Sandwich Tray	17 50
53	Incense Jar	3 50
54	Satsuma Vase	6 00
55	Medallion	

MRS. A. A. FRAZEE

919 Fine Arts Building

Chop Suey Service:

56	Chop Suey Bowl	$18 00
57	Rice Bowl	15 00
58	Half-dozen Chop Suey Plates	35 00
59	Half-dozen Rice Plates	10 00
60	Half-dozen Tea Bowls	10 00
61	Suey Bean Sauce Jug	8 00

4

MRS. A. A. FRAZEE—*Continued*

62	Vase	18 00
63	Vase (small)	3 50
64	Trinket Jar (small)	4 00
65	Conserve Jar	12 00
66	Hand Carved Incense	25 00
67	Footed Incense	6 00
68	Box, Satsuma	4 00
69	Box, Satsuma	4 00
70	Box, Satsuma	2 00
71	Box, Satsuma	6 00
72	Box, Satsuma	6 00
73	Box, Satsuma	4 00
74	Box, Satsuma	4 00
75	Box, Satsuma	4 00

MRS. H. CHARLES FREYTOG

3142 Logan Blvd.

76	Satsuma Tea Pot	
77	Small Satsuma Lamp Vase	
78	Satsuma Lamp Vase	
79	Small Desk Lamp (hand carved)	
80	Conserve Dish, Satsuma (for tea cart)	
81	Satsuma Bonbon Box	
82	Satsuma Incense Burner	
83	Satsuma Powder Box	

MRS. C. A. GALE

2119 Lincoln St., Evanston, Ill.

84	Sandwich Tray	$12 00
85	Lamp Vase, Satsuma (loaned by Mrs. LeRoy Nilles)	
86	Satsuma Box	5 00
87	Olive Dish	2 50
88	Satsuma Bowl	3 00
89	Open Bonbon Dish	3 00
90	Tobacco Jar	10 00
91	Small Satsuma Tray	2 00

MRS. MIRIAM M. GLEASON

1125 E. 54th Place

92	Plate	
93	Card Tray, Satsuma	
94	Mayonnaise Set, Sedji	
95	Plate	
96	Box, Satsuma	

5

MRS. EMMA HUTCHINSON

220 W. Tenth St., Michigan City, Ind.

97 Large Vase, Satsuma

98 Brown Bowl

99 Satsuma Vase (one of a pair)

100 Satsuma Vase (one of a pair)

101 Luster and Enamel Pitcher

102 Nest of Candy Bowls, Satsuma

103 Bisque Vase

104 Cabinet Teapot

MRS. EOLAH A. KULP

8001 S. Peoria Street

105 Bread Plate

106 Cake Plate

107 Box

108 Pin Box

109 Tea Tile

110 Radish Dish

111 Tray

112 Plate

113 Plate

114 Plate

115 Plate

116 Hat Pin Holder

117 Card Tray

118 Powder Shaker

Edgewater 7244 X

ELLEN E. LOVGREN

5240 Kenmore Avenue

No.	Item	Price
119	Faience Fernery	$22 00
120	Rose or Incense Jar	18 00
121	Cabinet Piece	3 00
122	Satsuma Box	4 00
123	Mayonnaise Bowl and Plate	10 00
124	Trinket Box	2 50
125	Incense Jar	3 50
126	Set of 12 Tumbler Coasters	18 00
127	Satsuma Box	4 00
128	Belleek Vase	8 00
129	Cabinet Piece	3 75
130	Bonbon Box	12 00
131	Cake Plate	7 50
132	Satsuma Box	3 50
133	Satsuma Box	3 00

6

MISS EDITH R. LEVEDAHL

33 Hickory Ave., Aurora, Ill.

134 Syrup Jug and Plate

135 Sedji Bowl

136 Sugar Shaker

137 Small Satsuma Box

138 Satsuma Bonbon

139 Small Satsuma Bowl

140 Tea Pot, Satsuma

141 Pitcher

142 Satsuma Box

MRS. FRANK C. LETZ

314 Sibley St., Hammond, Ind.

143 Dresser Tray, Satsuma

144 Incense Burner, Satsuma

145 Trinket Box, Satsuma

146 Small Bowl, Satsuma

147 Pin Tray, Satsuma

148 Cake Plate

149 Japanese Sweetmeat Box

150 Pottery Vase

151 Relish Dish

Ravenswood 7819 X

MRS. FRANCES M. LOWES

4615 N. Hermitage Avenue

No.	Item	Price
152	Service Plate	$ 8 00
153	Service Plate	8 00
154	Round Bonbon Box, Satsuma	
155	Cabinet Piece, Satsuma	
156	Shaving Mug	3 00
157	Relish Dish	
158	Bread and Butter Plate	1 50
159	Bread and Butter Plate	1 50
160	Square Box, Satsuma	4 00
161	Chop Platter	15 00
162	Plate	
163	Compote	
164	Cup, Saucer and Plate	5 00
165	Lamp Vase, Satsuma	
166	Small Satsuma Box	2 50
167	Box, Satsuma	3 00
168	Box, Satsuma	3 00
169	Bonbon Box, Satsuma	
170	Tea Tile	2 50
171	Pair Salt and Pepper Shakers	3 00

7

MRS. WILL B. LATHROP

85 N. Lake St., Aurora, Ill.

No.	Item	Price
172	Fruit Bowl, Satsuma	
	Dresser Set, Satsuma:	
173	Comb and Brush Tray	
174	Powder Box	
175	Trinket Box	
176	Lamp Base, Satsuma	
177	Salt and Pepper	
178	Stamp Box, Satsuma	
179	Faience Bowl	
180	Trinket Box, Satsuma	
181	Salad Plates	
182	Bonbon Box, Satsuma	

MRS. MELINA MAXSON

3707 Ellis Park

No.	Item	Price
183	Vase	$12 00
184	Large Plate	8 00
185	Satsuma Jewel Box	7 00
186	Satsuma Trinket Box	6 00
187	Satsuma Trinket Box	3 50
188	Japanese Lunch Box	10 00
189	Handle Bonbon	3 50
190	Marmalade Jar (Pottery)	2 50
191	Marmalade Jar (Pottery)	2 00
192	Jelly Jar (Pottery)	2 50
193	Jelly Jar (Pottery)	2 00
194	Pin Tray	2 50
195	Tray	Not for Sale

GLENNIE MOSELY

570 Arbor Vitae Road, Winnetka, Ill.

No.	Item	Price
196	Lamp Vase	
197	Cake Plate, Faience	$15 00
198	Handled Bonbon, Faience	5 00
199	Bowl, Sedji	6 50
200	Bowl	5 00
200	Vase, Satsuma	5 00
201	Trinket Box, Satsuma	3 50
202	Pitcher	10 00
	Part of Dinner Set:	
203	Dinner Plate	
204	Soup Bowl	

8

Edge 8052

MRS. BERTHA PARK

817 Galt Avenue

No.	Item	Price
205	Satsuma Box	$ 3 00
206	Satsuma Box	25 00
207	Cake Plate	10 00
208	Bowl	5 00
209	Salad Plates ....each	4 50
210	Satsuma Box	4 00
211	Cabinet Piece, Satsuma	3 50
212	Incense, Satsuma	3 00
213	Salad Plates ....each	4 50
214	Table Piece, Satsuma	15 00
215	Cabinet Piece	3 00
216	Jelly Dish	3 00

Irving 4247

MRS. ALFRED J. PRUDEN

4436 N. Sawyer Avenue

No.	Item	Price
217	Satsuma Set—Sugar and Creamer	$25 00
218	Satsuma Box	10 00
219	Satsuma Lamp Vase	25 00
220	Bisque Vase	15 00
221	Open Bonbon or Nut Dish ....Loaned	
222	Celery Tray	8 00
223	Faience Plate ....Loaned	
224	Tobacco Jar ....Loaned	
225	Relish Basket	6 00
226	Child's Mug	2 50
227	Sherbet Cup	3 50

MRS. ANNA SENGE

6416 Glenwood Ave., Rogers Park

No.	Item	Price
228	Vase, Satsuma	$65 00
229	Box, Satsuma	20 00
230	Box, Satsuma	8 00
231	Box, Satsuma	6 00
232	Service Plate	15 00
233	Service Plate	15 00
234	Service Plate	15 00
235	Service Plate	15 00
236	Service Plate	15 00
237	Service Plate	15 00
238	Service Plate	15 00
239	Service Plate	15 00
240	Service Plate	20 00
241	Dessert Plate ....per dozen	40 00
242	Dessert Plate	3 50
243	Sugar and Creamer	15 00

9

MRS. S. W. SEXTON

3105 Palmer Square

244	Vase, Belleek	$12 00
245	Sugar Shaker	4 00
246	Mug	Not for Sale
247	Vase (small)	Sold
248	Vase (small)	Sold
249	Butter Tub	Sold

MRS. W. E. VAN DOREN

443 E. 50th Street

250	Lamp Vase, Satsuma	
251	Bisque Vase	
252	Small Vase, Satsuma	
253	Small Vase, Satsuma	
254	Powder Box, Satsuma	
255	Trinket Box, Satsuma	
256	Trinket Box, Satsuma	
257	Trinket Box, Satsuma	
258	Glaced Fruit Bonbon, Satsuma	

MRS. ADA WARD

Desplaines, Ill.

259	Tea Set, Belleek	
260	Teapot, Sugar and Creamer	$35 00
261	Tea Cup and Saucer, Belleek	3 00
262	Bonbon Basket, Faience	8 00
263	Trinket Box, Satsuma	3 00
264	Box, Satsuma	3 00
265	Tea Tile	3 00
266	Vase, Belleek	10 00
267	Plate	2 50
268	Plate	2 50
269	Tea Caddy, Belleek	10 00
270	Mayonnaise Dish, Belleek	8 00

MRS. GEORGE R. WARNER

274 Spruce St., Aurora, Ill.

271	Cigar Jar, Satsuma	
272	Vase, Satsuma	
273	Rose Jar, Satsuma	$7 50
274	Card Tray, Satsuma	3 50
275	Powder Box, Satsuma	4 00
276	Small Plate, Satsuma	
277	Trinket Box, Satsuma	3 50
278	Small Tray, Satsuma	2 00

10

MISS ELEANOR H. WIESE

2111 Lipton Park Avenue

279	Set of Six Plates	
280	Table Fernery	
281	Set of Service Trays	
282	Satsuma Box	
283	Salt and Peppers	
284	Mustard Pot	
285	Sedji Hot Water Pot	

11

DEVOE

Keramic Supply Department

Everything for the Use of the
China Decorator or the Oil and
Water Color Artist

Devoe Oils, Mediums, Brushes, Etc., Etc.

Hasburg's Phoenix Golds

Coover's Outlines for China

White Enamel in Packages

Mrs. Katherine Cherry's Enamels and Dusting Colors

Mrs. Dorothea Warren O'Hara's New Enamel Colors

CHINA FIRING

is one of the special features of this department. We fire successfully Enamel Colors applied to soft glazes of all kinds.

PICTURE FRAMES MADE TO ORDER

Sample Line includes the latest
and most Artistic Styles

Devoe & Raynolds Company, Inc.

14-16 W. Lake Street, near State

Hasburg's New Style Improved Phoenix Gold Package

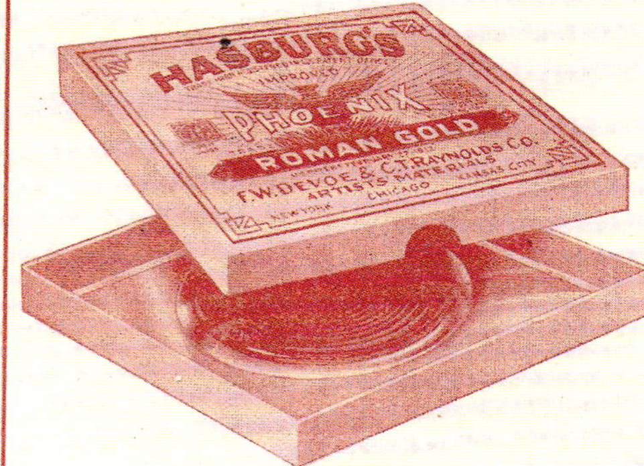

HERMETICALLY SEALED

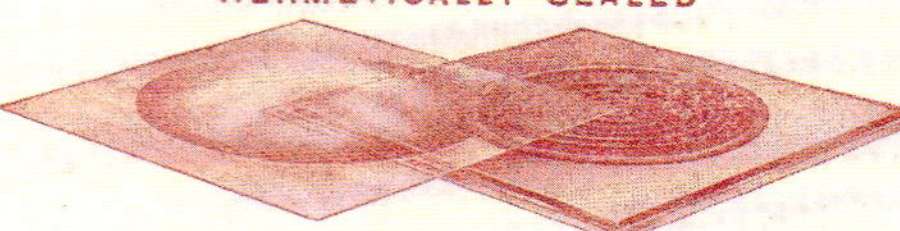

Six cardinal points which make
Hasburg's Phoenix Golds
superior to all others

First The only hermetically sealed package on the market.

Second Scientifically weighed so each box contains an accurate quantity.

Third Corrugated spread for holding the turpentine.

Fourth Colored background indicating color of gold after firing.

Fifth The unexcelled quality of all materials and processes which have been acquired by over thirty years' experience.

Sixth Made in the largest exclusive ceramic gold manufacturing plant in the world.

DISTRIBUTORS

F. W. Devoe & C. T. Raynolds Co.

NEW YORK CHICAGO KANSAS CITY

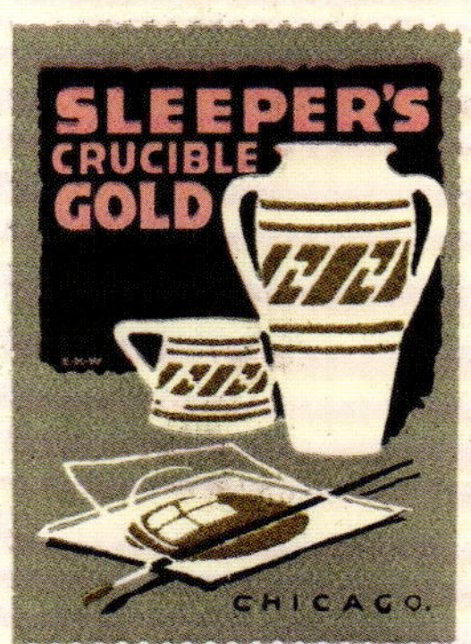

W. E. CLOW & CO.

Diamonds, Watches, Jewelry and Silverware

EXPERT ADJUSTING OF
FINE AND COMPLICATED WATCHES
OUR SPECIALTY

Ask to see Mr. Clow personally

COLUMBUS MEMORIAL BUILDING
Room 405
Telephone Central 225

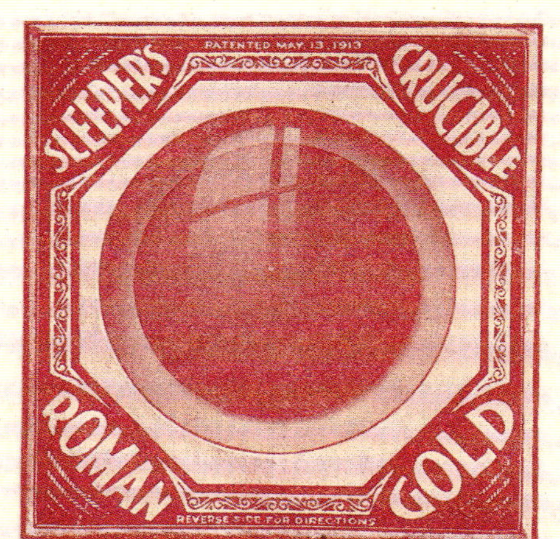

Sleeper's
Crucible Gold

IN THE NEW PATENT
ENVELOPE PACKAGE

AN INSURANCE POLICY
AGAINST FAILURE

All possibility of metallic contamination eliminated; thus giving full play to the splendid qualities of the gold.

FAVOR, RUHL & CO.
DISTRIBUTORS
New York Chicago

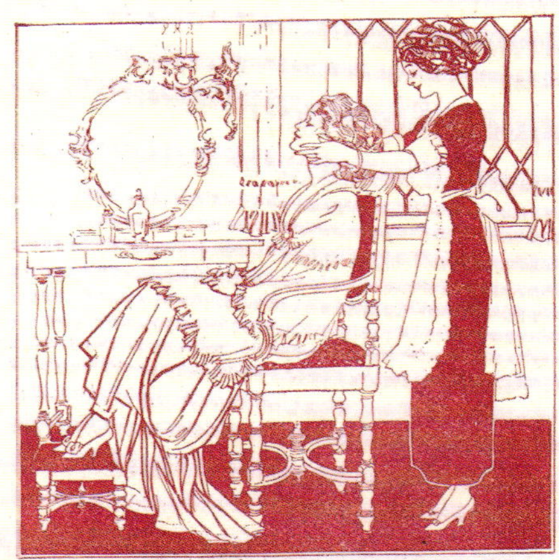

Mrs. Gervaise Graham's
Salon de Beauté

Suite 1432 Stevens Building
17 No. State Street

Facial and Scalp Treatments
Hair Dressing Manicuring
Hair Dyeing Electrolysis

Manufacturer of

Kosmeo Cream
Kosmeo Face Powder

Established 1888

Mrs. Graham's Hair Color

for restoring gray hair to its natural color has been in use for nearly a third of a century by millions of women in this country and abroad.

FOR SALE BY ALL DRUGGISTS AND AT
Mrs. Graham's Salon de Beaute
1432 STEVENS BUILDING

ONE-THIRD OFF
ON
Satsuma Ware

VASES, BOXES, BOWLS
NAPPIES, ROSE JARS
CUPS AND SAUCERS, ETC.

A. H. Abbott & Co.

Artists' Materials of Every Description

Fourth Floor, 208 S. Wabash Avenue
CHICAGO

Kaspar State Bank

LIBERTY BONDS
and accruing interest taken care of without charge.

1900 BLUE ISLAND AVE.
CHICAGO

Toyo Art Shop

DIRECT IMPORTERS OF

JAPANESE AND CHINESE ARTS

AND ART OBJECTS

Holiday Goods a Specialty

White Satsuma

Japanese Drawing Brushes

300 South Michigan Avenue

CHICAGO

Telephone Harrison 3484

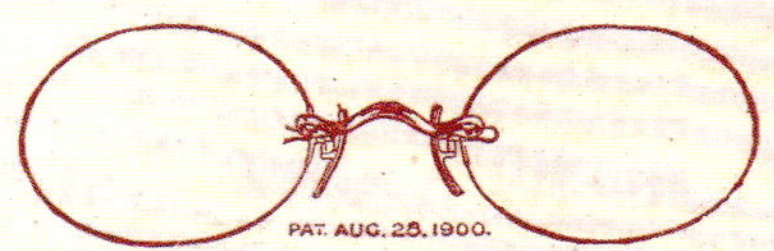

DR. ARTHUR G. FRENCH

REFRACTING OPTICIAN

Spectacles and Eye Glasses Scientifically Fitted
Oculists' Prescriptions Accurately Filled

31 N. State Street
Suite, 712 Columbus Memorial Bldg.
Phone Randolph 4049 CHICAGO

Mrs. A. Berglund

TEACHER OF CERAMICS

4117 N. CRAWFORD AVE.

Phone Irving 3038

Studio Phone Harrison 3375
Residence Phone Stewart 5063

Mrs. A. A. Frazee

Enamel Work on China

CLASSES IN PRACTICAL DESIGN
MONDAY, TUESDAY, THURSDAY

Studio 919 Fine Arts Bldg.

410 Michigan Boulevard, South

Phone Sunnyside 9295

Mrs. E. L. Humphrey

5644 WAYNE AVENUE

Classes in Construction of Conventional Design will begin January 2nd and 4th

FIVE DOLLARS FOR A TERM OF TEN LESSONS

Telephone Aurora 845R

Mrs. Paul G. Hoelscher

CERAMICS

609 GARFIELD AVENUE

AURORA, ILL.

Class Days—Mondays and Tuesdays

Phone Midway 171

Mrs. Leroy T. Steward

1535 East 60th Street

STUDIO

Flat Enamel Decorations on China

WITH SUGGESTIONS FOR COLOR SCHEMES AND DESIGNING, $1.00

The Enameled China in this exhibition illustrates what the book teaches, giving formulas for mixing, etc.

CLASS DAYS ARRANGED TO SUIT THE CONVENIENCE OF PUPILS

Mrs. Helen Wolf

4325 N. Ashland Avenue

SHAMPOOING — HAIR DRESSING
MANICURING — FACIAL MASSAGE

And a New Cleansing and Whitening Paste

Phone Lake View 5107

The Keramic Studio

IS A HELPFUL MAGAZINE FOR ALL CHINA PAINTERS

201 GIFFORD STREET

SYRACUSE, N. Y.

Notes

Introduction

1. As quoted in Cynthia A. Brandimarte, "Somebody's Aunt and Nobody's Mother: The American China Painter and Her Work, 1870–1920," *Winterthur Portfolio* 23, no. 4 (Winter 1988): 203–224.
2. John W. Hasburg, "A Glimpse into the Manufacture of Ceramic Colors," *Arts for America* 8, no. 2 (November 15, 1898): 100–102, 105.
3. Ellen Paul Denker, "The Grammar of Nature: Arts and Crafts China Painting," *The Substance of Style; Perspectives on the Arts and Crafts Movement*, 1990 Winterthur Conference Report, edited by Bert R. Denker (Winterthur, DE: Henry Francis du Pont Winterthur Museum, 1996), 281–300.
4. Brandimarte, "Somebody's Aunt and Nobody's Mother," 203–224.
5. The exhibition included a porcelain bowl decorated by Dorothea Warren O'Hara of New York and a porcelain vase decorated by Kathryn E. Cherry of Missouri. See Wendy Kaplan, *"The Art That Is Life": The Arts and Crafts Movement in America, 1875–1920* (Boston: Museum of Fine Arts, 1987).
6. Mabel C. Dibble, Vase, 1916, 1991.105; Ida Spech Ma Whinney (misattributed to Nellie K. McWhinney), Vase, 1920, 1981.126. Neither artist is identified as an Atlan Ceramic Art Club member.
7. "Ceramic Boarding School," *Ceramic Monthly* 1, no. 4 (May 1895): 10.

Chapter One

1. Steward gives the number of organizational members at fourteen, but lists the names of fifteen women, including herself. Mrs. Florence Steward, "The History of the Atlan Ceramic Art Club of Chicago, Ill., 1893–1902, Written for The Chicago Historical Society," typescript, unpaginated, Chicago History Museum (hereafter cited throughout as Steward, "History").
2. Susan Stuart Goodrich Frackelton (1848–1932) was born in Milwaukee, Wisconsin, where she studied landscape painting and crafts before focusing on ceramics in 1876. After marrying London-born Richard Frackelton in 1869, she became mother of four children. In 1883, she founded the Frackelton China and Decorating Works to supplement her husband's failing china import business and support the family; she sued for divorce

Cornelia Hooker Mann, 1893–1894

1. "A Skilled China Painter," *Art Interchange* 34, no. 4 (April 1895): 117.
2. "In Memoriam," *Ceramic Monthly* 1, no. 4 (May 1895): 8–9.
3. "Ceramics Their Fad," *Clay Record* 1, no. 3 (August 12, 1892): 85.
4. "A Skilled China Painter," 117, "Marcia Louise Vase" illustration on p. 116.
5. *1870 Milwaukee, Wisconsin, City Directory*, 150.
6. "The Chicago Exhibition, 1891," *China Decorator* 9, no. 6 (November 1891): 125–130.
7. "Hints on Green in China Painting," *Chicago Tribune*, November 17, 1894, 4.
8. "In Memoriam," 8.

in 1899. In addition to her successful 1886 publication, she patented a line of mineral paints and a home kiln for firing ceramics. In 1892, Frackelton founded the National League of Mineral Painters, with chapters across the United States. Trying her hand at pottery, she developed a salt-glazed ware and became known for her "Blue and Grey," a blue painted ware with a gray glaze. She won medals at the 1893 Chicago World's Fair, as well as numerous awards for her works in the 1880s and 1890s. After moving to Chicago in 1902, she opened a studio in the Fine Arts Building where she and her daughter focused on creating illuminated manuscripts, which were often exhibited in Chicago Arts and Crafts exhibitions; she remained a popular lecturer and writer. For a concise biography see, Nancy Owen, "Frackelton, Susan Stuart Goodrich," in *Women Building Chicago, 1790–1990: A Biographical Dictionary*, edited by Rima Lunin Schultz and Adele Hast (Bloomington: University of Indiana Press, 2001). Henceforth she will be referenced as a "ceramist."

3. "The Atlan Club," *Ceramic Monthly* 1, no. 1 (February 1895): 11.
4. Steward, "History." The club's symbolism is also described in "The Atlan Club," *Ceramic Monthly* 1, no. 1 (February 1895): 11.
5. Steward, "History." The formation of club is also described in "The Atlan Club."
6. Eva E. Adams, "A Tribute to Mabel C. Dibble," *Keramic Studio* 19, no. 11 (March 1918): 170.
7. Group 91, Ceramics and Mosaics, *Official Catalogue of Exhibits, World's Columbian Exposition, 1893*: pt. XIV, Woman's Building (World's Columbian Exposition, Chicago, 1893), 25–27.
8. "A Skilled China Painter," *Art Interchange* 34, no. 4 (April 1895): 117.
9. "Open to the People," *Chicago Daily Tribune*, May 18, 1893, 9.
10. "Chicago Women at Work," *Tennessean* (Nashville), May 3, 1897, 1.
11. "An Artistic Affair," *Inter Ocean* (Chicago), September 26, 1893, 4.
12. Steward, "History." Mrs. Henry M. Shepard, wife of a Cook County Superior Court Judge, organized the Chicago chapter of the Daughters of the American Revolution, the first local chapter in the United States.
13. "China Painters' Notes," *Standard Union* (Brooklyn), December 9, 1893, 7.
14. Mabel C. Dibble, "The Atlan Ceramic Art Club of Chicago," *Brush and Pencil* 4, no. 1 (April 1899): 34–35.

Chapter Two

1. "Ceramics Their Fad," *Clay Record* 1, no. 3 (August 12, 1892): 84. In 1897, the estimate was 1,500 in "Hand-Painted China Shown," *Inter Ocean* (Chicago), September 22, 1897, 6.
2. "Ceramics Their Fad," *Clay Record* 1 no. 3 (August 12, 1892): 84; "Ceramics," Art and Artists, *Chicago Tribune*, December 6, 1880, 5.
3. "Decorative China," *Inter Ocean* (Chicago), January 22, 1881, 8.
4. For a concise overview of china painting as a hobby and occupation, see Cynthia A. Brandimarte, "Somebody's Art and Nobody's Mother: The American China Painter and Her Work, 1870–1920," *Winterthur Portfolio* 23, no. 4 (Winter 1988): 203–224.
5. "China Painting Is Growing in Favor; Chicago Is Now the Headquarters of the Ceramic Cult in This Country," *Chicago Tribune*, April 11, 1896, 16.

Grunewald's contribution to china painting is also mentioned in Henrietta B. Paist, "Looking Backward," *Keramic Studio* 20, nos. 3–4 (July–August 1918): 29, 32.

6. Burley & Tyrrell Co. was the retail division of Chicago's ceramics importer Burley & Co.; the company reunited its retail and wholesale divisions under the name of Burley & Co. in 1907. For a brief history of the company, founded in Chicago in 1838, see "Reunite at End of 25 Years," *Chicago Tribune*, March 22, 1907, 3.
7. M. Louise McLaughlin, *China Painting: A Practical Manual for the Use of Amateurs in the Decoration of Hard Porcelain* (Cincinnati, OH: Robert Clarke & Co., 1877); S. S. Frackelton, *Tried by Fire: A Work on China-Painting* (New York: D. Appleton & Company, 1886).
8. According to Thomas W. Brunk, *Pewabic Pottery: The American Arts and Crafts Movement Expressed in Clay* (East Lansing: Michigan State University Press, 2021), 35: "Susan S. Frackelton invented and patented a 'china-firing apparatus' in 1886. Two years later she patented an improved model that enjoyed wide acceptance. Her egg-shaped, double-walled kiln was insulated with a sand lining."
9. Jeanne Madeline Weimann mentions the 25,000 figure and briefly discusses the artistic importance of china painting and pottery in *The Fair Women; The Story of the Woman's Building, World's Columbian Exposition, Chicago 1893* (Chicago: Academy Chicago, 1981), 416–420.
10. "Well Housed at Last: After Many Vicissitudes the Chicago Athenaeum Has a Home of Its Own," *Inter Ocean* (Chicago), May 10, 1891, 1; "Warming Its New Home, the Chicago Athenaeum Throws Open Its Doors to the Public," *Chicago Tribune*, May 10, 1891, 1.
11. D. M. Campana, "When Grandma Painted China," *Chicago Tribune*, October 2, 1941, 12.
12. "Tenth-Floor Colony Exhibit," *Chicago Record*, November 8, 1895, 3.
13. "Held a Reception and Sale, Artistic China Offered the Public by the Chicago Ceramic Association," *Chicago Daily Tribune*, April 8, 1892, 3.
14. "The Academy of Design Classes," *Inter Ocean* (Chicago), July 13, 1878, 7.
15. "Decorative Pottery Work Can Now Be Done Wholly at Home," *Chicago Daily Tribune*, November 13, 1881, 10.
16. "Mrs. Preussner [*sic*] and Her Pupils," *Chicago Tribune*, April 30, 1882, 24.
17. For a concise overview of Chicago's growth and industrialization, see Olivia Mahoney, *Chicago: Crossroads of America* (Chicago: Chicago History Museum, 2006).

Chapter Three

1. "An Artistic Affair," *Inter Ocean* (Chicago), December 15, 1893, 4.
2. "In Memoriam," *Ceramic Monthly* 1, no. 4 (May 1895): 9–10.
3. "A Skilled China Painter," *Art Interchange* 34, no. 4 (April 1895): 117, 116 (vase).
4. Editors Notes, *China Decorator* 13, no. 4 (September 1893): 70.
5. "Local Tone," *Arts for America* 3, no. 9 (1894): 265. *Arts for America*, the organ of the Central Art Association, was published from an office in the Auditorium Tower.
6. Steward, "History."

Eva Eliza Adams, 1893–1904

1. "The Dearborn Seminary," *Chicago Evening Post*, June 27, 1873, 4; "Musical Notes," *Daily Inter Ocean* (Chicago), January 3, 1877, 8.
2. Around Town Slips, *Daily Inter Ocean* (Chicago), January 20, 1881, 8; "Summer Villages," *The Traverse Region, Historical and Descriptive, with Illustrations of Scenery and Portraits and Biographical Sketches of Some of Its Prominent Men and Pioneers* (Chicago: H. R. Page & Co., 1884), 206.
3. Eva E. Adams, December 30, 1905, U.S. Passport Applications, 1795–1905, Ancestry.com.
4. "A Tribute to Mabel C. Dibble," *Keramic Studio* 19, no. 11 (March 1918): 170.
5. "Former Conklin Pastor Passes at Charlevoix," *Grand Rapids Press* (Grand Rapids, MI), September 22, 1942, 9.
6. "Art Show Is Opened," *Petoskey News-Review* (Petoskey, MI), November 18, 1941, 1.
7. "Mrs. Eva Sass Dies After Being Ill for A Week," *Petoskey News-Review* (Petoskey, MI), January 8, 1943, 3.

Chapter Four

1. Steward, "History."
2. "Large Reception by Ladies of the Atlan Club," *Inter Ocean* (Chicago), December 19, 1894, 8; also "Atlan Ceramic Exhibition," *Chicago Record*, December 19, 1894, 7.
3. "Large Reception by Ladies of the Atlan Club," *Inter Ocean* (Chicago), December 19, 1894, 8.
4. "The Atlan Club Exhibition," *Arts for America* 3, no. 7 (January 1895): 201–202.
5. Steward, "History."
6. "Some Fine Work on China," *Chicago Chronicle*, November 20, 1895, 5.
7. Modern dollar figures given in parentheses throughout as of 2023, using the inflation calculator at www.officialdata.org/us/inflation.
8. "China Painting Is Growing in Favor; Chicago Is Now the Headquarters of the Ceramic Cult in This Country," *Chicago Tribune*, April 11, 1896, 16; also, "China Painting in Chicago," *Crockery and Glass Journal* 43, no. 24 (June 11, 1896).

Chapter Five

1. Steward, "History."
2. "Music for Charity," *Inter Ocean* (Chicago), May 29, 1896, 8.
3. "Rare Work on China," *Inter Ocean* (Chicago), November 18, 1896, 3.
4. "Ceramics," *Inter Ocean* (Chicago), November 22, 1896, 35.
5. "In the Art Studios," *Chicago Daily Tribune*, November 22, 1896, 34.
6. "Another Gold Medal Awarded," *Arts for America* 6, no. 4 (December 1896): 122.
7. Steward, "History"; Art, *Chicago Daily Tribune*, November 21, 1897, 39; Art News in General, *Inter Ocean* (Chicago), November 21, 1897, 39. The decorated plates appear as illustrations in the *Art Interchange*, 40, no. 1 (January 1898): 23, accompanying "Notes for China Painters," 24.
8. "Atlan Ceramic Art Club," *American Art Annual 1898*, 1 (New York: Macmillan Company, 1899), 163.
9. Art News in General, *Inter Ocean* (Chicago), November 21, 1897, 39.
10. "Gen. LeRoy [*sic*] T. Steward Dies at Paw Paw Lake Estate," *News-Palladium* (Benton Harbor, MI), 1, 16.
11. "LeRoy T. Steward Chosen for Chief," *Chicago Daily Tribune*, August 15, 1909, 1.

Chapter Six

1. Steward, "History."
2. Steward, "History."
3. Steward, "History."
4. While affiliated with the Art Institute, Louis Julian Millet founded its Chicago School of Architecture in 1893, with multidisciplinary studies offered with coursework at the Art Institute and Armour Institute of Technology; later, he served as chief of mural and decorative painting for the world's fairs in Chicago (1893) and St. Louis (1904). After retiring from the Art Institute in 1918, he devoted his energies to the design and

Florence Cary Koehler: Honorary Member, 1898

1. Steward, "History."
2. "Koehler-Cary; the Quiet Marriage of a Well Known Society Couple," *Kansas City Evening Star* (Kansas City, MO), February 6, 1884, 1.
3. Frederick Koehler, *Kansas City, Missouri City Directory*, 1887, 387
4. "The Kansas City Art School," *Kansas City Times*, July 31, 1892, 10; "Art's Progress in this City," *Kansas City Times*, November 13, 1892, 11; "The Public's Loss," *Kansas City Star*, January 13, 1893, 1. "Her love of art was innate, and her art education was chiefly acquired in roaming through the old collections of Chinese and Japanese faience in the Metropolitan museum [*sic*] in New York," according to "Two Kansas City Women," *Kansas City Star*, September 13, 1897, 5.
5. In the Social World, *Kansas City Times*, January 9, 1895, 3; repeated in Here and There, *Kansas City Times*, January 13, 1895, 10.
6. "The Reflective Woman," *Kansas City Star*, December 14, 1895, 8.; "Two Kansas City Women," *Kansas City Star*, September 13, 1897, 5.
7. Catalogue of the Arts and Crafts Society in *Catalogue of the Eleventh Annual Exhibition by the Chicago Architectural Club at the Art Institute of Chicago, March Twenty-Third to April Tenth*, 1898, 133.
8. Mrs. Grundy's Budget of News, *Kansas City Journal*, April 3, 1898, 14. Bertha L. Holden's impressions of the sea voyage and London were published in "A. Letter; Recording a Voyage and First Impressions of London," *Kansas City Star*, July 31, 1898, 5. Holden (1868–1951) boarded with Edith Sheridan while in Chicago in 1900, according to the 1900 U.S. federal census.
9. In Society, *Kansas City Star*, April 6, 1902, 20; Many of the Pottery and Porcelain Society members were founders of the city's Arts and Crafts Society in 1904; see "Arts and Crafts Society," *Kansas City Star*, May 29, 1904, 3.
10. Passport application, October 2, 1922, Ancestry.com.
11. Peg Weiss, "Florence Koehler and Mary Elizabeth Sharpe: An American Saga of Art and Patronage," *Arts Magazine* 4 (December 1978): 108–117. Florence remained married to Frederick Koehler, who was living in New Jersey in 1922, according to her passport application.
12. Weiss, "Florence Koehler," 115; A. Clinton Landsberg, *Portrait of an Artist: The Paintings and Jewelry of Florence Koehler 1861–1944* (Rhode Island School of Design, 1947).

manufacture of art glass for churches and other buildings. For an overview of his career, see David Hanks, "Louis J. Millet and the Art Institute of Chicago," *Bulletin of the Art Institute of Chicago* (1973–1982) 67, no. 2 (1973): 13–19, https://doi.org/10.2307/4111224. For Millet's contributions to art glass, see Sharon S. Darling, *Chicago Ceramics & Glass* (Chicago: Chicago Historical Society, 1979), 104–110.

5. "Decorative Designing," *Inter Ocean* (Chicago), October 8, 1885, 4.

6. Mrs. Edith Whitehead Sheridan and Mrs. Louis [*sic*] (Florence Cary) Koehler had been on the faculty of the Kansas City Western Art League, absorbed by the Kansas City Art Association and School of Design, incorporated in 1887. The entire equipment of the school was destroyed by fire in 1893. Newly widowed, Sheridan, former head of the design department, joined Koehler in Chicago. See Mazee Bush Owens and Frances S. Bush, *Kansas City Art Institute and School of Design: A History of Community Achievement, 1885–1964* (Kansas City, MO: Kansas City Art Institute, 1965), 7; Carrie Westlake Whitney, *Kansas City, Missouri: Its History and Its People 1808–1908*, Vol. 1 (Kansas City, MO: S. J. Clarke, 1908), 599.

7. "Exhibit of Ceramic Decoration by Members of the Chicago Ceramic Club and Others," *Catalogue, Eighth Annual Exhibition, Chicago Architectural Club, Art Institute Chicago, May 23 to June 10, 1895*, unpaginated. Atlan members included Helen M. Clark, N. A. Cross, Mable C. Dibble, Helen Frazee, Marie McCreery, Grace H. Peck, and Mary A. Phillips.

8. For a discussion of the design influences on china painters, see Ellen Paul Denker, "The Grammar of Nature: Arts and Crafts China Painting," in Bert Denker, ed., *The Substance of Style; Perspectives on the Arts and Crafts Movement* (Winterthur, DE: Henry Francis du Pont Winterthur Museum, 1996).

9. Owen Jones, *The Grammar of Ornament* (New York: Van Nostrand Reinhold Company, reprint 1972), 154. For an analysis of Jones's theory and application in his work, see John Kresten Jespersen, *Owen Jones and the Conventionalization of Ornament* (Rhode Island College Faculty Book Gallery, October 25, 2010), https://digitalcommons.ric.edu/book_gallery/1.

10. *The Anatomy of Pattern* (London: B. T. Batsford, 1887); *The Planning of Ornament* (London: B. T. Batsford, 1887). Books by Lewis F. Day were still popular in 1905 when the Sketch Book Publishing Co. of Chicago advertised *Lettering in Ornament* (1902), *Ornament and Its Application* (1904), *Pattern Design* (1905), and *Nature and Ornament* (1908–1909).

11. Mabel C. Dibble, "The Atlan Ceramic Art Club of Chicago," *Brush and Pencil* 4, no. 1 (April 1899): 36–39. Also, Steward, "History."

12. *Catalogue, The Chicago Arts and Crafts Society, Formed at Hull House Oct. 22, 1897* (1898), 123–124. The society's catalog was issued as part of the *Catalogue of the Eleventh Annual Exhibition by the Chicago Architectural Club at the Art Institute of Chicago, March Twenty-Third to April Tenth*, 1898, 133.

13. T. Vernette Morse, "Arts and Crafts," *Arts for America* 7, no. 8 (April 1898): 491–492, 494.

14. E. K., "The Arts and Crafts Exhibition," *House Beautiful* 3, no. 6 (May 1898): 201–205.

15. "Art Life in Chicago; Practical Work Being Done by Arts and Crafts Society," *Inter Ocean* (Chicago), March 27, 1898, 26.

16. George Twose, "The Chicago Arts and Crafts Society's Exhibition," *Brush and Pencil* 5 (May 1898): 74. As quoted in Eileen Boris, "'Dreams of Brotherhood and Beauty': The Social Ideas of the Arts and Crafts

Movement," in Wendy Kaplan, *"The Art That Is Life": The Arts & Crafts Movement in America, 1875–1920* (Boston: Museum of Fine Arts, 1987), 219.

17. Dibble, "The Atlan Ceramic Art Club of Chicago," 35.
18. Dibble, "The Atlan Ceramic Art Club of Chicago," 33–34.
19. Steward, "History."
20. Steward, "History."
21. *Catalogue, Sixth Annual Exhibition of Atlan Ceramic Art Club, Art Institute, November 17th until 28th, 1898*, unpaginated.
22. Art, *Chicago Daily Tribune*, November 20, 1898, 36.
23. "The Atlan Ceramic Art Club," in *American Art Annual, 1898*, Vol. 1 (New York: MacMillan Company, 1899), 163.
24. Steward, "History."
25. Steward, "History."

Chapter Seven

1. "The Atlan Club Exhibition," *Art Interchange* 42, no. 1 (January 1899): 22.
2. Steward, "History."
3. Steward, "History."
4. "Medals Awarded to China Painters," Art Notes, *Inter Ocean* (Chicago), September 27, 1896, 31.
5. "Another Gold Medal Awarded," *Arts for America* 6, no. 4 (December 1896): 122.
6. "Ceramic Exhibit in Chicago, National League of Mineral Painters Will Display Its Work at the Art Institute This Week," *Chicago Tribune*, May 14, 1899, 5; "Mineral Paintings On View," *Inter Ocean* (Chicago), May 26, 1899, 6.
7. Art, *Chicago Tribune*, June 4, 1899, 42.
8. "The Atlan Club of Chicago," *Keramic Studio* 1, no 4 (August 1899): 75–76. Illustrations were supplied by *Brush and Pencil*.
9. "Plate Design by H. F. Frazee," *Keramic Studio* 1, no. 4 (August 1899): 79, treatment, 86; "Treatment Indo-Persian Design by Mabel C. Dibble," *Keramic Studio* 1, no. 5 (September 1899): 106; "A. A. Frazee: Treatment for Bon-Bon and Cup Design," *Keramic Studio* 1, no. 6 (October 1899): 119; "Helen M. Topping, Chafing Dish Bowl," *Keramic Studio* 1, no. 7 (November 1899): 146–147.
10. "The Social World," *Inter Ocean* (Chicago), November 5, 1899, 18.
11. "Club News," *Keramic Studio* 1, no. 7 (November 1899): 141. The CAA exhibit was held November 10–19. "While marking the seventh annual showing, this is really the first gathering of the work of the club displayed solely by itself as an art production. Formerly the exhibits were practically sales held at the Auditorium." "Chicago Ceramic Association," *Keramic Studio* 1, no. 9 (January 1900), 184. The difference in styles was evident: "The Chicago Ceramic Association allows a wider range of subjects to its members and encourages a closer following of nature in their work, hence we find more pieces decorated with flowers and fruit *au natural* [*sic*] in their collection; also portraits and figure pieces, and less attention to the merely conventional than with the Atlan Club, whose geometrical designs and copies and adaptations of historical ornamentation evince patient study." "Chicago Notes," *Art Interchange* 43, no. 6 (December 1899): 140.

Helen Maria Topping, 1895–1907

1. "Miss Helen M. Topping," *Alton Evening Telegraph* (Alton, IL), January 29, 1907, 8.

12. "In the Social World," *Inter Ocean* (Chicago), November 12, 1899, 18.
13. *Catalogue of the Seventh Exhibition of the Atlan Ceramic Art Club from November 21st to December 3rd, 1899* (Chicago: Art Institute of Chicago); Mabel C. Dibble, "Chicago Letter," *Keramic Studio* 1, no. 10 (February 1900): 204–206; "Chicago Ceramic Exhibitions," China Painting, *Art Interchange* 44, no. 1 (January 1900): 22, 24.
14. James William Pattison, "Ceramics for Paris," *Inter Ocean* (Chicago), November 26, 1899, 19; James William Pattison, "Chicago Ceramic Clubs," *Art Amateur* 42, no. 2 (January 1900): 46–47.
15. "What Interests Chicago," *New York Times*, December 3, 1899, 28.
16. *Chicago Times-Herald*, November 26, 1899, 131.
17. "Chicago Ceramic Exhibitions," *Art Interchange* 44, no. 1 (January 1900): 22, 24.
18. Dibble, "Chicago Letter," 205.

Chapter Eight

1. "In the Studios," *Keramic Studio* 2, no. 12 (April 1901): 257.
2. "League Notes," *Keramic Studio* 2, no. 6 (October 1900): 125.
3. Pattison's Art Notes, "Review of Ceramics Shown at the Paris Exposition," *Inter Ocean* (Chicago), November 18, 1900, 18.
4. Milton B. Marks, "The Atlan Club's Paris Display," *Art Interchange* 44 (January 1900): 24–25.
5. Steward, "History."
6. "Club News," *Keramic Studio* 1, no. 11 (March 1900): 229; Chicago Ceramic Association catalogue (Chicago: Art Institute of Chicago, 1900), 15. At the time, "organic architecture"—designing structures tailored to the function that served for their inhabitants or blending with their natural surroundings—was also a popular theory put forth by Chicago architect Louis H. Sullivan and his protege, Frank Lloyd Wright. Millet's course was described as "conventional designing appropriate to keramic work" in "Chicago Ceramic Exhibitions," *Art Interchange* 44, no. 1 (January 1900): 24.
7. "In the Studios," *Keramic Studio* 2, no. 1 (May 1900): 17.
8. "Club Notes," *Keramic Studio* 1, no. 11 (March 1900): 228; "Club News," *Keramic Studio* 1, no. 12 (April 1900): 250. For an example and brief overview of the work of Anna Burkhard Leonard (ca. 1860–1937), see Ellen Paul Denker, "Hot Bodies, Cool Colors: American China Painting in Two Centuries," *Ceramics in America 2014*, Chipstone, www.Chipstone.org.
9. "American Pottery at the National Arts Club," *Artist* 26 (October 1899–January 1900): 71.
10. "Notes for China Painters," *Art Interchange* 44, no. 5 (May 1900): 121–122.
11. Mary Adams, "The Chicago Arts and Crafts Society," *House Beautiful* 9, no. 2 (January 1901): 96, 98.
12. "At the Annual Art Institute Exhibition," *Chicago Daily Tribune*, November 1, 1900, 9.
13. "Atlan Club Exhibit" [extract from letter of Miss Mable C. Dibble], *Keramic Studio* 2, no. 9 (January 1901): 193.
14. "Exhibition by the Atlan Club," *Art Interchange* 46, no. 1 (January 1901): 23.
15. "Exhibition by the Atlan Club," 23.

16. *Catalogue of the Eighth Exhibition of the Atlan Ceramic Art Club, Art Institute from October 30th to November 13th, 1900* (Chicago: Art Institute of Chicago), unpaginated.
17. Personals, *Statesman* (Yonkers, NY), July 8, 1898, 4.

Chapter Nine

1. Steward, "History."
2. "Atlan Ceramic Art Club to Hold Annual Exhibit," *Chicago Daily Tribune*, November 5, 1911, 13.
3. Steward, "History."
4. "National League Exhibit at the Pan-American," *Keramic Studio* 3, no. 8 (December 1901): 174.
5. "Honorable Mention, United States, List of Prizes," *Buffalo Courier* (Buffalo, NY), October 10, 1901, 16.
6. "Ceramic Exhibition Begins," *Inter Ocean* (Chicago), November 1, 1901, 12.
7. *Catalogue of the Ninth Exhibition of the Atlan Ceramic Art Club, Art Institute from October 31st to November 13th, 1901* (Chicago: Art Institute), unpaginated.
8. *Chicago Chronicle*, November 1, 1901. Art Institute Scrapbook on microfilm, Ryerson Library, Art Institute of Chicago, Chicago.
9. William Vernon, *Chicago American*, November 4, 1901. Art Institute Scrapbook on microfilm, Ryerson Library, Art Institute of Chicago, Chicago.
10. Harriet Monroe, untitled newspaper clipping, October 31, 1901, in Art Institute Scrapbook on microfilm, Ryerson Library, Art Institute of Chicago, Chicago.
11. "Atlan Club Exhibit," *Keramic Studio* 3, no. 9 (January 1902): 203.
12. "Arts and Crafts Exhibit," *Chicago Tribune*, November 24, 1901, 8.
13. "Arts and Crafts in Chicago," *Minneapolis Journal*, December 12, 1901, 10.
14. Steward, "History"; "Reception at Industrial Art League's Rooms," *Chicago Daily Tribune*, December 20, 1901, 13.
15. For overview of Triggs and the Industrial Art League, see Christina Edith Ines Melk, "Oscar Lovell Triggs and the Industrial Art League of Chicago: A Chapter in the History of the Arts and Crafts Movement" (thesis/dissertation, English, Tufts University, 1983); also, Bruce Robert Kahler, "Art and Life: The Arts and Crafts Movement in Chicago, 1897–1910" (doctoral dissertation, Purdue University, 1986).
16. Oscar Lovell Triggs, *Chapters in the History of the Arts and Crafts Movement* (Chicago: Bohemia Guild of the Industrial Art League, 1902), 197; also mentioned in Oscar L. Triggs, "The Industrial Art League," *House Beautiful* 11, no. 3 (February 1902):198.
17. For a discussion of Dow's additive theory, see Richard D. Mohr, *"The Splendid Disarray of Beauty": The Boys, the Tiles, the Joy of Cathedral Oaks* (Rochester, NY: RIT Press, 2023), 18–21.
18. For the influence of Arthur Wesley Dow, see Nancy E. Green and Jessie Poesch, *Arthur Wesley Dow and American Arts and Crafts* (New York: Harry N. Abrams, 1999); Mary L. Battiata, "Elements of Influence: *Composition* and The Students of Arthur Wesley Dow" (thesis, Art Education, Corcoran College of Art + Design, 2014).
19. Mabel Key, "A New System of Art Education: Arranged and Directed by Arthur W. Dow," *Brush and Pencil* 4, no. 5 (August 1899): 258–271.

Mabel Caroline Dibble, 1893–1909

1. Mabel C. Dibble, "The Atlan Ceramic Art Club of Chicago," *Brush and Pencil* 4, no. 1 (April 1899): 33–39.
2. Letter from Mabel Caroline Dibble, Chicago, to Allen Whiting, Boston Society of Arts and Crafts, August 27, 1906, Society of Arts and Crafts, Boston, Collection, Boston Public Library.
3. "The Chicago Exhibition, 1891," *China Decorator* 9, no. 6 (November 1891): 125–130.
4. "Ceramics Their Fad," *Clay Record* 1, no. 3 (August 12, 1892): 85; "Ceramic Society Receives Friends," *Chicago Tribune*, December 7, 1893, 3.
5. "Awards at the Fair; More Exhibitors Listed for Bronze Medals," *Chicago Tribune*, October 23, 1893, 7.
6. "The Seventh Annual Exhibition of Decorated Porcelain in Chicago," *Art Interchange* 35, no. 5 (November 1895): 124–126.
7. Advertisement, Teachers Directory, *Keramic Studio* 3, no. 2 (June 1901): iv.
8. *Annual Report of the Society of Arts and Crafts of Boston, 1910* (Boston 1910), 4; Eva E. Adams, "A Tribute to Mabel C. Dibble," *Keramic Studio* 19, no. 11 (March 1918): 170; Studio Notes, *Keramic Studio* 12, no. 7 (November 1910): 135; Who's Who Among Craftsmen, Ceramics, *American Art Annual* 13 (1917): 411.
9. *The Artists Guild, An Illustrated Annual of Works by American Artists and Craft Workers, 1915–1916* Edward M. Ericson (Chicago: Artist Guild Galleries, 1916), 15. Dibble is listed as a professional ceramic worker.
10. *Keramic Studio* 8, no. 5 (September 1906): 97.
11. "What the Art Schools Are Doing," Special Ceramic Number, *Arts & Decoration* 1, no. 11 (September 1911): 450.
12. Advertisement, *Catalog of the 19th Annual Atlan Ceramic Art Club, 1911*, unpaginated.
13. Adams, "A Tribute to Mabel C. Dibble."

Grace Harriet Peck, 1893–1901

1. "Ceramic Art at the World's Fair," *Buffalo Courier* (Buffalo, NY), January 17, 1892, 11.
2. "Correction," *China Decorator* 12, no. 5 (April 1893): 97.
3. "China in the Woman's Building," *China Decorator* 13, no. 5 (October 1893): 97.
4. Passport, Grace Harriet Peck, March 13, 1922, U.S. Passport Applications, 1795–1925, Ancestry.com.
5. "Refinement of Taste in Table Embroideries," *Christian Science Monitor* (Boston), October 12, 1923, 14.

20. Frederick C. Moffatt, *Arthur Wesley Dow* (Washington, DC: Smithsonian Institution Press, 1977), 91.

Chapter Ten

1. Born in Cincinnati, Ohio, Bessie B. Bennett (1870–1939) was an 1898 graduate of Louis J. Millet's decorative design course at the Art Institute of Chicago. She was an instructor at the Art Institute before being appointed curator of decorative arts in 1914, a post she held until her death in 1939. She was instrumental in launching the museum's Arts and Crafts exhibitions in 1902.
2. *Kansas City Star*, April 6, 1902, 20. The four Atlan members residing in Kansas City were: Nannie E. (Mrs. W. G.) Baird, Lura Ward Fuller, Laura S. (Mrs. M. E.) Gerard, and Minna S. McDonald. The Kansas City Keramic Club's founding, first exhibition, and training of key members is described in "Ceramic Club's Exhibit," *Kansas City Journal*, May 7, 1899, 24.
3. Edward G. Holden, "Success of the Art Crafts," *Chicago Tribune*, December 28, 1902, 39.
4. "The Arts-Crafts Exhibition," *Inter Ocean* (Chicago), December 21, 1902, 40.
5. *Catalogue of the First Annual Exhibition of Original Designs for Decorations and Examples of Art Crafts Having Distinct Artistic Merit, the Art Institute of Chicago, December 16, 1903 to January 11, 1903* (Chicago: Art Institute of Chicago), 12–15.
6. "Oriental Ceramic Exhibit," *Kansas City Times*, May 23, 1903, 2. The newspaper refers to the club as the "Kansas City Pottery and Porcelain Club," although the women members are those listed with the Kansas City Keramic Club.
7. Rho Fisk Zueblin. "The Arts and Crafts Movement: The Education of the Producer and the Consumer," *Chautauquan* 37, no. 2 (May 1903): 175.

Chapter Eleven

1. James William Pattison, "Chicago Ceramic Clubs," *Art Amateur* 42, no. 2 (January 1899): 46.
2. "Swen Linderoth," in *History of the Swedes of Illinois*, Part II, *Biographical Sketches*, edited by Ernst W. Olson and Martin J. Engberg (Chicago: Engberg-Holmberg Publishing Company, 1908), 395–396. See also, "Ceramic Progress in Chicago," *Brick* 21, no. 2 (August 1904), 63–65.
3. "The Atlan Ceramic Art Club," *Brick* 19, no. 1 (July 1903): 39; also mentioned in "Ceramic Progress in Chicago," 64. Linderoth mentions the Atlan Club making pottery as late as 1907; however, it appears that the primary work occurred in 1903.
4. *Hull-House Bulletin* 6, no. 1 (Mid-Winter, 1903–1904), in Alice Bourland Coy, "Bibliography of the Arts and Crafts Movement in America" (thesis for the degree of Bachelor of Library Science in the State Library School in the University of Illinois, June 1904), appendix.
5. *Catalogue of the Second Annual Exhibition of Original Designs for Decorations and Examples of Art Crafts Having Distinct Artistic Merit, the Art Institute of Chicago, December 3, 1903 to December 20, 1903* (Chicago: Art Institute of Chicago).
6. "Club Note," *Keramic Studio* 7, no. 4 (August 1905): 73.
7. "Editorial," *Keramic Studio* 6, no. 11 (March 1905): 237.

Matilda Middleton, 1900-1903

1. Personals, *The Statesman* (Yonkers, NY), July 8, 1898, 4.
2. *Hull-House Bulletin* 6, no. 1 (Mid-Winter, 1903-1904), in Alice Bourland Coy, "Bibliography of the Arts and Crafts Movement in America" (thesis for the degree of Bachelor of Library Science in the State Library School in the University of Illinois, June 1904), appendix.
3. "Amateur Art Study Club Meets," *Daily Illinois State Journal* (Springfield, IL), August 7, 1909, 6.
4. Dorothy Biddle, "Ceramic Work of Matilda Middleton; Chinese Motifs and Methods Characteristic," *Arts & Decoration* 1, no. 8 (June 1911): 351-352, quote on p. 351.

8. "Louisiana Purchase Exposition Ceramics," *Keramic Studio* 7, no. 1 (May 1905): 7.
9. *Catalogue of the Third Annual Exhibition of Original Designs for Decorations and Examples of Art Crafts Having Distinct Artistic Merit, December 6, 1904, to December 21, 1904* (Chicago: Art Institute of Chicago, 1904).
10. Elizabeth Emery, "Arts and Crafts—Some Recent Work," *House Beautiful* 15, no. 3 (February 1904): 36.
11. *Catalogue of the Third Annual Exhibition of Original Designs for Decorations and Examples of Art Crafts Having Distinct Artistic Merit, December 6, 1904, to December 21, 1904.*

Chapter Twelve

1. "Chicago Art Echoes," *American Art News* 4, no. 6 (November 18, 1905): 1–8.
2. "Chicago Art Echoes," *American Art News* 4, no. 7 (November 25, 1905): 6.
3. "Ceramic Notes," *Brick* 23, no. 6 (December 1905): 228.
4. John Farson, "The Capital of the New West," *World To-Day* 8, no. 2 (February 1905): 204.
5. *Catalogue of the Fourth Annual Exhibition of Original Designs for Decorations and Examples of Art Crafts Having Distinct Artistic Merit, December 5, 1905, to December 21, 1905* (Chicago: Art Institute of Chicago), 11–12, Cross's entry is on p. 19.
6. "Ceramic Art at Exhibit Attractive," *Richmond Item* (Richmond, IN), June 14, 1906, 1.
7. "Social and Personal Mention," *Richmond Palladium* (Richmond, IN), June 20, 1906, 3.
8. Contributions from Margaret and Hannah are discussed in "Social Circles," *Richmond Item* (Richmond, IN), March 14, 1910, 3. For a study of Overbeck Pottery, see Kathleen R. Postle, *The Chronicle of the Overbeck Pottery* (Indianapolis: Indiana Historical Society, 1978).
9. "Interesting Meeting of the Indiana Keramic Association Held in Indianapolis This Week," *Indianapolis News*, May 16, 1903, mentions two potter members, Cora M. Day (Mrs. Walter S. Day) and "another member" (perhaps Elizabeth Overbeck) who studied at Alfred University in New York. The association's study courses were usually taught by member Roda E. Selleck (1847–1924), who headed the art department at Shortridge High School in Indianapolis for many years.
10. "Editorial Notes," *Keramic Studio* 8, no. 5 (September 1906): 97; "Editorial Notes," *Keramic Studio* 8, no. 6 (October 1906): 122.
11. *Catalog of the Thirteenth Exhibition of the Atlan Ceramic Art Club, Art Institute, From November 20th to December 2nd, 1906* (Chicago: Art Institute of Chicago).
12. A 1907 Atlan Club exhibition catalogue has not been located.
13. *Catalog for Fifteenth Annual Exhibition, Art Institute, November 17, 1908 to December 2, 1908* (Chicago: Art Institute of Chicago), 8. Steward also exhibited the tiles in the 1908 Art and Crafts exhibition at the Art Institute in December.
14. Margaret Watts Hughes, "Visible Sound," *Century Magazine* 42, no. 1 (May 1891): 38–40.

15. Marie Kingston, "Exhibit of Atlan Ceramic Art," *Chicago Daily Tribune*, November 28, 1909, B6.
16. *Catalogue of the Annual Exhibition of Original Designs and Examples of Art Crafts having Distinct Artistic Merit, December 8–22* (Chicago: Art Institute of Chicago, 1908).
17. "Exhibitions of 1908–09," in "Report of the Director," *The Art Institute of Chicago, Thirtieth Annual Report, June 1, 1908–June 1, 1909* (Chicago: Art Institute of Chicago), 36.
18. "Art Institute Exhibition," *Palette and Bench* 1, no. 6 (March 1909): 144. Also quoted in "Ceramics at the Art Institute of Chicago," *Keramic Studio* 10, no. 11 (March 1909): 251–252, 254.

Chapter Thirteen

1. "When the Poor Barbarian Visited the Exhibition of Ceramic Art," *Chicago Daily Tribune*, November 21, 1909, 13.
2. Mabel C. Dibble, *How to Use Enamels on China* (1911), mentioned in "What the Art Schools Are Doing," *Arts & Decoration* 1, no. 11 (September 1911): 450..
3. Advertisement, Anglo-French Art Co., *Catalogue of the Nineteenth Annual Atlan Ceramic Art Club* (Chicago: Art Institute of Chicago, 1911).
4. Anglo-French Art Co., "List of Publications Devoted to China Painting, et al," in *The Publishers' Trade List* (New York: R. R. Bowker Co., 1917).
5. Marie Kingston, "Exhibit of Atlan Ceramic Art Club," *Chicago Tribune*, November 28, 1909, 22, B6.
6. Harriet Monroe, "Talented Etcher Exhibits Art Work," *Chicago Tribune*, November 28, 1909, 22.
7. "Ceramics at the Art Institute, Chicago," *Keramic Studio* 10, no. 11 (March 1909), 251, 254.

Chapter Fourteen

1. "Ceramic Club Creates Life Post for Wife of Police Chief Steward," *Chicago Daily Tribune*, June 12, 1910, 7.
2. "Studio Notes," *Keramic Studio* 12, no. 7 (November 1910): 135. Dibble is also mentioned in Janet Koplos and Bruce Metcalf, *Makers: A History of Studio Craft* (Chapel Hill: University of North Carolina Press, 2010), 28–29.
3. Mabel Caroline Dibble, Chicago, to Allen Whiting, Society of Arts and Crafts, Boston, August 27, 1906. Collection of the Society of Arts and Crafts, Boston, Boston Public Library.
4. Mary S. Farrington, "League Notes," *Keramic Studio* 12, no. 1 (May 1910): 2.
5. For a detailed biography, see Lynette Korenic, "The Decorative Fire of Susan S. Frackelton: China Painting, Art Pottery, and Book Illuminations" (doctoral dissertation, University of California–Santa Barbara, 2006).
6. Roger Fry, "A Modern Jeweller," *Burlington Magazine* 17 (April–September 1910): 169–174.
7. *Catalog of the Seventeenth Annual Exhibition of the Atlan Ceramic Art Club, from November 15th to December 1st, 1910* (Chicago: Art Institute of Chicago).
8. Mira Burr Edson, "Ceramic Work of Mrs. Steward: Methods of the President of the Atlan Club of Chicago," *Arts & Decoration* 1, no. 7 (May 1911): 309.

Helga Mae Peterson, 1907–1922

1. Hilga [*sic*] Peterson, a bookkeeper, was living with her widowed mother and sister Josephine, a teacher, in the 1900 U.S. federal census, Ancestry.com; "Peterson, Helga M. Miss 518, 205 LaSalle" under "Notaries" in *Business Directory of Chicago, 1906*, 1435.
2. "League Notes," *Keramic Studio* 10, no. 11 (March 1909): 254.
3. Helga Peterson, teacher, arts and crafts, own account, in 1910 U.S. federal census, Ancestry.com.
4. "Critics Praise Exhibition of Ceramic Art," *Chicago Tribune*, September 11, 1910, 53; "A Ceramic Exhibition," *Keramic Studio* 12, no. 8 (December 1910): 172.
5. "Burley Exhibit," *Keramic Studio* 13, no. 9 (January 1912): 200, 201, 203.
6. Patent 1,060,022, April 29, 1913, *Official Gazette of the U. S. Patent Office*189 (April 1913), 1059.
7. *Chicago City Directory, 1915*, 1290.
8. Advertisement, *Keramic Studio* 18 (1916): viii.

9. H. Effa Webster, "Ceramic Art Club's Exhibit Social Event," *Chicago Examiner*, November 16, 1910, 7.
10. Fred W. Sandberg, "Atlan Club Offers Fine Exhibit of Ceramic Art in Art Institute," *Chicago Daily Tribune*, November 20, 1910, B7.
11. Sandberg, "Atlan Club Offers Fine Exhibit," B7.
12. A silver tray and water glasses engraved with national proverbs were available to complete the set. *Catalogue of the Ninth Annual Exhibition of Original Designs for Decorations and Examples of Art Crafts Having Distinct Artistic Merit. The Art Institute of Chicago, December 6,1910 to December 23, 1910* (unpaginated).
13. Others on the faculty were Adelaide and Samuel Robineau, publishers of *Keramic Studio*; English ceramic designer Frederick Hurten Rhead; and French potter Taxile Doat. For a brief overview of University City, see Koplos and Metcalf, *Makers*, 88–90.
14. "Ceramic Club Exhibit Ready," *Chicago Daily News*, November 6, 1911, 14.
15. Harriet Monroe, "Exhibition Opens Today of Atlan Ceramic Art Club," *Chicago Tribune*, November 7, 1911, 8.
16. "Burley Exhibit," *Keramic Studio* 13, no. 9 (January 1912): 200–203; "Critics Praise Exhibition of Ceramic Art," *Chicago Tribune*, September 11, 1910, 53; "A Ceramic Exhibition," *Keramic Studio* 12, no. 8 (December 1910): 172–175. Burley & Tyrrell Co. was the retail division of Chicago's ceramics importer Burley & Co; the company reunited its retail and wholesale divisions under the name of Burley & Co. in 1907. For a brief history of the company, founded in Chicago in 1838, see "Reunite at End of 25 Years," *Chicago Tribune*, March 22, 1907, 3.
17. Ad for Pickard China, *Herald and Review* (Decatur, IL), December 6, 1911, 48; Ad, *Reading Times* (Reading, PA), June 21, 1917, 2.
18. Frank E. Waska, "The Atlan Ceramic Art Club," *International Studio* 44, no. 175 (September 1911): li.
19. "Editorial Notes," *Keramic Studio* 12, no. 4 (August 1910): 67.
20. "Editorial Notes," *Keramic Studio* 13, no. 9 (January 1912): 183.
21. "Burley & Co.'s Exhibition," *Keramic Studio* 15, no. 8 (December 1913): 124–125.
22. "Indiana Keramic Club Work at Herron Art Institute," *Indianapolis News* (Indianapolis, IN), May 20, 1915, 7.
23. Maud M. Mason, "Exhibition of the New York Society of Keramic Arts," *Keramic Studio* 13, no. 1 (May 1911), 9. For a concise biography of Maud Mary Mason (1867–1956), see Ellen Paul Denker, "Hot Bodies, Cool Colors: American China Painting in Two Centuries," *Ceramics in America 2014*, Chipstone, www.Chipstone.org.
24. "Editorial Notes," *Keramic Studio* 13, no. 1 (May 1911): 1.
25. "New Keramic Society," *Brooklyn Daily Eagle* (Brooklyn, NY), February 2, 1912, 7.
26. H. Effa Webster, "Atlan Club Gives $1,000 to Institute," *Chicago Examiner*, April 27, 1912, 17; *Keramic Studio* 14, no. 2 (June 1912), 46.
27. "Spring Exhibitions," *International Studio* 46 (1912): cviii; "Past Exhibitions," *Bulletin of the Art Institute of Chicago* 10, no. 1 (January 1916): 124; "Atlan Exhibit," *Bulletin of the Art Institute of Chicago* 11, no. 1 (January 1917), 252.

Florence Jane Donovan Wilcox Pratt Steward, 1893–1921

1. Training in drawing and painting is mentioned in Mira Burr Edson, "Ceramic Work of Mrs. Steward" *Arts & Decoration* 1, no. 7 (May 1911): 308–309. Florence Steward's exhibit of four items with overglaze decoration and one pottery bowl is listed in the *Catalogue of the First Exhibition of Works by Former Students and Instructors of the Art Institute of Chicago, January 8–February 7, 1918*, entries 696–700, unpaginated.
2. "An Artistic Affair," *Inter Ocean* (Chicago), September 26, 1893, 4.
3. "Gen. LeRoy T. Steward Dies at Paw Paw Lake Estate," *News-Palladium* (Benton Harbor, MI), April 27, 1944, 1, 16; Steward, "History."
4. Steward, "History."
5. Fred W. Sandburg, "Atlan Club Offers Fine Exhibit of Ceramic Art in Art Institute," *Chicago Daily Tribune*, November 20, 1910, B7.
6. Mira Burr Edson, "Ceramic Work of Mrs. Steward; Methods of the President of the Atlan Club of Chicago," *Arts and Decoration* 1, no. 7 (May 1911):308–309.
7. *Annual Announcement of the Chicago Woman's Club* (Chicago, IL, 1922), 14.
8. "Mrs. Steward's Ceramic Treasures to Art Institute," *Chicago Tribune*, December 7, 1921, 7.
9. "Mrs. Florence Steward, Wife of Postal Official, Dies," *Chicago Daily Tribune*, November 30, 1921, 21.
10. Hamilton Park News, *Suburbanite Economist* (Chicago, IL), December 2, 1921, 9.

28. Illinois Federation of Women's Clubs, *Yearbook 1912–1913*, 23, 57. HathiTrust digital version of original at University of Illinois at Urbana-Champaign.

29. "Amateur Art Club Exhibit, Decorated China and Water Color Paintings to be Shown," *Daily Illinois State Journal* (Springfield, IL), November 17, 1912, 6.

30. "Invites Public to See Exhibit," *Daily Illinois State Journal* (Springfield, IL), September 7, 1919, 8.

31. "Shows Views of New Missouri State Capitol," *Daily Illinois Sate Journal* (Springfield, IL), March 2, 1923, 19.

32. Clara E. Dyer, "Art and Suffrage," *Detroit Times*, June 3, 1912, 14.

Chapter Fifteen

1. Haryot Holt Dey, "Decorating China in the Home," *Housewives Magazine* 11, no. 3 (March 1918): 7–8.

2. Art Notes, *Keramic Studio* 18, no. 9 (January 1917): 132; "Awards in Applied Arts Exhibition," *Bulletin of the Art Institute of Chicago* 11 (December 1917): 269. Ora Valetta White won the prize in 1914; Frances F. Newman, 1915; M. Etta Beede, 1916; Lula Lavell, 1917. In February 1919, Twin Cities Keramic Club changed its name to Minneapolis Keramic Art Club, according to "Keramic Club to Become Federated," *Star Tribune* (Minneapolis), February 23, 1929, 49.

3. Cheney and Paist are profiled in Marcia G. Anderson's essay, "Art for Life's Sake: The Handicraft Guild," in *Minnesota 1900: Art and Life on the Upper Mississippi, 1890–1915*, edited by Michael Conforti (Newark: University of Delaware Press, 1994), 122–213. See also Mary Dillon Fostle, "Henrietta Barclay Paist," *Who's Who Among Minnesota Women* (self-published, 1924), 246. For more about the Twin City Keramic Club's founding, see "Coming Art Events," *Minneapolis Journal* (Minneapolis), January 5, 1913, 43; "Local Keramic Club Honored," *Star Tribune* (Minneapolis), November 12, 1913, 15.

4. *Catalog of the Twenty-Second Annual Exhibition of the Atlan Ceramic Art Club, Art Institute from November 3rd to November 29th, 1914* (Chicago: Art Institute of Chicago), 2.

5. "American Ceramic Designs Sought," *Christian Science Monitor*, November 11, 1914, 7.

6. "Editorial Notes," *Keramic Studio* 16, no. 5 (September 1914): 93.

7. "Burley & Tyrrell Company's Exhibition," *Keramic Studio* 17, no. 1 (May 1915): 6–10.

8. "The Burley Exhibition," *Keramic Studio* 17, no. 9 (January 1916): 121–129. "The Recent Exhibition by Burley & Co. of Decorated China," *Arts and Decoration* 6, no. 2 (December 1915): 66, 68, 70, 71.

9. "Art Department," *The Torch* (Indiana: Valparaiso University, April 1915), 24.

10. *Keramic Studio* 17, no. 5 (September 1915): 59.

11. "Formal Design Is a Feature of Atlan Club Show," *Christian Science Monitor*, November 24, 1915, 7.

12. Art, *Chicago Daily Tribune*, November 18, 1916, 10. Also shown was her set of twelve cups, saucers, and bread and butter plates, most likely with similar decoration, with each three-piece set priced from $8 to $10 ($220 to $274).

13. Louise James Bargelt, Art, *Chicago Daily Tribune*, November 25, 1917, 48.

14. "Notes," *Bulletin of the Art Institute of Chicago* 11, no. 2 (February 1917): 272.

Helen Inez Fenton Frazee, 1893–1922

1. "List of the Awards, Illinois Exhibitors Who Won," *Chicago Record*, January 29, 1894; "Ceramics and Mosaics, Awards at the Fair," *Chicago Tribune*, October 23, 1893, 7.

2. "The Seventh Annual Exhibition of Decorated Porcelain in Chicago," *Art Interchange* 35, no. 5 (November 1895): 124–126. Many of the same items were exhibited at the Atlan Club's third exhibition in 1896, eliciting the comment that Helen "must be an indefatigable worker" for the collection included "numerous examples of almost all departments of effort in this art," in "Rare Work on China. Annual Exhibition by Members of the Atlan Club. Opens in Art Institute. Some Delicate Designs on Glass Are Shown," *Inter Ocean* (Chicago), November 18, 1896, 3.

3. "Another Gold Medal Awarded," *Arts for America* 6, no. 4 (December 1896): 122.

4. "Art Notes from Chicago," *Ceramic Monthly* 7, no. 6 (July 1898), n.p.

5. James William Pattison, "Ceramics for Paris," *Inter Ocean* (Chicago), November 26, 1899, 19; Milton B. Marks, "The Atlan Club's Paris Display," *Art Interchange* 44, no. 1 (January 1900): 24–25; *Keramic Studio* 1, no. 10 (February 1900): 206.

6. *Catalog of the 19th Annual Atlan Ceramic Art Club* (Chicago: Art Institute of Chicago, 1911), unpaginated.

7. Agnes Gertrude Richards, "Important Exhibition of American Ceramics," *Fine Arts Journal* 33, no. 4 (October 1915): 440; "The Recent Exhibition by Burley & Co. of Decorated China," *Arts & Decoration*, 6, no. 2 (December 1915): 70; "The Burley Exhibition," *Keramic Studio*, 17, no. 9 (January 1916): 122.

8. *American Art Annual 14* (American Federation of Arts, 1917), 89.

9. Eleanor Jewett, "Ceramic Exhibit on at Institute," News and Notes, *Chicago Daily Tribune*, October 12, 1919, F9.

10. Handwritten notes dated April 4, April 7, and September 20, 1922, in Frazee Family Papers (manuscript) 1858–1922, Chicago History Museum.

11. *Keramic Studio* 25, no. 2 (June 1923): 23; advertisement, A. A. Frazee, *Keramic Studio* 25, no. 11 (April 1924): vii.

15. "Accessions to the Museum," *Bulletin of the Art Institute of Chicago* 11, no. 2 (February 1917): 278; *Annual Report* (Chicago: Art Institute of Chicago, 1917): 17.

Chapter Sixteen

1. Associate membership is mentioned in Atlan Club catalogs, also "The Atlan Ceramic Art Club Exhibit," *International Studio*, 44, no. 175 (September 1911): li; "Formal Design Is a Feature of Atlan Club Show," *Christian Science Monitor*, November 24, 1915, 7; Louise James Bargelt, Art, *Chicago Daily Tribune*, November 25, 1917, 48; Mira Burr Edson, "Ceramic Work of Mrs. Steward," *Arts and Decoration* 1, no. 7 (May 1911), 309.
2. Burr Edson, "Ceramic Work of Mrs. Steward."
3. Gleason exhibited a "Bowl, Hammered Copper, Standard, made by a Roycrofter from Roycroft Shops, $25" in the Atlan exhibition in 1921; however, her connection with the Elbert Hubbard's craft community in East Aurora, New York, is unknown.
4. Johonnot's lecture is mentioned in "Chicago Ceramic Art Association," *American Art Annual* 13 (1917): 96; "Ralph Johonnot" *Wikipedia* entry includes the 1917 Atlan Ceramic Art Association, Chicago Art Institute exhibition in the list of his work, https://en.wikipedia.org/w/index.php?title=Ralph_Johonnot&oldid=1085387284.
5. "Chicago Ceramic Art Exhibit," *Keramic Studio* 19, no. 12 (April 1918): 186–189. For association study courses, see "Chicago Ceramic Art Association," *Keramic Studio* 17, no. 10 (February 1916): 136; "Chicago Ceramic Art Association," *Keramic Studio* 19, no. 2 (April 1918): 186–189; "Chicago Ceramic Art Association," *Keramic Studio* 20, no. 8 (December 1918): 108.
6. "Higher Ideals," *Keramic Studio* 19, no. 3 (July 1917), 40.
7. "Keramic Society Elects 1915–1916 Officers," *Brooklyn Daily Eagle* (Brooklyn, NY), May 31, 1915, 20.
8. Charles de Kay, "Keramic Society of Greater New York," *Art World* 2, no. 4 (July 1917): 400–402.
9. *American Art Directory 13* (New York: R. R. Bowker, 1917).

Chapter Seventeen

1. *Catalog of the Twenty-Seventh Annual Exhibition of the Atlan Ceramic Art Club, Art Institute from November 6th to November 30th, 1919* (Chicago: Art Institute of Chicago), 9–10.
2. Eleanor Jewett, "High Standards Maintained in American Exhibit," *Chicago Tribune*, November 9, 1919, 101.
3. "Chicago," *American Art News* 19, no. 8 (December 4, 1920): 5. The 1920 Atlan catalog is missing from the Chicago Art Institute's collection.
4. "Notes," *Bulletin of the Art Institute of Chicago* 15, no. 6 (November–December 1921): 180.
5. *Okmulgee Daily Democrat* (Okmulgee, OK), May 9, 1921, 3; Simon's exhibition is described in "Okmulgee Woman Finds Recreation in Painting China," *Okmulgee Daily Times* (Okmulgee, OK), May 15, 1921, 9.
6. "Announcement," *Chicago Tribune*, April 3, 1919, 5. Burley & Tyrell's wholesale business was acquired by hotel supplier Albert Pick & Co.

Anna Obermaier Senge, 1911–1922

1. "Artist Realizes Youthful Goal; Frank Senge Spends Life in Flowers," *American Florist: A Weekly Journal for the Trade* 70 (February 11, 1928): 19–20.
2. The Whirl of Society, *Inter Ocean* (Chicago), November 8, 1911, 6.
3. "The Burley Exhibition," *Keramic Studio* 17, no. 9 (January 1916): 121.
4. *Catalog of the Thirtieth Annual Exhibition of the Atlan Ceramic Art Club, Art Institute From November 2nd to November 19th, 1922* (Chicago: Art Institute of Chicago).
5. Frank C. Senge, accompanied by his wife Anna. *Passport issued August 19, 1924, U. S. Passport Applications, 1795–1925, Ancestry.com.*
6. Barb Triphahn and Sandra Scheck, interview with author, September 29, 2022.

Ellen Elizabeth Lovgren, 1915–1918

1. Art, *Chicago Daily Tribune* (Chicago), November 18, 1916, 10.
2. *American Art Annual* 17 (1920) (Washington, DC: American Federation of the Arts, 1921), 402.

Emma Amanda Lindquist Berglund, 1914–1922

1. *Who's Who in Chicago and Illinois* 8 (A. N. Marquis, 1945), 81.
2. *Who's Who in Michigan: A Biographical Dictionary of Leading Men and Women of the Commonwealth* (New York: Lewis Historical Publishing Co., 1947), 912; *Who's Who in Indiana* (New York: Lewis Historical Publishing Co., 1947), 912.
3. *Who's Who of American Women*, (Wilmette IL: Marquis-Who's Who, 1958), 14.

Elva Bryant Eichling, 1921–1922

1. James "Ike" Eichling (grandson of Elva), telephone conversation with author, February 16, 1923.
2. "Elva B. Eichling," *Naples Daily News* (Naples, FL), June 1, 1978, 18.

7. Published as *Keramic Studio* from 1899 to 1925, then renamed *Design Keramic Studio*; later, it became *Design for Arts in Education*.
8. "Would Extend Art League," *Chicago Daily News*, February 10, 1921,15; also mentioned in Eleanor Jewett, "Jacobean Room an Interesting Gift to the Art Institute," *Chicago Tribune*, February 20, 1921, 81; "Chicago," *Art News* 21, no. 36 (June 16, 1923), 8. According to Jewett's column, "The league is an association of active workers in the various applied arts. It holds meetings at the institute the first Friday of every month, when work is brought by the members for criticism of a constructive character. The object of the league is to improve the practice of design and decoration in practical objects, to improve artistically the productions of American industry, and to enrich life, in its broadest sense, by developing better expression in those matters which are of esthetic nature."
9. Marguerite B. Williams, "Ceremic [*sic*] Art," *Elmira Morning Telegram* (Elmira, NY), December 5, 1920.

Chapter Eighteen

1. Hamilton Park News, *Englewood Times* (*Suburbanite Economist*) (Chicago), December 2, 1921, 9. Her brief and inaccurate obituary in the *Chicago Daily Tribune* described her as "interested in art, being for years the president of the Chicago Ceramic club, which makes annual exhibits at the Art Institute," in "Mrs. Florence Steward, Wife of Postal Official Dies," *Chicago Daily Tribune*, November 30, 1921, 21.
2. "Notes," *Bulletin of the Art Institute of Chicago* 16, no. 1 (January–February 1922): 15.
3. "Mrs. Steward's Ceramic Treasures to Art Institute," *Chicago Tribune*, December 7, 1921, 7. Department of Decorative Arts, Art Institute of Chicago.
4. The Art Institute of Chicago receipt for the Mrs. LeRoy T. Steward Estate, dated May 22, 1922, lists forty ceramic pieces, a silver 1915 Panama-Pacific medal, and a typed history of the Atlan Ceramic Art Club, 1893–1902. Meeting on October 26, 1922, the museum's Decorative Arts Committee "voted not to accept" the Steward collection; all items were sold or disposed of on February 2, 1923. The committee was composed of Robert B. Harshe, museum director, Mrs. Potter Palmer II, and art-collecting philanthropist Russell Tyson. Office Files, Decorative Arts Committee Meeting 1921–1986, box 22, Art Institute of Chicago.
5. *Catalog of the Thirtieth Annual Exhibition of the Atlan Ceramic Art Club, Art Institute From November 2nd to November 19th, 1922* (Chicago: Art Institute of Chicago).
6. Barothy was listed in "Americans in Europe," *Chicago Tribune*, June 17, 1922, 11, and a passenger on a ship arriving in Philadelphia from Liverpool on September 29, 1922, on Ancestry.com.
7. *Catalog of the Thirtieth Annual Exhibition of the Atlan Ceramic Art Club, Art Institute from November 2nd to November 19th, 1922.*
8. Eleanor Jewett, "Realism Arrests the Eye Regarding Sargent's Canvas," *Chicago Daily Tribune*, November 12, 1922, 125.
9. "The Atlan Ceramic Art Club," *Christian Science Monitor*, November 25, 1922, 6.
10. "Would Extend Art League," *Chicago Daily News*, February 10, 1921, 15; mentioned in Eleanor Jewett, "Jacobean Room an Interesting Gift to the

Frances Alice Nessling Barothy, 1901–1921

1. Her presidency of the Technic Arts League is mentioned in "Beverly Club to Hear Talk on Russian Art," *Suburbanite Economist* (Chicago, IL), February 6, 1931, 3; "Woman's University Club Will Hear Art Talk Today," *Chicago Tribune*, December 14, 1943, 21.
2. "Frances A. Barothy," in *Who's Who in the Artists' Guild 1917* (Chicago: The Artists' Guild, 1917).
3. "Fremont News," *Omaha World-Herald* (Omaha, NE), February 23, 1891, 1; "Arpad Barothy, MD," *West Point Republican* (West Point, NE), May 25, 1894, 1.
4. *Thirteenth Annual Exhibition of Industrial Art Including the Work of Hungarian Peasant Potters and Weavers and a Collection of Tapestries and Weavings Made by Herter Looms of New York from October First to October Twenty-Fifth* (Chicago: Art Institute of Chicago, 1914). For a detailed analysis of the Hungarian exhibition, see Zoltan Fejos, "Hungarian Folk Art Exhibitions in the USA in 1914," *Hungarian Studies Review* 44, nos. 1–2 (Spring–Fall, 2017): 5–35.
5. Entries 417, "Bon-bon box, enamel on Satsuma," and 418, "Cold cream box, enamel, octagonal," *Catalogue of the Nineteenth Annual Exhibition of Applied Arts and the Exhibition of British Arts and Crafts, March Eighth to April Fifth* (Chicago: Art Institute of Chicago, 1921). Barothy was one of four Technic Art League exhibitors.
6. "Painter, 86, Teaches Art to Others; Widow Is Called 'Ageless One' by Friends," *Chicago Tribune*, February 14, 1957, 15.
7. "Sanitarium Erection Started at Walhalla by Chicago Physician," *Ludington Daily News* (Ludington, MI), November 9, 1930, 2.
8. "Beautiful Barothy Lodge, on Site Rich in Beauty, Formally Opened July 4," *Ludington Daily News* (Ludington, MI), July 5, 1931, 1, 8.
9. Tom McNally, "Angler Hooks a New Honduras Paradise," *Chicago Tribune,* March 25, 1964, B1. Email to author from Misha, Belize River Lodge, November 17, 2021.
10. Peter H. Falk, editor-in-chief, *Who Was Who in American Art 1564–1975: 400 Years of Artists in America*, 2nd ed., (Madison, CT: Sound View Press, 1999).

Art Institute," *Chicago Tribune*, February 20, 1921, 81; "Chicago," *Art News* 21, no. 36 (June 16, 1923): 8.

11. "Merger of Clubs, Atlan Ceramic Art and Chicago Ceramic Now Technic Arts League," *Oak Parker* (Oak Park, IL), July 14, 1923, 25.
12. "Technic Arts League," *Dixon Evening Telegraph* (Dixon, IL), November 21, 1923, 3. In 1922, the Technic Arts League offered a course in stage design, taught by Hermann Rosse, and an exercise in designing wallpaper based on old Chinese designs, according to notes in the Frazee manuscript collection at the Chicago History Museum.
13. Barothy's presidency is mentioned in "Beverly Club to Hear Talk on Russian Art," *Suburbanite Economist* (Chicago, IL), February 6, 1931, 3; "Woman's University Club Will Hear Art Talk Today," *Chicago Tribune*, December 14, 1943, 21.
14. "Returns from Meeting," *Daily Illinois State Journal* (Springfield, IL), June 19, 1949, 8.
15. "The Atlan Ceramic Art Club prize of $10 to J. Edgar Miller for overglaze bowl" in "Prizes and Honors in Exhibitions," *The Art Institute of Chicago Forty-Fifth Annual Report, 1923* (Chicago: Art Institute of Chicago), 44. In addition to three examples of overglaze china, Miller also exhibited batik-dyed textiles and woodcuts. *Catalogue of the Twenty-First Annual Exhibition of Applied Arts Under the Auspices of the Association of Arts and Industries and the Art Institute of Chicago, May the First to May Thirty-First Nineteen Hundred and Twenty-Three* (Chicago: Art Institute of Chicago), unpaginated.
16. Richard Cahan and Michael Williams, *Edgar Miller and the Handmade Home* (Chicago: City Files Press, 2009).
17. Listed in the Art Institute of Chicago exhibition archives, https://www.artic.edu/exhibitions/5244/atlan-ceramic-club-31st-annual, accessed May 14, 2022.
18. *Keramic Studio* 25, no. 2 (June 1923): 23.
19. Arthur Aman, "Painter, 86, Still Enthusiastic Over 'Delightful Hobby,'" *Chicago Daily Tribune*, February 14, 1957, N1.
20. Letter from Jane Van Doren Wright, Hotel Majestic, Paris, France, to Mrs. Howard Shaw, Chicago, postmarked May 20, 1933. Shaw-Wells Family Papers, 1792–1977, box 1: 4, Chicago History Museum 1979.0031.
21. For the evolution of Pickard China, see Alan B. Reed, *Collector's Encyclopedia of Pickard China* (Paducah, KY: Collector Books, 1995). He also includes brief profiles of many Chicago studios, including the Atlan Ceramic Art Club.
22. "Ceramists Go Modern at Exhibit of Pottery by Keramic Society," *Brooklyn Daily Eagle* (Brooklyn, NY), April 10, 1935, 7; also "Decorative Art Exhibition Opens," *Brooklyn Daily Eagle* (Brooklyn, NY), April 1, 1935, 10.
23. "Keramic Society to Exhibit at American Museum," *Brooklyn Daily Eagle* (Brooklyn, NY), March 9, 1930, 65.
24. "Woman Potter Sells Glazes; Defies Age," *Buffalo Evening News* (Buffalo, NY), June 14, 1941, 62.
25. "Marshall Fry," *Southampton Press* (Southampton, NY), September 23, 1965, 7; his obituary makes no mention of his career as a china painter.
26. Katherine Kelley, "Passing of Old Family Circle Hampers Child," *Chicago Tribune*, March 13, 1935, 17.

27. D. M. Campana, "When Grandma Painted China," *Chicago Tribune*, October 2, 1941, 12. In 2022, the D. M. Campana Art Co. was still in business in Pampa, Texas.

28. "Editorial," *Keramic Studio* 7, no. 3 (July 1905), 49.

29. Judy Chicago, "World of the China Painter," in Dextra Frankel (Compiler) *Overglaze Imagery Cone 019-016* (Fullerton: Visual Arts Center, California State University, 1977), 118. Born in Silesia, Franz B. Aulich (1860–1922) established a studio in the Auditorium Tower in the 1880s. He specialized in flowers, fruit, and figures in a style characteristic of the Royal Berlin factory. Trained in Vienna, Franz A. Bischoff (1864–1929), known for roses and grapes, often taught classes in Chicago while operating studios in New York, Detroit, and, after 1906, in South Pasadena, California.

30. Nettie Ethel Leist Pillet (1877–1975) of Pasadena, California, was the author of *China Painting* (privately printed, 1954) and *Kingdom of My Soul* (New York: Comet Press Books, 1955), an autobiography detailing her spiritual growth.

31. Dorothy Kamm, *American Painted Porcelain; Collector's Identification & Value Guide* (Paducah, KY: Collector Books, 1997), 13; Debby DuBay "Hand-Painted Porcelain: Women Played a Major Role," *Journal of Antiques and Collectibles* (February 2003). https://journalofantiques.com/features/hand-painted-porcelain-women-played-a-major-role.

32. "Pauline Salyer (1912–1991), Founder of the World Organization of China Painters," https://www.wocp.org/founder/2019-founder.html.; Pauline A. Salyer, *The Great Artists of China Decoration* (Salyer Pub. Co., 1964).

33. "The Dinner Party by Judy Chicago" is a long-term installation at the Elizabeth A. Sackler Center for Feminist Art at the Brooklyn Museum in Brooklyn, New York. For an overview, see Judy Chicago, *The Dinner Party* (New York: Penguin, 1996); David Colman (Editor), Carmen Hermo (Interviewer), Anne Pasternak (Introduction), Judy Chicago (Artist), Jeanne Greenberg Rohatyn (Contributor), *Judy Chicago: Roots of The Dinner Party: History in the Making* (New York: Salon 94 (Gallery), 2018).

34. U.S. Statutes at Large, vol. 94, part 1, 94 STAT.830, Public Law 96-299 (July 2, 1980).

35. World Organization of China Painters Museum, Oklahoma City, OK, telephone conversation with author, June 13, 2022.

36. Lucretia Donnell of Dallas, Texas, founded the National China Painting Teachers Association in 1958; the association's name was changed to International Porcelain Artists and Teachers, Inc., in 1990. See, https://www.ipatinc.org, accessed August 2, 2023.

37. Steward, "History."

Select Bibliography

Atlan Ceramic Art Club. Exhibition catalogs. Ryerson Library, Art Institute of Chicago, 6th (1898)–9th (1901), 12th (1905) –17th (1910), 19th (1911) –27th (1919), 29th (1921) –30th (1922).

Ball, L. Clarence. *Hasburg's Golds. A Glittering Trail.* Chicago: John W. Hasburg Company, 1913.

Barter, Judith A., ed. *Apostles of Beauty: Arts and Crafts from Britain to Chicago.* Chicago: Art Institute of Chicago, 2009.

Blaszczyk, Regina Lee. "The Aesthetic Moment: China Decorators, Consumer Demand, and Technological Change in the American Pottery Industry, 1865–1900." *Winterthur Portfolio* 29, no. 2/3 (1994): 121–153, pp. 125–126. http://www.jstor.org/stable/1181484, accessed August 6, 2023.

Brandimarte, Cynthia A. "Somebody's Aunt and Nobody's Mother: The American China Painter and Her Work, 1870–1920." *Winterthur Portfolio* 23 no. 4 (Winter 1988): 203–224.

Burke, Doreen Bolger, et al. *In Pursuit of Beauty: Americans and the Aesthetic Movement.* New York: Metropolitan Museum of Art/Rizzoli, 1986.

Chicago Ceramic Art Association. Catalogs, various dates, Ryerson Library, Art Institute of Chicago.

Clark, Michael, and Jill Thomas-Clark. "The Not-So-Lost Fine Art of the Arts and Crafts Movement." *Style:1900* 10, no. 4 (Fall/Winter 1997–98): 18–21.

Conforti, Michael, ed. *Minnesota 1900: Art and Life on the Upper Mississippi, 1890–1915.* Newark: University of Delaware Press, in association with the Minneapolis Institute of Arts, 1994.

Cordasco, Rachel S. "Tried by Fire: Susan Frackelton and the Arts and Crafts Movement in Wisconsin." *Wisconsin Magazine of History* 95, no. 4 (Summer 2012): 28–41.

Darling, Sharon S. *Chicago Ceramics and Glass: An Illustrated History from 1871 to 1933.* Chicago: Chicago Historical Society, 1979.

Declaration of China Painting as a Fine Art by President Jimmy Carter, January 3, 1980. https://indianawocp.com/president-carter's-declaration.

Denker, Ellen Paul. "Liberating the Creative Spirit, China Painters of Indiana." *Traces*, Winter 1994, 30–35. Published by the Indiana Historical Society, Indianapolis.

———. "The Grammar of Nature: Arts and Crafts China Painting." In *The Substance of Style: Perspectives on the Arts and Crafts Movement* (1990 Winterthur Conference Report), edited by Bert R. Denker, 281–300. Winterthur, DE: Henry Francis du Pont Winterthur Museum, 1996.

———. "Hot Bodies, Cool Colors: American China Painting in Two Centuries." In *Ceramics in America 2014.* https://chipstone.org/article.php/696/Ceramics-in-America-2014/?s=Denker.

Dyer, Joel S. "The Demise of the Chicago Academy of Design and the Rise of the Art Institute of Chicago." *Journal of the Illinois State Historical Society* 113, nos. 3–4 (Fall/Winter 2020): 7–39.

Ellis, Anita J. *The Ceramic Career of M. Louise McLaughlin*. Athens: Ohio University Press, 2003.

Falk, Peter Hastings, ed. *Who Was Who in American Art 1564–1975: 400 Years of Artists in America*. 3 vols. Madison, CT: Sound View Press, 1999.

Frankel, Dextra, compiler. *Overglaze Imagery, Cone 019–016*. Fullerton: Visual Arts Center, California State University, 1977.

Frelinghuysen, Alice Cooney. "Aesthetic Forms in Ceramics and Glass." In *In Pursuit of Beauty: Americans and the Aesthetic Movement*, Doreen Bolger Burke et al., 198–251. New York: Metropolitan Museum of Art/Rizzoli, 1986.

Frelinghuysen, Alice Cooney, and Martin Eidelberg. *Gifts from the Fire; American Ceramics, 1880–1950*. New York: Metropolitan Museum of Art, 2021.

Green, Nancy E., and Jessie Poesch. *Arthur Wesley Dow and American Arts and Crafts*. New York: Henry N. Abrams, 1999.

Jones, Owen. *The Grammar of Ornament: Illustrated by Examples from Various Styles of Ornament*. London: B. Quaritch, 1910. Reprint.

Kamm, Dorothy. *American Painted Porcelain; Collector's Identification & Value Guide*. Paducah, KY: Collector Books, 1997.

Kaplan, Wendy. *"The Art That Is Life": The Arts and Crafts Movement in America, 1875–1920*. Boston: Museum of Fine Arts, 1987.

Korenic, Lynette Marie. "The Decorative Fire of Susan S. Frackelton: China Painting, Art Pottery, and Book Illumination." Dissertation submitted in partial satisfaction of the requirements for the degree Doctor of Philosophy in Art History, University of California, Santa Barbara, June 2006.

Orr, Lynn Federle, and Stephen Calloway, eds. *The Cult of Beauty; The Victorian Avant-Garde 1860–1900*. London: V&A Publishing, 2011.

Ray, Marcia. *Collectible Ceramics: An Encyclopedia of Pottery and Porcelain*. Bloomington: Indiana University, 1974.

Reed, Alan B. *Collector's Encyclopedia of Pickard China*. Paducah, KY: Collector Books, 1995.

Smith, Avis Carol. "Changing Fortunes: The History of China Painting in South Australia." Thesis presented as requirement for the degree of Doctor of Philosophy, University of Adelaide, December 2008.

Vachon, Paula. "A Retrospective View of Hand Painted Porcelain in Canada (1880s to 1940s) from a Collector's Perspective." Hand Painted Porcelain in Canada. https://sites.google.com/site/handpaintedporcelainincanada/home/a-retrospective-view-of-the-hand-painted-porcelain-in-canada.

Veith, Barbara, and Alice Cooney Frelinghuysen. "Women China Decorators." Essay in Heilbrunn Timeline of Art History, Metropolitan Museum of Art (April 2013). Accessed August 6, 2023. https://www.metmuseum.org/toah/hd/woch/hd_woch.htm.

Weiss, Peg, ed. *Adelaide A. Robineau: Glory in Porcelain*. Syracuse, NY: Syracuse University Press, 1981.

Zipf, Catherine W. *Professional Pursuits: Women and the American Arts and Crafts Movement*. Knoxville: University of Tennessee Press, 2007.

Zukowski, Karen. *Creating the Artful Home: The Aesthetic Movement*. Layton, UT: Gibbs Smith, 2006.

Acknowledgments

I discovered the Atlan Ceramic Art Club in 1973, when I cataloged a collection of Helen Frazee ceramics and sketches bequeathed to the Chicago History Museum by her daughter Hazel. A history of the club, donated by Florence Steward in 1902, piqued my interest; I began collecting bits of information while I researched other projects. Fifty years later, thanks to digitized periodicals, newspapers, and the Internet, I finally had ample information to tell the club's story. But this book would not have come to fruition without the help, advice, support, and encouragement of many people.

Throughout the project, Richard D. Mohr served as a coach and mentor, providing valuable advice and sharing his wide knowledge of Arts and Crafts ceramics. Terri L. Sinnott was indefatigable in scanning documents, tracking down elusive periodicals, and reviewing copy. Tim Ingram and Olivia Mahoney read early drafts and shared constructive insights. Bridget A. Berglund, James "Ike" Eichling, Sandra Scheck, and Barbara Triphahn shared their memories of Atlan members. Institutional research assistance was graciously provided by Lesley Martin, Chicago History Museum; Elizabeth McGoey, Art Institute of Chicago; Brenda Norris, Michigan City Public Library; and Eve Griffin, Boston Public Library.

Robert W. Switzer and Mikell C. Darling shared their camera skills, while Tim Ingram and members of the Pickard Collectors Club networked to provide illustrations of Atlan ceramics. Exceptional photographic assistance was also provided by David Weidner, Dark Flowers Antiques; Colleen Layton, Chicago History Museum; John P. Walcher and Nick Stenzel, Toomey & Co. Auctioneers; and Sally-Ann Felgenhauer, Richard H. Driehaus Museum.

Sharing their professional expertise at RIT Press, Bruce Austin suggested essential revisions; Mary Safford Curioli provided expert copyediting; and Alexandra Hoff efficiently shepherded the book through production.

Illustration Credits

Natalie Ahlers, Ahlers & Ogletree Auction Gallery
Art Institute of Chicago
Marvin Venis Benjamin
Bridget A. Berglund
Tim Blackburn
Gus Bostrom, California Historical Design
Ronald Bry Collection
Chicago History Museum
Mikell C. Darling
Dark Flowers Antiques
Susan Hebert
Humler & Nolan
Tim Ingram
Ian Lawler, Estate Fresh Austin
James Johnson
Richard H. Driehaus Museum
Sue Phalen
Alan Reed Family
Sandra Scheck
Garret and Lee Smith
Grant Smith
Robert W. Switzer
Barbara Triphahn
Toomey & Co. Auctioneers
Treadway Toomey Auctions
David M. Weidner

Index

Note: Page numbers in *italics* indicate figures, and references following "n" refer to notes.

Colophon

Editor
Alexandra Hoff

Copy Editor
Mary Safford Curioli

Designer
Steve Boerner

Typefaces
Caslon 540 and Whitney

Production
Marnie Soom

Printing and Binding
Printing Partners

Paper
Anthem Plus Satin Text